Racial and Ethnic Diversity in the USA

Richard T. Schaefer

DePaul University

PEARSON

Boston   Columbus   Indianapolis   New York   San Francisco   Upper Saddle River
Amsterdam Cape Town   Dubai   London   Madrid   Milan   Munich   Paris   Montréal   Toronto
Delhi   Mexico   City   São Paulo   Sydney   Hong Kong   Seoul   Singapore   Taipei   Tokyo

Editor in Chief: Dickson Musslewhite
Publisher: Charlyce Jones Owen
Program Manager: Beverly Fong
Editorial Assistant: Maureen Diana
Director of Marketing: Brandy Dawson
Senior Marketing Manager: Maureen Prado Roberts
Marketing Assistant: Karen Tanico
Managing Editor: Ann Marie McCarthy
Project Manager: Frances Russello
Manufacturing Manager: Mary Fischer
Manufacturing Buyer: Diane Peirano
Design Manager: Blair Brown

Art Director, Interior: Anne Bonanno Nieglos
Interior and Cover Design: Tandem Creative, Inc.
Art Director, Cover: Jayne Conte
Manager, Text Rights and Permissions: Martha Shethar
Cover Art: Unclesam/Fotolia
Digital Media Director: Brian Hyland
Digital Media Editor: Alison Lorber
Media Project Manager: Nikhil Bramhavar
Full-Service Project Management: Anand Natarajan/Integra
Printer/Binder: LSC Communications
Cover Printer: LSC Communications
Text Font: 10/12, ITC New Baskerville Std

Credits appear on page 274, which constitutes an extension of the copyright page.

Library of Congress Cataloging-in-Publication Data
Schaefer, Richard T.
 Racial and ethnic diversity in the USA/Richard T. Schaefer.
  pages cm
 Includes bibliographical references.
 ISBN-13: 978-0-205-18188-9 (student edition: alk. paper)
 ISBN-10: 0-205-18188-0 (student edition: alk. paper)
 ISBN-13: 978-0-205-18221-3 (instructor's edition: alk. paper)
 ISBN-10: 0-205-18221-6 (instructor's edition: alk. paper)
 1. Minorities—United States. 2. Cultural pluralism—United States.
 3. Race awareness—United States. 4. Acculturation—United States.
 5. United States—Ethnic relations. 6. United States—Race relations. I. Title.
 E184.A1S28 2014
 305.800973—dc23

                                        2013010735

                               Student Edition ISBN-10:   0-205-18188-0
                                           ISBN-13: 978-0-205-18188-9
                       Instructor's Review Copy ISBN-10:   0-205-18221-6
                                           ISBN-13: 978-0-205-18221-3
                                À la Carte ISBN-10:   0-205-98616-1
                                           ISBN-13: 978-0-205-98616-3

To the students in my classes

who have assisted me in understanding

our multicultural society

Brief Contents

Contents

Features

Research Focus

- Multiracial Identity (Chapter 1)
- Islamophobia (Chapter 2)
- The Unequal Wealth Distribution (Chapter 3)
- Blended Identity and Self-Identifying as "Muslim American" and "Arab American" (Chapter 4)
- Learning the Navajo Way (Chapter 5)
- Moving On Up, or Not (Chapter 6)
- The Latino Family Circle: Familism (Chapter 7)
- Arranged Marriages in America (Chapter 8)
- Challenge to Pluralism: The Shark's Fin (Chapter 9)

Speaking Out

- Problem of the Color Line, by W. E. B. Du Bois (Chapter 1)
- National Media Should Stop Using Obscene Words, by Tim Giago (Chapter 2)
- The Enduring Relevance of Affirmative Action, by Randall Kennedy (Chapter 3)
- Chinese Exclusion Act of 1882, by Judy Chu (Chapter 4)
- Powwows and Karaoke, by Chris Eyre (Chapter 5)
- The New Jim Crow, by Michelle Alexander (Chapter 6)
- Puerto Ricans Cannot Be Silenced, by Luis Gutierrez (Chapter 7)
- Recognizing Native Hawaiians, by Daniel Akaka (Chapter 8)
- That Latino "Wave" Is Very Much American, by Galina Espinoza (Chapter 9)

Preface

The continuing and growing diversity in the United States emerges every day. People cheered on May 1, 2011, upon hearing that Osama bin Laden had been found and killed. However, the always-patriotic American Indian people were troubled to learn that the military had assigned the code name *Geronimo* to the infamous terrorist. The Chiricahua Apache of New Mexico were particularly disturbed to learn the name of their freedom fighter was used in this manner.

Barack Obama may be the son of an immigrant and the first African American president, but that is not the end of his ethnicity. On an official state visit to Ireland, the president made a side trip to the village of Moneygall in County Offaly, from where his great-great-grandfather Falmouth Kearney, a shoemaker's son, came to the United States in 1850.

Race and ethnicity are an important part of the national agenda. The contents of this agenda are constantly changing. Just one generation ago, the presence of a new immigrant group, the Vietnamese, was duly noted, and the efforts to define affirmative action were described. Today, we seek to describe the growing presence of El Salvadorans, Haitians, Tongans, and Arab Americans, all overseen by an African American president in the White House. The two-race White–Black paradigm that seemed to inform "race relations" in the twentieth century has now given way to a much more complex pattern and a rise to a growing proportion of biracial and multiracial individuals who actively embrace their heritages.

Specific issues may change over time, but they continue to play out against a backdrop of discrimination that is rooted in the social structure and changing population composition as influenced by immigration and reproduction patterns. One unanticipated change is that the breakup of the Soviet Union and erosion of power of totalitarian leaders in the Middle East have made ethnic, language, and religious divisions even more significant sources of antagonism between and within nations. Emotional divisions over religious dogma and cultural traditions have largely replaced the old ideological debates about communism and capitalism. These "foreign" issues impact migration patterns to and from the United States and become a focus of nationality groups in the United States following events in their home country.

Comprehensive Coverage

The objective of this book is to provide in just nine chapters broad coverage of race and ethnicity in the United States. Sufficient historical context is offered to place contemporary events in focus. Any constructive discussion of racial and ethnic minorities must do more than merely describe events. We begin by including the relevant theories and operational definitions that ground the study of race and ethnic relations in the social sciences. We specifically present the functionalist, conflict, and labeling theories of sociology in relation to the study of race and ethnicity. We show the relationship between subordinate groups and the study of stratification.

The extensive treatment of prejudice and discrimination covers anti-White prejudice as well as the more familiar topic of bigotry aimed at subordinate groups. Discrimination is analyzed from an economic perspective, including the latest efforts to document discrimination in environmental issues such as location of toxic waste facilities and the move to dismantle affirmative action. Immigration and the long history of White ethnic groups are advanced as ways to understand contemporary race and ethnicity. We consider how religion provides another layer of identify for a variety of groups in the United States.

Four separate chapters focus on the largest racial and ethnic groupings—American Indians, African Americans, Latinos, and Asian Americans. The continuing theme of diversity is reaffirmed in the concluding chapter that looks at the argument that we now live in a post-racialism era despite persistent prejudice and discrimination. Does success of some minority groups as some sort of "model minority" mean equality has been achieved? Why do people of different racial and ethnic backgrounds seem to talk past one another? By covering such topics in this book's closing sections, we are better equipped to understand the unpredictable future of diversity in a nation of more than three hundred million people.

Features to Aid Students

Several features are included in the textbook to facilitate student learning:

- A series of **chapter opening questions** appears at the beginning of each chapter to alert students to important issues and topics to be addressed.
- **Key Terms** are highlighted in bold when they are first introduced in the book.
- **Research Focus** and **Speaking Out** boxes help broaden understanding of text material.
- Inserts throughout the book point to students to further material found on **MySocLab**.
- To help students review, each chapter ends with a **Conclusion** and a numbered **Summary list**. The **Key Terms** are listed with page numbers at the end of each chapter.
- Periodically throughout the book, the **Spectrum of Intergroup Relations** first presented in Chapter 1 is repeated to reinforce major concepts while addressing the unique social circumstances of individual racial and ethnic groups. The Spectrum of Intergroup Relations in Chapter Nine offers a comprehensive review of the entire book.
- **Review Questions** and **Critical Thinking Questions** at the end of each chapter are intended to remind the reader of major points and encourage students to think more deeply about some of the major issues raised in the chapter.
- An end-of-book **Glossary** includes full definitions of **Key Terms** highlighted throughout the text and is referenced to text page numbers to help students locate the term in the book from the glossary and the end of the chapter.

Ancillary Materials

This book is accompanied by an extensive learning package to enhance the experience of both instructors and students.

Supplementary Material for Instructors

Instructor's Manual and Test Bank Each chapter in the Instructor's Manual offers a variety of the following resources: Chapter Summary, Chapter Outline, Learning Objectives, Critical Thinking Questions, Activities for Classroom Participation, Suggested Readings, and Suggested Films. Designed to make your lectures more effective and to save preparation time, this extensive resource gathers useful activities and strategies for teaching your course.

Also included in this manual is a test bank offering multiple-choice and short answer questions for each chapter. The Instructor's Manual and Test Bank is available to adopters for download at www.pearsonhighered.com/irc.

MyTest This computerized software allows instructors to create their own personalized exams, to edit any or all of the existing test questions, and to add new questions. Other special features of this program include random generation of test questions, creation of alternate versions of the same test, scrambling question sequence, and test preview before printing. For easy access, this software is available within the instructor section of the *MySocLab for Racial and Ethnic Diversity in the USA* or at www.pearsonhighered.com/irc.

PowerPoint Presentation The PowerPoint presentations are informed by instructional and design theory. You have the option in every chapter of choosing from Lecture and Illustration (figures, maps, and images) PowerPoints. The Lecture PowerPoint slides follow the chapter outline and feature images from the textbook integrated with the text. They are available to adopters via the MySocLab website for the text or at www.pearsonhighered.com.

Supplementary Material for Instructors and Students

MySocLab™

MySocLab is a state-of-the-art interactive and instructive solution designed to be used as a supplement to a traditional lecture course or to completely administer an online course. MySocLab provides access to a wealth of resources all geared to meet the individual teaching and learning needs of every instructor and every student. Highlights of MySocLab include the following:

- MySocLab for *Racial and Ethnic Diversity in the USA* provides all the tools you need to engage every student before, during, and after class. An assignment calendar and gradebook allow you to assign specific activities with due dates and to measure your students' progress throughout the semester.
- The **Pearson e-text** lets students access their textbook anytime, anywhere, and any way they want, including *listening online*. The e-Text for *Racial and Ethnic Diversity in the USA* features integrated videos, Social Explorer activities, additional readings, and interactive self-quizzes.
- A **Personalized Study Plan** for each student, based on Bloom's Taxonomy, arranges activities from those that require less complex thinking—like remembering and understanding—to more complex critical thinking—like applying and analyzing. This layered approach promotes better critical-thinking skills, helping students succeed in the course and beyond.

New Features of MySocLab

Two exciting new features of MySocLab are Social Explorer and MySocLibrary.

- **Social Explorer** activities connect with topics from the text, engaging students with data visualizations, comparisons of change over time, and data localized to their own communities.
- **MySocLibrary** available in the Pearson e-Text 200 classic and contemporary articles enables students to explore the discipline more deeply. Multiple-choice questions for each reading help students review what they've learned—and allow instructors to monitor their performance.

MySocLab and *Racial and Ethnic Diversity in the USA*

Correlations of the many resources in MySocLab are now included through icons in the margins that connect resources and content, making the integration of MySocLab even more flexible and useful to instructors for making assignments and for engaging students by giving them the opportunity to explore important sociological concepts and enhance their performance in this course.

Acknowledgments

This book has benefited from the thoughtful reaction of my students in classes as well as students who have communicated with me via email their experiences studying race and ethnicity in colleges across the country and overseas.

The book was improved by the suggestions of earlier manuscript drafts by the following people:

Annette Allen, Troy University, Montgomery
Amy Armenia, Randolph-Macon College
Michelle Bentz, Central Community College, Columbus
Shelly Brown-Jeffy, University of North Carolina, Greensboro
Henry Codjoe, Dalton State College
Mary Donaghy, Arkansas State University
Elena Ermolaeva, Marshall University
Dr. Loyd Ganey, College of Southern Nevada
Matasha Harris, Florida Memorial University
Kevin James, Indiana University South Bend
Tal Levy, Marygrove College
Enid Logan, University of Minnesota
CoSandra McNeal, Jackson State University
Kendra Murphy, University of Memphis
Vania Penha-Lopes, Bloomfield College
Jean Raniseski, Alvin Community College
Jan Rezek, West Virginia University Institute of Technology
Clara Senif, College of Southern Nevada
Tomecia Sobers, Fayetteville Technical Community College

Ann Strahm, California State University, Stanislaus

Madeline Troche-Rodriguez, Harry S. Truman College

Nivedita Vaidya, California State University, Los Angeles

Milton Vickerman, University of Virginia

George Wilson, University of Miami

I would like to especially thank my editor at Pearson, Charylce Jones-Owen, for developing this book and bringing fresh insights to the important topics covered in this book. I also am pleased to acknowledge the leadership of Dickson Musslewhite in championing this fresh approach to race and ethnicity in the United States. They make a great team in the production of academic books.

The truly exciting challenge of writing and researching has always been for me an enriching experience, mostly because of the supportive home I share with my wife, Sandy. She knows so well my appreciation and gratitude, now as in the past and in the future.

Richard T. Schaefer
http:schaeferrt@aol.com
www.schaefersociology.net

About the Author

Richard T. Schaefer grew up in Chicago at a time when neighborhoods were going through transitions in ethnic and racial composition. He found himself increasingly intrigued by what was happening, how people were reacting, and how these changes affected neighborhoods and people's jobs. In high school, he took a course in sociology. His interest in social issues caused him to gravitate to more sociology courses at Northwestern University, where he eventually received a BA in sociology.

"Originally, as an undergraduate I thought I would go on to law school and become a lawyer. But after taking a few sociology courses, I found myself wanting to learn more about what sociologists studied and was fascinated by the kinds of questions they raised," Dr. Schaefer says. "Perhaps most fascinating and, to me, relevant to the 1960s was the intersection of race, gender, and social class." This interest led him to obtain his MA and PhD in sociology from the University of Chicago. Dr. Schaefer's continuing interest in race relations led him to write his master's thesis on the membership of the Ku Klux Klan and his doctoral thesis on racial prejudice and race relations in Great Britain.

Dr. Schaefer went on to become a professor of sociology. He has taught sociology and courses on multiculturalism for 30 years. He has been invited to give special presentations to students and faculty on racial and ethnic diversity in Illinois, Indiana, Missouri, North Carolina, Ohio, and Texas.

Dr. Schaefer is the author of *Racial and Ethnicity in the United States*, seventh edition (Pearson, 2012) and *Racial and Ethnic Groups*, thirteenth edition (Pearson, 2012). Dr. Schaefer is the general editor of the three-volume *Encyclopedia of Race, Ethnicity, and Society* (2008). He also is the author of the thirteenth edition of *Sociology* (2012), the tenth edition of *Sociology: A Brief Introduction* (2013), the second edition of *Sociology: A Modular Approach* (2013), and the sixth edition of *Sociology Matters* (2013). Schaefer coauthored with William Zellner the ninth edition of *Extraordinary Groups* (2011). His articles and book reviews have appeared in many journals, including *American Journal of Sociology, Phylon: A Review of Race and Culture, Contemporary Sociology, Sociology and Social Research, Sociological Quarterly,* and *Teaching Sociology.* He served as president of the Midwest Sociological Society from 1994 to 1995. In recognition of his achievements in undergraduate teaching, he was named Vincent de Paul Professor of Sociology in 2004.

 Listen to Chapter 1 on MySocLab

1 Exploring Race and Ethnicity in the United States

1-1 Explain how groups are ranked in the United States.

1-2 Identify the four types of minority groups.

1-3 Discuss the social significance of race.

1-4 Address the impact of race on human behavior, identity, and interactions with others.

1-5 Identify how sociology assists in understanding race and ethnicity.

1-6 Explain the creation of subordinate-group status.

1-7 Discuss the consequences of subordinate-group status.

1-8 Describe the evolving nature of race and ethnic relations.

Lewiston, Maine, was dying. Now Lewiston is thriving, even in the midst of a national recession. This city changed its future. In 2000, the community of about 36,000, 96 percent White people, mostly of French and Irish descent, was going nowhere. The textile mills were shuttered and massive social welfare programs were created locally to meet the needs of the people. It was little wonder that nearby resident Stephen King often chose its abandoned mills and other buildings as inspiration for his suspense novels.

In February 2001, Black Africans originally from Somalia and of the Muslim faith, began to settle in Lewiston from other areas throughout the United States. With few job opportunities and well-known long, cold winters, it seemed like an unlikely destination for people whose homeland is hot and mostly arid. Better schools, little crime, cheap housing, and good social welfare programs attracted the initial arrivals. Once a small group was established, more and more Somalis arrived as the first group shared their positive experiences with friends and relatives. Not everyone stayed because of the winters or unrelated explanations, yet they continued to come.

The numbers of arrivals ebbed and flowed—the increased immigration regulations after 9/11 made entry difficult for Arab Muslims such as the Somali immigrants. One mayor in 2002 issued a public letter encouraging Somalis not to come; his actions were widely denounced. Another man threw a pig's head into a local mosque during evening prayers. Muslims by tradition cannot touch, much less eat, pork. Politicians continue to make unwelcoming comments, but they are quickly drowned out by those who are supportive of the 6,000-plus Somali community. For their part, the Somalis have settled in and are raising their children, but they are concerned that their sons and daughters identify more with being American than with being Somali. Despite their limited resources, as a community they send about $300,000 a month to friends and relatives in Somalia who continue to face incredible hardship.

For over ten years, they have come to Lewiston—10 to 30 *every week*. Lewiston is thriving in a state that continues to face many challenges. A decade is not a long time to reach conclusions about race, religion, and immigration. Somalis, who now account for about 15 percent of the population, have graduated from the local community college, run for office, and opened up dozens of previously shuttered businesses. Others commute the 20 miles to L.L.Bean warehouses to work (Canfield 2012; Cullen 2011; Hammond 2010; Huisman et al. 2011; Tice 2007).

In the pages and chapters that follow, several themes will emerge. The struggles of racial, ethnic, language, and religious minorities have often required their organized efforts to overcome inequities. Significant White support but also organized resistance typically mark these struggles. The various groups that make the United States diverse do not speak with one voice. For example, the Somalis of Maine are made up of different ethnic or tribal groups. Most are Bantu, who were targeted during the 1991 civil war, fled to refugee camps in Kenya, came to the United States, and resettled in Maine. They still see themselves as different from other ethnic groups from Somalia.

One aspect of the struggle to overcome inequality is the continuing effort to identify strategies and services to assist minorities in their struggle to overcome prejudice and discrimination. Among the beneficiaries of programs aimed at racial and ethnic minorities are White Americans, who, far from all being affluent themselves, have also experienced challenges in their lives.

Lewiston, Maine, a town undergoing difficult economic times over the last twenty years, received a boost from the arrival of Somalis from Africa who have now established a viable community.

The election and re-election of the nation's first African American president (who incidentally carried three states of the former Confederacy) presents the temptation to declare that issues of racial inequality are past or racism is limited to a few troublemakers. Progress has been made and expressions of explicit racism are rarely tolerated, yet challenges remain for immigrants of any color and racial, ethnic, and religious minorities (Massey 2011).

The United States is a diverse nation and is becoming even more so, as shown in Table 1.1. In 2010, approximately 33 percent of the population were members of racial minorities or were Hispanic. This represents one out of three people in the United States, without counting White ethnic groups or foreign-born Whites.

TABLE 1.1
Racial and Ethnic Groups in the United States

Classification	Number in Thousands	Percentage of Total Population
RACIAL GROUPS		
Whites (non-Hispanic)	194,553	63.1
Blacks/African Americans	34,658	11.2
Native Americans, Alaskan Natives	2,476	0.8
Asian Americans	15,899	5.2
Chinese	3,535	1.1
Asian Indians	2,919	1.0
Filipinos	2,650	0.9
Vietnamese	1,633	0.5
Koreans	1,464	0.5
Japanese	842	0.3
Pacific Islanders, Native Hawaiians, and other Asian Americans	2,856	0.9
ETHNIC GROUPS		
White ancestry (single or mixed, non-Hispanic)		
Germans	49,345	16.0
Irish	35,664	11.6
English	26,874	8.7
Italians	17,491	5.7
Poles	9,757	3.2
French	9,159	3.0
Scotch and Scotch-Irish	9,122	3.0
Jews	6,452	2.1
Hispanics (or Latinos)	50,478	16.4
Mexican Americans	31,798	10.3
Puerto Ricans	4,624	1.5
Cubans	1,785	0.6
Salvadorans	1,648	0.5
Dominicans	1,415	0.5
Guatemalans	1,044	0.3
Other Hispanics	8,164	2.7
TOTAL (ALL GROUPS)	308,746	

Note: All data are for 2010. Percentages do not total 100 percent, and when subcategories are added, they do not match totals in major categories because of overlap between groups (e.g., Polish American Jews or people of mixed ancestry such as Irish and Italian).

Source: 2008–2010. Three-year estimate from American Community Survey, 2010: Table B04003, B03001, C04006; Davidson and Pyle 2011:117; Ennis et al. 2011; Hoeffel et al. 2012; Humes et al. 2011.

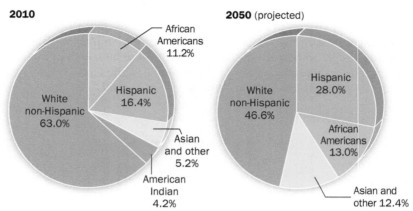

Explore the Map on MySocLab: Where the Minority-Majority Already Exists

FIGURE 1.1

Population of the United States by Race and Ethnicity, 2010 and 2050 (Projected)

According to projections by the Census Bureau, the proportion of residents of the United States who are White and non-Hispanic will decrease significantly by the year 2050. By contrast, the proportion of both Hispanic Americans and Asian Americans will rise significantly.

Source: Bureau of the Census 2012p: Table 6.

As shown in Figure 1.1, between 2010 and 2050, the Black, Hispanic, Asian, and Native American population in the United States is expected to increase to almost 54 percent. Although the composition of the population is changing, problems of prejudice, discrimination, and mistrust remain. This trend toward "majority-minority" got underway noticeably in 2011 when Latino and non-White babies outnumbered White newborns for the first time in the United States (Bureau of the Census 2012d).

Ranking Groups

In every society, not all groups are treated or viewed equally. Identifying a subordinate group or a minority in a society seems to be a simple task. In the United States, the groups readily identified as minorities—Blacks and Native Americans, for example—are outnumbered by non-Blacks and non–Native Americans. However, having minority status is not necessarily a result of being outnumbered. A social minority need not be a mathematical one. A **minority group** is a subordinate group whose members have significantly less control or power over their own lives than do the members of a dominant or majority group. In sociology, *minority* means the same as *subordinate*, and *dominant* is used interchangeably with *majority*.

Confronted with evidence that a particular minority in the United States is subordinate to the majority, some people respond, "Why not? After all, this is a democracy, so the majority rules." However, the subordination of a minority involves more than its inability to rule over society. A member of a subordinate or minority group experiences a narrowing of life's opportunities—for success, education, wealth, the pursuit of happiness—that goes beyond any personal shortcoming he or she may have. A minority group does not share in proportion to its numbers what a given society, such as the United States, defines as valuable.

Being superior in numbers does not guarantee a group has control over its destiny or ensure majority status. In 1920, the majority of people in Mississippi and South Carolina were African Americans. Yet African Americans did not have as much control over their lives as did Whites, let alone control of the states in which they lived. Throughout the United States today are counties or neighborhoods in which the majority of people are African American, Native American, or Hispanic, but White Americans are the dominant force. Nationally, 50.7 percent of the population is female, but males still dominate positions of authority and wealth well beyond their numbers.

A minority or subordinate group has five characteristics: unequal treatment, distinguishing physical or cultural traits, involuntary membership, awareness of subordination, and in-group marriage (Wagley and Harris 1958):

1. Members of a minority experience unequal treatment and have less power over their lives than members of a dominant group have over theirs. Prejudice, discrimination, segregation, and even extermination create this social inequality.

2. Members of a minority group share physical or cultural characteristics such as skin color or language that distinguish them from the dominant group. Each society has its own arbitrary standard for determining which characteristics are most important in defining dominant and minority groups.

3. Membership in a dominant or minority group is not voluntary: People are born into the group. A person does not choose to be African American or White.

4. Minority group members have a strong sense of group solidarity. William Graham Sumner, writing in 1906, noted that people make distinctions between members of their own group (the in-group) and everyone else (the out-group). When a group is the object of long-term prejudice and discrimination, the feeling of "us versus them" often becomes intense.

5. Members of a minority generally marry others from the same group. A member of a dominant group often is unwilling to join a supposedly inferior minority by marrying one of its members. In addition, the minority group's sense of solidarity encourages marriage within the group and discourages marriage to outsiders.

Although "minority" status is not about numbers, there is no denying that the White American majority is diminishing in size relative to the growing diversity of racial and ethnic groups, as illustrated in Figure 1.2.

Types of Groups

There are four types of minority or subordinate groups. All four, except where noted, have the five properties previously outlined. The four criteria for classifying minority groups are race, ethnicity, religion, and gender.

Racial Groups

The term **racial group** is reserved for minorities and the corresponding majorities that are socially set apart because of obvious physical differences. Notice the two crucial words in the definition: *obvious* and *physical*. What is obvious? Hair color? Shape of an earlobe? Presence of body hair? To whom are these differences obvious, and why? Each society defines what it finds obvious.

In the United States, skin color is one obvious difference. On a cold winter day when one has clothing covering all but one's head, however, skin color may be less obvious than hair color. Yet people in the United States have learned informally that skin color is important and hair color is unimportant. In the United States, people have traditionally

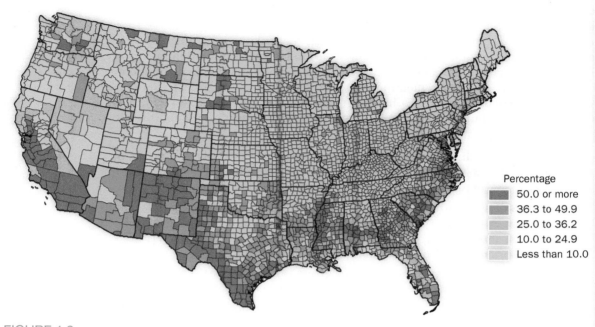

Percentage
- 50.0 or more
- 36.3 to 49.9
- 25.0 to 36.2
- 10.0 to 24.9
- Less than 10.0

FIGURE 1.2
Minority Population by County

In four states (California, Hawaii, New Mexico, and Texas) and the District of Columbia, as well as in about one-tenth of all counties, minorities constitute the numerical majority.

Source: Bureau of the Census 2011d.

classified themselves as either Black or White. There is no in-between state except for people readily identified as Native Americans or Asian Americans. Later in this chapter, we explore this issue more deeply and see how such assumptions about race have complex implications.

Other societies use skin color as a standard but may have a more elaborate system of classification. In Brazil, where hostility between races is less prevalent than in the United States, numerous categories identify people on the basis of skin color. In the United States, a person is Black or White. In Brazil, a variety of terms such as *cafuso, mazombo, preto,* and *escuro* are used to describe various combinations of skin color, facial features, and hair texture.

The designation of a racial group emphasizes physical differences as opposed to cultural distinctions. In the United States, minority races include Blacks, Native Americans (or American Indians), Japanese Americans, Chinese Americans, Arab Americans, Filipinos, Hawaiians, and other Asian peoples. The issue of race and racial differences has been an important one, not only in the United States but also throughout the entire sphere of European influence. Later in this chapter, we examine race and its significance more closely. We should not forget that Whites are a race, too. As we consider in Chapter 4, who is White has been subject to change over history when certain European groups were considered not worthy of being considered White. Partly to compete against a growing Black population, the "Whiting" of some European Americans has occurred. In Chapter 4, we consider how Italians and Irish for all intents and purposes were once considered *not* to be White by other Americans.

Some racial groups also may have unique cultural traditions, as we can readily see in the many Chinatowns throughout the United States. For racial groups, however, the physical distinctiveness and not the cultural differences generally prove to be the barrier to acceptance by the host society. For example, Chinese Americans who are faithful Protestants and know the names of all the members of the Baseball Hall of Fame may be bearers of American culture. Yet these Chinese Americans are still part of a minority because they are seen as physically different.

Ethnic Groups

Ethnic minority groups are differentiated from the dominant group on the basis of cultural differences such as language, attitudes toward marriage and parenting, and food habits. **Ethnic groups** are groups set apart from others because of their national origin or distinctive cultural patterns.

View the **Chart** on **MySocLab**: *U.S Racial-Ethnic Groups'*

Ethnic groups in the United States include a grouping that we call *Hispanics* or *Latinos*, which, in turn, include Mexican Americans, Puerto Ricans, Cubans, and other Latin American residents of the United States. Hispanics can be either Black or White, as in the case of a dark-skinned Puerto Rican who may be taken as Black in central Texas but may be viewed as Puerto Rican in New York City. The ethnic group category also includes White ethnics such as Irish Americans, Polish Americans, and Norwegian Americans.

The cultural traits that make groups distinctive usually originate from their homelands or, for Jews, from a long history of being segregated and prohibited from becoming a part of a host society. Once living in the United States, an immigrant group may maintain distinctive cultural practices through associations, clubs, and worship. Ethnic enclaves such as a Little Haiti or a Greektown in urban areas also perpetuate cultural distinctiveness.

Ethnicity and race have been long recognized as an important source of differentiation. More than a century ago, African American sociologist W. E. B. Du Bois, addressing an audience at a world antislavery convention in London in 1900, called attention to the overwhelming importance of the color line throughout the world. In "Speaking Out," we read the remarks of Du Bois, the first Black person to receive a doctorate from Harvard, who later helped organize the National Association for the Advancement of Colored People (NAACP). Du Bois's observations give us a historic perspective on the struggle for equality. We can look ahead, knowing how far we have come and speculating on how much further we have to go.

We also should appreciate the context of Du Bois's insight. He spoke of his "color-line" prediction in light of then-contemporary U.S. occupation of the Philippines and the relationship of "darker to lighter races" worldwide. So today, he would not only see that race matters not only in the sporadic hate crimes we hear about but also in global conflicts (Roediger 2009).

Religious Groups

Association with a religion other than the dominant faith is the third basis for minority-group status. In the United States, Protestants, as a group, outnumber members of all other religions. Roman Catholics form the largest minority religion. For people who are not a part of the Christian tradition, such as followers of Islam, allegiance to their faith often is misunderstood and stigmatizes people. This stigmatization became especially widespread and legitimated by government action in the aftermath of the attacks of September 11, 2001.

Religious minorities include groups such as the Church of Jesus Christ of Latter-day Saints (the Mormons), Jehovah's Witnesses, Amish, Muslims, and Buddhists. Cults or sects associated with practices such as animal sacrifice, doomsday prophecy, demon worship, or the use of snakes in a ritualistic fashion also constitute religious minorities. Jews are excluded from this category and placed among ethnic groups. Culture is a more important

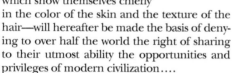

Speaking Out

Problem of the Color Line

In the metropolis of the modern world, in this the closing year of the nineteenth century, there has been assembled a congress of men and women of African blood, to deliberate solemnly upon the present situation and outlook of the darker races of mankind. The problem of the twentieth century is the problem of the color line, the question as to how far differences of race—which show themselves chiefly in the color of the skin and the texture of the hair—will hereafter be made the basis of denying to over half the world the right of sharing to their utmost ability the opportunities and privileges of modern civilization....

To be sure, the darker races are today the least advanced in culture according to European standards. This has not, however, always been the case in the past, and certainly the world's history, both ancient and modern, has given many instances of no despicable ability and capacity among the blackest races of men.

In any case, the modern world must remember that in this age when the ends of the world are being brought so near together, the millions of black men in Africa, America, and Islands of the Sea, not to speak of the brown and yellow myriads elsewhere, are bound to have a great influence upon the world in the future, by reason of sheer numbers and physical contact. If now the world of culture

W. E. B. Du Bois

bends itself towards giving Negroes and other dark men the largest and broadest opportunity for education and self-development, then this contact and influence is bound to have a beneficial effect upon the world and hasten human progress. But if, by reason of carelessness, prejudice, greed, and injustice, the black world is to be exploited and ravished and degraded, the results must be deplorable, if not fatal—not simply to them, but to the high ideals of justice, freedom and culture which a thousand years of Christian civilization have held before Europe....

Let the world take no backward step in that slow but sure progress which has successively refused to let the spirit of class, of caste, of privilege, or of birth, debar from life, liberty, and the pursuit of happiness a striving human soul.

Let not color or race be a feature of distinction between White and Black men, regardless of worth or ability....

Thus we appeal with boldness and confidence to the Great Powers of the civilized world, trusting in the wide spirit of humanity, and the deep sense of justice of our age, for a generous recognition of the righteousness of our cause.

Source: From W. E. B. Du Bois 1900 [1969a], *ABC of Color*, pp. 20–21, 23.

defining trait for Jewish people worldwide than is religious doctrine. Jewish Americans share a cultural tradition that goes beyond theology. In this sense, it is appropriate to view them as an ethnic group rather than as members of a religious faith.

Gender Groups

Gender is another attribute that creates dominant and subordinate groups. Males are the social majority; females, although numerous, are relegated to the position of the social minority. Women are considered a minority even though they do not exhibit all the characteristics outlined earlier (e.g., there is little in-group marriage). Women encounter prejudice and discrimination and are physically distinguishable. Group membership is involuntary, and many women have developed a sense of sisterhood.

Women who are members of racial and ethnic minorities face special challenges to achieving equality. They suffer from greater inequality because they belong to two separate minority groups: a racial or ethnic group plus a subordinate gender group.

Other Subordinate Groups

This book focuses on groups that meet a set of criteria for subordinate status. People encounter prejudice or are excluded from full participation in society for many reasons. Racial, ethnic, religious, and gender barriers are the main ones, but there are others. Age, disability status, physical appearance, and sexual orientation are among the factors that are used to subordinate groups of people.

Does Race Matter?

We see people around us—some of whom may look quite different from us. Do these differences matter? The simple answer is no, but because so many people have for so long acted as if differences in physical characteristics as well as geographic origin and shared culture do matter, distinct groups have been created in people's minds. Race has many meanings for many people. Often these meanings are inaccurate and based on theories scientists discarded generations ago. As we will see, race is a socially constructed concept (Young 2003).

Biological Meaning

The way the term *race* has been used by some people to apply to human beings lacks any scientific basis. Distinctive physical characteristics for groups of human beings cannot be identified the same way that scientists distinguish one animal species from another. The idea of **biological race** is based on the mistaken notion of a genetically isolated human group.

Absence of Pure Races   Even past proponents of the belief that sharp, scientific divisions exist among humans had endless debates over what the races of the world were. Given people's frequent migration, exploration, and invasions, pure genetic types have not existed for some time, if they ever did. There are no mutually exclusive races. Skin color among African Americans varies tremendously, as it does among White Americans. There is even an overlapping of dark-skinned Whites and light-skinned African Americans. If we grouped people by genetic resistance to malaria and by fingerprint patterns, then Norwegians and many African groups would be the same race. If we grouped people by lactose intolerance some Africans, Asians, and southern Europeans would be of one group and West Africans and northern Europeans of another (Leehotz 1995; Shanklin 1994).

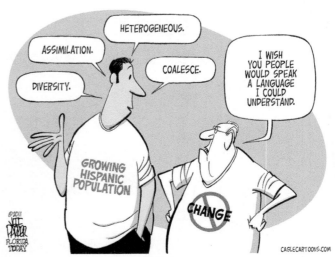

The changing landscape of the United States is hard to miss, but not all people equally embrace it.

Biologically, no pure, distinct races exist. Research as a part of the Human Genome Project mapping human deoxyribonucleic acid (DNA) has served to confirm genetic diversity only, with differences within traditionally regarded racial groups (e.g., Black Africans) much greater than that between groups (e.g., between Black Africans and Europeans). Contemporary studies of DNA on a global basis have determined that about 90 percent of human genetic variation is within "local populations," such as within the French or within the Afghan people. The remaining 10 percent of total human variation is what we think of today as constituting races and accounts for skin color, hair form, nose shape, and so forth (Feldman 2010).

Research has also been conducted to determine whether personality characteristics such as temperament and nervous habits are inherited among minority groups. It is no surprise that the question of whether races have different innate levels of intelligence has led to the most explosive controversies (Bamshad and Olson 2003; El-Haj 2007).

Intelligence Tests Typically, intelligence is measured as an **intelligence quotient (IQ)**, which is the ratio of a person's mental age to his or her chronological age, multiplied by 100, with 100 representing average intelligence and higher scores representing greater intelligence. It should be noted that there is little consensus over just what intelligence is, other than as defined by such IQ tests. Intelligence tests are adjusted for a person's age so that 10-year-olds take a different test from someone 20 years old. Although research shows that certain learning strategies can improve a person's IQ, generally IQ remains stable as one ages.

A great deal of debate continues over the accuracy of IQ tests. Are they biased toward people who come to the tests with knowledge similar to that of the test writers? Sceptics argue that questions in IQ tests do not truly measure intellectual potential. The question of cultural bias in tests remains a concern. The most recent research shows that differences in intelligence scores between Blacks and Whites are almost eliminated when adjustments are made for social and economic characteristics (Brooks-Gunn, Klebanov, and Duncan 1996; Kagan 1971; Young 2003).

In 1994, an 845-page book unleashed another national debate on the issue of IQ. This research effort of psychologist Richard J. Herrnstein and social scientist Charles Murray, published in *The Bell Curve* (1994), concluded that 60 percent of IQ is inheritable and that racial groups offer a convenient means to generalize about any differences in intelligence. Unlike most other proponents of the race–IQ link, the authors offered policy suggestions that included ending welfare to discourage births among low-IQ poor women and changing immigration laws so that the IQ pool in the United States is not diminished. Herrnstein and Murray even made generalizations about IQ levels among Asians and Hispanics in the United States, groups subject to even more intermarriage. In spite of *The Bell Curve* "research," it is not possible to generalize about absolute differences between groups, such as Latinos versus Whites, when almost half of Latinos in the United States marry non-Hispanics.

More than a decade later, the mere mention of the "bell curve" still signals to many people a belief in a racial hierarchy,

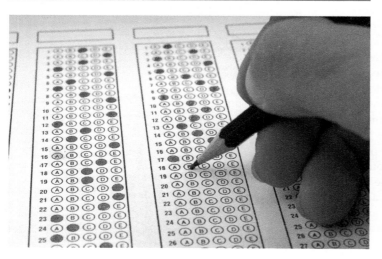

Listen to the Audio on MySocLab: Race and Intelligence

with Whites toward the top and Blacks near the bottom. The research present then and repeated today points to the difficulty in definitions: What is intelligence, and what constitutes a racial group, given generations (if not centuries) of intermarriage? How can we speak of definitive inherited racial differences if there has been intermarriage between people of every color? Furthermore, as people on both sides of the debate have noted, regardless of the findings, we would still want to strive to maximize the talents of each individual. All research shows that the differences within a group are much greater than any alleged differences between group averages.

Why does such IQ research reemerge if the data are subject to different interpretations? The argument that "we" are superior to "them" is appealing to the dominant group. It justifies receiving opportunities that are denied to others. We can anticipate that the debate over IQ and the allegations of significant group differences will continue. Policymakers need to acknowledge the difficulty in treating race as a biologically significant characteristic.

Social Construction of Race

If race does not distinguish humans from one another biologically, then why does it seem to be so important? It is important because of the social meaning people have attached to it. The 1950 (UNESCO) Statement on Race maintains, "for all practical social purposes 'race' is not so much a biological phenomenon as a social myth" (Montagu 1972:118). Adolf Hitler expressed concern over the "Jewish race" and translated this concern into the Holocaust and Nazi death camps. Winston Churchill spoke proudly of the "British race" and used that pride to spur a nation to fight. Evidently, race was a useful political tool for two very different leaders in the 1930s and 1940s.

Race is a social construction, and this process benefits the oppressor, who defines which groups of people are privileged and which groups are not. The acceptance of race in a society as a legitimate category allows racial hierarchies to emerge to the benefit of the dominant "races." For example, inner-city drive-by shootings are now seen as a race-specific problem worthy of local officials cleaning up troubled neighborhoods. Yet, school shootings are viewed as a societal concern and placed on the national agenda.

People could speculate that if human groups have obvious physical differences, then they could have corresponding mental or personality differences. No one disagrees that people differ in temperament, potential to learn, and sense of humor, among other characteristics. In its social sense, race implies that groups that differ physically also bear distinctive emotional and mental abilities or disabilities. These beliefs are based on the notion that humankind can be divided into distinct groups. We have already seen the difficulties associated with pigeonholing people into racial categories. Despite these difficulties, belief in the inheritance of behavior patterns and in an association between physical and cultural traits is widespread. It is called **racism** when this belief is coupled with the feeling that certain groups or races are inherently superior to others. Racism is a doctrine of racial supremacy that states one race is superior to another (Bash 2001; Bonilla-Silva 1996).

We questioned the biological significance of race in the previous section. In modern complex industrial societies, we find little adaptive utility in the presence or absence of prominent chins, epicanthic folds of the eyelids, or the comparative amount of melanin in the skin. It is of little importance that people are genetically different; what is important is that they approach one another with dissimilar perspectives. It is in the social setting that race is decisive. Race is significant because people have given it significance.

Race definitions are crystallized through what Michael Omi and Howard Winant (1994) called **racial formation**, a sociohistorical process by which racial categories are created, inhabited, transformed, and destroyed. Those in power define groups of people in a certain way that depends on a racist social structure. As in the United States, these definitions can become systematic and embedded in many aspects of society for a significant length of time. No one escapes the extent and frequency to which we are subjected to racial formation. The Native Americans and the creation of the reservation system for Native Americans in the late 1800s is an example of this racial formation. The federal American Indian policy combined previously distinctive tribes into a single group (Feagin and Elias 2012).

With rising immigration from Latin America in the latter part of the twentieth century, the fluid nature of racial formation is evident. As if it happened in one day, people in the United States have spoken about the Latin Americanization of the United States or stated that the biracial order of Black and White has been replaced with a *triracial* order. We examine this social context of the changing nature of diversity to understand how scholars have sought to generalize about intergroup relations in the United States and elsewhere (Bonilla-Silva and Dietrich 2011; Frank et al. 2010).

In the southern United States, the social construction of race was known as the "one-drop rule." This tradition stipulated that if a person had even a single drop of "Black blood," that person was defined and viewed as Black. Today, children of biracial or multi-racial marriages try to build their own identities in a country that seems intent on placing them in some single, traditional category—a topic we look at next.

Biracial and Multiracial Identity: Who Am I?

People are now more willing to accept and advance identities that do not fit neatly into mutually exclusive categories. Hence, increasing numbers of people are identifying themselves as biracial or multiracial or, at the very least, explicitly viewing themselves as reflecting a diverse racial and ethnic identity. Barack Obama is the most visible person with a biracial background. President Obama has explicitly stated he sees himself as a Black man, although his mother was White and he was largely raised by his White grandparents. Yet in 2010, he chose only to check the "(Black, African American, or Negro) box on his household's census form. Obviously, biracial does not mean biracial identity.

Read the Document on MySocLab: *Beyond Black and White: Remaking Race in America*

The diversity of the United States today has made it more difficult for many people to place themselves on the racial and ethnic landscape. It reminds us that racial formation continues to take place. Obviously, the racial and ethnic landscape, as we have seen, is constructed not naturally but socially and, therefore, is subject to change and different interpretations. Although our focus is on the United States, almost every nation faces the same problems.

The United States tracks people by race and ethnicity for myriad reasons, ranging from attempting to improve the status of oppressed groups to diversifying classrooms. But how can we measure the growing number of people whose ancestry is mixed by anyone's definition? In Research Focus, we consider how the U.S. Bureau of the Census dealt with this issue.

Besides the increasing respect for biracial identity and multiracial identity, group names undergo change as well. Within little more than a generation during the twentieth century, labels that were applied to subordinate groups changed from *Negroes* to *Blacks* to *African Americans*, from *American Indians* to *Native Americans* or *Native Peoples*. However, more Native Americans prefer the use of their tribal name, such as *Seminole*, instead of a collective label. The old 1950s statistical term of "people with a Spanish surname" has long been discarded, yet there is disagreement over a new term: *Latino* or *Hispanic*. Like Native Americans, Hispanic Americans avoid such global terms and prefer their native names, such as *Puerto Ricans* or *Cubans*. People of Mexican ancestry indicate preferences for a variety of names, such as *Mexican American*, *Chicano*, or simply *Mexican*.

Research Focus

Multiracial Identity

Approaching Census 2000, a movement was spawned by people who were frustrated by government questionnaires that forced them to indicate only one race. Take the case of Stacey Davis in New Orleans. The young woman's mother is Thai and her father is Creole, a blend of Black, French, and German. People seeing Stacey confuse her for a Latina, Filipina, or Hawaiian. Officially, she has been "White" all her life because she looks White. The census in 2000 for the first time gave people the option to check off one or more racial groups. "Biracial" or "multiracial" was not an option because pretests showed very few people would use it. This meant that in Census 2000 the government recognized different social constructions of racial identity—that is, a person could be Asian American and White.

Most people did select one racial category in Census 2000 and again in 2010. Overall, approximately 9 million people, or 2.9 percent of the total population, selected two or more racial groups in 2010. This was a smaller proportion than many observers had anticipated. In fact, not even the majority of mixed-race couples identified their children with more than one racial classification. As shown in Figure 1.3, Whites and African Americans were the most common multiple identity, with 1.8 million people or so selecting that response. As a group, American Indians were most likely to select a second category and Whites least likely. Race is socially defined.

Complicating the situation is that, in the Census, people are asked separately whether they are Hispanic or non-Hispanic. So a Hispanic person can be any race.

In the 2010 Census, 94 percent indicated they were one race, but 6 percent indicated two or more races; this proportion was twice as high than among non-Hispanics. Therefore, Latinos are more likely than non-Hispanics to indicate a multiracial ancestry.

Changes in measuring race and ethnicity are not necessarily over. Already Census officals are considering adding categories for people of Middle Eastern, North African, or Asian descent for 2020. "Hispanic" might even be added as a race category along with White, African-American, Asian, and American Indian/Alaska Native and Pacific Islander.

The Census Bureau's decisions do not necessarily resolve the frustration of hundreds of thousands of people such as Stacey Davis, who daily face people trying to place them in some racial or ethnic category that is convenient. However, it does underscore the complexity of social construction and trying to apply arbitrary definitions to the diversity of the human population. A symbol of this social construction of race can be seen in President Barack Obama, born of a White woman and a Black immigrant from Kenya. Although he has always identified himself as a Black man, it is worthy to note he was born in Hawaii, a state in which 23.6 percent of people see themselves as more than one race, compared to the national average of 2.9 percent.

Sources: DaCosta 2007; Dadei 2012; Grieco and Cassidy 2001; Humes 2011 et al. 2–11; Jones and Smith 2001; Saulny 2011; Welch 2011; Williams 2005.

Read the Document on MySocLab: Race Matters

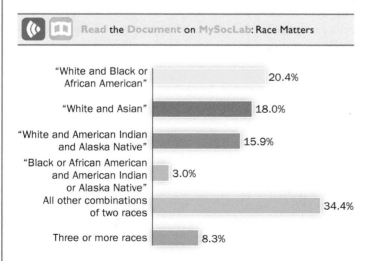

FIGURE 1.3

Multiple-Race Choices in Census 2010

This figure shows the percentage distribution of the 9 million people who chose two or more races (out of the total population of 309 million).

Source: Humes et al. 2011:10.

In the United States and other multiracial, multiethnic societies, **panethnicity**, the development of solidarity between ethnic subgroups, has emerged. The coalition of tribal groups as Native Americans or American Indians to confront outside forces, notably the federal government, is one example of panethnicity. Hispanics or Latinos and Asian Americans are other examples of panethnicity. Although it is rarely recognized by the dominant society, the very term *Black* or *African American* represents the descendants of many different ethnic or tribal groups, such as Akamba, Fulani, Hausa, Malinke, and Yoruba (Lopez and Espiritu 1990).

Is panethnicity a convenient label for *outsiders* or a term that reflects a mutual identity? Certainly, many people outside the group are unable or unwilling to recognize ethnic differences and prefer umbrella terms such as *Asian Americans*. For some small groups, combining with others is emerging as a useful way to make them heard, but there is always a fear that their own distinctive culture will become submerged. Although many Hispanics share the Spanish language and many are united by Roman Catholicism, only one in four native-born people of Mexican, Puerto Rican, or Cuban descent prefers a panethnic label to nationality or ethnic identity. Yet the growth of a variety of panethnic associations among many groups, including Hispanics, continues into the twenty-first century (de la Garza, DeSipio, Garcia, Garcia, and Falcon 1992; Espiritu 1992; Steinberg 2007).

Another challenge to identity is **marginality**: the status of being between two cultures, as in the case of a person whose mother is a Jew and father a Christian. A century ago, Du Bois (1903) spoke eloquently of the "double consciousness" that Black Americans feel—caught between being a citizen of the United States but viewed as something quite apart from the dominant social forces of society. Incomplete assimilation by immigrants also results in marginality. Although a Filipino woman migrating to the United States may take on the characteristics of her new host society, she may not be fully accepted and may, therefore, feel neither Filipino nor American. Marginalized individuals often encounter social situations in which their identities are sources of tension, especially when the expression of multiple identities is not accepted, and each finds him- or herself being perceived differently in different environments, with varying expectations (Park 1928; Stonequist 1937; Townsend, Markos, and Bergsieker 2009).

Yet another source of marginality comes from children of biracial or multiracial parental backgrounds and children adopted by parents of a different racial or ethnic background. For these children or adolescents, developing their racial or ethnic identity says more about society's desire to fix labels onto their own actions (Fryer et al. 2012).

As we seek to understand diversity in the United States, we must be mindful that ethnic and racial labels are just that: labels that have been socially constructed. Yet these social constructs can have a powerful impact, whether self-applied or applied by others.

Explore the Concept on MySocLab: *Social Constructions of Race and Ethnicity*

Sociology and the Study of Race and Ethnicity

Before proceeding further with our study of racial and ethnic groups, let us consider several sociological perspectives that provide insight into dominant–subordinate relationships. **Sociology** is the systematic study of social behavior and human groups, so it is aptly suited to enlarge our understanding of intergroup relations. The study of race relations has a long, valuable history in sociology. Admittedly, it has not always been progressive; indeed, at times it has reflected the prejudices of society. In some instances, sociology scholars who are members of racial, ethnic, and religious minorities, as well as women, have not been permitted to make the kind of contributions they are capable of making to the field.

Stratification by Class and Gender

That some members of society have unequal amounts of wealth, prestige, or power is a characteristic of all societies. Sociologists observe that entire groups may be assigned less or more of what a society values. The hierarchy that emerges is called **stratification**. Stratification is the structured ranking of entire groups of people that perpetuates unequal rewards and power in a society.

Much discussion of stratification identifies the **class**, or social ranking, of people who share similar wealth, according to sociologist Max Weber's classic definition. Mobility from one class to another is not easy to achieve. Movement into classes of greater wealth may be particularly difficult for subordinate-group members faced with lifelong prejudice and discrimination (Banton 2008; Gerth and Mills 1958).

Recall that the first property of subordinate-group standing is unequal treatment by the dominant group in the form of prejudice, discrimination, and segregation. Stratification is intertwined with the subordination of racial, ethnic, religious, and gender groups. Race has implications for the way people are treated; so does class. One also must add the effects of race and class together. For example, being poor and Black is not the same as being either one by itself. A wealthy Mexican American is not the same as an affluent Anglo American or Mexican Americans as a group.

Public discussion of issues such as housing or public assistance often is disguised as a discussion of class issues, when, in fact, the issues are based primarily on race. Similarly, some topics such as the poorest of the poor or the working poor are addressed in terms of race when the class component should be explicit. Nonetheless, the link between race and class in society is abundantly clear (Winant 2004).

Another stratification factor that we need to consider is gender. How different is the situation for women as contrasted with men? Returning again to the first property of minority groups—unequal treatment and less control—women do not receive treatment that equals that received by men. Whether the issue is jobs or poverty, education or crime, women typically have more difficult experiences. In addition, the situations women face in areas such as healthcare and welfare raise different concerns than they do for men. Just as we need to consider the role of social class to understand race and ethnicity better, we also need to consider the role of gender.

Watch the **Video** on **MySocLab**: *Social Stratification*

Read the **Document** on **MySocLab**: *Our Mother's Grief: Racial-Ethnic Women and the Maintenance of Families*

Theoretical Perspectives

Sociologists view society in different ways. Some see the world basically as a stable and ongoing entity. The endurance of a Chinatown, the general sameness of male–female roles over time, and other aspects of intergroup relations impress them. Some sociologists see society as composed of many groups in conflict, competing for scarce resources. Within this conflict, some people or even entire groups may be labeled or stigmatized in a way that blocks their access to what a society values. We examine three theoretical perspectives that are widely used by sociologists today: the functionalist, conflict, and labelling perspectives.

Functionalist Perspective In the view of a functionalist, a society is like a living organism in which each part contributes to the survival of the whole. The **functionalist perspective** emphasizes how the parts of society are structured to maintain its stability. According to this approach, if an aspect of social life does not contribute to a society's stability or survival, then it will not be passed on from one generation to the next.

It seems reasonable to assume that bigotry between races offers no such positive function, and so we ask, Why does it persist? Although agreeing that racial hostility is hardly to be admired, the functionalist would point out that it serves some positive functions from the perspective of the racists. We can identify five functions that racial beliefs have for the dominant group:

1. Racist ideologies provide a moral justification for maintaining a society that routinely deprives a group of its rights and privileges.

2. Racist beliefs discourage subordinate people from attempting to question their lowly status and why they must perform "the dirty work"; to do so is to question the very foundation of the society.

3. Racial ideologies not only justify existing practices but also serve as a rallying point for social movements, as seen in the rise of the Nazi party or present-day Aryan movements.

4. Racist myths encourage support for the existing order. Some argue that if there were any major societal change, the subordinate group would suffer even greater poverty, and the dominant group would suffer lower living standards.

5. Racist beliefs relieve the dominant group of the responsibility to address the economic and educational problems faced by subordinate groups.

As a result, racial ideology grows when a value system (e.g., that underlying a colonial empire or slavery) is being threatened (Levin and Nolan 2011:115–145; Nash 1962).

Prejudice and discrimination also cause definite dysfunctions. **Dysfunctions** are elements of society that may disrupt a social system or decrease its stability. Racism is dysfunctional to a society, including to its dominant group, in six ways:

1. A society that practices discrimination fails to use the resources of all individuals. Discrimination limits the search for talent and leadership to the dominant group.

2. Discrimination aggravates social problems such as poverty, delinquency, and crime and places the financial burden of alleviating these problems on the dominant group.

3. Society must invest a good deal of time and money to defend the barriers that prevent the full participation of all members.

4. Racial prejudice and discrimination undercut goodwill and friendly diplomatic relations between nations. They also negatively affect efforts to increase global trade.

5. Social change is inhibited because change may assist a subordinate group.

6. Discrimination promotes disrespect for law enforcement and for the peaceful settlement of disputes.

That racism has costs for the dominant group as well as for the subordinate group reminds us that intergroup conflict is exceedingly complex (Bowser and Hunt 1996; Feagin, Vera, and Batur 2000; Rose 1951).

Conflict Perspective   In contrast to the functionalists' emphasis on stability, conflict sociologists see the social world as being in continual struggle. The **conflict perspective** assumes that the social structure is best understood in terms of conflict or tension between competing groups. The result of this conflict is significant economic disparity and structural inequality in education, the labor market, housing, and healthcare delivery. Specifically, society is in a struggle between the privileged (the dominant group) and the exploited (the subordinate group). Such conflicts need not be physically violent and may take the form of immigration restrictions, real estate practices, or disputes over cuts in the federal budget.

The conflict model often is selected today when one is examining race and ethnicity because it readily accounts for the presence of tension between competing groups.

According to the conflict perspective, competition takes place between groups with unequal amounts of economic and political power. The minorities are exploited or, at best, ignored by the dominant group. The conflict perspective is viewed as more radical and activist than functionalism because conflict theorists emphasize social change and the redistribution of resources. Functionalists are not necessarily in favor of inequality; rather, their approach helps us understand why such systems persist.

Those who follow the conflict approach to race and ethnicity have remarked repeatedly that the subordinate group is criticized for its low status. That the dominant group is responsible for subordination is often ignored. William Ryan (1976) calls this an instance of **blaming the victim**: portraying the problems of racial and ethnic minorities as their fault rather than recognizing society's responsibility.

Conflict theorists consider the costs that come with residential segregation. Besides the more obvious cost of reducing housing options, racial and social class isolation reduces for people (including Whites) all available options in schools, retail shopping, and medical care. People, however, can travel to access services and businesses, and it is more likely that racial and ethnic minorities will have to make that sometimes costly and time-consuming trip (Carr and Kutty 2008).

Labeling Theory   Related to the conflict perspective and its concern over blaming the victim is **labeling theory**, a concept introduced by sociologist Howard Becker to explain why certain people are viewed as deviant and others engaging in the same behavior are not. Students of crime and deviance have relied heavily on labeling theory. According to labeling theory, a youth who misbehaves may be considered and treated as a delinquent if he or she comes from the "wrong kind of family." Another youth from a middle-class family who commits the same sort of misbehavior might be given another chance before being punished.

The labeling perspective directs our attention to the role that negative stereotypes play in race and ethnicity. The image that prejudiced people maintain of a group toward which they hold ill feelings is called a **stereotype**. Stereotypes are unreliable generalizations about all members of a group that do not take individual differences into account. The warrior image of Native American (American Indian) people is perpetuated by the frequent use of tribal names or even names such as "Indians" and "Redskins" for sports teams. In Chapter 2, we review some of the research on the stereotyping of minorities. This labeling is not limited to racial and ethnic groups, however. For instance, age can be used to exclude a person from an activity in which he or she is qualified to engage. Groups are subjected to stereotypes and discrimination in such a way that their treatment resembles that of social minorities. Social prejudice as a result of stereotyping exists toward ex-convicts, gamblers, alcoholics, lesbians, gays, prostitutes, people with AIDS, and people with disabilities, to name a few.

The labeling approach points out that stereotypes, when applied by people in power, can have negative consequences for people or groups identified falsely. A crucial aspect of the relationship between dominant and subordinate groups is the prerogative of the dominant group to define society's values. U.S. sociologist William I. Thomas (1923), an early critic of racial and gender discrimination, saw that the "definition of the situation" could mold the personality of the individual. In other words, Thomas observed that people respond not only to the objective features of a situation (or person) but also to the meaning these features have for them. So, for example, a lone walker seeing a young Black man walking toward him may perceive the situation differently than if the oncoming person is an older woman. Sociologist Elijah Anderson (2011) has long seen passers-by scrutinize him and other African American males more closely and suspiciously than they would women or White males. In this manner, we can create false images or stereotypes that become real in their social consequences.

Watch the Video on MySocLab: Racial Stereotypes and Discrimination

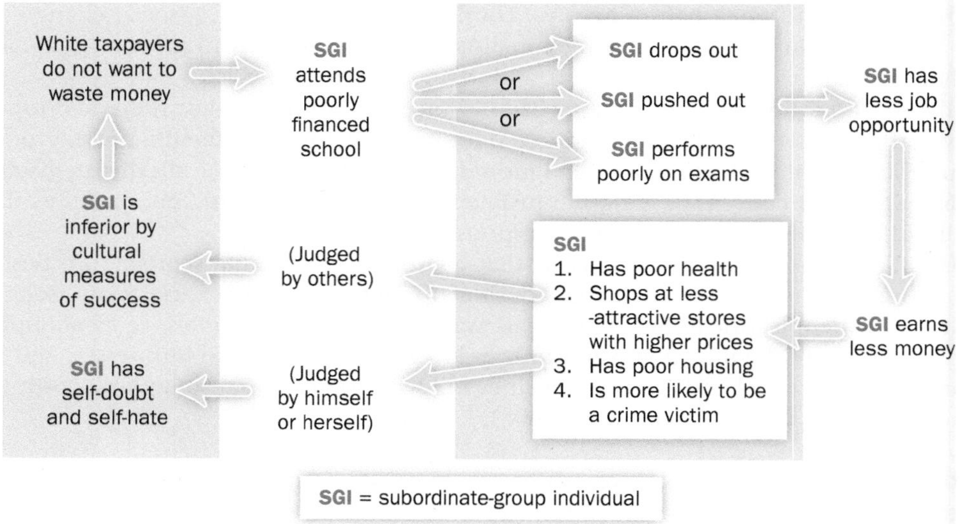

FIGURE 1.4
Self-Fulfilling Prophecy

The self-validating effects of dominant-group definitions are shown here. The subordinate-group individual attends a poorly financed school and is left unequipped to perform jobs that offer high status and pay. He or she then gets a low-paying job and must settle for a much lower level of society's standard of living. Because the person shares these societal standards, he or she may begin to feel self-doubt and self-hatred.

In certain situations, we may respond to negative stereotypes and act on them, with the result that false definitions become accurate. This is known as a **self-fulfilling prophecy**. A person or group described as having particular characteristics begins to display the very traits attributed to him or her. Thus, a child who is praised for being a natural comic may focus on learning to become funny to gain approval and attention.

Self-fulfilling prophecies can be devastating for minority groups (Figure 1.4). Such groups often find that they are allowed to hold only low-paying jobs with little prestige or opportunity for advancement. The rationale of the dominant society is that these minority people lack the ability to perform in more important and lucrative positions. Training to become scientists, executives, or physicians is denied to many subordinate-group individuals (SGIs), who are then locked into society's inferior jobs. As a result, the false definition of the self-fulfilling prophecy becomes real. The subordinate group becomes inferior because it was defined at the start as inferior and was, therefore, prevented from achieving the levels attained by the majority.

Because of this vicious circle, a talented subordinate-group person may come to see the fields of entertainment and professional sports as his or her only hope for achieving wealth and fame. Thus, it is no accident that successive waves of Irish, Jewish, Italian, African American, and Hispanic performers and athletes have made their mark on culture in the United States. Unfortunately, these very successes may convince the dominant group that its original stereotypes were valid—that these are the only areas of society in which subordinate-group members can excel. Furthermore, athletics and the arts are highly competitive areas. For every LeBron James and Jennifer Lopez who makes it, many, many more SGIs will end up disappointed.

The Creation of Subordinate-Group Status

Three situations are likely to lead to the formation of a relationship between a subordinate group and the dominant group. A subordinate group emerges through migration, annexation, and colonialism.

Migration

People who emigrate to a new country often find themselves a minority in that new country. Cultural or physical traits or religious affiliation may set the immigrant apart from the dominant group. Immigration from Europe, Asia, and Latin America has been a powerful force in shaping the fabric of life in the United States. **Migration** is the general term used to describe any transfer of population. **Emigration** (by emigrants) describes leaving a country to settle in another. **Immigration** (by immigrants) denotes coming into the new country. As an example, from Vietnam's perspective, the "boat people" were emigrants from Vietnam to the United States, but in the United States they were counted among this nation's immigrants.

Although some people migrate because they want to, leaving one's home country is not always voluntary. Millions have been transported as slaves against their will. Conflict and war have displaced people throughout human history. In the twentieth century, we saw huge population movements caused by two world wars; revolutions in Spain, Hungary, and Cuba; the partition of British India; conflicts in Southeast Asia, Korea, and Central America; and the confrontations between Arabs and Israelis.

In all types of movement, even when a U.S. family moves from Ohio to Florida, but especially regarding emigration, two sets of forces operate: push factors and pull factors. Push factors discourage a person from remaining where he or she lives. Religious persecution and economic factors such as dissatisfaction with employment opportunities are possible push factors. Pull factors, such as a better standard of living, friends and relatives who have already emigrated, and a promised job, attract an immigrant to a particular country.

Although generally we think of migration as a voluntary process, much of the population transfer that has occurred in the world has been involuntary. Such forced movement of people into another society guarantees a subordinate role. Involuntary migration is no longer common; although enslavement has a long history, all industrialized societies today prohibit such practices. Of course, many contemporary societies, including the United States, bear the legacy of slavery.

Migration has taken on new significance in the twenty-first century partly because of **globalization**, or the worldwide integration of government policies, cultures, social movements, and financial markets through trade and the exchange of ideas. The increased movement of people and money across borders has made the distinction between temporary and permanent migration less meaningful. Although migration has always been fluid, people in today's global economy are connected across societies culturally and economically as never before. Even after they have relocated, people maintain global linkages to their former country and with a global economy (Richmond 2002).

Annexation

Nations, particularly during wars or as a result of war, incorporate or attach land. This new land is contiguous to the nation, as in the German annexation of Austria and Czechoslovakia in 1938 and 1939 and in the U.S. Louisiana Purchase of 1803. The Treaty of Guadalupe Hidalgo that ended the Mexican–American War in 1848 gave the United

States California, Utah, Nevada, most of New Mexico, and parts of Arizona, Wyoming, and Colorado. The indigenous peoples in some of this huge territory were dominant in their society one day, only to become minority-group members the next.

When annexation occurs, the dominant power generally suppresses the language and culture of the minority. Such was the practice of Russia with the Ukrainians and Poles and of Prussia with the Poles. Minorities try to maintain their cultural integrity despite annexation. Poles inhabited an area divided into territories ruled by three countries but maintained their own culture across political boundaries.

Colonialism

Colonialism has been the most common way for one group of people to dominate another. **Colonialism** is the maintenance of political, social, economic, and cultural dominance over people by a foreign power for an extended period (Bell 1991). Colonialism is rule by outsiders but, unlike annexation, does not involve actual incorporation into the dominant people's nation. The long-standing control that was exercised by the British Empire over much of North America, parts of Africa, and India is an example of colonial domination (see Figure 1.5).

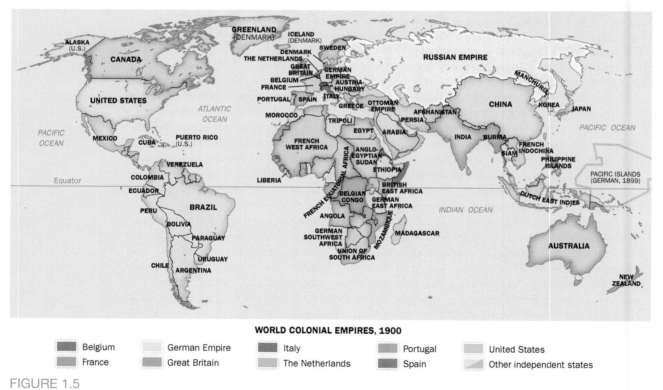

WORLD COLONIAL EMPIRES, 1900

Belgium	German Empire	Italy	Portugal	United States
France	Great Britain	The Netherlands	Spain	Other independent states

FIGURE 1.5

World Colonial Empires (1900)

Events of the nineteenth century increased European dominance over the world. By 1900, most independent African nations had disappeared, and the major European powers and Japan took advantage of China's internal weakness to gain both trading ports and economic concessions.

Source: Divine, Breen, Williams, Gross and Brands 2013: v. 2.

Societies gain power over a foreign land through military strength, sophisticated political organization, and investment capital. The extent of power may also vary according to the dominant group's scope of settlement in the colonial land. Relations between the colonizing nation and the colonized people are similar to those between a dominant group and exploited subordinate groups. Colonial subjects generally are limited to menial jobs and the wages from their labor. The natural resources of their land benefit the members of the ruling class.

By the 1980s, colonialism, in the sense of political rule, had become largely a phenomenon of the past, yet industrial countries of North America and Europe still dominated the world economically and politically. Drawing on the conflict perspective, sociologist Immanuel Wallerstein (1974) views the global economic system of today as much like the height of colonial days. Wallerstein has advanced the **world systems theory**, which views the global economic system as divided between nations that control wealth and those that provide natural resources and labor. The limited economic resources available in developing nations exacerbate many of the ethnic, racial, and religious conflicts noted at the beginning of this chapter. In addition, the presence of massive inequality between nations only serves to encourage immigration generally and, more specifically, the movement of many of the most skilled from developing nations to the industrial nations.

The Consequences of Subordinate-Group Status

A group with subordinate status is faced with several consequences. These differ in their degree of harshness, ranging from physical annihilation to absorption into the dominant group. In this section, we examine six consequences of subordinate-group status: extermination, expulsion, secession, segregation, fusion, and assimilation. The following figure illustrates how these consequences can be defined using the Spectrum of Intergroup Relations.

SPECTRUM OF INTERGROUP RELATIONS

EXPULSION	SEGREGATION	ASSIMILATION
INCREASINGLY UNACCEPTABLE		MORE TOLERABLE
EXTERMINATION SECESSION	FUSION	PLURALISM
or genocide or partitioning	or amalgamation or melting pot	or multiculturalism

Extermination

The most extreme way to deal with a subordinate group is to eliminate it. Today, the term **genocide** is used to describe the deliberate, systematic killing of an entire people or nation. This term is often used in reference to the Holocaust, Nazi Germany's extermination of 12 million European Jews and other ethnic minorities during World War II. The **Holocaust** was the state-sponsored systematic persecution and annihilation of European Jewry by Nazi Germany and its collaborators. The move to eliminate Jews from the European continent started slowly, with Germany gradually restricting the rights of Jews:

preventing them from voting, living outside the Jewish ghetto, and owning businesses. Much anti-Semitic cruelty was evident before the beginning of the war. *Kristallnacht*, or the "Night of Broken Glass," in Berlin on November 9, 1938, was a dramatic turning point toward genocide. Ninety Berlin Jews were murdered, hundreds of homes and synagogues were set on fire or ransacked, and thousands of Jewish store windows were broken.

Despite the obvious intolerance they faced, Jews desiring to immigrate were often turned back by government officials in Europe and the Americas (Institute for Jewish and Community Research 2008; DellaPergola 2007).

The term **ethnic cleansing** refers to the forced deportation of people, accompanied by systematic violence, including death. The term was introduced in 1992 to the world's vocabulary as ethnic Serbs instituted a policy intended to "cleanse"—eliminate—Muslims from parts of Bosnia. Again in 1994, a genocidal war between the Hutu and Tutsi people in Rwanda left 300,000 school-age children orphaned (Chirot and Edwards 2003; Naimark 2004).

Genocide also appropriately describes White policies toward Native Americans in the nineteenth century. In 1800, the American Indian population in the United States was approximately 600,000; by 1850, it had been reduced to 250,000 through warfare with the U.S. Army, disease, and forced relocation to inhospitable environments.

In 2008, the Australian government officially apologized for past treatment of its native people, the Aboriginal population. Not only did this involve brutality and neglect, but also a quarter of their children, the so-called lost generation, were taken from their families and placed in orphanages, foster homes, or put up for adoption by White Australians until the policy was finally abandoned in 1969 (Johnston 2008).

Expulsion

Dominant groups may choose to force a specific subordinate group to leave certain areas or even vacate a country. Expulsion, therefore, is another extreme consequence of minority-group status. European colonial powers in North America and eventually the U.S. government itself drove almost all Native Americans out of their tribal lands and into unfamiliar territory.

More recently, beginning in 2009, France expelled over 10,000 ethnic Roma (or Gypsies), forcing their return to their home countries of Bulgaria and Romania. This appeared to violate the European Union's (EU) ban against targeting ethnic groups as well as Europe's policy of "freedom of movement." In 2011, the EU withdrew its threat of legal action against France when the government said it would no longer expel Roma in particular but only those living in "illegal camps," which many observers felt was only a technical way for the country to get around long-standing human rights policies.

Stigmatizing and expelling minority groups is not an action of the distance past. Here, police in Paris round up Roma (Gypsies) for subsequent expulsion from the country.

Secession

A group ceases to be a subordinate group when it secedes to form a new nation or moves to an already-established nation, where it becomes dominant. After Great

Britain withdrew from Palestine, Jewish people achieved a dominant position in 1948, attracting Jews from throughout the world to the new state of Israel. Similarly, Pakistan was created in 1947 when India was partitioned. The predominantly Muslim areas in the north became Pakistan, making India predominantly Hindu. Throughout this century, minorities have repudiated dominant customs. In this spirit, the Estonian, Latvian, Lithuanian, and Armenian peoples, not content to be merely tolerated by the majority, all seceded to form independent states after the demise of the Soviet Union in 1991. In 1999, ethnic Albanians fought bitterly for their cultural and political recognition in the Kosovo region of Yugoslavia.

Some African Americans have called for secession. Suggestions dating back to the early 1700s supported the return of Blacks to Africa as a solution to racial problems. The settlement target of the American Colonization Society was Liberia, but proposals were also advanced to establish settlements in other areas. Territorial separatism and the emigrationist ideology were recurrent and interrelated themes among African Americans from the late nineteenth century well into the 1980s. The Black Muslims, or Nation of Islam, once expressed the desire for complete separation in their own state or territory within the modern borders of the United States. Although a secession of Blacks from the United States has not taken place, it has been proposed.

Segregation

Segregation is the physical separation of two groups in residence, workplace, and social functions. Generally, the dominant group imposes segregation on a subordinate group. Segregation is rarely complete; however, intergroup contact inevitably occurs even in the most segregated societies.

Sociologists Douglas Massey and Nancy Denton wrote *American Apartheid* (1993), which described segregation in U.S. cities on the basis of 1990 data. The title of their book was meant to indicate that neighborhoods in the United States resembled the segregation of the rigid government-imposed racial segregation that prevailed for so long in the Republic of South Africa.

Analysis of census data shows continuing segregation despite racial and ethnic diversity in the United States. Scholars use a segregation index to measure separation. This index ranges from 0 (complete integration) to 100 (complete segregation), where the value indicates the percentage of the minority group that needs to move to be distributed exactly like Whites. So a segregation index of 60 for Blacks–Whites would mean that 60 percent of all African Americans would have to move to be residing just like Whites.

In Table 1.2, we look at the most segregated metropolitan areas with large African American, Latino, and Asian American populations. Backs and Whites are most separated from each other in Detroit, the Los Angeles/Long Beach metropolitan area finds Whites and Latinos most living apart, and the New Brunswick, New Jersey, area is where Asians and Whites are most segregated from each other. Typically half to three quarters of the people would have to move to achieve even distribution throughout the city and surrounding suburbs.

Over the last forty years, Black–White segregation has declined modestly. Hispanic–White segregation, while lower, has not changed significantly in the last thirty years. Asian–White segregation is even a bit lower but also has been mostly unchanged over the three decades. Even when we consider social class, the patterns of minority segregation persist. Despite the occasional multiracial neighborhood, segregation prevails (Bureau of the Census 2010b; Krysan, Farley, and Couper 2008; Frey 2011; Wilkes and Iceland 2004).

TABLE 1.2
Segregated Metro America

BLACK–WHITE

1. Detroit	79.6
2. Milwaukee	79.6
3. New York/White Plains	79.1
4. Newark	78.0
5. Chicago/Naperville	75.9
6. Philadelphia	73.7
7. Miami/Miami Beach	73.0
8. Cleveland	72.6

HISPANIC–WHITE

1. Los Angeles/Long Beach	63.4
2. New York/White Plains	63.1
3. Newark	62.6
4. Boston	62.0
5. Salinas, CA	60.0
6. Philadelphia	58.8
7. Chicago/Naperville	57.0
8. Oxford/Venture, CA	54.5

ASIAN–WHITE

1. Edison/New Brunswick, NJ	63.7
2. New York/White Plains	49.5
3. Houston	48.7
4. Boston	47.4
5. Sacramento, CA	46.8
7. San Francisco	46.7
8. Warren/Farmington Hills, MI	46.3

Note: The higher the value, the more segregated the metropolitan area.

Source: Logan and Stults 2011.

This focus on metropolitan areas should not cause us to ignore the continuing legally sanctioned segregation of Native Americans on reservations. Although the majority of our nation's first inhabitants live outside these tribal areas, the reservations play a prominent role in the identity of Native Americans. Although it is easier to maintain tribal identity on the reservation, economic and educational opportunities are more limited in these areas, which are segregated from the rest of society.

A particularly troubling pattern has been the emergence of **resegregation**, or the physical separation of racial and ethnic groups reappearing after a period of relative integration. Resegregation has occurred in neighborhoods and schools after a transitional period of desegregation. For example, in 1954, only one in 100,000 Black students attended a majority White school in the South. Thanks to the civil rights movement and a series of civil rights measures, by 1968, the percentage of Black students in White majority schools rose to 23 percent and then to 47 percent by 1988.

The latest analysis, however, shows continuing racial isolation. A 2012 report documents that nationwide, 43 percent of Latinos and 38 percent of Blacks attend schools in which fewer than 10 percent of their classmates are White (Orfield 2007; Orefield, Kucsera and Siegel-Hawley 2012; Orfield and Lee 2005; Rich 2008).

Given segregation patterns, many Whites in the United States have limited contact with people of other racial and ethnic backgrounds. In one study of 100 affluent powerful White men that looked at their experiences past and present, it was clear they had lived in a "White bubble"—their neighborhoods, schools, elite colleges, and workplaces were overwhelmingly White. The continuing pattern of segregation in the United States means our diverse population grows up in very different nations (Bonilla-Silva and Embrick 2007; Feagin and O'Brien 2003).

Segregation by race, ethnicity, religion, tribal or clan affiliation, and sometimes even language grouping occurs throughout the world. The most dramatic government-engineered segregation in recent memory was in South Africa. In 1948, the United Kingdom granted South Africa its independence, and the National Party, dominated by a White minority, assumed control of the government. The rule of White supremacy, well under way as the custom in the colonial period, became more and more formalized into law. To deal with the multiracial population, the Whites devised a policy called apartheid to ensure their dominance. **Apartheid** (in Afrikaans, the language of the White Afrikaners, it means *separation* or *apartness*) came to mean a policy of separate development, euphemistically called *multinational development* by the government. Black South Africans were relegated to impoverished urban townships or rural areas and their mobility within the country strictly regulated. Events took a significant turn in 1990, when the South African Prime Minister legalized once-banned Black organizations and freed Nelson Mandela, leader of the African National Congress (ANC), after 27 years of imprisonment. Mandela's triumphant return was soon followed by him becoming head of the government, and a half-century of Apartheid came to an end.

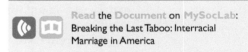

Read the Document on MySocLab: Breaking the Last Taboo: Interracial Marriage in America

Fusion

Fusion occurs when a minority and a majority group combine to form a new group. This combining can be expressed as A + B + C → D, where A, B, and C represent the groups present in a society and D signifies the result, an ethnocultural–racial group that shares some of the characteristics of each initial group. Mexican people are an example of fusion, originating as they do from the mixing of Spanish and indigenous Indian cultures. Theoretically, fusion does not entail intermarriage, but it is very similar to **amalgamation**, or the process by which a dominant group and a subordinate group combine through intermarriage into a new people. In everyday speech, the words *fusion* and *amalgamation* are rarely used, but the concept is expressed in the notion of a human **melting pot** in which diverse racial or ethnic groups form a new creation, a new cultural entity (Newman 1973).

The analogy of the cauldron, the "melting pot," was first used to describe the United States by the French observer Crèvecoeur in 1782. The phrase dates back to the Middle Ages, when alchemists attempted to change less-valuable metals into gold and silver. Similarly, the idea of the human melting pot implied that the new group would represent only the best qualities and attributes of the different cultures contributing to it. The belief in the United States as a melting pot became widespread in the early twentieth century. This belief suggested that the United States had an almost divine mission to destroy artificial divisions and create a single kind of human. However, the dominant group had indicated its unwillingness to welcome such groups as Native Americans, Blacks, Hispanics, Jews, Asians, and Irish Roman Catholics into the melting pot. It is a mistake to think of the United States as an ethnic mixing bowl. Although superficial signs of fusion are present, as in a cuisine that includes sauerkraut and spaghetti, most contributions of subordinate groups are ignored (Gleason 1980).

Marriage patterns indicate the resistance to fusion. People are unwilling, in varying degrees, to marry outside their own ethnic, religious, and racial groups. Until relatively recently, interracial marriage was outlawed in much of the United States. At the time that President Barack Obama's White mother and Black father were married in Hawaii, their union would have been illegal and unable to occur in 22 other states. Surveys show that 20–50 percent of various White ethnic groups report single ancestry. When White ethnics do cross boundaries, they tend to marry within their religion and social class. For example, Italians are more likely to marry Irish, who are also Catholic, than they are to marry Protestant Swedes.

Although it may seem that interracial matches are everywhere, there is only modest evidence of a fusion of races in the United States. Racial intermarriage has been increasing. In 1980, there were 651,000 interracial marriages, but by 2010, there were 5.4 million. That is still less than 7 percent of married couples but it is increasing significantly. Among unmarried couples it rises to 14 percent and among same-sex couples to 15 percent.

Among couples in which at least one member is Hispanic, marriages with a non-Hispanic partner account for 28 percent. Taken together, all interracial and Hispanic–non-Hispanic marriages account for 10 percent of married opposite-sex couples today. But this includes decades of marriages. Among new couples, about 15 percent of marriages are between people of different races or between Hispanics and non-Hispanics (Bureau of the Census 2010a: Table 60; Lofquist et al. 2012; Taylor et al. 2010).

Assimilation

Assimilation is the process by which a subordinate individual or group takes on the characteristics of the dominant group and is eventually accepted as part of that group. Assimilation is a majority ideology in which $A + B + C \rightarrow A$. The majority (A) dominates in such a way that the minorities (B and C) become indistinguishable from the dominant group. Assimilation dictates conformity to the dominant group, regardless of how many racial, ethnic, or religious groups are involved (Newman 1973:53).

To be complete, assimilation must entail an active effort by the minority-group individual to shed all distinguishing actions and beliefs and the unqualified acceptance of that individual by the dominant society. In the United States, dominant White society encourages assimilation. The assimilation perspective tends to devalue alien culture and to treasure the dominant. For example, assimilation assumes that whatever is admirable among Blacks was adapted from Whites and that whatever is bad is inherently Black. The assimilation solution to Black–White conflict has been typically defined as the development of a consensus around White American values.

Assimilation is very difficult. The person being assimilated must forsake his or her cultural tradition to become part of a different, often antagonistic culture. However, assimilation should not be viewed as if immigrants are extraterrestrials. Cross-border movement is often preceded by adjustments and awareness of the culture that awaits the immigrant (Skrentny 2008).

Assimilation does not occur at the same pace for all groups or for all individuals in the same group. Typically, the assimilation process is not completed by the first generation—the new arrivals. Assimilation tends to take longer under the following conditions:

- The differences between the minority and the majority are large.
- The majority is not receptive, or the minority retains its own culture.
- The minority group arrives over a short period of time.
- The minority-group residents are concentrated rather than dispersed.
- The arrival is recent, and the homeland is accessible.

Assimilation is not a smooth process (Warner and Srole 1945).

Many people view assimilation as unfair or even dictatorial. However, members of the dominant group see it as reasonable that subordinate people shed their distinctive cultural traditions. In public discussions today, assimilation is the ideology of the dominant group in forcing people how to act. Consequently, the social institutions in the United States—the educational system, economy, government, religion, and medicine—all push toward assimilation, with occasional references to the pluralist approach.

The Pluralist Perspective

Thus far, we have concentrated on how subordinate groups cease to exist (removal) or take on the characteristics of the dominant group (assimilation). The alternative to these relationships between the majority and the minority is pluralism. **Pluralism** implies that various groups in a society have mutual respect for one another's culture, a respect that allows minorities to express their own culture without suffering prejudice or discrimination. Whereas the assimilationist or integrationist seeks the elimination of ethnic boundaries, the pluralist believes in maintaining many of them.

There are limits to cultural freedom. A Romanian immigrant to the United States cannot expect to avoid learning English and still move up the occupational ladder. To survive, a society must have a consensus among its members on basic ideals, values, and beliefs. Nevertheless, there is still plenty of room for variety. Earlier, fusion was described as A + B + C → D and assimilation as A + B + C → A. Using this same scheme, we can think of pluralism as A + B + C → A + B + C, with groups coexisting in one society (Manning 1995; Newman 1973; Simpson 1995).

In the United States, cultural pluralism is more an ideal than a reality. Although there are vestiges of cultural pluralism—in the various ethnic neighborhoods in major cities, for instance—the rule has been for subordinate groups to assimilate. Yet as the minority becomes the numerical majority, the ability to live out one's identity becomes a bit easier. African Americans, Hispanics, American Indians, and Asian Americans already outnumber Whites in most of the largest cities. The trend is toward even greater diversity. Nonetheless, the cost of cultural integrity throughout the nation's history has been high. The various Native American tribes have succeeded to a large extent in maintaining their heritage, but the price has been bare subsistence on federal reservations.

The United States is experiencing a reemergence of ethnic identification by groups that had previously expressed little interest in their heritage. Groups that make up the dominant majority also are reasserting their ethnic heritages. Various nationality groups are rekindling interest in almost forgotten languages, customs, festivals, and traditions. In some instances, this expression of the past has taken the form of a protest against exclusion from the dominant society. For example, Chinese youths chastise their elders for forgetting the old ways and accepting White American influence and control.

Watch the Video on MySocLab: *Michael Kimmel: What Is Multiculturalism?*

Explore the Concept on MySocLab: *How Diverse Is American Society?*

The most visible expression of pluralism is language use. As of 2008, nearly one in every five people (19.1 percent) over age five speaks a language other than English at home. Later, in Chapter 4, we consider how language use figures into issues relating to immigration and education (American Community Survey 2009: Table S1601).

Facilitating a diverse and changing society affects just about every aspect of that society. Yet another nod to pluralism, although not nearly so obvious as language to the general population, has been the changes within the funeral industry. Where Christian and Jewish funeral practices once dominated, funeral home professionals are now being trained to accommodate a variety of practices. Latinos often expect 24-hour viewing of their deceased, whereas Muslims may wish to participate in washing the deceased before burial in a grave pointing toward Mecca. Hindu and Buddhist requests to participate in cremation are now being respected (Brulliard 2006).

Resistance and Change

By virtue of wielding power and influence, the dominant group may define the terms by which all members of society operate. This is particularly evident in a slave society, but even in contemporary industrialized nations, the dominant group has a disproportionate role in shaping immigration policy, the curriculum of the schools, and the content of the media.

Subordinate groups do not merely accept the definitions and ideology proposed by the dominant group. A continuing theme in dominant–subordinate relations is the minority group's challenge to its subordination. Resistance by subordinate groups is well documented as they seek to promote change that will bring them more rights and privileges, if not true equality. Often, traditional notions of racial formation are overcome not only through panethnicity but also because Black people, along with Latinos and sympathetic Whites, join in the resistance to subordination (Moulder 1996; Winant 2004).

Resistance can be seen in efforts by racial and ethnic groups to maintain their identity through newspapers and organizations and in today's technological age through cable

Through recent efforts of collective action, African American farmers successfully received Congressional approval in 2010 for compensation denied them in the latter 1900s by the Department of Agriculture.

television stations, blogs, and Internet sites. Resistance manifests itself in social movements such as the civil rights movement, the feminist movement, and gay rights efforts. The passage of such legislation as the Age Discrimination Act or the Americans with Disabilities Act marks the success of oppressed groups in lobbying on their own behalf.

Resistance efforts may begin through small actions. For example, residents of a reservation question why a toxic waste dump is to be located on their land. Although it may bring in money, they question the wisdom of such a move. Their concerns lead to further investigations of the extent to which American Indian lands are used disproportionately as containment areas for dangerous materials. This action in turn leads to a broader investigation of the ways in which minority-group people often find themselves "hosting" dumps and incinerators. As we discuss later, these local efforts eventually led the Environmental Protection Agency to monitor the disproportionate placement of toxic facilities in or near racial and ethnic minority communities. There is little reason to expect that such reforms would have occurred if the reservation residents had relied on traditional decision-making processes alone.

Change has occurred. At the beginning of the twentieth century, lynching was practiced in many parts of the country. At the beginning of the twenty-first century, laws punishing hate crimes were increasingly common and embraced a variety of stigmatized groups. Although this social progress should not be ignored, the nation still must focus concern on the significant social inequalities that remain. It is too easy to look at the accomplishments of Barack Obama and Hillary Clinton and conclude "mission accomplished" in terms of racial and gender injustices (Best 2001).

An even more basic form of resistance is to question societal values. In this book, we avoid using the term *American* to describe people of the United States because geographically, Brazilians, Canadians, and El Salvadorans are Americans as well. It is easy to overlook how our understanding of today has been shaped by the way institutions and even the very telling of history have been presented by members of the dominant group. African American studies scholar Molefi Kete Asante (2007, 2008) has called for an **Afrocentric perspective** that emphasizes the customs of African cultures and how they have pervaded the history, culture, and behavior of Blacks in the United States and around the world. Afrocentrism seeks to balance Eurocentrism and works toward a multiculturalist or pluralist orientation in which no viewpoint is suppressed. The Afrocentric approach could become part of our school curriculum, which has not adequately acknowledged the importance of this heritage.

The Afrocentric perspective has attracted much attention in education. Opponents view it as a separatist view of history and culture that distorts both past and present. Its supporters counter that African peoples everywhere can come to full self-determination only when they are able to overthrow the dominance of White or Eurocentric intellectual interpretations (Conyers 2004).

The remarkable efforts by members of racial and ethnic minorities working with supportive White Americans beginning in the 1950s through the early 1970s successfully targeted overt racist symbols or racist and sexist actions. Today's targets are more intractable and tend to emerge from institutional discrimination. Sociologist Douglas Massey (2011) argued that a central goal must be to reform the criminal justice system by demanding repeal of the following: the three-strikes law, mandatory minimum sentencing, and harsher penalties for crack than for powdered cocaine. Such targets are quite different from laws that prevented Blacks and women from serving on juries.

In considering the inequalities present today, as we do in the chapters that follow, it is easy to forget how much change has taken place. Much of the resistance to prejudice and discrimination in the past, either to slavery or to women's prohibition from voting, took the active support of members of the dominant group. The indignities still experienced by subordinate groups continue to be resisted as subordinate groups and their allies among the dominant group seek further change.

Conclusion

One hundred years ago, sociologist and activist W. E. B. Du Bois took another famed Black activist, Booker T. Washington, to task for saying that the races could best work together apart, like fingers on a hand. Du Bois felt that Black people had to be a part of all social institutions and not create their own. Now with an African American elected to the presidency, Whites, African Americans, and other groups continue to debate what form society should take. Should we seek to bring everyone together into an integrated whole? Or do we strive to maintain as much of our group identities as possible while working as cooperatively as necessary?

In this chapter, we have attempted to organize our approach to subordinate–dominant relations in the United States. We observed that subordinate groups do not necessarily contain fewer members than the dominant group. Subordinate groups are classified into racial, ethnic, religious, and gender groups. Racial classification has been of interest, but scientific findings do not explain contemporary race relations. Biological differences of race are not supported by scientific data. Yet as the continuing debate over standardized tests demonstrates, attempts to establish a biological meaning of race have not been swept entirely into the dustbin of history. However, the social meaning given to physical differences is very significant. People have defined racial differences in such a way as to encourage or discourage the progress of certain groups.

Subordinate-group members' reactions include the seeking of an alternative avenue to acceptance and success: "Why should we forsake what we are, to be accepted by them?" In response to this question, there continues to be strong ethnicity identification. A result of this maintenance of ethnic and racial identity, complementary, and occasionally competing, images of what it means to be a productive member of a single society persist. Pluralism describes a society in which several different groups coexist, with no dominant or subordinate groups. People individually choose what cultural patterns to keep and which to let go.

Subordinate groups have not and do not always accept their second-class status passively. They may protest, organize, revolt, and resist society as defined by the dominant group. Patterns of race and ethnic relations are changing, not stagnant. Indicative of the changing landscape, biracial and multiracial children present us with new definitions of identity emerging through a process of racial formation, reminding us that race is socially constructed.

In the twenty-first century, we are facing new challenges to cooperation. There has been a marked increase in the population of minority racial and ethnic groups to the point that collectively they will be in the majority well before today's college students reach middle-age.

Continuing immigration and the explosive growth of the Hispanic population—more than double since 1990—fuels this growth. Latinos are now settling in to the point that the Spanish-language Telemundo network is now introducing English-language subtitles to ensure their Latino viewers can fully comprehend their programming.

Barack Obama's historic campaign and becoming the forty-fourth president of the United States in January 2009 marks a significant time in U.S. history. The fact that he is the first African American (and also the first non-White person) to serve as president demonstrates how much progress has been achieved in race relations in this country. It also underscores both how long it has taken and how much more needs to be accomplished for the United States to truly be "a more perfect union," as stated in the Constitution.

The two significant forces that are absent in a truly pluralistic society are prejudice and discrimination. In an assimilation society, prejudice disparages out-group differences, and discrimination financially rewards those who shed their past. In the next two chapters, we explore the nature of prejudice and discrimination in the United States.

MySocLab   Study and Review on MySocLab

Summary

1. When sociologists define a minority group, they are concerned primarily with the economic and political power, or powerlessness, of the group.

2. A racial group is set apart from others primarily by physical characteristics; an ethnic group is set apart primarily by national origin or cultural patterns.

3. People cannot be sorted into distinct racial groups, so race is best viewed as a social construct that is subject to different interpretations over time.

4. A small but still significant number of people in the United States—more than 7 million—readily see themselves as having a biracial or multiracial identity.

5. The study of race and ethnicity in the United States often considers the role played by class and gender.

6. Functionalists point out that discrimination is both functional and dysfunctional for a society. Conflict theorists see racial subordination through the presence of tension between competing groups. Labeling theory directs our attention to the role that negative stereotypes play in race and ethnicity.

7. Subordinate-group status has emerged through migration, annexation, and colonialism. The social consequences of subordinate-group status include extermination, expulsion, secession, segregation, fusion, assimilation, and pluralism.

8. Racial, ethnic, and other minorities maintain a long history of resisting efforts to restrict their rights.

Key Terms

Afrocentric perspective, p. 29

amalgamation, p. 25

apartheid, p. 25

assimilation, p. 26

biological race, p. 9

blaming the victim, p. 17

class, p. 15

colonialism, p. 20

conflict perspective, p. 16

dysfunction, p. 16

emigration, p. 19

ethnic cleansing, p. 22

ethnic group, p. 7

functionalist perspective, p. 15

fusion, p. 25

genocide, p. 21

globalization, p. 19

Holocaust, p. 21

immigration, p. 19

intelligence quotient (IQ), p. 10

labeling theory, p. 17

marginality, p. 14

melting pot, p. 25

migration, p. 19

minority group, p. 4

panethnicity, p. 14

pluralism, p. 27

racial formation, p. 11

racial group, p. 5

racism, p. 11

resegregation, p. 24

segregation, p. 23

self-fulfilling prophecy, p. 18

sociology, p. 14

stereotypes, p. 17

stratification, p. 15

world systems theory, p. 21

Review Questions

1. In what different ways is race viewed?

2. How do the concepts of "biracial" and "multiracial" relate to W. E. B. Du Bois's notion of a "color line"?

3. How do the conflict, functionalist, and labeling approaches apply to the social construction of race?

Critical Thinking

1. How diverse is your city? Can you see evidence that some group is being subordinated? What social construction of categories do you see that may be different in your community as compared to elsewhere?

2. Select a racial or ethnic group and apply the Spectrum of Intergroup Relations on page xy. Can you provide an example today or in the past where each relationship occurs?

3. Identify some protest and resistance efforts by subordinated groups in your area. Have they been successful? Even though some people say they favor equality, why are they uncomfortable with such efforts? How can people unconnected with such efforts either help or hinder such protests?

Listen to Chapter 2 on MySocLab

2 Prejudice

2-1 Examine the differences between prejudice and discrimination.

2-2 Explain the function(s) of White-Privilege.

2-3 Compare and contrast the four theories of prejudice.

2-4 Discuss stereotyping and its effect on social interactions.

2-5 Define color-blind racism and explain its impact on society.

2-6 Discuss the prevalence of prejudice and discrimination in modern day society.

2-7 Address the concept of Intergroup Hostility.

2-8 Identify individual and collective strategies to reduce prejudice.

The first day of college—it is an exciting but often traumatic day for students and those close to them. Catherine Donnelly's mother, a single White science teacher from New Orleans, was understandably proud in 1981 when she dropped her daughter off for her first day at Princeton University. During dinner with Catherine that first night, however, her mom was shocked to learn of her daughter's first visitor. Craig Robinson, a junior and a Princeton basketball player, dropped by the dorm looking for his sister whom Catherine had not yet met. Craig was Black.

Growing up in the South, Donnelly attended school with a few black classmates, but living together was another thing. Donnelly quickly warmed to her new roommate Michelle Robinson, with her big sense of humor and riveting stories. But she was worried that her mother, who Donnelly said had grown up in a racist family, would not react well. She was right.

The next day, in an effort to get Catherine a new room assignment, her mother telephoned influential Princeton alums in New Orleans and also headed to the housing office. University officials said no room change was possible until the second semester. Catherine got along with her roommate Michelle for that term but barely acknowledged her on campus. Eventually, Catherine graduated with a major in psychology and now practices real estate law in Atlanta. For nearly thirty years, Michelle was unaware of the reason her freshman roommate moved out.

When 17-year-old Michelle entered Princeton, she was one of 94 Black students in a class of 1,141. Michelle majored in sociology and her senior thesis was "Princeton-Educated Blacks and the Black Community." While not specifically mentioning the slighting by her first-semester roommate, Michelle did write how experiences at Princeton made her far more aware of her "Blackness." She wrote that she interviewed Black Princeton alumni who had similar experiences but upon graduation, these successful men and women comfortably interacted with equally successful White men and women.

Now almost 50 years old, Catherine admits that she gave up a chance of a lifetime by not taking the opportunity to get to know Michelle Robinson, now known as Michelle Obama, wife of the president of the United States.

"Michelle early on began to hang out with other Black students," said Donnelly. "Princeton was just a very segregated place. I wish now that I had pushed harder to be friends, but by the same token she did not invite me to do things either." Michelle, for her part, wrote this in her thesis that at Princeton, "No matter how liberal and open minded some of my White professors and classmates try to be toward me, I sometimes feel like a visitor on campus; as if I really don't belong" (Felsenthal 2009; Fryer Law Firm 2012; Jacobs 2008; Robinson 1985).

The prevalence of social media means that high school seniors and their parents no longer must wait until move-in day to meet their roommates. Colleges know that soon after students get their roommate's contact information in August, they friend them on Facebook or do some "detective work" via social networking sites. As a result, colleges now must screen all requests for new roommates to make sure such requests are not based on race, sexual orientation, religion, or national origin (Conley 2011, Michigan State University 2012).

Prejudice is so prevalent that it is tempting to consider it inevitable or, even more broadly, part of human nature. Such a view ignores its variability from individual to individual and from society to society. People learn prejudice as children before they exhibit it as adults. Therefore, prejudice is a social phenomenon, an acquired characteristic. A truly pluralistic society would lack unfavorable distinctions made through prejudicial attitudes among racial and ethnic groups.

Holding ill feelings based on a person's race or ethnicity is more of an issue because our nation is so increasingly diverse. In Figure 2.1, we look at the increase in minority

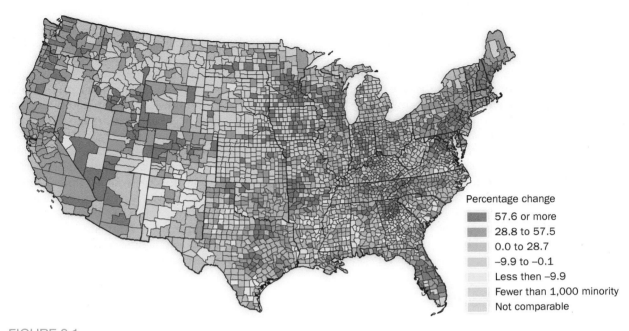

FIGURE 2.1
Change in Minority Population by County, 2000–2010

Growth in the minority population has occurred in the last decade across the country, including in many areas that previously had few members of racial and ethnic minorities.

Source: Humes, Jones and Ramirez 2011:21.

presence in the first decade of the twenty-first century. Many counties far removed from urban centers or historic areas with Black and Latino populations saw population increases in the years from 2000 to 2010. The likelihood that prejudices will be expressed, dealt with, or hidden is beginning a truly nationwide phenomenon as majority-minority interaction pervades more and more communities.

Ill feeling among groups of different races, ethnicities, or cultures may result from **ethnocentrism**, or the tendency to believe that one's culture and way of life are superior to all others'. The ethnocentric person judges other groups and other cultures by the standards of his or her own group. This attitude makes it quite easy for people to view other cultures as inferior. We see a woman wearing a veil and may regard it as strange and backward, yet we are baffled when other societies think U.S. women in short skirts are dressed inappropriately. Ethnocentrism and other expressions of prejudice are often voiced, but unfortunately, such expressions sometimes become the motivation for criminal acts.

Explore the Map on MySocLab: *The View from Down-Under*

Prejudice and Discrimination

Prejudice and discrimination are related concepts but are not the same. **Prejudice** is a negative attitude toward an entire category of people. The important components in this definition are *attitude* and *entire category*. Prejudice involves attitudes, thoughts, and beliefs, not actions. Prejudice often is expressed using **ethnophaulisms**, or ethnic slurs, which include derisive nicknames such as *honky*, *gook*, and *wetback*. Ethnophaulisms also include speaking to or about members of a particular group in a condescending way, such as saying, "José does well in school for a Mexican American" or referring to a middle-aged woman as "one of the girls."

A prejudiced belief also leads to categorical rejection. Prejudice means you dislike someone not because you find his or her behavior objectionable; it means you dislike an entire racial or ethnic group, even if you have had little or no contact with that group. A college student is not prejudiced because he requests a room change after three weeks of enduring his roommate's sleeping all day, playing loud music all night, and piling garbage on his desk. However, he is displaying prejudice if he requests a change after arriving at school and learning his new roommate is of a different nationality.

Prejudice is a belief or attitude; discrimination is action. **Discrimination** is the denial of opportunities and equal rights to individuals and groups because of prejudice or for other arbitrary reasons. Unlike prejudice, discrimination involves *behavior* that excludes members of a group from certain rights, opportunities, or privileges. Like prejudice, it is categorical, except for a few rare exceptions. If an employer refuses to hire an illiterate Italian American as a computer analyst, that is not discrimination. If an employer refuses to hire all Italian Americans because he or she thinks they are incompetent and makes no effort to determine if an applicant is qualified, that is discrimination.

Merton's Typology

Prejudice does not necessarily coincide with discriminatory behavior. In exploring the relationship between negative attitudes and negative behavior, sociologist Robert Merton (1949, 1976) identified four major categories (Figure 2.2). The label added to each of Merton's categories may more readily identify the type of person described:

1. The unprejudiced nondiscriminator—or all-weather liberal
2. The unprejudiced discriminator—or reluctant liberal
3. The prejudiced nondiscriminator—or timid bigot
4. The prejudiced discriminator—or all-weather bigot

As the term is used in types 1 and 2, liberals are committed to equality among people. The all-weather liberal believes in equality and practices it. Merton was quick to observe that all-weather liberals may be far removed from any real competition with subordinate groups such as African Americans or women. Furthermore, such people may be content with their own behavior and do little to change themselves. The reluctant liberal is not completely committed to equality between groups. Social pressure may cause such a person to discriminate. Fear of losing employees may lead a manager to avoid promoting women to supervisory capacities. Equal-opportunity legislation may be the best way to influence a reluctant liberal.

Types 3 and 4 do not believe in equal treatment for racial and ethnic groups, but they vary in their willingness to act. The timid bigot, type 3, will not discriminate if discrimination costs money or reduces profits or if peers or the government apply pressure against doing so. The all-weather bigot acts without hesitation on the prejudiced beliefs he or she holds.

LaPiere's Study

Merton's typology points out that attitudes should not be confused with behavior. People do not always act as they believe. More than a half-century ago, Richard LaPiere (1934, 1969) exposed the relationship between racial attitudes and social conduct. From 1930 to 1932, LaPiere traveled throughout the United States with a Chinese couple. Despite an alleged climate of intolerance of Asians, LaPiere observed that the couple was treated

✳ **Explore** the **Concept** on **MySocLab:** Prejudice and Discrimination: The Vicious Circle'

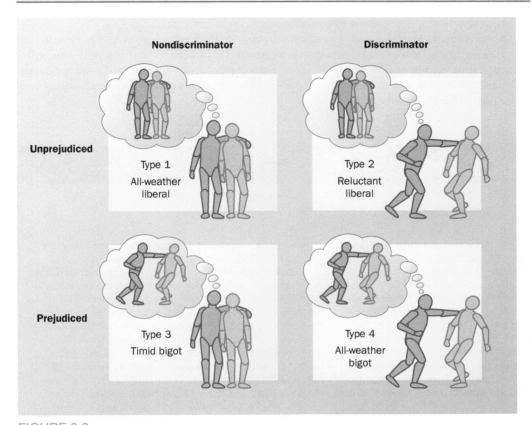

FIGURE 2.2
Prejudice and Discrimination

As sociologist Robert Merton's formulation shows, prejudice and discrimination are related but are not the same.

courteously at hotels, motels, and restaurants. He was puzzled by the good reception they received; all the conventional attitude surveys showed extreme prejudice by Whites toward the Chinese.

Was it possible that LaPiere was fortunate during his travels and consistently stopped at places operated by tolerant members of the dominant group? To test this possibility, he sent questionnaires asking the places at which they had been served whether the owner would "accept members of the Chinese race as guests in your establishment." More than 90 percent responded no, even though LaPiere's Chinese couple were treated politely at all of these establishments. How can this inconsistency be explained? People who returned questionnaires reflecting prejudice were unwilling to act based on those asserted beliefs; they were timid bigots.

The LaPiere study is not without flaws. First, he had no way of knowing whether the respondent to the questionnaire was the person who had served him and the Chinese couple. Second, he accompanied the couple, but the questionnaire suggested that the guests would be unescorted (and, in the minds of some, uncontrolled) and might consist of many Chinese people. Third, personnel may have changed between the time of the visit and the mailing of the questionnaire (Deutscher, Pestello, and Pestello 1993).

The LaPiere technique has been replicated with similar results. This technique questions whether attitudes are important if they are not reflected in behavior. But if attitudes are not important in small matters, they are important in other ways: Lawmakers legislate and courts may reach decisions based on what the public thinks.

This is not just hypothetical. Legislators in the United States often are persuaded to vote a certain way by what they perceive are changed attitudes toward immigration, affirmative action, and prayer in public schools. Sociologists have enumerated some of prejudice's functions. For the majority group, prejudice maintains privileged occupations and more power for its members.

 ## Research Focus

Islamophobia

In what ways do prejudice and discrimination manifest themselves with respect to Muslim and Arab Americans? In form and magnitude, they are much like that shown to other subordinate groups. Regrettably, this situation has gone beyond orientalism, in which one sees a group of people as "the other" and as somewhat frightening. Islamophobia refers to a range of negative feelings toward Muslims and their religion. Those feelings range from generalized intolerance to hatred. These current expressions of hostility are strikingly different because, in the twenty-first century, they have taken on a decidedly patriotic fervor; that is, many people who overtly express anti-Muslim or anti-Arab feelings also believe themselves to be pro-American.

Few normalizing or positive images are available. Rarely are Arab and Muslim Americans exhibiting normal behavior such as shopping, attending a sporting event, or even eating without the subtext of terrorism literally lurking in the shadows. Furthermore, the interests of the United States are depicted either as leaning against the Arabs and Muslims, as in the Israeli–Palestinian violence, or presented as hopelessly dependent on them, as in the case of our reliance on foreign oil production.

Evidence of hate crimes and harassment toward Arab and Muslim Americans rose sharply after 9/11, compared to studies done in the mid-1990s. Hate crimes and harassment remained high through 2008, according to more recent studies. Incidents have ranged from beatings to vandalism of mosques to organized resistance to Arabic school openings. Muslim Americans also have received unwarranted eviction notices. Surveys show a complex view of Arab and Muslim Americans exists in the United States. Surveys since 2001 show that one in four people believe several anti-Muslim stereotypes, for example, that Islam teaches violence and hatred. It is curious that even as they harbor such views, people do not recognize that Arab Americans are poorly treated. Still by 2012, only 40 percent of people had a favorable image of Islam compared to 41 percent who viewed it unfavorably.

A major flashpoint has been the proposed "Ground Zero Mosque." A mosque that has operated since 1985, twelve blocks from the World Trade Center (WTC) site, planned to move into an empty retail area to accommodate its growing congregation and out of a desire to create an interfaith outreach center. However, the new site, initially approved by the local community, brought it within two blocks of the WTC site. By 2009, the plan became a national controversy and many people saw Muslims, in general, as being insensitive to the significance of Ground Zero. National surveys showed 61 percent opposed to a mosque near Ground Zero and barely 25 percent favoring the location. Plans were set aside as advocates tried to explain they intended to reach out to the nation, not try to divide it.

Arab Americans and Muslim Americans, like other subordinate groups, have not responded passively to their treatment. Their communities have created organizations to counter negative stereotypes and to offer schools material responding to the labeling that has occurred. Even before 2001, Arab Americans and Muslim Americans were becoming active in both major political parties in the United States. However, during the 2000 campaign, candidates had already distanced themselves from campaign contributions made by Muslim and Arab organizations.

Given the presence of Islamophobia, the position of being Arab or Muslim in the United States grew more complex and contentious in the wake of the events of September 11, 2001, despite the public efforts of many Arabs and Muslims to proclaim their loyalty to the United States.

Sources: Ghosh 2010; Halstead 2008; Lugo et al. 2011; Mohamed and O'Brien 2011; Pew Forum on Religion and Public Life 2011; Zogby 2012.

What might a contemporary version of the Lapiere study look like? Instead of using a Chinese couple, one might look at the treatment of a Muslim man accompanied by his veiled wife. While such a study has yet to be conducted, we already have existing information about attitudes toward Muslim Americans, as indicated in the Research Focus section titled Islamaphobia.

The following sections examine theories of why prejudice exists and discuss the content and extent of prejudice today.

White Privilege

White travelers, unlike LaPiere's Chinese couple, rarely, if ever, would be concerned about second-class treatment because of race. Being White in the United States may not assure success and wealth, but it does limit encounters with intolerance.

White privilege refers to the rights or immunities granted as a particular benefit or favor for being White. This advantage exists unconsciously and is often invisible to the White people who enjoy it (Ferber 2008).

Scholar Peggy McIntosh of the Wellesley College Center for Research on Women looked at the privilege that comes from being White and the added privilege of being male. The other side of racial oppression is the privilege enjoyed by dominant groups. Being White or being successful in establishing a White identity carries with it distinct advantages. Among those that McIntosh (1988) identified were the following:

- Being considered financially reliable when using checks, credit cards, or cash
- Taking a job without having coworkers suspect it came about because of race

 Watch the Video on MySocLab: Woody Doan: White Privilege in the United States

Being White means having distinct advantages, which has been called *White privilege*. For example, one can seek assistance and assume your race will not work against you.

- Never having to speak for all the people of your race
- Watching television or reading a newspaper and seeing people of your own race widely represented
- Speaking effectively in a large group without being called a credit to your race
- Assuming that if legal or medical help is needed, your race will not work against you

Whiteness does carry privileges, but most White people do not consciously think of them except on the rare occasions when they are questioned.

Typically, White people do not see themselves as privileged in the way many African Americans and Latinos see themselves as disadvantaged. When asked to comment on their "Whiteness," White people most likely see themselves devoid of ethnicity ("no longer Irish," for example), stigmatized as racist, and victims of reverse discrimination. Privilege for many White people may be easy to exercise in one's life, but it is difficult to acknowledge (McKinney 2008).

Theories of Prejudice

Prejudice is learned. Friends, relatives, newspapers, books, movies, television, and the Internet all teach it. Awareness of the differences among people that society judges to be important begins at an early age. Several theories have been advanced to explain the rejection of certain groups in a society. We examine four theoretical explanations. The first two, scapegoating and authoritarian personality, are psychological and emphasize why a particular person harbors ill feelings. The second two, exploitation and normative, are sociological and view prejudice in the context of our interaction in a larger society.

Scapegoating Theory

People use some expressions of prejudice so they can blame others and refuse to accept responsibility. **Scapegoating theory** says that prejudiced people believe they are society's victims.

The term *scapegoat* comes from a biblical injunction telling the Hebrews to send a goat into the wilderness to symbolically carry away the people's sins. Similarly, the theory of scapegoating suggests that, rather than accepting guilt for some failure, a person transfers the responsibility for failure to a vulnerable group.

In the major tragic twentieth-century example, Adolf Hitler used the Jews as the scapegoat for all German social and economic ills in the 1930s. This premise led to the passage of laws restricting Jewish life in pre–World War II Germany and eventually escalated into the mass extermination of Europe's Jews. Scapegoating of Jews persists. A national survey in 2009 showed that one out of four people in the United States blame "the Jews" for the recent financial crisis. **Anti-Semitism**—anti-Jewish prejudice and discrimination—remains a very real phenomenon (Malhotra and Margalit 2009).

Today in the United States, both legal and illegal immigrants often are blamed by "real Americans" for their failure to secure jobs or desirable housing. The immigrant becomes the scapegoat for one's own lack of skills, planning, or motivation. It is so much easier to blame someone else.

Authoritarian Personality Theory

Prejudice may be influenced by one's upbringing and the lessons taught—and learned—early in life. Several efforts have been made to detail the prejudiced personality, but the most comprehensive effort culminated in a volume titled *The Authoritarian Personality*

(Adorno et al. 1950). Using a variety of tests and relying on more than 2,000 respondents, ranging from middle-class Whites to inmates of San Quentin State Prison (California), the authors claimed they had isolated the characteristics of the authoritarian personality.

In Adorno and colleagues' (1950) view, the **authoritarian personality** has basic characteristics that mean it is a personality type that is likely to be prejudiced. It encompasses adherence to conventional values, uncritical acceptance of authority, and concern with power and toughness. With obvious relevance to the development of intolerance, the authoritarian personality also was characterized by aggressiveness toward people who did not conform to conventional norms or obey authority. According to the researchers, this personality type developed from experiencing harsh discipline in early childhood. A child with an authoritarian upbringing was obedient to authority figures and then later treated others as he or she had been raised.

This study has been widely criticized, but the very existence of such wide criticism indicates the influence of the study. Critics have attacked the study's equation of authoritarianism with right-wing politics (although liberals also can be rigid); its failure to see that prejudice is more closely related to other individual traits, such as social class, than to authoritarianism as it was defined; the research methods used; and the emphasis on extreme racial prejudice rather than on more-common expressions of hostility.

Despite these concerns about specifics in the study, which was completed 60 years ago, annual conferences continue to draw attention to how authoritarian attitudes contribute to racism, sexism, and even torture (Kinloch 1974; O'Neill 2008).

Exploitation Theory

Racial prejudice is often used to justify keeping a group in a subordinate economic position. Conflict theorists, in particular, stress the role of racial and ethnic hostility as a way for the dominant group to keep its position of status and power intact. Indeed, this approach maintains that even the less-affluent White working class uses prejudice to minimize competition from upwardly mobile minorities.

This **exploitation theory** is clearly part of the Marxist tradition in sociological thought. Karl Marx emphasized exploitation of the lower class as an integral part of capitalism. Similarly, the exploitation or conflict approach explains how racism can stigmatize a group as inferior to justify the exploitation of that group. As developed by Oliver Cox (1942), exploitation theory saw prejudice against Blacks as an extension of the inequality faced by the entire lower class.

The exploitation theory of prejudice is persuasive. Japanese Americans were the object of little prejudice until they began to enter occupations that brought them into competition with Whites. The movement to keep Chinese out of the country became strongest during the late nineteenth century, when Chinese immigrants and Whites fought over dwindling numbers of jobs. Both the enslavement of African Americans and the removal westward of Native Americans were to a significant degree economically motivated.

Normative Approach

Although personality factors are important contributors to prejudice, normative or situational factors also must be given serious consideration. The **normative approach** takes the view that prejudice is influenced by societal norms and situations that encourage or discourage the tolerance of minorities.

Analysis reveals how societal influences shape a climate for tolerance or intolerance. Societies develop social norms that dictate not only what foods are desirable (or forbidden) but also what racial and ethnic groups are to be favored (or despised). Social forces

TABLE 2.1
Theories of Prejudice

No single explanation of why prejudice exists is satisfactory, but several approaches taken together offer insight.

Theory	Explanation	Example
Scapegoating	People blame others for their own failures.	An unsuccessful applicant assumes that a minority member or a woman got "his" job.
Authoritarian	Childrearing leads one to develop intolerance as an adult.	The rigid personality type dislikes people who are different.
Exploitation	People use others unfairly for economic advantage.	A minority member is hired at a lower wage level.
Normative	Peer and social influences encourage tolerance or intolerance.	A person from an intolerant household is more likely to be openly prejudiced.

operate in a society to encourage or discourage tolerance. The force may be widespread, such as the pressure on White Southerners to oppose racial equality even though there was slavery or segregation, which would seem to make concerns about equality irrelevant. The influence of social norms may be limited, as when one man finds himself becoming more sexist as he competes with three women for a position in a prestigious law firm.

The four approaches to prejudice summarized in Table 2.1 are not mutually exclusive. Social circumstances provide cues for a person's attitudes; personality determines the extent to which people follow social cues and the likelihood that they will encourage others to do the same. Societal norms may promote or deter tolerance; personality traits suggest the degree to which a person will conform to norms of intolerance. To understand prejudice, we must use all four approaches together.

Stereotypes

On Christmas Day 2001, Arab American Walied Shater boarded an American Airlines flight from Baltimore to Dallas carrying a gun. The cockpit crew refused to let him fly, fearing that Shater would take over the plane and use it as a weapon of mass destruction. However, Walied Shater carried documentation identifying him as a Secret Service agent, and calls to Washington, DC, confirmed that he was flying to join a presidential protection force at President George W. Bush's ranch in Texas. Nevertheless, the crew could not get past the stereotype of Arab American men posing a lethal threat (Leavitt 2002).

What Are Stereotypes?

Explore the Concept on MySocLab: *Prejudices and Stereotypes*

In Chapter 1, we saw that stereotypes play a powerful role in how people come to view dominant and subordinate groups. **Stereotypes** are unreliable generalizations about all members of a group and do not take individual differences into account. Numerous scientific studies have been made of these exaggerated images. This research has shown the willingness of people to assign positive and negative traits to entire groups of people, which are then applied to particular individuals. Stereotyping causes people to view Blacks as superstitious, Whites as uncaring, and Jews as shrewd. Over the last 80 years of such research, social scientists have found that people have become less willing to express such views openly, but prejudice persists, as we will see later in this chapter (Quillian 2006).

If stereotypes are exaggerated generalizations, then why are they so widely held, and why are some traits assigned more often than others? Evidence for traits may arise out of real conditions. For example, more Puerto Ricans live in poverty than Whites, so the prejudiced mind associates Puerto Ricans with laziness. According to the New Testament, some Jews were responsible for the crucifixion of Jesus, so, to the prejudiced mind, all Jews are Christ killers. Some activists in the women's movement are lesbians, so all feminists are seen as lesbians. From a kernel of fact, faulty generalization creates a stereotype.

In "Speaking Out," journalist Tim Giago, born a member of the Oglala Sioux tribe on the Pine Ridge Reservation, comments on college and professional teams having mascots patterned after American Indians. He finds the use neither harmless nor providing honor to the tribal people of the United States.

 ## Speaking Out

National Media Should Stop Using Obscene Words

I am just sick and tired of hearing students and faculty from schools using Indians as mascots say they are doing it to "honor us...."

Who or what is a redskin? It is a derogatory name for a race of people. It's as simple as that. It is akin to the racist names "nigger" or "gook" or "kike" or "wop." It is not, I repeat NOT, an honor to be called a racist name nor is it an honor to see football fans dressed in supposed Indian attire nor to hear them trumpeting some ludicrous war chant nor to see them mimic or ape our dress, culture, or person.

When I saw the Florida State fans doing the ridiculous "tomahawk chop" and heard their Johnny-one-note band play that asinine version of an Indian song over and over, I was heartsick. I was also highly embarrassed for the people of the Seminole Nation of Florida for allowing their good name to be taken in vain.

I am also sick and tired of fanatical sports fans telling Indians who object to this kind of treatment to "lighten up." You know, I didn't hear those same White folks saying this to African Americans in the 1960s when they were objecting to the hideous Black caricature at Sambo's Restaurants or to the Step-in-Fetch-It character used so often in the early movie days to portray Blacks as dimwitted, shiftless people. I didn't hear anybody tell them to "lighten up."

Tim Giago

However, 2000 did give us (Indians) a little reprieve. The Cleveland Indians and their hideous mascot were clobbered and didn't make the playoffs. The Washington Redskins turned into the Washington "Deadskins." The Kansas City Chiefs were real losers. And almost best of all, the Florida State Seminoles were steamrolled by an Oklahoma team with real Indians serving as bodyguards to the Oklahoma coach Bob Stoops. My thrill at watching the Seminoles lose was topped only by watching Ted Turner's Atlanta Braves get "tomahawked" this year. Now that was truly an "honor."...

Webster's Ninth New Collegiate Dictionary, note the word "collegiate" here, reads the word *redskin* quite simply as "American Indian usually taken to be offensive."

"Usually taken to be offensive." Now what is so hard to understand about this literal translation of the word "redskin"?

Attention major newspapers, CNN, Fox, ABC, CBS and NBC: the word "redskin" is an obscenity to Indians and to people who are sensitive to racism. It is translated by *Webster's* to be offensive. Now what other proof do you need to discontinue its usage?

Source: "National Media Should Stop Using Obscene Words" by Tim Giago, as reprinted in *The Denver Post*, January 21, 2001. Copyright © 2001 by Tim Giago. Reprinted by permission of Tim Giago.

 Listen to the **Audio** on **MySocLab:** *When is the 'N-Word' Not a Racial Slur?*

Labeling individuals through negative stereotypes has strong implications for the self-fulfilling prophecy. Studies show that people are all too aware of the negative images others have of them. When asked to estimate the prevalence of hard-core racism among Whites, one in four Blacks agrees that more than half "personally share the attitudes of groups like the Ku Klux Klan toward Blacks"; only one Black in ten says "only a few" share such views. Stereotypes not only influence how people feel about themselves but also, and perhaps equally important, affect how people interact with others. If people feel that others hold incorrect, disparaging attitudes toward them, then it undoubtedly makes it difficult to have harmonious relations (Sigelman and Tuch 1997).

Although explicit expressions of stereotypes are becoming less common, it is much too soon to write the obituary of racial and ethnic stereotypes. In addition, stereotyping is not limited to racial and ethnic groups. Other groups are subjected to stereotyping. Probably easiest to see in daily life and the mass media is sexism. **Sexism** is the ideology that one sex is superior to the other. Images and descriptions of women and even girls often reinforce sexism. **Homophobia**, the fear of and prejudice toward homosexuality, is present in every facet of life: the family, organized religion, the workplace, official policies, and the mass media. Like the myths and stereotypes of race and gender, those about homosexuality keep gay men and lesbian women oppressed as a group and may also prevent sympathetic members of the dominant group, the heterosexual community, from supporting them. We next consider the use of stereotypes in the contemporary practice of racial profiling.

Stereotyping in Action: Racial Profiling

A Black dentist, Elmo Randolph, testified before a state commission that he was stopped dozens of times in the 1980s and 1990s while traveling the New Jersey Turnpike to work. Invariably state troopers asked, "Do you have guns or drugs?" "My parents always told me, be careful when you're driving on the turnpike," said Dr. Randolph, age 44. "White people don't have that conversation" (Purdy 2001:37; see also Fernandez and Fahim 2006).

Little wonder that Dr. Randolph was pulled over. Although African Americans accounted for only 17 percent of the motorists on that turnpike, they were 80 percent of the motorists pulled over. Such occurrences gave rise to the charge that a new traffic offense was added to the books: DWB, or "driving while Black" (Bowles 2000).

Read the **Document** on **MySocLab**: *Explaining and Eliminating Racial Profiling*

In recent years, the government has given its attention to a social phenomenon with a long history: racial profiling. According to the Department of Justice, **racial profiling** is any police-initiated action based on race, ethnicity, or national origin rather than the person's behavior. Generally, profiling occurs when law enforcement officers, including customs officials, airport security, and police, assume that people fitting certain descriptions are likely to be engaged in something illegal. In 2012, national attention was drawn to the incident of a man on a neighborhood watch patrol shooting dead 17-year-old Trayvon Martin, a black youth visiting his father's fiancée in a gated Florida community. While the legal system slowly investigated, many felt the boy would still be alive had he been White and the shooter immediately arrested if Black. So unsettling was the event that it prompted President Obama in the midst of his public nomination for the World Bank to express sympathy for Martin's parents and say, "If I had a son, he'd look like Trayvon" (White House 2012).

Racal profiling persists despite overwhelming evidence that it is not a predictive approach toward identifying potential troublemakers. Whites are more likely to be found with drugs in the areas in which minority group members are disproportionately targeted.

A federal study made public in 2005 found little difference nationwide in the likelihood of being stopped by law enforcement officers, but African Americans were twice as likely to have their vehicles searched, and Latinos were five times more likely. A similar pattern emerged in the likelihood of force being used against drivers: It was three times more likely for Latinos and Blacks than White drivers. A study of New York City police officers released in 2011 found that racial minorities accounted for 87 percent of people who were stopped and frisked, but it was 50 percent more likely that Whites were found to be carrying weapons (Center for Constitutional Rights 2011; Herbert 2010; Tomaskovic-Devey and Warren 2009).

Back in the 1990s, increased attention to racial profiling led not only to special reports and commissions but also to talk of legislating against it. This proved difficult. The U.S. Supreme Court in *Whren v. United States* (1996) upheld the constitutionality of using a minor traffic infraction as an excuse to stop and search a vehicle and its passengers. Nonetheless, states and other government units are discussing policies and training that would discourage racial profiling. At the same time, most law enforcement agencies reject the idea of compiling racial data on traffic stops, arguing that it would be a waste of money and staff time.

Efforts to stop racial profiling came to an abrupt end after the September 11, 2001, terrorist attacks on the United States. Suspicions about Muslims and Arabs in the United States became widespread. Foreign students from Arab countries were summoned for special questioning. Legal immigrants identified as Arab or Muslim were scrutinized for any illegal activity and were prosecuted for routine immigration violations that were ignored for people of other ethnic backgrounds and religious faiths (Withrow 2006).

National surveys have found little change since 2001 in support for profiling Arab Americans at airports. In 2010, 53 percent of Americans favored "ethnic and religious profiling," even for U.S. citizens, and want requirements that Arab Americans undergo special and more-intensive security checks before boarding planes in the United States (Zogby 2010).

Read the Document on MySocLab: *Racism in Toyland*

Color-Blind Racism

Over the last three generations, nationwide surveys have consistently shown growing support by Whites for integration, interracial dating, and having members of minority groups attain political office, including becoming president of the United States. Yet how can this be true when the hatred described at the beginning of the chapter persists and thousands of hate crimes occur annually?

Color-blind racism refers to the use of race-neutral principles to defend the racially unequal status quo. Yes, "no discrimination for college admission" should exist, yet the disparity in educational experiences means that formal admissions criteria will privilege White high school graduates. "Healthcare is for all," but if you do not have workplace insurance, you likely cannot afford it.

Color-blind racism has also been referred to as laissez-faire, postracialism, or aversive racism, but the common theme is that notions of racial inferiority are rarely expressed and that proceeding color-blind into the future will perpetuate inequality. In the post–civil rights era and with the election of President Barack Obama, people are more likely to assume discrimination is long past and express views that are more proper—that is, lacking the overt expressions of racism of the past.

An important aspect of color-blind racism is the recognition that race is rarely invoked in public debates on social issues. Instead, people emphasize lower social class, the lack of citizenship, or illegal aliens; these descriptions serve as proxies for race. Furthermore, the emphasis is on individuals failing rather than recognizing patterns of groups being disadvantaged. This leads many White people to declare they are not racist and that they do not know anyone who is racist. It also leads to the mistaken conclusion that more progress has been made toward racial and ethnic equality and even tolerance than has really taken place.

When we survey White attitudes toward African Americans, three conclusions are inescapable. First, attitudes are subject to change; during periods of dramatic social upheaval, dramatic shifts can occur within one generation. Second, less progress was made in the late twentieth and beginning of the twentieth-first centuries than was made in the relatively brief period of the 1950s and 1960s. Third, the pursuit of a color-blind agenda has created lower levels of support for politics that could reduce racial inequality if implemented.

Economically less-successful groups such as African Americans and Latinos have been associated with negative traits to the point that issues such as urban decay, homelessness, welfare, and crime are viewed as race issues even though race is rarely mentioned explicitly. Besides making it harder to resolve difficult social issues, this is another instance of blaming the victim. These perceptions come at a time when the willingness of the government to address domestic ills is limited by increasing opposition to new taxes and continuing commitments to fight terrorism here and abroad. The color line remains, even if more people are unwilling to accept its divisive impact on everyone's lives (Ansell 2008; Bonilla-Silva 2006; Bonilla-Silva and Seamster 2011; Kang and Lane 2010; Mazzocco et al. 2006; Quillian 2006; Winant 2004:106–108).

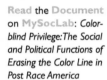

Read the Document on MySocLab: *Color-blind Privilege:The Social and Political Functions of Erasing the Color Line in Post Race America*

The Mood of the Oppressed

Sociologist W. E. B. Du Bois relates an experience from his youth in a largely White community in Massachusetts. He tells how, on one occasion, the boys and girls were exchanging cards, and everyone was having a lot of fun. One girl, a newcomer, refused his card as soon as she saw that Du Bois was Black. He wrote:

> *Then it dawned upon me with a certain suddenness that I was different from others...shut out from their world by a vast veil. I had therefore no desire to tear down that veil, to creep through; I held all beyond it in common contempt and lived above it in a region of blue sky and great wandering shadows.* (1903:2)

In using the image of a veil, Du Bois describes how members of subordinate groups learn they are being treated differently. In his case and that of many others, this leads to feelings of contempt toward all Whites that continue for a lifetime.

Opinion pollsters have been interested in White attitudes on racial issues longer than they have measured the views of subordinate groups. This neglect of minority attitudes reflects, in part, the bias of the White researchers. It also stems from the contention that the dominant group is more important to study because it is in a better position to act on its beliefs. The results of a nationwide survey conducted in the United States offer insight into sharply different views on the state of race relations today (Figure 2.3). Latinos, African Americans, and Asian Americans all have strong reservations about the state of race relations in the United States. They are sceptical about the level of equal opportunity and perceive a lot of discrimination. It is interesting to note that Hispanics and Asian Americans, overwhelmingly immigrants, are more likely to feel they will succeed if they work hard. Yet the majority of all three groups have a positive outlook for the next ten years (New America Media 2007; Preston 2007).

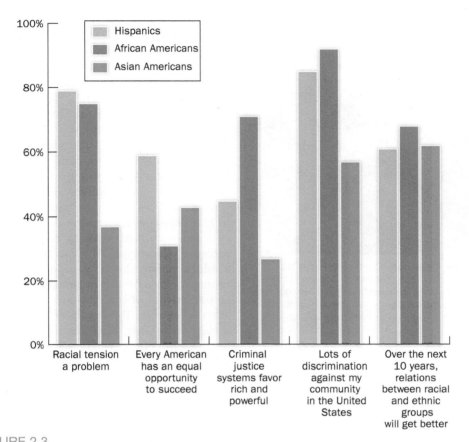

What Is the State of Race Relations? Three Views

Note: Answers mean respondent believes "very important problem" or "strongly agree" regarding the statements listed. Based on 1,105 interviews in August–September 2007, with bilingual questioners used as necessary.

Source: New America Media 2007:6, 12, 14, 24, 26.

National surveys showed that the 2008 successful presidential bid of Senator Barack Obama led to a sense of optimism and national pride among African Americans, even though political observers noted that Obama ran a race-neutral campaign and rarely addressed issues specifically of concern to African Americans. Unlike Whites or Hispanics, Black voters still saw President Obama's campaign as addressing issues important to the Black community. Survey researchers closely followed these perceptions after the 2008 election.

Optimism about the present and future increased significantly among African Americans during the Obama campaign and first year of his presidency. Ironically, White optimism about positive racial change was even more optimistic during the early period of the Obama administration. Yet other data show little evidence of a new nationwide perspective on race following the election. For example, only 35.3 percent of first-year college students in September 2012 indicated a goal of "helping to promote racial understanding" compared to 46 percent in 1992 (Pew Research Center 2010; Pryor, Blake, Hurtado, Berdan, and Case 2012:43).

We have focused so far on what comes to mind when we think about prejudice: one group hating another group. But there is another form of prejudice that has been

How do children come to develop an image about themselves? Toys and playthings have an important role, and for many children of racial and ethnic minorities, it is unusual to find toys that look like them. In 2005, a new doll was released called Fulla—an Arab who reflects modesty, piety, and respect, yet underneath she wears chic clothes that might be typically worn by a Muslim woman in private.

proposed in the past: A group may come to hate itself. Members of groups held in low esteem by society may, as a result, either hate themselves or have low self-esteem, as many social scientists once believed. Research literature of the 1940s through the 1960s emphasized the low self-esteem of minorities. Usually, the subject was African American, but the argument also has been generalized to include any subordinate racial, ethnic, or nationality group.

This view is no longer accepted. We should not assume that minority status influences personality traits in either a good or a bad way. First, such assumptions may create a stereotype. We cannot describe a Black personality any more accurately than we can a White personality. Second, characteristics of minority-group members are not entirely the result of subordinate racial status; they also are influenced by low incomes, poor neighborhoods, and so forth. Third, many studies of personality imply that certain values are normal or preferable, but the values chosen are those of dominant groups.

If assessments of a subordinate group's personality are so prone to misjudgements, then why has the belief in low self-esteem been so widely held? Much of the research rests on studies with preschool-age Black children who were asked to express their preferences for dolls with different facial colors. Indeed, one such study by psychologists Kenneth and Mamie Clark (1947) was cited in the arguments before the U.S. Supreme Court in the landmark 1954 case *Brown v. Board of Education*. The Clarks' study showed that Black children preferred White dolls, a finding that suggested the children had developed a negative self-image. Although subsequent doll studies have sometimes shown Black children's preference for white-faced dolls, other social scientists contend that this shows a realization of what most commercially sold dolls look like rather than documenting low self-esteem (Bloom 1971; Powell-Hopson and Hopson 1988).

Because African American children, as well as other subordinate groups' children, realistically see that Whites have more power and resources and, therefore, rate them higher does not mean that they personally feel inferior. Children who experience overt discrimination are more likely to continue to display feelings of distress and anxiety later in life. However, studies, even those with children, show that when the self-images of middle-class or affluent African Americans are measured, their feelings of self-esteem are more positive than those of comparable Whites (Coker et al. 2009; Gray-Little and Hafdahl 2000).

Intergroup Hostility

Prejudice is as diverse as the nation's population. It exists not only between dominant and subordinate peoples but also among specific subordinate groups. Unfortunately, until recently little research existed on this subject except for a few social distance scales administered to racial and ethnic minorities.

A national survey revealed that, like Whites, many African Americans, Hispanic Americans, and Asian Americans held prejudiced and stereotypical views of other racial and ethnic minority groups:

- Majorities of Black, Hispanic, and Asian American respondents agreed that Whites are "bigoted, bossy, and unwilling to share power." Majorities of these non-White groups also believed that they had less opportunity than Whites to obtain a good education, a skilled job, or decent housing.
- Forty-six percent of Hispanic Americans and 42 percent of African Americans agreed that Asian Americans are "unscrupulous, crafty, and devious in business."
- Sixty-eight percent of Asian Americans and 49 percent of African Americans believed that Hispanic Americans "tend to have bigger families than they are able to support."
- Thirty-one percent of Asian Americans and 26 percent of Hispanic Americans agreed that African Americans "want to live on welfare."

Members of oppressed groups have adopted the widely held beliefs of the dominant culture concerning oppressed groups. At the same time, the survey also revealed positive views of major racial and ethnic minorities:

- More than 80 percent of respondents admired Asian Americans for "placing a high value on intellectual and professional achievement" and "having strong family ties."
- A majority of all groups surveyed agreed that Hispanic Americans "take deep pride in their culture and work hard to achieve a better life."
- Large majorities from all groups stated that African Americans "have made a valuable contribution to American society and will work hard when given a chance" (National Conference of Christians and Jews 1994).

Do we get along? Although this question often is framed in terms of the relationships between White Americans and other racial and ethnic groups, we should recognize the prejudice between groups. In a national survey conducted in 2000, people were asked whether they felt they could generally get along with members of other groups. In Figure 2.4, we can see that Whites felt they had the most difficulty getting along with Blacks. We also see the different views that Blacks, Latinos, Asian Americans, and American Indians hold toward other groups.

It is curious to find that some groups feel they get along better with Whites than with other minority groups. Why would that be? Often, low-income people compete daily with other low-income people and do not readily see the larger societal forces that contribute to their low status. The survey results reveal that many Hispanics are more likely to believe Asian Americans are getting in their way than the White Americans who are the real decision makers in their community.

Most troubling is when intergroup hostility becomes violent. Ethnic and racial tensions among African Americans, Latinos, and immigrants may become manifest in hate crimes. Violence can surface in neighborhoods where people compete for scarce resources such as jobs and housing. Gangs become organized along racial lines, much like private clubs "downtown." In recent years, Los Angeles has been particularly concerned about rival Black and Hispanic gangs. Conflict theorists see this violence as resulting from larger structural forces, but for the average person in such areas, life itself becomes more of a challenge (Archibold 2007).

Read the Document on MySocLab: Racism Without "Racists"

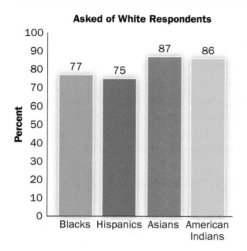

Asked of White Respondents

Blacks	77
Hispanics	75
Asians	87
American Indians	86

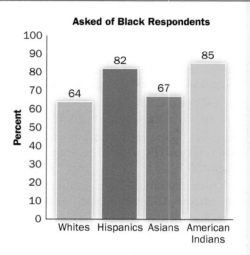

Asked of Black Respondents

Whites	64
Hispanics	82
Asians	67
American Indians	85

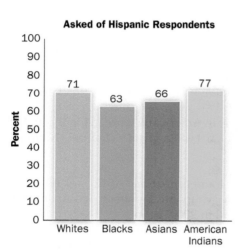

Asked of Hispanic Respondents

Whites	71
Blacks	63
Asians	66
American Indians	77

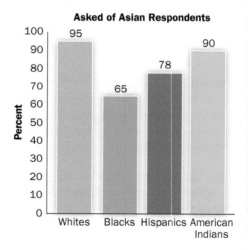

Asked of Asian Respondents

Whites	95
Blacks	65
Hispanics	78
American Indians	90

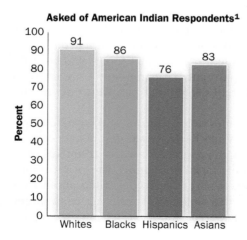

Asked of American Indian Respondents[1]

Whites	91
Blacks	86
Hispanics	76
Asians	83

FIGURE 2.4

Do We Get Along?

Percentage saying groups get along with each other ("Don't Knows" excluded).

[1]Sample size for American Indians is very small and subject to large sample variance.

Note: The wording of the question was, "We hear a lot these days about how various groups in society get along with each other. I'm going to mention several groups and ask whether you think they generally get along with each other or generally do not get along with each other." So, in the "Asked of White Respondents" graph, Whites are asked how Whites get along with each ethnic group; in the "Asked of Black Respondents" graph, Blacks are asked how Blacks get along with each ethnic group, and so on.

Source: Smith 2006:65. Reprinted by permission of the author.

Reducing Prejudice

Focusing on how to eliminate prejudice involves an explicit value judgment: Prejudice is wrong and causes problems for those who are prejudiced and for their victims. As individuals, we can act to stop prejudice, as indicated in Table 2.2. The important thing to remember is not to ignore prejudice when you witness it.

The obvious way to eliminate prejudice is to eliminate its causes: the desire to exploit, the fear of being threatened, and the need to blame others for one's own failure. These might be eliminated by personal therapy, but therapy, even if it works for every individual, is no solution for an entire society in which prejudice is a part of everyday life.

The answer appears to rest with programs directed at society as a whole. Prejudice is attacked indirectly when discrimination is attacked. Despite prevailing beliefs to the contrary, we *can* legislate against prejudice: Statutes and decisions do affect attitudes. In the past, people firmly believed that laws could not overcome norms, especially racist ones. Recent history, especially after the civil rights movement began in 1954, has challenged that once-common belief. Laws and court rulings that have equalized the treatment of Blacks, and Whites have led people to reevaluate their beliefs about what is right and wrong. The increasing tolerance by Whites during the civil rights era from 1954 to 1965 supports this conclusion.

Much research has been done to determine how to change negative attitudes toward groups of people. The most encouraging findings point to education, mass media, intergroup contact, and workplace training programs.

TABLE 2.2
Ways to Fight Prejudice

1. *Act.* Do something. In the face of hatred, apathy will be taken as acceptance, even by the victims of prejudice themselves.

2. *Unite.* Call a friend or coworker. Organize a group of like-thinking friends from school or your place of worship or club. Create a coalition that is diverse and includes the young, the old, law enforcement representatives, and the media.

3. *Support the victims.* Victims of hate crimes are especially vulnerable. Let them know you care by words, in person, or by e-mail. If you or your friend is a victim, report it.

4. *Do your homework.* If you suspect a hate crime has been committed, do your research to document it.

5. *Create an alternative.* Never attend a rally where hate is a part of the agenda. Find another outlet for your frustration, whatever the cause.

6. *Speak up.* You, too, have First Amendment rights. Denounce the hatred, the cruel jokes. If you see a news organization misrepresenting a group, speak up.

7. *Lobby leaders.* Persuade policymakers, business heads, community leaders, and executives of media outlets to take a stand against hate.

8. *Look long term.* Participate or organize events such as annual parades or cultural fairs to celebrate diversity and harmony. Supplement it with a Web site that can be a 24/7 resource.

9. *Teach acceptance.* Prejudice is learned, and parents and teachers can influence the content of curriculum. In a first-grade class in Seattle, children paint self-portraits, mixing colors to match their skin tone.

10. *Dig deeper.* Look into the issues that divide us—social inequality, immigration, and sexual orientation. Work against prejudice. Dig deep inside yourself for prejudices and stereotypes you may embrace. Find out what is happening and act!

Source: Author, based on Southern Poverty Law Center 2010; Willoughby 2004.

Education

Research on education and prejudice considers special programs aimed at promoting mutual respect as well as what effect more formal schooling generally has on expressions of bigotry.

Most research studies show that well-constructed programs have a positive effect on reducing prejudice, at least temporarily. The reduction is rarely as much as one might want, however. The difficulty is that a single program is insufficient to change lifelong habits, especially if little is done to reinforce the program's message once it ends. Persuasion to respect other groups does not operate in a clear field because, in their ordinary environments, people are still subjected to situations that promote prejudicial feelings. Children and adults are encouraged to laugh at Polish jokes and cheer for a team named *Redskins*. Black adolescents may be discouraged by peers from befriending a White youth. All this undermines the effectiveness of prejudice-reduction programs (Allport 1979).

Studies document that increased formal education, regardless of content, is associated with racial tolerance. Research data show that highly educated people are more likely to indicate respect and liking for groups different from themselves. Why should more education have this effect? It might promote a broader outlook and make a person less likely to endorse myths that sustain racial prejudice. Formal education teaches the importance of qualifying statements such as, "Even though they have lower test scores, you need to remember the neighborhoods from which they come." Education introduces one to the almost indefinite diversity of social groups and the need to question rigid categorizations, if not reject them altogether. Colleges increasingly include a graduation requirement that students complete a course that explores diversity or multiculturalism. Another explanation is that education does not reduce intolerance but instead makes people more careful about revealing it. Formal education may simply instruct people in the appropriate responses. Despite the lack of a clear-cut explanation, either theory suggests that the continued trend toward a better-educated population will contribute to a reduction in overt prejudice.

However, college education may not reduce prejudice uniformly. For example, some White students might believe that minority students did not earn their admission into college. Students may feel threatened to see large groups of people of different racial and cultural backgrounds congregating and forming their own groups. Racist confrontations do occur outside the classroom and, even if they involve only a few individuals, the events will be followed by hundreds more. Therefore, some aspects of the college experience may only foster "we" and "they" attitudes (Schaefer 1986, 1996).

"I'M IN FAVOR OF LIFTING RESTRICTIONS ON IMMIGRATION — THEY'RE WILLING TO WORK CHEAP WITH NO BENEFITS."

Many people express tolerant beliefs such as "I'm in favor of lifting restrictions on immigration," while still harboring stereotypes generalized to an entire group of people.

Source: LALO ALCARAZ ©2001 Dist. by UNIVERSAL UCLICK. Reprinted with permission. All rights reserved.

Mass Media

Mass media, like schools, may reduce prejudice without requiring specially designed programs. Television, radio, motion pictures, newspapers, magazines, and the Internet present only a portion of real life, but what effect do they have on prejudice if the content is racist or antiracist, sexist or antisexist? As with measuring the influence of programs designed to reduce prejudice, coming to strong conclusions on mass media's effect is hazardous, but the evidence points to a measurable effect.

Today, over 56 percent of all youth younger than 14 years of age in the United States are children of color, yet few faces they see on television reflect their race or cultural heritage. What is more, the programs shown earlier in the evening, when young people are most likely to watch television, are the least diverse of all.

Why the underrepresentation? Incredibly, network executives seemed surprised by the research demonstrating an all-White season. Producers, writers, executives, and advertisers blamed each other for the alleged oversight. In recent years, the rise of cable television and the Internet has fragmented the broadcast entertainment market, siphoning viewers away from the general-audience sitcoms and dramas of the past. With the proliferation of cable channels such as Black Entertainment Television (BET) and the Spanish-language Univision and Web sites that cater to every imaginable taste, there no longer seems to be a need for a broadly popular series such as *The Cosby Show*, whose tone and content appealed to Whites as well as Blacks in a way that newer series do not. The result of these sweeping technological changes has been a sharp divergence in viewer preferences. Black comedian and director Tyler Perry is an immensely popular and successful actor, director, and producer but his popularity is limited to the African American community.

The absence of racial and ethnic minorities in television is well documented. They are less likely to play recurring roles and are far underrepresented in key decision-making positions such as directors, producers, and casting agents. Television series are

only part of the picture. News broadcasting is done predominantly by Whites, and local news emphasizes crime, often featuring Black or Hispanic perpetrators; print journalism is nearly the same. This is especially troubling given another finding in a research study creating simulations where the participants can choose to act in a possible crime situation. Research showed that people were quicker to "shoot" an armed Black person than a White man in a video simulation. In another variation of that same study, the researchers showed subjects fake newspaper articles describing a string of armed robberies that showed either Black or White suspects. The subjects were quicker to "shoot" the armed suspect if he was Black but reading the articles had no impact on their willingness to "shoot" the armed White criminal. This is a troubling aspect of the potential impact of media content (Correll et al. 2007a, 2007b; Park, Judd, Wittenbrink, Sadler, and Keesee 2007a, 2007b).

Reality or unscripted television programs have dominated prime time television for the last few years. Popular with consumers and relatively inexpensive to produce, broadcast and cable networks alike rushed into production

Who does the guy pick on *The Bachelor*? Who does the gal pick on *The Bachelorette*? If the first 24 seasons of the two shows are any indication, the person choosing will definitely be White and the choices will most likely be White.

Watch the Video on **MySocLab**: *ABC News: Tough Talk from America's Number 1 TV Dad*

TABLE 2.3
Stereotyping in the Twenty-First Century

When asked to identify the role a person of a particular ethnic or racial background would be most likely to play in a movie or on television, teenagers cited familiar stereotypes.

Group	Media Roles Identified
African American	Athlete, gang member, police officer
Arab American	Terrorist, convenience store clerk
Asian American	Physician, lawyer, CEO, factory worker
Hispanic	Gang member, factory worker
Irish American	Drunkard, police officer, factory worker
Italian American	Crime boss, gang member, restaurant worker
Jewish American	Physician, lawyer, CEO, teacher
Polish American	Factory worker

Note: Based on national survey of 1,264 people between ages 13 and 18.
Source: Zogby 2001.

shows that featured everyday people or, at least, C-list celebrities thrust into challenges. While unscripted shows have been routinely criticized on many artistic grounds, it is hard not to see the diverse nature of the participants. Reality programs have been analyzed as representing the diversity of the population. They represent a new and significant exception to television dominated by White actors and actresses.

In one area of unscripted television, the color line remains in place. Reality shows that promote creation of romantic partnerships such as *The Bachelor* and *The Bachelorette* do so in an all-white dating gallery—at least that has been the case for the first 24 seasons through late 2012. Meanwhile, back on scripted television, in a recent year, only four of the nearly 70 pilot projects under development by the four major networks had a minority person cast in a starring role (Belton 2009; Braxton 2009; National Association for the Advancement of Colored People 2008; Ratledge 2012; Wyatt 2009).

It is not surprising that young people quickly develop expectations of the roles that various racial and ethnic group members play in mass media such as television and motion pictures. A national survey of teens (ages 12–18) asked what characters members of racial and ethnic groups would be likely to play. The respondents' perception of media, as shown in Table 2.3, shows a significant amount of stereotyping occurring in their minds, in the media, or both.

Avoidance versus Friendship

Is prejudice reduced or intensified when people cross racial and ethnic boundaries? Two parallel paths have been taken to look at this social distance and equal-status contact.

The Social Distance Scale Robert Park and Ernest Burgess (1921:440) first defined **social distance** as the tendency to approach or withdraw from a racial group. Emory Bogardus (1968) conceptualized a scale that could measure social distance empirically. His social distance scale is so widely used that it is often called the **Bogardus scale**.

The scale asks people how willing they would be to interact with various racial and ethnic groups in specified social situations. The situations describe different degrees of social contact or social distance. The items used, with their corresponding distance scores, follow. People are asked whether they would be willing to work alongside someone or be a neighbor to someone of a different group, and, showing the least amount of social distance, be related through marriage. Over the 70-year period in which the tests were administered, certain patterns emerged. In the top third of the hierarchy are White Americans and northern Europeans. Held at greater social distance are eastern and southern Europeans, and generally near the bottom are racial minorities (Bogardus 1968; Song 1991; Wark and Galliher 2007).

Explore the Concept on MySocLab: *Bogardus Social Distance Research*

Generally, the researchers also found that among the respondents who had friends of different racial and ethnic origins, they were more likely to show greater social distance—that is, they were less likely to have been in each other's homes, shared in fewer activities, and were less likely to talk about their problems with each other. This is unlikely to promote mutual understanding.

Equal Status Contact   An impressive number of research studies have confirmed the **contact hypothesis**, which states that intergroup contact between people of equal status in harmonious circumstances causes them to become less prejudiced and to abandon previously held stereotypes. The importance of equal status in interaction cannot be stressed enough. If a Puerto Rican is abused by his employer, little interracial harmony is promoted. Similarly, the situation in which contact occurs must be pleasant, making a positive evaluation likely for both individuals. Contact between two nurses, one Black and the other White, who are competing for one vacancy as a supervisor may lead to greater racial hostility. On the other hand, being employed together in a harmonious workplace or living in the same neighborhood would work against harboring stereotypes or prejudices (Krysan, Farley, and Couper 2008; Schaefer 1976).

The key factor in reducing hostility, in addition to equal-status contact, is the presence of a common goal. If people are in competition, as already noted, contact may heighten tension. However, bringing people together to share a common task has been shown to reduce ill feelings when these people belong to different racial, ethnic, or religious groups. A study released in 2004 traced the transformations that occurred over the generations in the composition of the Social Service Employees Union in New York City. Always a mixed membership, the union was founded by Jews and Italian Americans, only to experience an influx of Black Americans. More recently in other parts of the United States, it comprises Latin Americans, Africans, West Indians, and South Asians. At each transformation, the common goals of representing the workers effectively overcame the very real cultural differences among the rank and file of Mexican and El Salvadoran immigrants in Houston. The researchers found that when the new arrivals had contact with African Americans, intergroup relations generally improved, and the absence of contact tended to foster ambivalent, even negative, attitudes (Fine 2008; Foerstrer 2004; Paluck and Green 2009).

The limited amount of intergroup contact is of concern given the power of the contact hypothesis. If there is no positive contact, then how can we expect a decrease in prejudice? National surveys show prejudice directed toward Muslim Americans, but social contact bridges that hatred. In a 2006 survey, 50 percent of people who were not acquainted with a Muslim favored special identification for Muslim Americans, but only 24 percent of those who knew a Muslim embraced that same view. Similarly, people personally familiar with Muslims are more than one-third less likely to endorse special security checks just for Muslims and are less nervous to see Muslim men on the same flight with themselves. Although negative views are common toward Muslim Americans today, they are much less likely to be endorsed by people who have had intergroup contact (Saad 2006).

As African Americans and other subordinate groups slowly gain access to better-paying and more-responsible jobs, the contact hypothesis takes on greater significance. Usually, the availability of equal-status interaction is taken for granted; yet in everyday life, intergroup contact does not conform to the equal-status idea of the contact hypothesis. Furthermore, as we have seen, in a highly segregated society such as the United States, contact tends to be brief and superficial, especially between Whites and minorities. The apartheid-like friendship patterns prevent us from learning firsthand not just how to get along but also how to revel in interracial experiences (Bonilla-Silva and Embrick 2007; Miller 2002).

Avoidance Via the Internet   The emergence of the Internet, smartphones, and social media are often heralded as transforming social behavior by allowing us to network globally. While this may be the case in some instances, avoiding people online who are racially, ethnically, and religiously different is just another means of doing what one's parents and grandparents did face-to-face.

Take dating, for example. While in the past, one avoided people who looked different at social occasions, Internet daters have a new tool for such avoidance. Studies document that people who use Internet dating services typically use filters or respond to background questions to exclude contact with people different from themselves. While many daters use such means, Whites are least open to dating racial and ethnic groups different from themselves, African Americans are most open, and Latinos and Asian Americans are somewhere between the two extremes (Robnett and Feliciano 2011).

Sometimes the avoidance is not necessarily initiated by people but by the helpful technology.

There is growing concern that because of an increasingly wired world, in a more subtle fashion we are less likely to benefit from intergroup contacts, not to mention friendships, in the future. Through Facebook, Classmate, and LinkedIn, the Internet allows us to reach out to those who are different from ourselves—or does it? The search engines we use to navigate the Internet are personalized. Google, for example, uses as many as 57 sources of information, including a person's location and past searches, to make calculated guesses about the sites a person might like to visit. Its searches have been personalized in this way since 2009. Keep in mind that Google accounts for 82 percent of the global Internet searches and captures 98 percent of the mobile/cell phone searches. In 2012, Google carried the process one step further by collecting information from the websites that people "friend" or "like" through social media, and then use that information to direct their web searches.

Although Google's approach may at first sound convenient, critics charge that it can trap users in their own worlds by routing them ever more narrowly in the same direction. In his book, *The Filter Bubble,* online political activist Eli Pariser (2011a, 2011b) contends that when a search engine filters our searches, it encloses us in a kind of "invisible bubble" or "walled garden" that limits what we see to what we are already familiar with. Thus, we are not likely to discover people, places, and ideas that are outside our comfort zone. Secure in our online bubble, which we may not even realize is there, we have little interaction with people different from ourselves (Katz 2012; Zitrain 2008).

What is wrong with that? Given a choice, most of us go only to restaurants whose food we enjoy and read and listen to only those books and radio programs we know we like. Yet, wasn't the Internet supposed to open new vistas to us? If we are investigating a major news event, shouldn't we all see the same information when we search for it? Pariser describes what happened when two friends searched for the term "BP" in the spring of 2010, during the Deepwater Horizon oil rig's accidental discharge of crude oil into the Gulf of Mexico. Using the same browser, the two friends got very different results. One saw links to information about the oil spill; the other saw links to information about BP's CEO, intended for investors.

Corporate Response: Diversity Training

Prejudice carries a cost. This cost is not only to the victim but also to any organization that allows prejudice to interfere with its functioning. Workplace hostility can lead to lost productivity and even staff attrition. Furthermore, if left unchecked, an organization—whether a corporation, government agency, or nonprofit enterprise—can develop a reputation for having a "chilly climate."

If a business has a reputation that it is unfriendly to people of color or to women, qualified people are discouraged from applying for jobs there and potential clients might seek products or services elsewhere.

In an effort to improve workplace relations, most organizations have initiated some form of diversity training. These programs are aimed at eliminating circumstances and relationships that cause groups to receive fewer rewards, resources, or opportunities. Typically, programs aim to reduce ill treatment based on race, gender, and ethnicity. In addition, diversity training may deal with (in descending order of frequency) age, disability, religion, and language as well as other aspects, including citizenship status, marital status, and parental status (Society for Human Resource Management 2008).

"Oh, you'll love working here. Nobody treats you any differently just because of your age, race, or gender."

Many employment situations do not afford the opportunity to learn about a diverse workforce. Explicit efforts to learn about diversity are important especially in these situations.

Source: Mike Lester.

It is difficult to make broad generalization about the effectiveness of diversity-training programs because they vary so much in structure between organizations. At one extreme are short presentations that seem to have little support from management. People file into the room feeling it is something they need to get through quickly. Such training is unlikely to be effective and may be counterproductive by heightening social tensions. At the other end of the continuum is a diversity training program that is integrated into initial job training, reinforced periodically, and presented as part of the overall mission of the organization, with full support from all levels of management. In such businesses, diversity is a core value, and management demands a high degree of commitment from all employees (Dobbin, Kalev, and Kelly 2007).

Remarkably, the prevalence of any diversity programs in organizations remains slow (10 to 30 percent), even in the 30-plus years after the diversity-management paradigm was first widely viewed as good for business. Even inexpensive steps are not widely adopted. Unfortunately, corporations with lower representation of women and minorities are less likely to embrace diversity programs.

Research into different corporate policies has found two that are particularly effective. Diversity task forces that bring together people from different departments to brainstorm about opening up hiring opportunities appear to eventually increase the diversity in upper management. A second successful policy is the diversity mentoring programs designed for aspiring women and minorities, as well as White men, to achieve their career goals. Unfortunately, research suggests that if White men perceive African Americans are

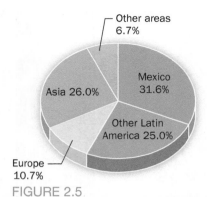

FIGURE 2.5

Foreign-Born Workers in the United States, by Country

About 16 percent of the civilian labor force is foreign-born, with Mexico the largest source.

Source: Data for 2010 from the Bureau of the Census 2011k: Table 3.6.

the primary organizers of such efforts, networking progress can actually have a negative impact (Dobbin et al. 2011; Kaler et al. 2006).

As shown in Figure 2.5, the workforce is becoming more diverse, and management is taking notice. An increasing proportion of the workforce is foreign-born, and the numbers of U.S.-born African Americans, Latinos, and Asian Americans also are growing. Growing research in business and the social sciences documents that diversity is an asset in bringing about creative changes. The benefits of workplace diversity are especially true at management levels where leadership teams can develop innovative solutions and creative ideas. However, it is troubling to note that organizations that have the least diverse leadership are less likely to adopt any kind of diversity program, whatever its effectiveness (DiTomaso, Post, and Parks-Yancy 2007; Dobbin, Kim, and Kalev 2011; Leung et al. 2008; Page 2007).

It is not in an organization's best interests if employees start to create barriers based on, for example, racial lines. Earlier, we learned that equal-status contact can reduce hostility. However, in the workplace, people compete for promotions, desirable work assignments, and better office space, to name a few sources of friction. When done well, an organization undertakes diversity training to remove ill feelings among workers, which often reflect the prejudices present in larger society.

To have a lasting impact, diversity training also should not be separated from other aspects of the organization. For example, even the most inspired program will have little effect on prejudice if the organization promotes a sexist or ethnically offensive image in its advertising. The University of North Dakota launched an initiative in 2001 to become one of the top institutions for Native Americans in the nation. Yet at almost the same time, the administration reaffirmed its commitment, despite tribal objections, to have the "Fighting Sioux" as its mascot for athletic teams. It does little to present diversity training if overt actions by an organization propel it in the opposite direction. In 2005, the National Collegiate Athletic Association began to review logos and mascots that could be considered insulting to Native Americans. Some colleges have resisted suggestions to change or alter their publicity images, although others have abandoned the practice (University of North Dakota 2008).

Despite the problems inherent in confronting prejudice, an organization with a comprehensive, management-supported program of diversity training can go a long way toward reducing prejudice in the workplace. The one major qualifier is that the rest of the organization must also support mutual respect.

Conclusion

This chapter has examined theories of prejudice and measurements of its extent. Prejudice has a long history in the United States. Whispering campaigns suggested that presidents Martin Van Buren and William McKinley were secretly working with the pope. This whispering emerged into the national debate when John F. Kennedy became the first Roman Catholic to become president. Much more recently, in 2010,

18 percent of Americans believed President Obama to be a Muslim and only 34 percent a Christian (Kristof 2010; Pew Forum on Religion and Public Life 2010).

Are some minority groups now finally being respected? People cheered on May 1, 2011, on hearing that Osama bin Laden had been found and killed. However, the always-patriotic American Indian people were troubled to learn that the military had assigned the code name "Geronimo" to the operation to capture the terrorist. The Chiricahua Apache of New Mexico were particularly disturbed to learn that the name of their freedom fighter was associated with a global terrorist. In response, the U.S. Defense Department said no disrespect was meant to Native Americans. Of course, one can imagine that the operation never would have been named "Operation Lafayette" or "Operation Jefferson" (Dally 2011).

Several theories try to explain why prejudice exists. Theories for prejudice include two that tend to be psychological—scapegoating and authoritarian personality—and emphasize why a particular person harbors ill feelings. Others are more sociological—exploitation and normative—and view prejudice in the context of our interaction in a larger society.

Surveys conducted in the United States over the past 60 years point to a reduction of prejudice as measured by the willingness to express stereotypes or maintain social distance. Survey data also show that African Americans, Latinos, Asian Americans, and American Indians do not necessarily feel comfortable with each other. They have adopted attitudes toward other oppressed groups similar to those held by many White Americans.

The absence of widespread public expression of prejudice does not mean prejudice itself is absent. Recent prejudice aimed at Hispanics, Asian Americans, and large recent immigrant groups such as Arab Americans and Muslim Americans is well documented. Issues such as immigration and affirmative action reemerge and cause bitter resentment. Furthermore, ill feelings exist between subordinate groups in schools, on the streets, and in the workplace. Color-blind racism allows one to appear to be tolerant while allowing racial and ethnic inequality to persist.

Equal-status contact may reduce hostility between groups. However, in a highly segregated society defined by inequality, such opportunities are not typical. The mass media can help reduce discrimination, but they have not done enough and may even intensify ill feelings by promoting stereotypical images.

Even though we can be encouraged by the techniques available to reduce intergroup hostility, sizable segments of the population still do not want to live in integrated neighborhoods, do not want to work for or be led by someone of a different race, and certainly object to the idea of their relatives marrying outside their own group. People still harbor stereotypes toward one another, and this tendency includes racial and ethnic minorities having stereotypes about one another.

Reducing prejudice is important because it can lead to support for policy change. There are steps we can take as individuals to confront prejudice and overcome hatred. Another real challenge and the ultimate objective are to improve the social condition of oppressed groups in the United States. To consider this challenge, we turn to discrimination in Chapter 3. Discrimination's costs are high to both dominant and subordinate groups. With this fact in mind, we examine some techniques for reducing discrimination.

MySocLab ✓ Study and Review on MySocLab

Summary

1. Prejudice consists of negative attitudes, and discrimination consists of negative behavior toward a group.

2. Typically unconsciously, White people accept privileges automatically extended to them in everyday life.

3. Robert Merton's formulation clarifies how individuals may be prejudiced and not necessarily discriminatory and finds they act in discriminatory ways while not harboring prejudices.

4. Although evidence indicates that the public expression of prejudice has declined, ample evidence exists that people are expressing race-neutral principles or color-blind racism that still serves to perpetuate inequality in society.

5. Among explanations for prejudice are the theories of scapegoating, authoritarian personality, and exploitation as well as the normative approach.

6. Typically, members of minority groups have a significantly more negative view of social inequality and are more pessimistic about the future compared to Whites.

7. Not only do people in dominant positions direct prejudice at racial and ethnic minorities but intergroup hostility among the minorities themselves also persists and may become violent.

8. Various techniques are utilized by the corporate sector to reduce prejudice, including educational programs, mass media, friendly intergroup contact, and diversity-training programs.

Key Terms

anti-Semitism, p. 40

authoritarian personality, p. 41

Bogardus scale, p. 54

color-blind racism, p. 45

contact hypothesis, p. 55

discrimination, p. 36

ethnocentrism, p. 35

ethnophaulisms, p. 35

exploitation theory, p. 41

homophobia, p. 44

Islamophobia, p. 38

normative approach, p. 41

prejudice, p. 35

racial profiling, p. 44

scapegoating theory, p. 40

sexism, p. 44

social distance, p. 54

stereotypes, p. 42

White privilege, p. 39

Review Questions

1. How are prejudice and discrimination both related and unrelated to each other?

2. How do theories of prejudice relate to different expressions of prejudice?

3. How is color-blind racism expressed?

4. Can you identify any steps that have been taken against prejudice in your community?

Critical Thinking

1. What privileges do you have to which you do not give much thought? Are they in any way related to race, ethnicity, religion, or social class?

2. Identify stereotypes associated with a group of people such as older adults or people with physical disabilities.

3. Consider the television programs you watch the most. In terms of race and ethnicity, how well do the programs you watch reflect the diversity of the population in the United States?

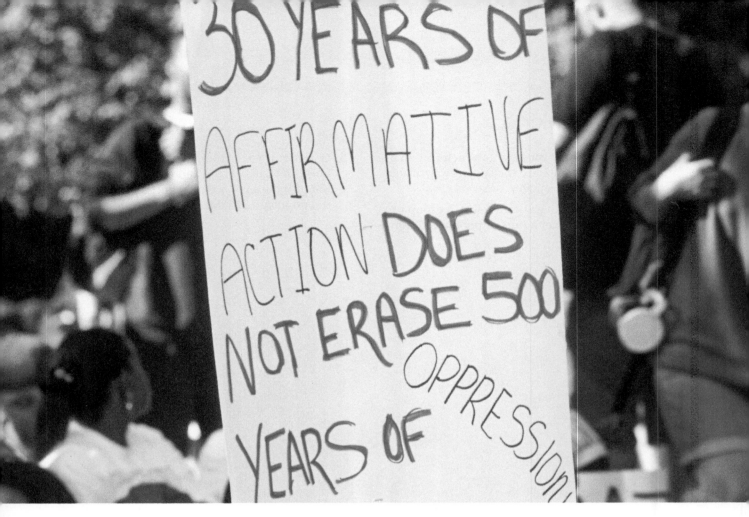

3 Discrimination

- 3-1 Explain the implications of discrimination in our society.
- 3-2 Define and summarize the origin of hate crimes.
- 3-3 Identify the discriminatory patterns of institutions
- 3-4 Address the prevalence of discrimination in the United States.
- 3-5 Discuss distribution of income and wealth among racial and ethnic groups.

- 3-6 Summarize environmental justice and identify present-day concerns.
- 3-7 Explain affirmation action and its effects on discrimination.
- 3-8 Describe the origin and consequences of reverse discrimination.
- 3-9 Compare and contrast glass ceilings, glass walls, and glass escalators.

"I didn't get the job" is a frequent complaint that soon leads to reasons "I" did not get the job for which I applied. Sometimes people think it's because of their race. Is discrimination still the case? Consider two pairs of job applicants—two women, Emily and Lakisha, and two men, Greg and Jamal—who headed out into the job market. Two economists sent out resumes with names that either "sound White" or "sound Black" to 1,300 job ads in *The Boston Globe* and *The Chicago Tribune*.

The results were startling. Welcome the Carries and Kristens but maybe not Aisha and Tamika. White names got about one callback per 10 resumes; black names got one per 15. Having a higher-quality resume featuring more skills and experience, made a White-sounding names 30 percent more likely to elicit a callback but only 9 percent more likely for Black-sounding names. Even employers who specified "equal opportunity employer" in their advertisements showed bias.

Getting a callback does not mean you are hired, but you certainly cannot get a job for which you are never interviewed.

It is not much better when you look for housing. Two communication scholars sent more than 1,100 identically worded e-mail inquiries to Los Angeles-area landlords asking about vacant apartments advertised online. The inquiries were signed randomly, with an equal number signed Patrick McDougall, Tyrell Jackson, or Said Al-Rahman. The fictional McDougall received positive or encouraging replies from 89 percent of the landlords, while Al-Rahman was encouraged by about 66 percent of the landlords. Only 56 percent, however, responded positively to Jackson.

"We thought there might be a discrepancy between the Anglo-sounding name and the other two," professor William Loges said, "but we were surprised by the severity of the reaction—especially to Tyrell Jackson. He was the only one to get any responses directly questioning whether he could really afford the apartment" (Oregon State University 2006).

In either study, we don't know from whom the negative or absence of positive responses came, but evidently it is not easy being Jackson, Tamika, Tyrell, or Said (Bertrand and Mullainathan 2004; Carpusor and Loges 2006).

Another dramatic confirmation of discrimination came with research begun by sociologist Devah Pager in 2003. She sent White, Black, and Latino men out as trained "testers" to look for entry-level jobs in Milwaukee and New York City that required no experience or special training. Each tester was in his twenties and was college educated, but each one presented himself as having only a high school diploma and similar job history.

The job-seeking experiences with different employers were vastly different among the men. Why? Besides having different racial and ethnic backgrounds, some testers indicated in the job application that they had served 18 months in jail for a felony conviction (possession of cocaine with intent to distribute). As you can see in Figure 3.1, applicants with a prison record received significantly fewer callbacks. Although a criminal record made a dramatic difference, race was clearly more important. In another study, she documented that Latino job applicants were at a disadvantage similar to that of the African American testers (Pager, Western, and Bonikowski 2009; Paher and Western 2012).

The differences were so pointed that a White job applicant with a jail record received more callbacks for further consideration than a Black man with no criminal record. Whiteness has a privilege even

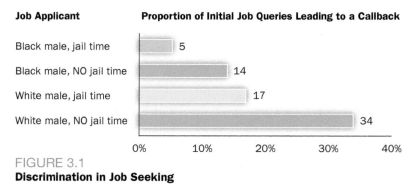

Job Applicant   **Proportion of Initial Job Queries Leading to a Callback**

FIGURE 3.1
Discrimination in Job Seeking

Source: Pager 2003:958. Reprinted by permission of the University of Chicago.

when it comes to jail time; race, it seems, was more of a concern to potential employers than a criminal background. It is no surprise that an analysis of labor patterns after release from prison finds that wages grow at a 21 percent slower rate for Black compared to White ex-inmates.

"I expected there to be an effect of race, but I did not expect it to swamp the results as it did," Pager told an interviewer. Her finding was especially significant because one in three African American men and one in six Hispanic men are expected to serve time in prison during their lifetime compared to one in 17 White men (Greenhouse 2012; Kroeger 2004).

Pager's research, which was widely publicized, eventually contributed to a change in public policy. In his 2004 State of the Union address, and specifically referring to Pager's work, President George W. Bush announced a $300 million monitoring program for ex-convicts who are attempting to reintegrate into society.

Discrimination has a long history, right up to the present, of taking its toll on people. **Discrimination** is the denial of opportunities and equal rights to individuals and groups because of prejudice or other arbitrary reasons. We examine the many faces of discrimination, its many victims, and the many ways scholars have documented its presence today in the United States. We not only return to more examples of discrimination in housing but also look at differential treatment in employment opportunities, wages, voting, vulnerability to environmental hazards, and even access to membership in private clubs.

Understanding Discrimination

Explore the
Activity on
MySocLab:
Discrimination

People in the United States find it difficult to see discrimination as a widespread phenomenon. "After all," it is often said, "these minorities drive cars, hold jobs, own their homes, and even go to college." An understanding of discrimination in modern industrialized societies such as the United States must begin by distinguishing between relative and absolute deprivation.

Conflict theorists have said correctly that it is not absolute, unchanging standards that determine deprivation and oppression. Although minority groups may be viewed as having adequate or even good incomes, housing, healthcare, and educational opportunities, it is their position relative to some other group that offers evidence of discrimination.

Relative deprivation is defined as the conscious experience of a negative discrepancy between legitimate expectations and present actualities. After settling in the United

States, immigrants often enjoy better material comforts and more political freedom than were possible in their old countries. If they compare themselves with most other people in the United States, however, they will feel deprived because, although their standards have improved, the immigrants still perceive relative deprivation.

Absolute deprivation, on the other hand, implies a fixed standard based on a minimum level of subsistence below which families should not be expected to exist. Discrimination does not necessarily mean absolute deprivation. A Japanese American who is promoted to a management position may still be a victim of discrimination if he or she had been passed over for years because of corporate reluctance to place an Asian American in a highly visible position.

Dissatisfaction also is likely to arise from feelings of relative deprivation. The members of a society who feel most frustrated and disgruntled by the social and economic conditions of their lives are not necessarily worse off in an objective sense. Social scientists have long recognized that what is most significant is how people perceive their situations. Karl Marx pointed out that although the misery of the workers was important in reflecting their oppressed state, so was their position relative to the ruling class. In 1847, Marx wrote, "Although the enjoyment of the workers has risen, the social satisfaction that they have has fallen in comparison with the increased enjoyment of the capitalist" (Marx and Engels 1955:94).

This statement explains why the groups or individuals who are most vocal and best organized against discrimination are not necessarily in the worst economic and social situation. However, they are likely to be those who most strongly perceive that, relative to others, they are not receiving their fair share. Resistance to perceived discrimination, rather than the actual amount of absolute discrimination, is the key.

Hate Crimes

Although prejudice certainly is not new in the United States, it is receiving increased attention as it manifests itself in hate crimes in neighborhoods, at meetings, and on college campuses. The Hate Crime Statistics Act, which became law in 1990, directs the Department of Justice to gather data on hate or bias crimes.

What Are Hate Crimes?

The government defines an ordinary crime as a **hate crime** when offenders are motivated to choose a victim because of some characteristic—for example, race, ethnicity, religion, sexual orientation, or disability—and provide evidence that hatred prompted them to commit the crime. Hate crimes also are sometimes referred to as *bias crimes.*

The Hate Crime Statistics Act created a national mandate to identify such crimes, whereas previously only 12 states had monitored hate crimes. The act has since been amended to include disabilities, physical and mental, as well as sexual orientation as factors that could be considered a basis for hate crimes.

In 2012, law enforcement agencies released hate crime data submitted by police agencies. Even though many, many hate crimes are not reported (fewer than one in seven participating agencies reported an incident), a staggering number of offenses that come to law agencies' attention were motivated by hate. While most incidents receive relatively little attention, some become the attention of headlines and online sites for days. Such was the case in 2009 when a Maryland man with a long history of ties to neo-Nazi groups walked into the U.S. Holocaust Memorial Museum in Washington, DC, and opened fire, killing a security guard.

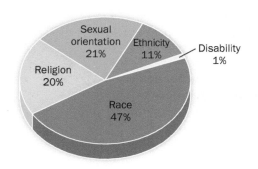

FIGURE 3.2
Distribution of Reported Hate Crimes

Source: Incidents reported for 2011 in Federal Bureau of Investigation 2012.

Official reports noted more than 6,200 hate crimes and bias-motivated incidents in 2011. As indicated in Figure 3.2, race was the apparent motivation for the bias in approximately 47 percent of the reports, and religion, sexual orientation, and ethnicity accounted for 11–20 percent each. Vandalism against property and intimidation were the most common crimes, but among the more than 4,600 crimes directed against people, 44 percent involved assault, rape, or murder.

The vast majority of hate crimes are directed by members of the dominant group toward those who are, relatively speaking, powerless. Only one in five bias incidents based on race are anti-White. Hate crimes, except for those that are most horrific, receive little media attention, and anti-White incidents probably receive even less. Hostility based on race knows no boundaries (Department of Justice 2011; Witt 2007).

The official reports of hate or bias crimes appear to be only the tip of the iceberg. Government-commissioned surveys conducted over a national cross section indicate that 192,000 people annually report they have been victims of hate crimes, but only half of these are reported to police. Of these, only one out of ten, according to the victims, are confirmed as hate crimes. Although definitions vary, a considerable amount of racial hostility in this country becomes violent (Harlow 2005; Perry 2003).

National legislation and publicity have made *hate crime* a meaningful term, and we are beginning to recognize the victimization associated with such incidents. A current proposal would make a violent crime a federal crime if it were motivated by racial or religious bias. Although passage is uncertain, the serious consideration of the proposal indicates a willingness to consider a major expansion of federal jurisdiction. Currently, federal law prohibits crimes motivated by race, color, religion, or national origin only if they violate a federally guaranteed right such as voting.

Victimized groups do more than experience and observe hate crimes and other acts of prejudice. Watchdog organizations play an important role in documenting bias-motivated violence; among such groups are the Anti-Defamation League, the National Institute Against Prejudice and Violence, the Southern Poverty Law Center, and the National Gay and Lesbian Task Force.

To further their agenda, established hate groups have even set up propaganda sites on the World Wide Web. This also creates opportunities for previously unknown haters and hate groups to promote themselves. However, hate crime legislation does not affect such outlets because of legal questions involving freedom of speech. An even more recent technique of hate groups has been to use instant messaging software, which enables Internet users to create a private chat room with another individual. Enterprising bigots use directories to target their attacks through instant messaging, much as harassing telephone calls were placed in the past. Even more creative and subtle are people who have constructed Web sites to attract people who are surfing for information on Martin Luther King, Jr., only to find sites that look educational but savagely discredit the civil rights activist. A close inspection reveals that a White-supremacist organization hosts the sites (Davis 2008; Simon Wiesenthal Center 2008; Working 2007).

Why Do Hate Crimes Carry Harsher Penalties?

Frequently, one hears the identification of a crime as a hate crime being questioned. After all, is not hate involved in every assault or act of vandalism? While many non-hate crimes may include a motivation of hatred toward an individual or organization, a hate or bias crime toward a minority is intended to carry a message well beyond the individual victim. When a person is assaulted because they are gay or lesbian, the act is meant to terrorize all gay and lesbians. Vandalizing a mosque or synagogue is meant to warn all Muslims or Jews that they are not wanted and their religious faith is considered inferior.

In many respects, today's hate crimes are like the terrorist efforts of the Ku Klux Klan of generations ago. Targets may be randomly selected, but the group being terrorized is carefully chosen. In many jurisdictions, having a crime classified as a hate crime can increase the punishment. For example, a misdemeanor like vandalism can be increased to a felony. A felony that is a hate crime can carry a greater prison sentence. These sanctions were upheld by the Supreme Court in the 1993 decision *Mitchell v. Wisconsin*, which recognized that greater harm may be done by hate-motivated crimes (Blazak 2011).

Institutional Discrimination

Individuals practice discrimination in one-on-one encounters, and institutions practice discrimination through their daily operations. Indeed, a consensus is growing today that institutional discrimination is more significant than acts committed by prejudiced individuals.

Social scientists are particularly concerned with how patterns of employment, education, criminal justice, housing, healthcare, and government operations maintain the social significance of race and ethnicity. **Institutional discrimination** is the denial of opportunities and equal rights to individuals and groups that results from the normal operations of a society.

Civil rights activist Stokely Carmichael and political scientist Charles Hamilton are credited with introducing the concept of institutional racism. *Individual discrimination* refers to overt acts of individual Whites against individual Blacks; Carmichael and Hamilton reserved the term *institutional racism* for covert acts committed collectively against an entire group. From this perspective, discrimination can take place without an individual intending to deprive others of privileges and even without the individual being aware that others are being deprived (Ture and Hamilton 1992).

View the **Figure** on **MySocLab**: *Race-Ethnicity and Mortgages*

How can discrimination be widespread and unconscious at the same time? A few documented examples of institutional discrimination follow:

1. Standards for assessing credit risks work against African Americans and Hispanics who seek to establish businesses because many lack conventional credit references. Businesses in low-income areas where these groups often reside also have much higher insurance costs.

2. IQ testing favors middle-class children, especially the White middle class, because of the types of questions included.

3. The entire criminal justice system, from the patrol officer to the judge and jury, is dominated by Whites who find it difficult to understand life in poverty areas.

4. Hiring practices often require several years' experience at jobs only recently opened to members of subordinate groups.

5. Many jobs automatically eliminate people with felony records or past drug offenses, a practice that disproportionately reduces employment opportunities for people of color.

Institutional discrimination is so systemic that it takes on the pattern of what has been termed "woodwork racism" in that racist outcomes become so widespread that African Americans, Latinos, Asian Americans, and others endure them as a part of everyday life (Feagin and McKinney 2003).

Read the Document on MySocLab: *Race and Class in the American Criminal Justice System*

At the beginning of this chapter, we noted how employers routinely pass over job applicants who are felons. This may seem reasonable to casual observers; however, Black and Latino job applicants are more likely to be passed over than Whites. This is a form of institutional discrimination.

Recognizing this, the Equal Opportunity Commission ruled in 2012 that while employers may consider criminal records, a policy that excludes all applicants with a conviction could violate employment discrimination laws because of this differential impact. This does not mean employers must hire ex-felons, only that blanket exclusions are to be avoided (Greenhouse 2012).

Despite the positive step, concern grows over another potential example of institutional discrimination—the requirement of a government-issued ID to vote. Eleven states enacted laws requiring voters to show a photo ID, presumably to prevent voter fraud. However, there is little evidence that people have been impersonating eligible voters at the polls. Courts have been reluctant to uphold such laws, contending that accessibility is not ensured for all eligible voters to obtain such a credential. Such laws disproportionately disenfranchise members of minority groups simply because they do not have a driver's license. National surveys found 25 percent of African Americans and 16 percent of Latino citizens do not have a valid government-issued photo ID compared to 8 percent of White citizens (Brennan Center 2006, 2013; Dade 2012).

In other cases, even apparently neutral institutional standards can lead a college's policy to have discriminatory effects. African American students at a Midwestern state university protested a policy under which fraternities and sororities that wanted to use campus facilities for a dance were required to post a $150 security deposit to cover possible damage. The Black students complained that this policy had a discriminatory impact on minority student organizations. Campus police countered that the university's policy applied to all student groups interested in using these facilities. However, because almost all White fraternities and sororities at the school had their own houses, which they used for dances, the policy affected only African American and other subordinate groups' organizations.

Institutional discrimination continuously imposes more hindrances on and awards fewer benefits to certain racial and ethnic groups than it does to others. This is the underlying and painful context of American intergroup relations.

Discrimination Today

Discrimination continues to be widespread in the United States. It sometimes results from prejudices held by individuals but more significantly, it is found in institutional discrimination. We first look at measuring discrimination in terms of income and then look at efforts that are being made to eliminate or at least reduce it.

Discrimination Hits the Wallet

How much discrimination is there? As in measuring prejudice, problems arise when trying to quantify discrimination. Measuring prejudice is hampered by the difficulties in assessing attitudes and by the need to take many factors into account. It is further limited by the initial challenge of identifying different treatment. A second difficulty of measuring discrimination is assigning a cost to discrimination.

An important measure of economic well-being for any household is their annual income and the wealth they have to draw upon in cases of emergency. **Income** refers to salaries, wages, and other money received; **wealth** is a more inclusive term that encompasses all of a person's material assets, including land and other types of property. We first consider income and then look at wealth later in this chapter.

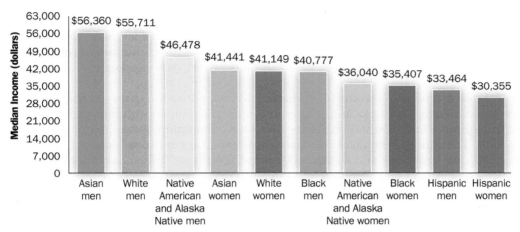

Read the Document on MySocLab: Racial Stratification and Education in the United States: Why Inequality Persists

FIGURE 3.3

Median Income by Race, Ethnicity, and Gender

Even at the very highest levels of schooling, the income gap remains between Whites and Blacks. Education also has little apparent effect on the income gap between male and female workers. Even a brief analysis reveals striking differences in earning power between White men and other groups in the United States. Furthermore, greater inequality is apparent for African American and Hispanic women.

Note: Data released in 2012 for income earned in 2011. Median income is from all sources and is limited to year-round, full-time workers at least 25 years old. Data for White men and women are for non-Hispanics.

Source: Bureau of the Census 2012b; DeNavas-Walt, Proctor, and Smith 2012: PINC-03.

Some tentative conclusions about discrimination can be made looking at income and wealth data. Figure 3.3 uses income data to show the vivid disparity in income between African Americans and Whites and also between men and women. This encompasses all full-time workers. White men, with a median income of $55,711, earn one-third more than Black men and almost twice what Hispanic women earn in wages.

Yet Asian American men are at the top and edge out White males by a little less than $200 a year. Why do Asian American men earn so much if race serves as a barrier? The economic picture is not entirely positive. Some Asian American groups such as Laotians and Vietnamese have high levels of poverty. However, a significant number of Asian Americans with advanced educations have high-earning jobs, which brings up the median income. However, as we will see, given their high levels of schooling, their incomes should be even higher.

Clearly, regardless of race or ethnicity, men outpace women in annual income. This disparity between the incomes of Black women and White men has remained unchanged over the more than 50 years during which such data have been tabulated. It illustrates yet another instance of the greater inequality experienced by minority women. Also, Figure 3.3 includes data only for full-time, year-round workers; it excludes homemakers and the unemployed. Even in this comparison, the deprivation of Blacks, Hispanics, and women is confirmed again.

We might be drawn to the fact that Asian American income appears to slightly overtake that of Whites. However, as we will see, this is due to Asian Americans collectively having much more formal schooling than Whites as a group and deriving some benefits from that achievement.

Are these differences entirely the result of discrimination in employment? No. Individuals within the four groups are not equally prepared to compete for high-paying jobs. Past discrimination is a significant factor in a person's current social position. As discussed previously and illustrated in Figure 3.3, past discrimination continues to take a toll on modern victims. Taxpayers, predominantly White, were unwilling to subsidize the public education of African Americans and Hispanics at the same levels as White pupils. Even as these actions have changed, today's schools show the continuing results of this uneven spending pattern from the past. Education clearly is an appropriate variable to control.

In Table 3.1, median income is compared, holding education constant, which means that we can compare Blacks and Whites and men and women with approximately the same amount of formal schooling. More education means more money, but the disparity remains. The gap between races does narrow somewhat as education increases. However, both African Americans and women lag behind their more affluent counterparts. The contrast remains dramatic: Women with a master's degree typically receive $60,304, which means they earn more than $6,000 less than men who complete only a bachelor's degree.

Thinking over the long term, a woman with a bachelor's degree will work full-time for three years to earn $147,000. The typical male can work a little more than 27 months, take over 9 months off without pay, and still exceed the woman's earnings. Women, regardless of race, pay at every point. They are often hired at lower starting salaries in jobs comparable to those held by men. Salary increases come slower. And by their 30s, they rarely recover from even short maternity leaves (Dey and Hill 2007; Gittell and McKinney 2007; Jacobs 2008).

✳ **Explore** the **Concept** on **MySocLab:** Who Ends Up Poor? Poverty by Education/Race

---

TABLE 3.1
Median Income by Race and Sex, Holding Education Constant

Even at the very highest levels of schooling, the income gap remains between Whites and Blacks. Education also has little apparent effect on the income gap between male and female workers (income values in dollars).

	Race				Sex	
	White Families	Black Families	Asian Families	Hispanic Families	Male	Female
Total	69,829	40,495	72,996	40,061	50,655	38,909
High School						
Nongraduate	35,970	20,768	37,118	30,868	30,423	21,113
Graduate	53,478	32,699	49,658	39,451	40,447	30,611
College						
Associate Degree	71,735	49,989	66,921	53,386	50,928	39,286
Bachelors degree	97,442	76,444	87,704	70,849	66,196	49,108
Master's degree	111,071	80,184	111,871	87,956	83,027	60,304
Doctorate degree	125,059	111,535	114,662	115,434	100,766	77,458

Note: Data released in 2012 for income earned in 2011. Figures are median income from all sources except capital gains. Included are public assistance payments, dividends, pensions, unemployment compensation, and so on. Incomes are for all workers 25 years of age and older. High school graduates include those with GEDs. Data for Whites are for White non-Hispanics. "Some college" excludes associate degree holders. Family data above bachelor's degree are derived from median incomes, and data for doctorate-holders' families are author's estimate.

Source: DeNavas-Walt, Proctor, and Smith 2012: FINC-01, PINC-01.

Note what happens to Asian American households. Although highly educated Asian Americans earn a lot of money, they trail well behind their White counterparts. With a doctorate degree holder in the family, the typical Asian American household earns an estimated $114,662, compared to $125,059 in a White household.

This is the picture today, but is it getting better? According to a Census Bureau report released in 2011, the answer is no. During the early years of the twenty-first century, Blacks were more likely to stay poor than Whites and those African Americans in the top rung of income were more likely to fall than their White counterparts among the wealthy. The inequality is dramatic and the trend is not diminishing (Hisnanick and Giefer 2011).

Now that education has been held constant, is the remaining gap caused by discrimination? Not necessarily. Table 3.1 uses only the amount of schooling, not its quality. Racial minorities are more likely to attend inadequately financed schools. Some efforts have been made to eliminate disparities between school districts in the amount of wealth available to tax for school support, but they have met with little success.

The inequality of educational opportunity may seem less important in explaining sex discrimination. Although women usually are not segregated from men, educational institutions encourage talented women to enter fields that pay less (nursing or elementary education) than other occupations that require similar amounts of training. Even when they do enter the same occupation, the earnings disparity persists. Even controlling for age, a study of census data showed that female physicians and surgeons earned 69 percent of what their male counterparts did. Looking at broad ranges of occupations, researchers in the last few years have attributed between one-quarter and one-third of the wage gap to discrimination rather than personal choices, skill preparation, and formal schooling (Reskin 2012; Weinberg 2007).

Eliminating Discrimination

Two main agents of social change work to reduce discrimination: voluntary associations organized to solve racial and ethnic problems and the federal government, including the courts. The two are closely related: Most efforts initiated by the government were urged by associations or organizations that represent minority groups and followed vigorous protests by African Americans against racism. Resistance to social inequality by subordinate groups has been the key to change. Rarely has any government on its own initiative sought to end discrimination based on such criteria as race, ethnicity, and gender.

All racial and ethnic groups of any size are represented by private organizations that are, to some degree, trying to end discrimination. Some groups originated in the first half of the twentieth century, but most have been founded since World War II or have become significant forces in bringing about change only since then. These include church organizations, fraternal social groups, minor political parties, and legal defense funds, as well as more militant organizations operating under the scrutiny of law enforcement agencies. The purposes, membership, successes, and failures of these resistance organizations dedicated to eliminating discrimination are discussed throughout this book.

The judiciary, charged with interpreting laws and the U.S. Constitution, has a much longer history of involvement in the rights of racial, ethnic, and religious minorities. However, its early decisions protected the rights of the dominant group, as in the 1857 U.S. Supreme Court's *Dred Scott* decision, which ruled that slaves remained slaves even when living or traveling in states where slavery was illegal. Not until the 1940s did the Supreme Court revise earlier decisions and begin to grant African Americans the same rights as those held by Whites. The 1954 *Brown v. Board of Education* decision, which stated that "separate but equal" facilities—including education—were unconstitutional, heralded a new series of rulings, arguing that distinguishing between races in order to segregate was inherently unconstitutional.

The most important legislative effort to eradicate discrimination was the Civil Rights Act of 1964. This act led to the establishment of the Equal Employment Opportunity Commission (EEOC), which had the power to investigate complaints against employers and to recommend action to the Department of Justice. If the justice department sued and discrimination was found, then the court could order appropriate compensation. The act covered employment practices of all businesses with more than 25 employees and nearly all employment agencies and labor unions. A 1972 amendment broadened the coverage to employers with as few as 15 employees.

The Civil Rights Act of 1964 prohibited discrimination in public accommodations—that is, hotels, motels, restaurants, gasoline stations, and amusement parks. Publicly owned facilities such as parks, stadiums, and swimming pools were also prohibited from discriminating. Another important provision forbade discrimination in all federally supported programs and institutions such as hospitals, colleges, and road construction projects.

Read the Document on MySocLab:
Fences and Neighbors: Segregation in Twenty-First-Century America

The Civil Rights Act of 1964 was not perfect. Since 1964, several acts and amendments to the original act have been added to cover the many areas of discrimination it left untouched, such as criminal justice and housing. Even in areas singled out for enforcement in the act, discrimination still occurs. Federal agencies charged with enforcement complain that they are underfunded or are denied wholehearted support by the White House. Also, regardless of how much the EEOC may want to act in a particular case, the person who alleges discrimination has to pursue the complaint over a long time that is marked by lengthy periods of inaction. Despite these efforts, devastating forms of discrimination persist. African Americans, Latinos, and others fall victim to **redlining**, or the pattern of discrimination against people trying to buy homes in minority and racially changing neighborhoods.

People living in predominantly minority neighborhoods have found that companies with delivery services refuse to go to their area. In one case that attracted national attention in 1997, a Pizza Hut in Kansas City refused to deliver 40 pizzas to an honors program at a high school in an all-Black neighborhood. A Pizza Hut spokesperson called the neighborhood unsafe and said that almost every city has "restricted areas" to which the company will not deliver. This admission was particularly embarrassing because the high school already had a $170,000-a-year contract with Pizza Hut to deliver pizzas as a part of its school lunch program. Service redlining covers everything from parcel deliveries to repair people as well as food deliveries. The red pencil continues to exist in cities throughout the United States (Fuller 1998; Rusk 2001; Schwartz 2001; Turner et al. 2002; Yinger 1995).

Although civil rights laws often have established rights for other minorities, the Supreme Court made them explicit in two 1987 decisions involving groups other than African Americans. In the first of the two cases, an Iraqi American professor asserted that he had been denied tenure because of his Arab origins; in the second, a Jewish congregation brought suit for damages in response to the defacement of its synagogue with derogatory symbols. The Supreme Court ruled unanimously that, in effect, any member of an ethnic minority may sue under federal prohibitions against discrimination. These decisions paved the way for almost all racial and ethnic groups to invoke the Civil Rights Act of 1964 (Taylor 1987).

A particularly insulting form of discrimination seemed finally to be on its way out in the late 1980s. Many social clubs had limitations that forbade membership to minorities, Jews, and women. For years, exclusive clubs argued that they were merely selecting friends, but, in fact, a principal function of these clubs is as a forum to transact business. Denial of membership meant more than the inability to attend a luncheon; it also seemed to exclude certain groups from part of the marketplace. In 1988, the Supreme Court ruled unanimously in *New York State Clubs Association v. City of New York* that states and cities may ban sex discrimination by large private clubs where business lunches and similar activities take place. Although the ruling does not apply to all clubs and leaves the issue of racial and ethnic barriers unresolved, it did chip away at the arbitrary exclusiveness of private groups (Steinhauer 2006; Taylor 1988).

Memberships and restrictive organizations remain perfectly legal. The rise to national attention of professional golfer Tiger Woods, of mixed Native American, African, and Asian ancestry, made the public aware that he would be prohibited from playing at a minimum of 23 golf courses by virtue of race. In 2002, women's groups tried unsuccessfully to have the golf champion speak out because the Master's and British Open were played on courses closed to women as members. Ten years later, the Augusta National Golf Club, home of the Masters, opened its membership to women (Scott 2003; Martin, Dawsey, and McKay 2012; Sherwood 2010).

Proving discrimination, even as outlined for generations in legislation, continues to be difficult. In the 2007 *Ledbetter v. Goodyear Tire and Rubber Co.* ruling, the Supreme Court affirmed that victims had to file a formal complaint within 180 days of the alleged discrimination. This set aside thousands of cases where employees learned their initial pay was lower to comparably employed White or male workers only after they had been in a job for years. Given the usual secrecy in workplaces around salaries, it would have made it difficult for potential cases of pay disparity to be effectively advanced. Two years later, Congress enacted the Lilly Ledbetter Fair Pay Act, which gives victims more time to file a lawsuit.

The inability of the Civil Rights Act, similar legislation, and court decisions to end discrimination does not result entirely from poor financial and political support, although it does play a role. The number of federal employees assigned to investigate and prosecute bias cases is insufficient. Many discriminatory practices, such as those described as institutional discrimination, are seldom subject to legal action.

A setback in antidiscrimination lawsuits came when the Supreme Court told Lilly Ledbetter, in effect, that she was "too late." Ledbetter had been a supervisor for many years at the Gadsden, Alabama, Goodyear Tire Rubber plant when she realized that she was being paid $6,500 less per year than the lowest-paid male supervisor. The Court ruled that she must sue within 180 days of the initial discriminatory paycheck even though it had taken years before she even knew of the differential payment. Congress later enacted legislation eliminating the 180-day restriction.

Wealth Inequality: Discrimination's Legacy

Discrimination that has occurred in the past carries into the present and future. As noted in Figure 3.1, a lack of inherited wealth is one element of the past. African American and other minority groups have had less opportunity to accumulate assets such as homes, land, and savings that can insulate them, and later their children, from economic setbacks.

Watch the **Video** on **MySocLab:** *Social Inequalities: Race and Ethnicity*

Wealth is a more inclusive term than income and encompasses all of a person's material assets, including land, stocks, and other types of property. Wealth allows one to live better; even modest assets provide insurance against the effects of job layoffs, natural disasters, and long-term illness, and they afford individuals much better interest rates when they need to borrow money. Wealth allows children to graduate from college with little or no debt. This reminds us that for many people, wealth is not always related to assets but also can be measured by indebtedness.

Studies document that the disparities in income we have seen are even greater when wealth is considered. In 2010, only 6 percent of homebuyers were African Americans and another 6 percent Latino. This is, unfortunately, to be expected, because if individuals experience lower incomes throughout their lives, they are less likely to be able to put anything aside for a down payment. They are more likely to have to pay for today's expenses rather than save for their future or their children's future.

In the Research Focus "The Unequal Wealth Distribution," we consider the latest findings regarding the relative assets among White, Black, and Latino Americans.

Research Focus

The Unequal Wealth Distribution

There is widespread consensus that African Americans typically have fewer assets and other wealth than Whites. However, recent research suggests that the gap is widening.

Using government data, a team of researchers at Brandeis University found that over two decades, the difference in wealth (excluding homes) grew from $20,000 less for the typical Black household to $95,000 less, as shown in Figure 3.4. This growing gap is the result of long-term economic affects but also recent policy changes such as lowering taxes on investment income and inheritances that benefit the more affluent, who are more likely to be White.

While the wealth gap has grown, so has debt. As indicated in Figure 3.5, among the least wealthy—the bottom 10 percent—the African American typically is $3600 in debt, while the least wealthy White families are able to average $100 to the good. Other researchers have confirmed these findings and show further that the recession of the last few years has made the gaps even greater. While many people have lost their homes—the most significant asset for most families—the proportion of Black homeowners who lost homes through foreclosure or bankruptcy is much higher than among White families.

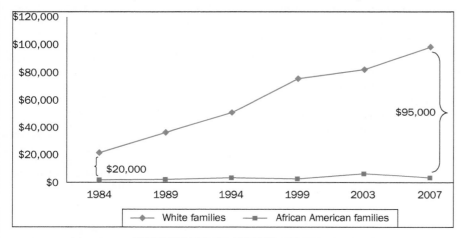

FIGURE 3.4
Median Wealth Holdings 1984–2007 (Not including home equity)

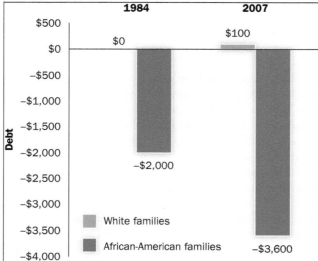

FIGURE 3.5
Bottom 10 Percent of Wealth Holdings, 1984 and 2007

Sources: Bernard 2012; Kochhar, Fry and Taylor 2011; Shapiro, Meschede, and Sullivan 2010.

 Read the Document on MySocLab: *Doubly Divided: The Racial Wealth Gap*

Read the Document
on MySocLab: *Race
Matters*

A 2009 study among the affluent shows the wealth gap will continue. For people earning more than $120,000, Whites typically had set aside $223,000 in retirement accounts—Asian Americans $62,000 less, African Americans $69,000 less, and Latinos $73,000 less.

It is little wonder then that White children are more likely to surpass their parents' income than Black children. Furthermore, White children are more likely to move up the economic social class ladder than are Black children, who also are more likely to fall back in absolute terms. As adults, well-off Black Americans are less likely to have acquired knowledge from their parents about how to invest wisely and more likely will make "safe" economic decisions for the future of themselves and their children.

A close analysis of wealth shows that African American families typically have $95,000 less in wealth than their White counterparts, even when households are comparably educated and employed. The median wealth of White households is 20 times that of Black households and 18 times that of Latino households.

Evidence indicates that this inequality in wealth has been growing; the wealth gap between White and African American families has more than quadrupled over the course of a generation (Ariel/Hewitt 2009; Bowman 2011; Economic Mobility Project 2007; Kochhar, Fry, and Taylor 2011; Lautz 2011; Oliver and Shapiro 2006; Shapiro 2004, 2010; Shapiro, Meschede, and Sullivan 2010).

Environmental Justice

Discrimination takes many forms and is not necessarily apparent, even when its impact can be far reaching. Take the example of Kennedy Heights, a well-kept working-class neighborhood nestled in southeastern Houston. This community faces a real threat, and it is not from crime or drugs. The threat that community residents fear is right under their feet in the form of three oil pits abandoned by Gulf Oil in 1927. The residents, mostly African American, argue that they have suffered high rates of cancer, lupus, and other illnesses because the chemicals from the oil fields poison their water supply. The residents first sued Chevron USA in 1985, and the case is still making its way through the courtrooms of no fewer than six states and the federal judiciary.

Lawyers and other representatives for the residents say that the oil company is guilty of environmental racism because it knowingly allowed a predominantly Black housing development to be built on the contaminated land. They are able to support this charge with documents, including a 1954 memorandum from an appraiser who suggested that the oil pits be drained of any toxic substances and the land filled for "low-cost houses for White occupancy." When the land did not sell right away, an oil company official in a 1967 memorandum suggested a tax-free land exchange with a developer who intended to use the land for "Negro residents and commercial development." For this latter intended use by African Americans, no mention was made of any required environmental cleanup of the land. The oil company counters that it assumed the developer would do the necessary cleanup of the pits (Maning 1997; Sze and London 2008).

The conflict perspective sees the case of the Houston suburb as one in which pollution harms minority groups disproportionately. **Environmental justice** refers to the efforts to ensure that hazardous substances are controlled so that all communities receive protection regardless of race or socioeconomic circumstance. After the Environmental Protection Agency and other organizations documented discrimination in the location of hazardous waste sites, an executive order was issued in 1994 that requires all federal agencies to ensure that low-income and minority communities have access to better information about their environment and have an opportunity

to participate in shaping government policies that affect their communities' health. Initial efforts to implement the policy have met widespread opposition, including criticism from some proponents of economic development who argue that the guidelines unnecessarily delay or altogether block locating new industrial sites.

Low-income communities and areas with significant minority populations are more likely to be adjacent to waste sites than are affluent White communities. Studies in California show the higher probability that people of color live closer to sources of air pollution. Another study concluded that grade schools in Florida nearer to environmental hazards are disproportionately Black or Latino. People of color jeopardized by environmental problems also lack the resources and political muscle to do something about it (Pastor, Morello-Frosch, and Saad 2005; Pellow and Brulle 2007; Stretesky and Lynch 2002).

Issues of environmental justice are not limited to metropolitan areas. Another continuing problem is abuse of Native American reservation land. Many American Indian leaders are concerned that tribal lands are too often regarded as toxic waste dumping grounds that go to the highest bidder. On the other hand, the economic devastation faced by some tribes in isolated areas has led one tribe in Utah to seek out becoming a depot for discarded nuclear waste (Jefferies 2007).

Read the Document on MySocLab: *Dumping in Dixie: Race, Class, and the Politics of Place*

As with other aspects of discrimination, experts disagree. There is controversy within the scientific community over the potential hazards, and there is even some opposition within the subordinate communities being affected. This complexity of the issues in terms of social class and race is apparent, as some observers question the wisdom of an executive order that may slow economic development coming to areas in dire need of employment opportunities. On the other hand, some observers counter that such businesses typically employ only a few unskilled workers and make the environment less liveable for those left behind. Despite such varying viewpoints, environmental justice is an excellent example of resistance and change in the 1990s that the civil rights workers of the 1950s could not have foreseen.

Affirmative Action

Affirmative action is the positive effort to recruit subordinate-group members, including women, for jobs, promotions, and educational opportunities. The phrase *affirmative action* first appeared in an executive order issued by President John F. Kennedy in 1961. The order called for contractors to "take affirmative action to ensure that applicants are employed, and that employees are treated during employment, without regard to their race, creed, color, or national origin." However, at that time, no enforcement procedures were specified. Six years later, the order was amended to prohibit discrimination on the basis of sex, but affirmative action was still defined vaguely.

Today, affirmative action has become a catchall term for racial preference programs and goals. It also has become a lightning rod for opposition to any programs that suggest special consideration of women or racial minorities.

Affirmative Action Explained

Affirmative action has been viewed as an important tool for reducing institutional discrimination. Whereas previous efforts were aimed at eliminating individual acts of discrimination, federal measures under the heading of affirmative action have been aimed at procedures that deny equal opportunities, even if they are not intended to be overtly discriminatory. This policy has been implemented to deal with both current discrimination and past discrimination, outlined earlier in this chapter.

Affirmative action has been aimed at institutional discrimination in areas such as the following:

- Height and weight requirements that are unnecessarily geared to the physical proportions of White men without regard to the actual characteristics needed to perform the job and that therefore exclude women and some minorities.
- Seniority rules, when applied to jobs historically held only by White men, that make more recently hired minorities and females more subject to layoff—the "last hired, first fired" employee—and less eligible for advancement.
- Nepotism-based membership policies of some unions that exclude those who are not relatives of members who, because of past employment practices, are usually White.
- Restrictive employment leave policies, coupled with prohibitions on part-time work or denials of fringe benefits to part-time workers, that make it difficult for the heads of single-parent families, most of whom are women, to get and keep jobs and also meet the needs of their families.
- Rules requiring that only English be spoken at the workplace, even when not a business necessity, which result in discriminatory employment practices toward people whose primary language is not English.
- Standardized academic tests or criteria geared to the cultural and educational norms of middle-class or White men when these are not relevant predictors of successful job performance.
- Preferences shown by law and medical schools in admitting children of wealthy and influential alumni, nearly all of whom are White.
- Credit policies of banks and lending institutions that prevent granting mortgages and loans in minority neighborhoods or that prevent granting credit to married women and others who have previously been denied the opportunity to build good credit histories in their own names.

Employers also have been cautioned against asking leading questions in interviews, for example, "Did you know you would be the first Black to supervise all Whites in that factory?" or "Does your husband mind your working on weekends?" Furthermore, the lack of minority-group or female employees may in itself represent evidence for a case of unlawful exclusion (Commission on Civil Rights 1981; see also Bohmer and Oka 2007).

The Legal Debate

How far can an employer go in encouraging women and minorities to apply for a job before it becomes unlawful discrimination against White men? Since the late 1970s, several bitterly debated cases on this difficult aspect of affirmative action have reached the U.S. Supreme Court. The most significant cases are summarized in Table 3.2.

In the 1978 *Bakke* case (*Regents of the University of California v. Bakke*), by a narrow 5–4 vote, the Court ordered the medical school of the University of California at Davis to admit Allan Bakke, a qualified White engineer who had originally been denied admission solely on the basis of his race. The justices ruled that the school had violated Bakke's constitutional rights by establishing a fixed quota system for minority students. However, the Court added that it was constitutional for universities to adopt flexible admission programs that use race as one factor in making decisions.

Colleges and universities responded with new policies designed to meet the *Bakke* ruling while broadening opportunities for traditionally underrepresented minority students.

TABLE 3.2
Key Decisions on Affirmative Action

In a series of split and often very close decisions, the Supreme Court has expressed a variety of reservations in specific situations.

Year	Favorable (+) or Unfavorable (−) to Policy	Case	Vote	Ruling
1971	+	*Griggs v. Duke Power Co.*	9–0	Private employers must provide a remedy where minorities were denied opportunities, even if unintentional.
1978	−	*Regents of the University of California v. Bakke*	5–4	Prohibited holding a specific number of places for minorities in college admissions.
1979	+	*United Steelworkers of America v. Weber*	5–2	Okay for union to favor minorities in special training programs.
1984	−	*Firefighters Local Union No. 1784 (Memphis, TN) v. Stotts*	6–1	Seniority means recently hired minorities may be laid off first in staff reductions.
1986	+	*International Association of Firefighters v. City of Cleveland*	6–3	May promote minorities over more-senior Whites.
1986	+	*New York City v. Sheet Metal*	5–4	Approved specific quota of minority workers for union.
1987	+	*United States v. Paradise*	5–4	Endorsed quotas for promotions of state troopers.
1987	+	*Johnson v. Transportation Agency, Santa Clara, CA*	6–3	Approved preference in hiring for minorities and women over better-qualified men and Whites.
1989	−	*Richmond v. Croson Company*	6–3	Ruled a 30 percent set-aside program for minority contractors unconstitutional.
1989	−	*Martin v. Wilks*	5–4	Ruled Whites may bring reverse discrimination claims against Court-approved affirmative action plans.
1990	+	*Metro Broadcasting v. FCC*	5–4	Supported federal programs aimed at increasing minority ownership of broadcast licenses.
1995	−	*Adarand Constructors Inc. v. Peña*	5–4	Benefits based on race are constitutional only if narrowly defined to accomplish a compelling interest.
1996	−	*Texas v. Hopwood*	*	Let stand a lower court decision covering Louisiana, Mississippi, and Texas that race could not be used in college admissions.
2003	+	*Grutter v. Bollinger*	5–4	Race can be a limited factor in admissions at the University of Michigan Law School.
2003	−	*Gratz v. Bollinger*	6–3	Cannot use a strict formula awarding advantage based on race for admissions to the University of Michigan.
2009	−	*Ricci v. DeStefano*	5–4	May not disregard a promotion test because Blacks failed to qualify for advancement.
2013	−	*Fisher v. University of Texas*	7–1	Referred back to lower courts saying colleges needed to more explicitly justify race-based policies.

*U.S. Court of Appeals Fifth Circuit decision

In 2012, the Supreme Court heard arguments in *Fisher v. University of Texas at Austin* arguing that a White woman, Abigail Fisher, missed out of automatic admission under a Texas provision that extended admissions to the top 10 percent of a high school graduating class. While she was not in the top tenth, she contended that non-Whites who did not have comparable academic preparation were admitted and that the top 10 percent provision leaves any further racial consideration unnecessary. Ultimately the Court sent it back to a lower court for consideration, but placed greater responsibility on colleges to justify consideration of race in applicants.

Has affirmative action actually helped alleviate employment inequality on the basis of race and gender? This question is difficult to answer, given the complexity of the labor market and the fact that other anti-discrimination measures are in place, but it does appear that affirmative action has had a significant impact in the sectors where it has been applied. Sociologist Barbara Reskin (1998) reviewed available studies looking at workforce composition in terms of race and gender in light of affirmative action policies. She found that gains in minority employment could be attributed to affirmative action policies. This includes firms mandated to follow affirmative action guidelines and those that took them on voluntarily. There is also evidence that some earnings gains can be attributed to affirmative action. Economists M. V. Lee Badgett and Heidi Hartmann (1995), reviewing 26 other research studies, came to similar conclusions: Affirmative action and other federal compliance programs have had a modest impact, but it is difficult to assess, given larger economic changes such as recessions or the rapid increase in women in the paid labor force.

Scholars of labor force patterns still make a case for affirmative action even if few, if any, political leaders are likely to publicly endorse the policy. In the "Speaking Out" section, Harvard law professor Randall Kennedy makes the case for the necessity of an aggressive program of affirmative action.

Speaking Out

The Enduring Relevance of Affirmative Action

One of the most notable accomplishments of liberalism over the past 20 years is something that didn't happen: the demise of affirmative action. Contrary to all predictions, affirmative action has survived. This is a triumph not only for race relations but also for the liberal vision of an inclusive society with full opportunity for all....

Conservatives charged that affirmative action amounts to "reverse racism"; discriminates against "innocent whites"; stigmatizes its putative beneficiaries; erodes the incentives that prompt individuals to put forth their best efforts; lowers standards; produces inefficiencies; goes to those racial minorities who need it least; and generates racial resentments. This indictment

Randall Kennedy

and the backlash it rationalized resonated not only with Republicans but also with Democrats, some of whom [sic] shared the conservatives' philosophical objections to the policy, while others worried that supporting it meant electoral suicide.

Writing...in 1990, sociologist William Julius Wilson asserted that "the movement for racial equality needs a new political strategy...that appeals to a broader coalition." Eschewing affirmative action (though he has subsequently changed his mind), Wilson championed redistributive reforms through "race-neutral policies," contending that they could help the Democratic Party regain lost political support while simultaneously benefiting those further down within minority groups ....

(continued)

One key Democrat attracted to this critique is Barack Obama. Writing in *The Audacity of Hope*, he did not expressly condemn affirmative action, but he did consign it to a category of exhausted programs that "dissect[s] Americans into 'us' and 'them' " and that "can't serve as the basis for the kinds of sustained, broad-based political coalitions needed to transform America." As president, Obama has repeatedly eschewed race targeting (with respect most notably to employment policy) in favor of "universal" reforms that allegedly lift all boats.

Over the years, affirmative action has been truncated by judicial rulings and banned by voters in some states. In one guise or another, however, special efforts to assist marginalized racial minorities remain a major force in many schools and firms, foundations, and governments. Affirmative action survived principally because many rightly believe what President Bill Clinton declared on July 19, 1995, in what is (thus far) the only presidential address wholly devoted to the subject: "Affirmative action has been good for America" (Richter 1995). Clinton argued that ongoing injuries of past racial wrongs require redress; that affirmative action can usefully serve to prevent new invidious discrimination that is difficult, if not impossible, to reach through litigation; that the adverse consequences of affirmative action on whites are often grossly exaggerated and can easily be minimized; and that better learning and decision making arise in environments that are racially diverse.

The amorphous and malleable idea of "diversity" provided much needed buoyancy to affirmative action, especially in the 2003 University of Michigan affirmative-action cases when 65 major companies, including American Express, Coca Cola, and Microsoft, asserted that maintaining racial diversity in institutions of higher education is vital to their efforts to hire and maintain a diverse workforce. A group of former high-ranking officers and civilian leaders of the military concurred, declaring that "a highly qualified, racially diverse officer corps...is essential to the military's ability to fulfil its principal mission to provide national security." Even Theodore Olson, the Bush administration's solicitor general, took pains to defer to "diversity" in a brief on the case....

Liberals have been key supporters of the modern struggle for racial equality. Affirmative action is both a major strategy and central accomplishment of that struggle. Its status is paradoxical. The election of the first African American president represents a coming of age of the "affirmative-action babies," but the right has so successfully vilified the policy that Obama is embarrassed by it. He has yet to say forthrightly what Bill Clinton aptly declared: Affirmative action is good for America.

This observation is not necessarily a criticism of Obama. The president should be pragmatic. If quietude about affirmative action serves its purposes or is essential to him retaining office, then by all means he should remain quiet. Fortunately, though, Obama's acts and omissions, justifiable or not, will not prove decisive. The true measure of affirmative action's staying power is that its absence now is virtually inconceivable.

Source: Kennedy 2010:31–33.

Reverse Discrimination

Although researchers debated the merit of affirmative action, the public—particularly Whites but also some affluent African Americans and Hispanics—questioned the wisdom of the program. Particularly strident were the charges of reverse discrimination: that government actions cause better-qualified White men to be bypassed in favor of women and minority men. **Reverse discrimination** is an emotional term because it conjures up the notion that somehow women and minorities will subject White men in the United States to the same treatment received by minorities during the last three centuries. Such cases are not unknown, but they are uncommon.

Increasingly, critics of affirmative action call for color-blind policies that would end affirmative action and, they argue, allow all people to be judged fairly. However, will that end institutional practices that favored Whites? For example, according to the latest data, 40 percent of applicants who are children of Harvard's alumni, who are almost all White, are admitted to the university, compared to 11 percent of nonalumni children.

By contrast, at the competitive California Institute of Technology, which specifically does not use legacy preferences, only 1.5 percent of students are children of alumni. Ironically, studies show that students who are children of alumni are far more likely than either minority students or athletes to run into academic trouble (Kahlenberg 2010; Massey and Mooney 2007; Pincus 2003, 2008).

Is it possible to have color-blind policies prevail in the United States in the twenty-first century? Supporters of affirmative action contend that as long as businesses rely on informal social networks, personal recommendations, and family ties, White men will have a distinct advantage built on generations of being in positions of power. Furthermore, an end to affirmative action should also mean an end to the many programs that give advantages to certain businesses, homeowners, veterans, farmers, and others. Most of these preference holders are White.

Consequently, by the 1990s and into the twenty-first century, affirmative action had emerged as an increasingly important issue in state and national political campaigns. As noted earlier, in 2003, the Supreme Court reviewed the admission policies at the University of Michigan, which may favor racial minorities (see Table 3.2). In 2006, Michigan citizens, by a 58 percent margin, voted to restrict all their state universities from using

Does affirmative action represent an overdue just solution to a centuries-old problem or an undeserved outright reward for the current generation?

affirmative action in their admissions policies. Generally, discussions have focused on the use of quotas in hiring practices. Supporters of affirmative action argue that hiring goals establish "floors" for minority inclusion but do not exclude truly qualified candidates from any group. Opponents insist that these "targets" are, in fact, quotas that lead to reverse discrimination (Lewin 2006; Mack 1996).

The State of California, in particular, was a battleground for this controversial issue. The California Civil Rights Initiative (Proposition 209) was placed on the ballot in 1996 as a referendum to amend the state constitution and prohibit any programs that give preference to women and minorities for college admission, employment, promotion, or government contracts. Overall, 54 percent of the voters backed the state proposition.

In 2009, the Supreme Court ruled 5–4 in the *Ricci v. DeStefano* case in favor of White firefighters. Many observers felt this outcome recognized reverse racism. In 2003, in New Haven, Connecticut, firefighters took an examination to identify possible promotions but no African Americans taking the test qualified to be eligible for advancement. Rather than select all White (including one Hispanic) firefighters, the city threw out the test results. The qualifying firefighters sued that they were victims of discrimination and the Court eventually concurred. The decision was limited in its applications because the justices seemed to say that possible test bias could be considered in the design stage of a test, but others saw it as "impeding" the use of race in hiring even advantaged minorities.

The Glass Ceiling

We have discussed racial and ethnic groups primarily as if they have uniformly failed to keep pace with Whites. Although this notion is accurate, tens of thousands of people of color have matched and even exceeded Whites in terms of income. For example, in 2011, more than 235,000 Black households and over 245,000 Hispanic households earned more than $200,000. What can we say about financially better-off members of subordinate groups in the United States (DeNavas-Walt, Proctor, and Smith 2012:Table HINC-01)?

Prejudice does not necessarily end with wealth. Black newspaper columnist De Wayne Wickham (1993) wrote of the subtle racism he had experienced. He heard a White clerk in a supermarket ask a White customer whether she knew the price of an item the computer would not scan; when the problem occurred while the clerk was ringing up Wickham's groceries, she called for a price check. Affluent subordinate-group members routinely report being blocked as they move toward the first-class section aboard airplanes or seek service in upscale stores. Another journalist, Ellis Cose (1993), has called these insults the soul-destroying slights to affluent minorities that lead to the "rage of a privileged class."

Discrimination persists for even educated and qualified people from the best family backgrounds. As subordinate-group members are able to compete successfully, they sometimes encounter attitudinal or organizational bias that prevents them from reaching their full potential. They have confronted what has come to be called the **glass ceiling**. This refers to the barrier that blocks the promotion of a qualified worker because of gender or minority membership (Figure 3.6). Often, people entering nontraditional areas of employment become marginalized and are made to feel uncomfortable, much like the situation of immigrants who feel like they are part of two cultures, as we discussed in Chapter 1.

 Read the Document on MySocLab: From Summer Camps to Glass Ceilings

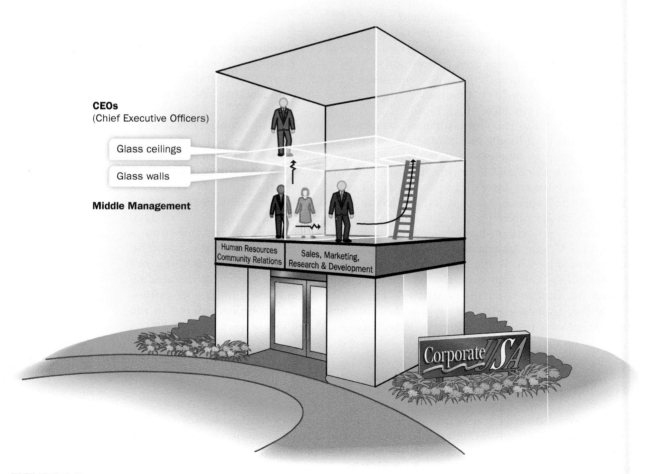

FIGURE 3.6
Glass Ceilings and Glass Walls

Women and minority men are moving up in corporations but encounter glass ceilings that block entry to top positions. In addition, they face glass walls that block lateral moves to areas from which executives are promoted. These barriers contribute to women and minority men not moving into the ultimate decision-making positions in the nation's corporate giants.

Reasons for glass ceilings are as many as the occurrences. It may be that one Black or one woman vice president is regarded as enough, so the second potential candidate faces a block to movement up through management. Decision makers may be concerned that their clientele will not trust them if they have too many people of color or may worry that a talented woman could become overwhelmed with her duties as a mother and wife and thus perform poorly in the workplace.

Concern about women and minorities climbing a broken ladder led to the formation in 1991 of the Glass Ceiling Commission, with the U.S. secretary of labor chairing the twenty-one-member group. Initially, it regarded the following as some of the glass ceiling barriers:

- Lack of management commitment to establishing systems, policies, and practices for achieving workplace diversity and upward mobility
- Pay inequities for work of equal or comparable value
- Sex-, race-, and ethnicity-based stereotyping and harassment
- Unfair recruitment practices
- Lack of family-friendly workplace policies
- "Parent-track" policies that discourage parental leave policies
- Limited opportunities for advancement to decision-making positions

This significant underrepresentation of women and minority males in managerial positions results in large part from the presence of glass ceilings. Sociologist Max Weber wrote more than a century ago that the privileged class monopolizes the purchase of high-priced consumer goods and wields the power to grant or withhold opportunity from others. To grasp just how White and male the membership of this elite group is, consider the following: 71 percent of the 1,219 people who serve on the boards of directors of *Fortune* 100 corporations are White non-Hispanic males. For every 82 White men on these boards, there are two Latinos, two Asian Americans, three African Americans, and eleven White women (Alliance for Board Diversity 2009; Weber [1913–1922] 1947).

Read the **Document** on **MySocLab**: *Race-Specific Policies and the Truly Disadvantaged*

Glass ceilings are not the only barrier. Glass walls also block minorities. Catalyst, a non-profit research organization, conducted interviews in 1992 and again in 2001 with senior and middle managers from larger corporations. The study found that even before glass ceilings are encountered, women and racial and ethnic minorities face **glass walls** that keep them from moving laterally. Specifically, the study found that women tend to be placed in staff or support positions in areas such as public relations and human resources and are often directed away from jobs in core areas such as marketing, production, and sales. Women are assigned to and, therefore, trapped in jobs that reflect their stereotypical

SPECTRUM OF INTERGROUP RELATIONS

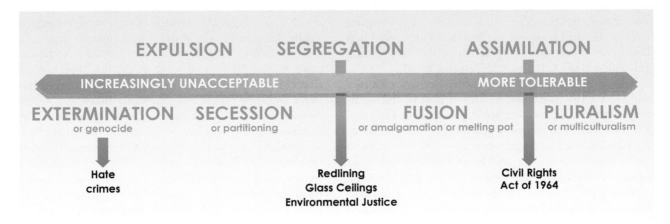

helping nature and encounter glass walls that cut off access to jobs that might lead to broader experience and advancement (Bjerk 2008; Catalyst 2001; Lopez 1992).

Researchers have documented a differential impact the glass ceiling has on White males. It appears that men who enter traditionally female occupations are more likely to rise to the top. Male elementary teachers become principals, and male nurses become supervisors. The **glass escalator** refers to the White male advantage experienced in occupations dominated by women. Whereas females may become tokens when they enter traditionally male occupations, men are more likely to be advantaged when they move out of sex-typical jobs. In summary, women and minority men confront a glass ceiling that limits upward mobility and glass walls that reduce their ability to move into fast-track jobs leading to the highest reaches of the corporate executive suite. Meanwhile, White men who do choose to enter female-dominated occupations are often rewarded with promotions and positions of responsibility coveted by their fellow female workers (Budig 2002; Cognard-Black 2004).

Conclusion

What is it like to experience discrimination over and over again? Not just an occasional slight or a possible instance of discrimination but constantly seeing yourself dealt with differently because of race, ethnicity, or gender? W. E. B. Du Bois (1903:9) wrote in his classic *The Souls of Black Folk*, "To be a poor man is hard, but to be a poor race in a land of dollars is the very bottom of hardships." Not all members of racial and ethnic minorities, much less all women, are poor, of course, but virtually all can recall instances where they were treated as second-class citizens, not necessarily by White men, but even by members of their own group or by other women.

One job advertisement read "African Americans and Arabians tend to clash with me so that won't work out." Sound like it was from your grandfather's era? Actually, it appeared on the popular Craigslist Web site in 2006 and is just one example of how explicit discrimination thrives even in the digital age. Similar charges have been made concerning "no minorities" wording in housing advertisements. Courts have not held Craigslist responsible and accepted the Web site's argument that it cannot screen out all racism in online advertising (Hughlett 2006; U.S. Court of Appeals 2008).

Discrimination takes its toll, whether or not a person who is discriminated against is part of the informal economy or looking for a job on the Internet. Even members of minority groups who are not today overtly discriminated against continue to fall victim to past discrimination. We also have identified the costs of discrimination to members of the privileged group.

From the conflict perspective, it is not surprising to find the widespread presence of the informal economy proposed by the dual labor market model and even an underclass. Derrick Bell (1994), an African American law professor, has made the sobering assertion that "racism is permanent." He contends that the attitudes of dominant Whites prevail, and society is willing to advance programs on behalf of subordinate groups only when they coincide with needs as perceived by those Whites.

The surveys presented in Chapter 2 show gradual acceptance of the earliest efforts to eliminate discrimination, but that support is failing as color-blind racism takes hold, especially as it relates to affirmative action. Indeed, concerns about doing something about alleged reverse discrimination are as likely to be voiced as concerns about racial or gender discrimination or glass ceilings and glass walls.

Institutional discrimination remains a formidable challenge in the United States. Attempts to reduce discrimination by attacking institutional discrimination have met with staunch resistance. Partly as a result of this outcry from some of the public, especially White Americans, the federal government gradually deemphasized its affirmative action efforts, beginning in the 1980s and continuing into the twenty-first century. Most of the material in this chapter has been about racial groups, especially Black and White Americans. It would be easy to see intergroup hostility as a racial phenomenon, but that would be incorrect. Throughout the history of the United States, relations between some White groups have been characterized by resentment and violence. The next two chapters examine the ongoing legacy of immigration and the nature and relations of White ethnic groups.

MySocLab ✓ **Study** and **Review** on **MySocLab**

Summary

1. Discrimination is likely to result in feelings of relative deprivation, not necessarily absolute deprivation.

2. Hate crimes highlight hostility that culminates in a criminal offense.

3. Institutional discrimination results from the normal operations of a society.

4. Discrimination in hiring is documented through job-testing experiments.

5. Inequality continues to be apparent in the analysis of annual incomes, controlling for the amount of education attained and wealth, and even in the absence of environmental justice.

6. Presidential executive orders, legislative acts, and judicial decisions have all played a part in reducing discrimination.

7. For over 60 years, affirmative action as a remedy to inequality has been a hotly contested issue, with its critics contending it amounts to reverse discrimination.

8. Upwardly mobile professional women and minority males may encounter a glass ceiling and be thwarted in their efforts by glass walls to become more attractive candidates for advancement.

Key Terms

absolute deprivation, p. 65

affirmative action, p. 76

discrimination, p. 64

environmental justice, p. 75

glass ceiling, p. 82

glass escalator, p. 84

glass wall, p. 83

hate crime, p. 65

income, p. 68

institutional discrimination, p. 67

redlining, p. 72

relative deprivation, p. 64

reverse discrimination, p. 80

wealth, p. 68

Review Questions

1. Why might people feel disadvantaged even though their incomes are rising and their housing circumstances have improved?

2. Why does institutional discrimination sometimes seem less objectionable than individual discrimination?

3. In what way might national income data point to discrimination?

4. Why are questions raised about affirmative action even though inequality persists?

5. Distinguish among glass ceilings, glass walls, and glass escalators. How do they differ from more obvious forms of discrimination in employment?

Critical Thinking

1. Discrimination can take many forms. Select a case of discrimination that you think almost everyone would agree is wrong. Then describe another incident in which the alleged discrimination was subtler. Who is likely to condemn and who is likely to overlook such situations?

2. Resistance is a continuing theme of intergroup race relations. Discrimination implies the oppression of a group, but how can discrimination also unify the oppressed group to resist such unequal treatment? How can acceptance, or integration, for example, weaken the sense of solidarity within a group?

3. Voluntary associations such as the National Association for the Advancement of Colored People (NAACP) and government units such as the courts have been important vehicles for bringing about a measure of social justice. In what ways can the private sector—corporations and businesses—also work to bring about an end to discrimination?

4 Immigration and Ethnicity

4-1 Discuss the current patterns of immigration in the United States.

4-2 Identify today's foreign-born population.

4-3 Explain early immigration patterns to the United States.

4-4 Describe the increase of the restrictionist sentiment.

4-5 Identify present social concerns with immigration.

4-6 Summarize the challenges surrounding illegal immigration.

4-7 Describe the United States' policies toward refugees.

4-8 Explain the level of ethnic diversity in the United States.

4-9 Discuss the concept of Whiteness and explain how it is studied.

4-10 Examine the rediscovery of ethnicity.

4-11 Define and explain religious pluralism.

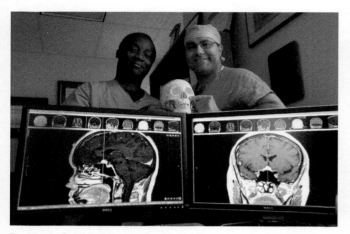

Dr. Alfredo Quiñoes-Hinojosa (on the right)

The story of Alfredo the immigrant is not typical, but then every immigrant who comes to the United States has a unique story. Alfredo Quiñoes-Hinojosa came to the United States as an illegal immigrant in 1987 at the age of nineteen. Caught the first time, he succeeded the second time on the same day. (The majority of immigrants apprehended at the border have been caught previously.) One of six children, Alfredo had frequently come across the border from his native Mexico to work as a farmhand pulling weeds in the fields to help support his five younger brothers and sisters. Eventually, he settled with relatives in Stockton, California. He tried other jobs: sweeping floors, shoeing horses, and soldering metal. He learned English and eventually applied and was accepted to the local San Joaquin Delta College.

His next big step was when he accepted an offer to study at the University of California at Berkeley. Alfredo dreamed of becoming a doctor, and nothing was going to stop him.

After graduating from Berkeley, Alfredo was accepted to Harvard Medical School, where he graduated with honors, but he also became a citizen along the way.

While Quiñoes-Hinojosa, and later his parents, had entered the United States as an undocumented worker, under an amnesty provision passed under President Reagan, he was able to secure a green card legally allowing him to work and continue his education. In 1997, he became a U.S. citizen.

Today, married with three children, he heads the Brain Tumor Surgery Program at Johns Hopkins Medical Center and is actively engaged in research as to the causes of brain cancer. It has not been easy. His hands now perform brain surgery, but they bear the scars of farmwork. He endured prejudice: People strongly suggested he change his name to something easier to pronounce. While reluctant to speak out in the immigration debate, he recognizes that many people today want to exclude from the United States people exactly like he was fewer than 30 years ago (Cave 2011; Gupta 2012; Ramos 2010; Quiñoes-Hinojosa with Rivas 2011).

The world is now a global network. The core and periphery countries, described in world systems theory (see Chapter 1), link not only commercial goods but also families and workers across political borders. Social forces that cause people to emigrate are complex. The most important have been economic, such as the case of Alfredo Quiñoes-Hinojosa: financial failure in the old country and expectations of higher incomes and standards of living in the new land. Other factors include dislike of new political regimes in their native lands, being victims of racial or religious bigotry, and a desire to reunite families. All these factors push people from their homelands and pull them to other nations such as the United States. Immigration into the United States, in particular, has been facilitated by cheap ocean transportation and by other countries' removal of restrictions on emigration.

Patterns of Immigration to the United States

Immigration to the United States has three unmistakable patterns: (1) the number of immigrants has fluctuated dramatically over time largely because of government policy changes, (2) settlement has not been uniform across the country but centered in certain

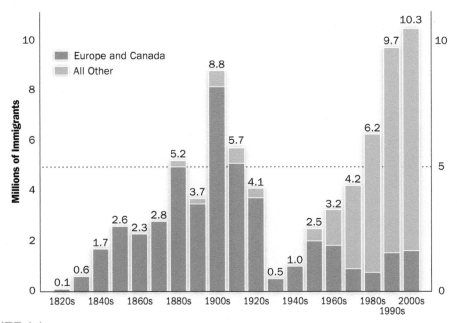

FIGURE 4.1
Legal Immigration to the United States, 1820–2010

Source: Office of Immigration Statistics 2011.

regions and cities, and (3) the immigrants' countries of origin have changed over time. First, we look at the historical picture of immigrant numbers.

Vast numbers of immigrants have come to the United States. Figure 4.1 indicates the high but fluctuating number of immigrants who arrived during every decade from the 1820s through the beginning of the twenty-first century. The United States received the largest number of legal immigrants during the first decade of the 1900s; that number likely will be surpassed in the first decade of the twenty-first century. However, the country was much smaller in the period from 1900 through 1910, so the numerical impact was even greater then.

Immigrants to this country have not always received a friendly reception. Open bloodshed, restrictive laws, and the eventual return of almost one-third of immigrants and their children to their home countries attest to some Americans' uneasy feelings toward strangers who want to settle here. Opinion polls in the United States from 1999 through 2012 have never shown more than 21 percent of the public in favor of more immigration, and usually about 42–50 percent want less (Jones 2012).

Today's Foreign-Born Population

Before considering the sweep of past immigration policies, let us consider today's immigrant population. About 13 percent of the nation's people are foreign-born— a level not reached since the 1920s. As recently as 1979, this proportion was just 4.7 percent. By global comparisons, the foreign-born population in the United States is large but not unusual. Whereas most industrial countries have a foreign population

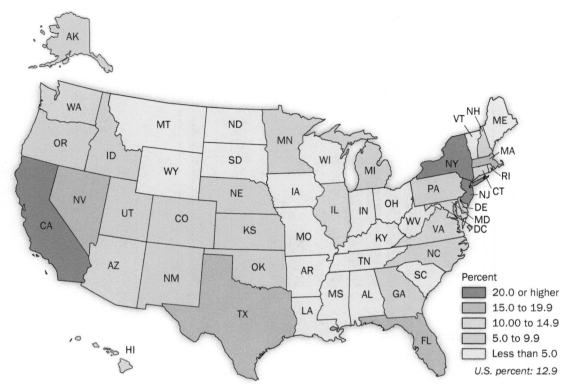

FIGURE 4.2
Foreign-Born Population in the United States

Source: Grieco et al. 2012:4.

Percent

■	20.0 or higher
▨	15.0 to 19.9
▢	10.00 to 14.9
▢	5.0 to 9.9
□	Less than 5.0

U.S. percent: 12.9

of around 5 percent, Canada's foreign population is 19 percent and Australia's is 25 percent.

As noted earlier, immigrants have not settled evenly across the nation. As shown in the map in Figure 4.2, six states—California, New York, Texas, Florida, New Jersey, and Illinois—account for two-thirds of the nation's total foreign-born population but less than 40 percent of the nation's total population.

Cities in these states are the destinations of the foreign-born population. Almost half (43.3 percent) live in the central city of a metropolitan area, compared with about one-quarter (27 percent) of the nation's population. More than one-third of residents in the cities of Miami, Los Angeles, San Francisco, San Jose, and New York are now foreign born.

The source countries of immigrants have changed. First, settlers came from Europe, then Latin America, and, now, increasingly, Asia. The majority of today's 38.5 million foreign-born people are from Latin America rather than Europe, as was the case through the 1950s. Primarily, they are from Central America and, more specifically, Mexico. By contrast, Europeans, who dominated the early settlement of the United States, now account for fewer than one in seven of the foreign born today. The changing patterns of immigration have continued into the twenty-first century. Beginning in 2010, the annual immigration from Asia exceeded the level of annual immigration from Latin America for the first time (Grieco et al. 2012; Pew Social and Demographic Trends 2012; Semple 2012).

✸ Explore the
Concept on
MySocLab:
*Foreign-Born
Population and
Percent of Total
Population for the
United States:
1850–200*

Early Immigration

Settlers, the first immigrants to the Western Hemisphere, soon followed European explorers of North America. The Spanish founded St. Augustine, Florida, in 1565, and the English founded Jamestown, Virginia, in 1607. Protestants from England emerged from the colonial period as the dominant force numerically, politically, and socially. The English accounted for 60 percent of the 3 million White Americans in 1790. Although exact statistics are lacking for the early years of the United States, the English were soon outnumbered by other nationalities as the numbers of Scotch-Irish and Germans, in particular, swelled. However, the English colonists maintained their dominant position, as Chapter 5 examines.

Throughout American history, immigration policy has been politically controversial. The policies of the English king, George III, were criticized in the U.S. Declaration of Independence for obstructing immigration to the colonies. Toward the end of the nineteenth century, the American republic itself was criticized for enacting immigration restrictions. In the beginning, however, the country encouraged immigration. Legislation initially fixed the residence requirement for naturalization at five years; although briefly, under the Alien Act of 1798, it was 14 years, and so-called dangerous people could be expelled. Despite this brief harshness, immigration was unregulated through most of the 1800s, and naturalization was easily available. Until 1870, naturalization was limited to "free white persons" (Calavita 2007).

Although some people hold the mistaken belief that concerns about immigration are something new, some people also assume that immigrants to the United States rarely reconsider their decision to come to a new country. Analysis of available records, beginning in the early 1900s, suggests that about 35 percent of all immigrants to the United States eventually emigrated back to their home country. The proportion varies, with the figures for some countries being much higher, but the overall pattern is clear: About one in three immigrants to this nation eventually chooses to return home (Wyman 1993).

The relative absence of federal legislation from 1790 to 1881 does not mean that all new arrivals were welcomed. **Xenophobia** (the fear or hatred of strangers or foreigners) led naturally to **nativism** (beliefs and policies favoring native-born citizens over immigrants). Although the term *nativism* has largely been used to describe nineteenth-century sentiments, anti-immigration views and organized movements have continued into the twenty-first century. Political scientist Samuel P. Huntington (1993, 1996) articulated the continuing immigration as a "clash of civilizations" that could be remedied only by significantly reducing legal immigration, not to mention closing the border to illegal arrivals. His view, which enjoys support, is that the fundamental world conflicts of the new century are cultural in nature rather than ideological or even economic (Citrin, Lerman, Murakami, and Pearson 2007; Schaefer 2008b).

The most dramatic outbreak of nativism in the nineteenth century was aimed at the Chinese. If any doubt remained by the mid-1800s that the United States could harmoniously accommodate all and was some sort of melting pot, debate on the Chinese Exclusion Act negatively ended that doubt.

The Anti-Chinese Movement

Before 1851, official records show that only 46 Chinese had immigrated to the United States. Over the next 30 years, more than 200,000 came to this country, lured by the discovery of gold and the opening of job opportunities in the West. Overcrowding, drought, and warfare in China also encouraged them to take a chance in the United States. Another important factor was improved oceanic transportation; it was cheaper to travel from Hong Kong to San Francisco than from Chicago to San Francisco. The frontier communities of the West, particularly in California, looked on the Chinese as a valuable resource to

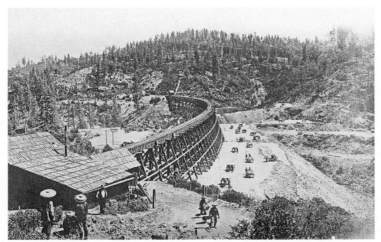

Chinese workers, such as these pictured in 1844, played a major role in building railroads in the West.

fill manual jobs. As early as 1854, so many Chinese wanted to emigrate that ships had difficulty handling the volume.

In the 1860s, railroad work provided the greatest demand for Chinese labor until the Union Pacific and Central Pacific railroads were joined at Promontory Summit, Utah, in 1869. The Union Pacific relied primarily on Irish laborers, but 90 percent of the Central Pacific's labor force were Chinese because Whites generally refused to do the backbreaking work over the Western terrain. Despite the contribution of the Chinese, White workers physically prevented them from attending the driving of the golden spike to mark the joining of the two railroads.

With the dangerous railroad work largely completed, people began to rethink the wisdom of encouraging Chinese to immigrate to do the work no one else would do. Reflecting their xenophobia, White settlers found the Chinese immigrants, their customs, and religion difficult to understand. Indeed, few people tried to understand these immigrants from Asia. Although they had had no firsthand contact with Chinese Americans, Easterners and legislators soon jumped on the anti-Chinese bandwagon as they read sensationalized accounts of the lifestyle of the new arrivals.

Even before the Chinese immigrated, stereotypes of them and their customs were prevalent. American traders returning from China, European diplomats, and Protestant missionaries consistently emphasized the exotic and sinister aspects of life in China. **Sinophobes**, people who fear anything associated with China, appealed to the racist theory developed during the slavery controversy that non-Europeans were subhuman. Americans also were becoming more conscious of biological inheritance and disease, so it was not hard to conjure up fears of alien genes and germs. The only real challenge the anti-Chinese movement faced was convincing people that the negative consequences of unrestricted Chinese immigration outweighed any possible economic gain. Earlier, racial prejudice was subordinated to industrial dependence on Chinese labor for the work that Whites shunned, but acceptance of the Chinese was short-lived. The fear of the "yellow peril" overwhelmed any desire to know more about Asian peoples and their customs (Takaki 1989).

Employers were glad to pay the Chinese low wages, but non-Chinese laborers began directing their resentment against the Chinese rather than against their compatriots' willingness to exploit the Chinese. Only a generation earlier, the same concerns were felt about the Irish, but with the Chinese, the hostility reached new heights because of another factor.

Although many arguments were voiced, racial fears motivated the anti-Chinese movement. Race was the critical issue. The labor market fears were largely unfounded, and most advocates of restrictions at that time knew that. There was no possibility of the Chinese immigrating in numbers that would match those of Europeans at that time, so it is difficult to find any explanation other than racism for their fears (Winant 1994).

From the sociological perspective of conflict theory, we can explain how the Chinese immigrants were welcomed only when their labor was necessary to fuel growth in the United States. When that labor was no longer necessary, the welcome mat for the immigrants was withdrawn. Furthermore, as conflict theorists point out, restrictions were not applied evenly: Americans focused on a specific nationality (the Chinese) to reduce the number of foreign workers in the nation. Because decision making at that time rested in the hands of the descendants of European immigrants, the steps taken were most likely to be directed against the least powerful: immigrants from China who, unlike Europeans seeking entry, had few allies among legislators and other policymakers.

In 1882, Congress enacted the Chinese Exclusion Act, which outlawed Chinese immigration for ten years. It also explicitly denied naturalization rights to the Chinese in the United States; that is, they were not allowed to become citizens. There was little debate in Congress, and discussion concentrated on how to best handle suspending Chinese immigration. No allowance was made for spouses and children to be reunited with their husbands and fathers in the United States. Only brief visits of Chinese government officials, teachers, tourists, and merchants were exempted.

The rest of the nineteenth century saw the remaining loopholes allowing Chinese immigration closed. Beginning in 1884, Chinese laborers could not enter the United States from any foreign place, a ban that also lasted ten years. Two years later, the Statue of Liberty was dedicated, with a poem by Emma Lazarus inscribed on its base. To the Chinese, the poem welcoming the tired, the poor, and the huddled masses must have seemed a hollow mockery.

In 1892, Congress extended the Exclusion Act for another ten years and added that Chinese laborers had to obtain certificates of residence within a year or face deportation. After the turn of the century, the Exclusion Act was extended again. With immigration restrictions, like many other laws, the ill effects last generations. Judy Chu, born of Chinese immigrants, was first elected to Congress in 2009 from suburban Los Angeles. A psychology professor and school board member before going to Washington, she was keenly aware of the toll that one of the most restrictive immigration laws ever passed in the United States had on Chinese Americans. In "Speaking Out," we hear the Congresswoman's case for a resolution apologizing for the passage of the Chinese Exclusion Act. In 2012, Congress passed the resolution unanimously. This marked only the fourth official apology in the last twenty-five years—the other three were slavery, the internment of Japanese Americans during World War II, and mistreatment of native Hawaiians and the overthrow of their rule of the islands (Chu 2012, Nahm 2012).

Restrictionist Sentiment Increases

As Congress closed the door to Chinese immigration, the debate on restricting immigration turned in new directions. Prodded by growing anti-Japanese feelings, the United States entered into the so-called gentlemen's agreement, which was completed in 1908. Japan agreed to halt further immigration to the United States, and the United States agreed to end discrimination against the Japanese who had already arrived. The immigration ended, but anti-Japanese feelings continued. Americans were growing uneasy that the "new immigrants" would overwhelm the culture established by the "old immigrants." The earlier immigrants, if not Anglo-Saxon, were from similar groups such as the Scandinavians, the Swiss, and the French Huguenots. These people were more experienced in democratic political practices and had a greater affinity with the dominant Anglo-Saxon culture. By the end of the nineteenth century, however, more and more immigrants were neither English speaking nor Protestant and came from dramatically different cultures.

The National Origin System

Beginning in 1921, a series of measures was enacted that marked a new era in American immigration policy. Whatever the legal language, the measures were drawn up to block the growing immigration from southern Europe (from Italy and Greece, for example) and also to block all Asian immigrants by establishing a zero quota for them.

To understand the effect of the national origin system on immigration, it is necessary to clarify the quota system. Quotas were deliberately weighted to favor immigration from

((ψ)) Speaking Out

Chinese Exclusion Act of 1882

A century ago, the Chinese came here in search of a better life; but they faced harsh conditions, particularly in the Halls of Congress. Congress passed numerous laws to restrict Chinese Americans, starting from the 1882 Chinese Exclusion Act, to stop the Chinese from immigrating, from becoming naturalized citizens, and from ever having the right to vote.

Judy Chu

These were the only such laws to target a specific ethnic group. The Chinese were the only residents that had to carry papers on them at all times. They were often harassed and detained. If they couldn't produce the proper documents, authorities threw them into prison or out of the country, regardless of their citizenship status. Political cartoons and hateful banners...were hung in towns and cities and printed in papers. At that time of this hateful law, the Chinese were called racial slurs, were spat upon in the streets, and even brutally murdered.

Only after China became an ally of the United States in World War II was this law repealed in 1943, 60 years after its passage. It has never been formally acknowledged by Congress as incompatible with America's founding principles.

That is why, as the first Chinese American woman elected to Congress, and whose grandfather was a victim of this law, I stand on the very floor where the Chinese Exclusion Act was passed and announce that I have introduced a resolution calling for a formal acknowledgment and expression of regret for the Chinese exclusion laws.

When the exclusion laws were first introduced, there was a great deal of debate in Congress over their merits. The U.S. had just abolished slavery. The 14th and 15th Amendments had recently been ratified. Slavery had been defeated, and freedom seemed more certain. The national atmosphere led many in Congress to stand up against the discriminatory anti-Chinese laws. But over the years, those standing for justice almost all disappeared. By the time 1882 came around, Members of Congress were fighting over who deserved the most credit for getting the most discriminatory laws passed and standing against the "Mongolian horde."....

But there were a brave few, a small minority who fought hard against prejudice and principles of freedom. One such man was Senator George Frisbie Hoar, whose statue now stands proudly in the Capitol. He stood up to all of the Chinese exclusion laws and voted against each. He said in 1904 when the laws were made permanent, "I cannot agree with the principle that this legislation or any legislation on the subject rests. All races, all colors, all nationalities contain persons entitled to be recognized everywhere as equals of other men. I am bound to record my protest, if I stand alone."

And stand alone he did. The final vote against the Chinese in the Senate was 76–1. What Senator Hoar stood up for is what I am asking Congress to stand up for today: that all people, no matter the color of their skin, or the nation of origin, are the equals of every other man or woman.

America came to be what it is today through immigrants who came from all corners of the world. Chinese immigrants were amongst them. They sought a place to live that was founded upon liberty and equality. They came in search of the American Dream—that if you worked hard, you could build a good life. It is why my grandfather came to the United States.

But when the Chinese Exclusion Act was passed, the truths that this Nation holds as self-evident—that all are endowed with the inalienable rights of life, liberty and the pursuit of happiness—were discounted by the very ones elected to uphold them.

And so for a generation of our ancestors, like my grandfather, who were told for six decades by the U.S. government that the land of the free wasn't open to them, it is long past time that Congress officially and formally acknowledges these ugly laws that targeted Chinese immigrants, and express sincere regret for these actions.

With my resolution, Congress will acknowledge the injustice of the Chinese Exclusion Act, express regret for the lives it destroyed, and make sure that the prejudice that stained our Nation is never repeated again. And it will demonstrate that today is a different day and that today we stand side by side for a stronger America.

Chu 2011.

northern Europe. Because of the ethnic composition of the country in 1920, the quotas placed severe restrictions on immigration from the rest of Europe and other parts of the world. Immigration from the Western Hemisphere (i.e., Canada, Mexico, Central and South America, and the Caribbean) continued unrestricted. The quota for each nation was set at 3 percent of the number of people descended from each nationality recorded in the 1920 census. Once the statistical manipulations were completed, almost 70 percent of the quota for the Eastern Hemisphere went to just three countries: Great Britain, Ireland, and Germany.

The absurdities of the system soon became obvious, but it was nevertheless continued. British immigration had fallen sharply, so most of its quota of 65,000 went unfilled. However, the openings could not be transferred, even though countries such as Italy, with a quota of only 6,000, had 200,000 people who wanted to enter. However one rationalizes the purpose behind the act, the result was obvious: Any English person, regardless of skill and whether related to anyone already here, could enter the country more easily than, say, a Greek doctor whose children were American citizens. The quota for Greece was 305, with the backlog of people wanting to come reaching 100,000.

By the end of the 1920s, annual immigration had dropped to one-fourth of its pre–World War I level. The worldwide economic depression of the 1930s decreased immigration still further. A brief upsurge in immigration just before World War II reflected the flight of Europeans from the oppression of expanding Nazi Germany. The war virtually ended transatlantic immigration. The era of the great European migration to the United States had been legislated out of existence.

 Explore the Concept on MySocLab: Immigration Through the Years

Ellis Island
Although it was not opened until 1892, New York Harbor's Ellis Island—the country's first federal immigration facility—quickly became the symbol of all migrant streams to the United States. By the time it was closed in late 1954, it had processed 17 million immigrants. Today, their descendants number over 100 million Americans.

The 1965 Immigration and Nationality Act

The national origin system was abandoned with the passage of the 1965 Immigration and Nationality Act, signed into law by President Lyndon B. Johnson at the foot of the Statue of Liberty. The primary goals of the act were to reunite families and to protect the American labor market. The act also initiated restrictions on immigration from Latin America. After the act, immigration increased by one-third, but the act's influence was primarily on the composition rather than the size of immigration. The sources of immigrants now included Italy, Greece, Portugal, Mexico, the Philippines, the West Indies, and South America.

The lasting effect is apparent when we compare the changing sources of immigration over the last 190 years, as shown in Figure 4.3. The most recent period shows that Asian and Latin American immigrants combined to account for 78 percent of the people who

Explore the Concept on MySocLab: Hispanic and Asian Immigration and Settlement Patterns

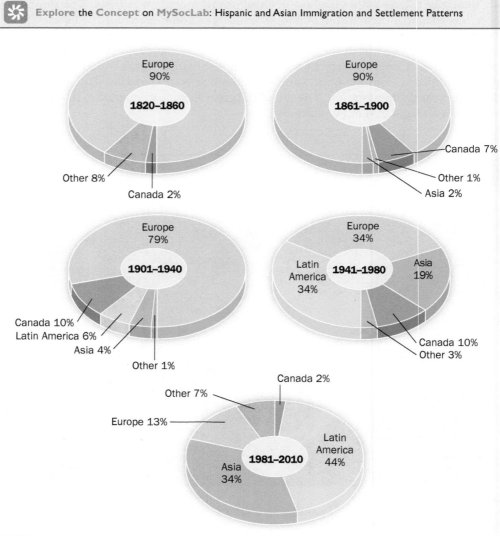

FIGURE 4.3

Legal Immigrants Admitted to the United States by Region of Last Residence, 1820–2010

Source: Office of Immigration Statistics 2011.

were permitted entry. This contrasts sharply with early immigration, which was dominated by arrivals from Europe.

The nature of immigration laws is exceedingly complex and is subjected to frequent,
often minor, adjustments. In 2000 and 2010, between 840,000 and 1,270,000 people were
legally admitted each year. For 2010, people were admitted for the following reasons:

- Relatives of citizens   57%
- Relatives of legal residents   9%
- Employment based   14%
- Refugees/people seeking political asylum   13%
- Diversity (lottery among applications from
  nations historically sending few immigrants)   5%
- Other   2%

Overall, two-thirds of immigrants come to join their families, one-seventh because of
skills needed in the United States, and another one-seventh because of special refugee
status (Martin and Yankay 2012).

Contemporary Social Concerns

Although our current immigration policies are less restrictive than other nations', they
are the subjects of great debate. Table 4.1 summarizes the benefits and concerns regarding immigration to the United States. We now consider five continuing criticisms relating
to our immigration policy: the brain drain, population growth, mixed status, English language acquisition, and illegal immigration. All five, but particularly illegal immigration,
have provoked heated debates on the national level and continuing efforts to resolve
them with new policies. We then consider the economic impact of immigration, followed
by the nation's policy toward refugees, a group distinct from immigrants.

The Brain Drain

How often have you identified your science or mathematics teacher or your physician as
someone who was not born in the United States? This nation has clearly benefited from
attracting human resources from throughout the world, but this phenomenon has had
its price for the nations of origin.

TABLE 4.1
Immigration Benefits and Concerns

Potential Benefits	Areas of Concern
Provide needed skills	Drain needed resources from home country
Contribute to taxes	Send money home
May come with substantial capital to start business	Less-skilled immigrants compete with already disadvantaged residents
Maintain growth of consumer market	Population growth
Diversify the population (intangible gain)	Language differences
Maintain ties with countries throughout the world	May complicate foreign policy by lobbying the government
	Illegal immigration

Brain drain is the immigration to the United States of skilled workers, professionals, and technicians who are desperately needed by their home countries. In the mid-twentieth century, many scientists and other professionals from industrial nations, principally Germany and Great Britain, came to the United States. More recently, however, the brain drain has pulled emigrants from developing nations, including India, Pakistan, the Philippines, and several African nations. They are eligible for H-1B visas that qualify them for permanent work permits.

Listen to the Audio on MySocLab: *Study: Immigrant Entrepreneurs Boost Economy*

Currently, 65,000 foreigners with at a least a bachelor's degree and a specialized skill receive the H-1B visa. Another 20,000 such visas go to foreign nationals with advanced degrees from U.S. universities. In these cases, a person comes to the United States on a student visa, secures a degree, say in engineering, and then may apply for the H-1B.

More than one out of four physicians (27 percent) in the United States is foreign-born and plays a critical role in serving areas with too few doctors. Thousands of doctors have sought to enter the United States, pulled by the economic opportunity. Persons born in India, Philippines, and China account for the largest groups of foreign-born physicians. The pay differential is so great that, beginning in 2004, when foreign physicians were no longer favored with entry to the United States, physicians in the Philippines retrained as nurses so that they could immigrate to the United States where, employed as nurses, they would make four times what they would as doctors in the Philippines. By 2010, one-third of the foreign-born workers employed as registered nurses were born in the Philippines (McCabe 2012; *New York Times* 2005b).

Many foreign students say they plan to return home. Fortunately for the United States, many do not and make their talents available in the United States. One study showed that the majority of foreign students receiving their doctorates in the sciences and engineering remain here four years later. Critics note, however, that this foreign supply means that the United States overlooks its own minority scholars. Currently, for every African American and Latino doctorate, a foreign citizen also receives this degree in the United States. More encouragement must be given to African Americans and Latinos to enter high-tech career paths.

Conflict theorists see the current brain drain as yet another symptom of the unequal distribution of world resources. In their view, it is ironic that the United States gives foreign aid to improve the technical resources of African and Asian countries while maintaining an immigration policy that encourages professionals in such nations to migrate to our shores. These very countries have unacceptable public health conditions and need native scientists, educators, technicians, and other professionals. In addition, by relying on foreign talent, the United States is not encouraging native members of subordinate groups to enter these desirable fields of employment (National Center for Education Statistics 2013: Table 307; Pearson 2006; Wessel 2001; West 2010).

Population Growth

The United States, like a few other industrial nations, continues to accept large numbers of permanent immigrants and refugees. Although such immigration has increased since the passage of the 1965 Immigration and Nationality Act, the nation's birth rate has decreased. Consequently, the contribution of immigration to population growth has become more significant. As citizen "baby boomers" age, the country has increasingly depended on the economically younger population fueled by immigrants (Meyers 2007).

Immigration, legal and illegal, is projected to account for nearly 50 percent of the nation's growth from 2005 to 2050 with the children and grandchildren of immigrants accounting for another 35 percent. To some observers, the United States is already overpopulated. Environmentalists have weighed in on the immigration issue, questioning immigration's possible negative impact on the nation's natural resources. We consider that aspect of the immigration debate later in this chapter. Thus far, the majority of environmentalists have indicated a desire to keep a neutral position rather than enter the politically charged immigration debate (Kotkin 2010; Livingston and Cohn 2012).

The patterns of uneven settlement by immigrants in the United States are expected to continue, so future immigrants' impact on population growth will be felt much more in certain areas, for example, California and New York rather than Wyoming or West Virginia. Although immigration and population growth may be viewed as national concerns, their impact is localized in certain areas, such as Southern California and large urban centers nationwide (Camarota and Jensenius 2009; Passel and Cohn 2009).

Read the Document on MySocLab: *Sixteen Impacts of Population Growth*

Mixed-Status Families

Little is simple when it comes to immigration. This is particularly true regarding the challenge of mixed status. **Mixed status** refers to families in which one or more members are citizens and one or more are noncitizens. This especially becomes problematic when the noncitizens are illegal or undocumented immigrants.

The problem of mixed status emerges on two levels. On the macro level, when policy debates are made about issues that seem clear to many people—such as whether illegal immigrants should be allowed to attend state colleges or whether illegal immigrants should be immediately deported—the complicating factor of mixed-status families quickly emerges. On the micro level, the daily toll on members of mixed-status households is difficult. Often, the legal resident or even the U.S. citizen in a household finds daily life limited for fear of revealing the undocumented status of a parent or brother or even a son.

Watch the Video on MySocLab: *ABC Nightline: How Stinky Beat MIT*

About three-quarters of illegal immigrants' children were born in the United States and thus are citizens. This means that perhaps half of all adult illegal immigrants have a citizen in their immediate family. This proportion has grown in recent years. Therefore, some of the issues facing illegal immigrants, whom we discuss later, also affect the citizens in the families because they avoid bringing attention to themselves for fear of revealing the illegal status of their mother or father (Gonzalez 2009; Passel and Cohn 2009).

Language Barriers

For many people in the United States, the most visible aspects of immigration are non–English speakers, businesses with foreign-language storefronts, and even familiar stores assuring potential customers that their employees speak Spanish or Polish or Chinese or another foreign language. Non–English speakers cluster in certain states, but bilingualism attracts nationwide passions. The release in 2006 of "Nuestro Himno," the Spanish-language version of "The Star-Spangled Banner," led to a strong reaction, with 69 percent of people saying it was appropriate to be sung only in English. Yet at least one congressman who decried the Spanish version sang the anthem himself in English with incorrect lyrics (Carroll 2006; Koch 2006b).

About 20 percent of the population speaks a language other than English, as shown in Figure 4.4. Indeed, 32 different languages are spoken at home by at least 200,000 residents. As of 2008, about half of the 38 million people born abroad spoke English less than "very well." This rises to 74 percent among those born in Mexico. Nationally, about 64 percent of Latino schoolchildren report speaking Spanish at home (American Community Survey 2009: Tables S0501 and S0506; Shin and Kominski 2010).

The myth of Anglo superiority has rested in part on language differences. (The term *Anglo* in the following text means all non-Hispanics but primarily Whites.) First, the criteria for economic and social achievement usually include proficiency in English. By such standards, Spanish-speaking pupils are judged less able to compete until they learn English. Second, many Anglos believe that Spanish is not an asset occupationally. Only

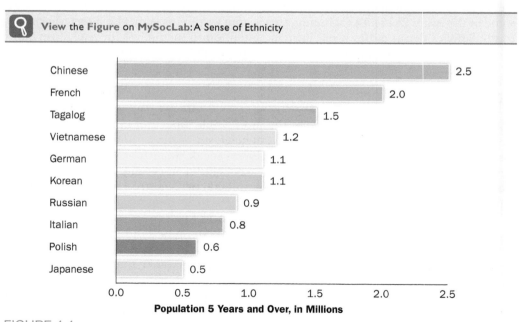

FIGURE 4.4

Ten Languages Most Frequently Spoken at Home, Other Than English and Spanish

Source: Data for 2007 in Shin and Kominski 2010.

recently, as government agencies belatedly began serving Latino people and as businesses recognized the growing Latino consumer market, have Anglos recognized that knowing Spanish is not only useful but also necessary to carry out certain tasks.

Until the last 40 years, a conscious effort was made to devalue Spanish and other languages and to discourage the use of foreign languages in schools. In the case of Spanish, this practice was built on a pattern of segregating Hispanic schoolchildren from Anglos. In the recent past in the Southwest, Mexican Americans were assigned to Mexican schools to keep Anglo schools all-White. These Mexican schools, created through de jure school segregation resulting from residential segregation, were substantially underfunded compared with the Anglo public schools. Legal action against such schools dates back to 1945, but it was not until 1970 that the U.S. Supreme Court ruled, in *Cisneros v. Corpus Christi Independent School District*, that segregation of Mexican Americans was unconstitutional. Appeals delayed implementation of that decision, and not until September 1975 was the de jure plan forcibly overturned in Corpus Christi, Texas (Commission on Civil Rights 1976).

Is it essential that English be the sole language of instruction in schools in the United States? **Bilingualism** is the use of two or more languages in places of work or educational facilities and accords each language equal legitimacy. Thus, a program of **bilingual education** may instruct children in their native language (such as Spanish) while gradually introducing them to the language of the dominant society (English). If such a program also is bicultural, it will teach children about the culture of both linguistic groups. Bilingual education allows students to learn academic material in their own language while they learn a second language. Proponents believe that, ideally, bilingual education programs should also allow English-speaking pupils to be bilingual, but generally they are directed only at making non–English speakers proficient in more than one language.

The immigration debates range from loosening to tightening the flow of immigrants, whether illegal immigrants who came here as children and went to school should be allowed a pathway to citizenship (the proposed DREAM act), and whether states such as Arizona have overstepped their bounds in trying to identity illegal immigrants.

Do bilingual programs help children learn English? It is difficult to reach firm conclusions on the effectiveness of the bilingual programs in general because they vary so widely in their approach to non–English-speaking children. The programs differ in the length of the transition to English and how long they allow students to remain in bilingual classrooms. A major study analyzed more than three decades of research, combining 17 different studies, and found that bilingual education programs produce higher levels of student achievement in reading. The most successful are paired bilingual programs—those offering ongoing instruction in a native language and English at different times of the day (Slavin and Cheung 2003; Soltero 2008).

Attacks on bilingualism in voting and education have taken several forms and have even broadened to question the appropriateness of U.S. residents using any language other than English. Federal policy has become more restrictive. Local schools have been given more authority to determine appropriate methods of instruction; they also have been forced to provide more of their own funding for bilingual education. In the United States, as of 2011, 30 states have made English their official language. Repeated efforts have been made to introduce a constitutional amendment declaring English as the nation's official language. Even such an action would not completely outlaw bilingual or multilingual government services. It would, however, require that such services be called for specifically as in the Voting Rights Act of 1965, which requires voting information to be available in multiple languages (U.S. English 2010).

Illegal Immigration

The most bitterly debated aspect of U.S. immigration policy has been the control of illegal or undocumented immigrants. These immigrants and their families come to the United States in search of higher-paying jobs than their home countries can provide.

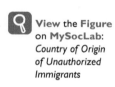

View the Figure on MySocLab: *Country of Origin of Unauthorized Immigrants*

Because by definition illegal immigrants are in the country illegally, the exact number of these undocumented or unauthorized workers is subject to estimates and disputes. Based on the best available information in 2013, more than 11.1 million illegal or unauthorized immigrants live in the United States. This compares with about 3.5 million in 1990. With employment opportunities drying up during the economic downturn beginning in 2008, significantly fewer people tried to enter illegally, and many unauthorized immigrants returned to their countries (Passel and Cohn 2011; Pew Hispanic Center 2013).

The public has tied illegal immigrants, and even legal immigrants, to almost every social problem in the nation. They become the scapegoats for unemployment; they are labeled "drug runners" and, especially since September 11, 2001, "terrorists." Their vital economic and cultural contribution to the United States is generally overlooked, as it has been for more than a hundred years.

The cost of the federal government's attempt to police the nation's borders and locate illegal immigrants is sizable. There are significant costs for aliens—that is, foreign-born noncitizens—and for other citizens. Civil rights advocates have expressed concern that the procedures used to apprehend and deport people are discriminatory and deprive many aliens of their legal rights. American citizens of Hispanic or Asian origin, some of whom were born in the United States, may be greeted with prejudice and distrust, as if their names automatically imply that they are illegal immigrants. Furthermore, these citizens and legal residents of the United States may be unable to find work because employers wrongly believe that their documents are forged.

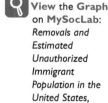

View the Graph on MySocLab: *Removals and Estimated Unauthorized Immigrant Population in the United States, Fiscal Years 1986–2008'*

In the context of this illegal immigration, Congress approved the Immigration Reform and Control Act of 1986 (IRCA) after debating it for nearly a decade. The act marked a historic change in immigration policy compared with earlier laws, as summarized in Table 4.2. Amnesty was granted to 1.7 million illegal immigrants who could document that they had

TABLE 4.2
Major Immigration Policies

Policy	Target Group	Impact
Chinese Exclusion Act, 1882	Chinese	Effectively ended all Chinese immigration for more than 60 years
National Origin System, 1921	Southern Europeans	Reduced overall immigration and significantly reduced likely immigration from Greece and Italy
Immigration and Nationality Act, 1965	Western Hemisphere and the less skilled	Facilitated entry of skilled workers and relatives of U.S. residents
Immigration Reform and Control Act of 1986	Illegal immigrants	Modest reduction of illegal immigration
Illegal Immigration Reform and Immigrant Responsibility Act of 1996	Illegal immigrants	Greater border surveillance and increased scrutiny of legal immigrants seeking benefits

established long-term residency in the United States. Under the IRCA, hiring illegal aliens became illegal, and employers became subject to fines and even prison sentences. Little workplace enforcement occurred for years, but beginning in 2009, federal agents concentrated on auditing large employers rather than raiding workplaces (Simpson 2009).

Many illegal immigrants continue to live in fear and hiding, subject to even more severe harassment and discrimination than before. From a conflict perspective, these immigrants, primarily poor and Hispanic or Asian, are being firmly lodged at the bottom of the nation's social and economic hierarchies. However, from a functionalist perspective, employers, by paying low wages, are able to produce goods and services that are profitable for industry and more affordable to consumers. Despite the poor working conditions often experienced by illegal immigrants here, they continue to come because it is still in their best economic interest to work here in disadvantaged positions rather than seek wage labor unsuccessfully in their home countries.

Amidst heated debate, Congress reached a compromise and passed the Illegal Immigration Reform and Immigrant Responsibility Act of 1996, which emphasized increasing efforts to keep immigrants from entering the country illegally. The act prevented illegal immigrants from having access to such programs as Social Security and welfare. Legal immigrants would still be entitled to such benefits, although social service agencies were required to verify their legal status. Another significant element was to increase border control and surveillance.

Illegal aliens or undocumented workers are not necessarily transient. One estimate indicates 63 percent had been here for at least ten years. Many have established homes, families, and networks with relatives and friends in the United States whose legal status might differ. These are the mixed-status households noted earlier. For the most part, their lives are not much different from legal residents, except when they seek services that require documentation proving citizenship status (Pew Hispanic Center 2011).

Another often-overlooked issue is that the presence of illegal immigrants is not merely the result of illegal border crossings. About 40 percent came here legally as tourists or students and simply never left, overstaying their visas (Murray 2013).

Policymakers continue to avoid the only real way to stop illegal immigration: discourage employment opportunities. This has certainly been the approach in recent years. The Immigration and Customs Enforcement (ICE) notifies major companies that it will soon audit its employment records looking for illegal immigrants. If found, such

Listen to the Audio on MySocLab:
Immigrants' First U.S. Christmas: The Montagnards

employees can lead to civil and criminal penalties against the business. The workers themselves are subject to deportation. This has led corporations such as American Apparel and Chipotle Mexican Grill to look closer and fire hundreds of employees lacking sufficient documentation. In 2011, about 150,000 people had been deported, but because of the slowdown in illegal border crossing, this is a significant decline from just a few years earlier (Migration News 2012).

The public often thinks in terms of controlling illegal immigration through greater surveillance at the border. After the terrorist attacks of September 11, 2001, greater control of border traffic took on a new sense of urgency, even though almost all the hijackers had entered the United States legally. It also is very difficult to secure the vast boundaries that mark the United States on land and sea.

Numerous civil rights groups and migrant advocacy organizations have expressed alarm regarding people who cross into the United States illegally and perish in the attempt. Some die in deserts, in isolated canyons, and while concealed in containers or locked in trucks during smuggling attempts. Several hundred die annually in the Southwest by seeking ever more dangerous crossing points because border control has increased. However, this death toll has received so little attention that one journalist likened it to a jumbo jet crashing between Los Angeles and Phoenix every year without anyone giving it much notice (Del Olmo 2003; Sullivan 2005).

The immigration policy debate was largely absent from the recent presidential race and was replaced by concerns over the economy. Locally, however, concerns continued. Erecting a 700-mile-long double concrete wall hardened the Mexico–United States border. This action, which was heavily supported by the general public, still brought concerns that desperate immigrants would take even more chances with their lives in order to work in the United States. Legal measures to make unauthorized crossings more difficult are being augmented by self-appointed border guards such as the Minuteman movement. Sometimes these armed volunteers engage in surveillance that leads to more violence and an atmosphere of suspicion and incidents of racial profiling along the United States–Mexican border.

An immigration-related issue that began being raised in 2010 has been concern over illegal immigrants' children who are born here and thus regarded as citizens at birth. Public opinion polls reveal that about half of the population has concerns regarding these children. Some people want to alter the Fourteenth Amendment to revise the "birthright citizenship" that was intended for children of slaves but has

since been long interpreted to cover anyone born in the United States regardless of their parents' legal status. While such a movement is unlikely to succeed, it is yet another example of a relatively minor issue that sidetracks any substantive discussion of immigration reform (Gomez 2010).

So what is the future of immigration reform? It is unlikely to be resolved in any satisfying way because the issues are complex and are wrapped up in economic interests, humanitarian concerns, party politics, constitutional rights, and even foreign policy. Alongside immigration policy is how the nation is to accommodate people escaping political and religious persecution.

Refugees

Refugees are people who live outside their country of citizenship for fear of political or religious persecution. Approximately 11 million refugees exist worldwide, enough to populate an entire "nation." That nation of refugees is larger than Belgium, Sweden, or Cuba. The United States has touted itself as a haven for political refugees. However, political refugees have not always received an unqualified welcome.

The United States makes the largest financial contribution of any nation to worldwide assistance programs. As such, it resettles about 60,000 refugees annually and has hosted over one million refugees between 1990 and 2011 (See Table 4.3). Following 9/11, the procedures have become much more cumbersome for foreigners to acquire refugee status and gain entry to the United States. Many other much smaller and poorer nations have much larger numbers of refugees, with Jordan, Iran, and Pakistan hosting more than one million refugees each (Martin and Yankay 2012; United Nations High Commission on Refugees 2008).

The United States, insulated by distance from wars and famines in Europe and Asia, has been able to be selective about which and how many refugees are welcomed. Since the arrival of refugees uprooted by World War II, through the 1980s the United States allowed three groups of refugees to enter in numbers greater than regulations would ordinarily permit: Hungarians, Cubans, and Southeast Asians.

Despite periodic public opposition, the U.S. government is officially committed to accepting refugees from other nations. In Table 4.3, we consider the major sources of refugees. According to the United Nations treaty on refugees, which our government ratified in 1968, countries are obliged to refrain from forcibly returning people to territories where their lives or liberty might be endangered. However, it is not always clear whether a person is fleeing for his or her personal safety or to escape poverty. Although people in the latter category may be of humanitarian interest, they do not meet the official definition of refugees and are subject to deportation.

Refugees are people who are granted the right to enter a country while still residing abroad. **Asylees** are foreigners who have already entered the United States and seek protection because of persecution or a well-founded fear of persecution. This persecution may be based on the individual's race, religion, nationality, membership in a particular social group, or political opinion. Asylees are eligible to adjust to lawful permanent resident status after one year of continuous presence in the United States. Asylum is granted to about 12,000 people annually.

Because asylees, by definition, are already here, they are either granted legal entry or returned to their home country. The practice of deporting people who are fleeing poverty has been the subject of criticism. The United States has a long tradition of facilitating the arrival of people leaving Communist nations, such as the Cubans. Mexicans who are refugees from poverty, Liberians fleeing civil war, and Haitians running from despotic rule are not similarly welcomed. The plight of Haitians is of particular concern.

Haitians began fleeing their country, often on small boats, in the 1980s. The U.S. Coast Guard intercepted many Haitians at sea, saving some of these boat people from death in their rickety and overcrowded wooden vessels. The Haitians said they feared detentions, torture, and execution if they remained in Haiti. Yet both Republican and Democratic administrations viewed most Haitian exiles as economic migrants rather than

TABLE 4.3				
Top Sources of Refugees				
	2000		2011	
1. Bosnia-Herzegovina	22,699	Burma	16,972
2. Yugoslavia (former)	14,280	Bhutan	14,991
3. Vietnam	9,622	Iraq	9,388
4. Ukraine	8,649	Somalia	3,161
5. Russia	4,386	Eritrea/Iran	2,032
Total:	85,076		56,384

Note: In 2011, Eritrea and Iran tied with 2,032 refugees apiece.

Source: Martin and Yankey 2012.

political refugees and opposed granting them asylum and permission to enter the United States. Once apprehended, the Haitians are returned. In 1993, the U.S. Supreme Court, by an 8–1 vote, upheld the government's right to intercept Haitian refugees at sea and return them to their homeland without asylum hearings.

The devastating 2010 earthquake in Haiti made the government reconsider this policy. Indeed, the United States halted deportations of 30,000 Haitians that were about to occur for at least 18 months. The moratorium also applied to the more than 100,000 Haitians believed to be living in the United States. As more residents of Haiti with U.S. citizenship or dual citizenship arrived from the island nation in the aftermath of the earthquake, the Haitian community increased. Despite continuing obstacles, the Haitian American community exhibits pride in those who have succeeded, from a Haitian American Florida state legislator and professional athletes to hip-hop musician Wyclef Jean. In fact, the initial earthquake refugees tended to come from the Haitian middle class or higher. Some even expressed annoyance at the quality of the public schools their children attended in America compared to the private ones in Haiti (Buchanan et al. 2010; Office of Immigration Statistics 2011; Preston 2010; Winerip 2011).

New foreign military campaigns often bring new refugee issues. Large movements of Iraqis throughout the country and the region accompanied the occupation of Iraq, beginning in 2003. It is hoped that most will return home, but some want to relocate to the United States. As was true in Vietnam, many Iraqis who aided the U.S.-led mission have increasingly sought refuge in the West, fearing for their safety if they remain in Iraq or even in the Middle East. Gradually, the United States has begun to offer refugee status to Iraqis; some 18,000 arrived in 2010 and another 9,000 in 2011 to join an Iraqi American community of 90,000. The diverse landscape of the United States has taken on yet another nationality group in large numbers (Martin and Yankay 2012).

Ethnic Diversity

The ethnic diversity of the United States at the beginning of the twenty-first century is apparent to almost everyone. Passersby in New York City were undoubtedly surprised once when two street festivals met head-to-head. The procession of San Gennaro, the patron saint of Naples, marched through Little Italy, only to run directly into a Chinese festival that originated in Chinatown. Teachers in many public schools often encounter students who speak only one language, and it is not English. Students in Chicago are taught in Spanish, Greek, Italian, Polish, German, Creole, Japanese, Cantonese, or a Native American tribal language. In the Detroit metropolitan area, classroom instruction is conveyed in 21 languages, including Arabic, Portuguese, Ukrainian, Latvian, Lithuanian, and Serbian. In many areas of the United States, you can refer to special yellow pages and find a driving instructor who speaks Portuguese or a psychotherapist who will talk to you in Hebrew.

Studying Whiteness

Race is socially constructed, as we learned in Chapter 1. Sometimes we define race in a clear-cut manner. A descendant of a Pilgrim is White, for example. But sometimes race is more ambiguous: Children of an African American and Vietnamese American union are biracial, mixed, or whatever they come to be seen by others. Our recognition that race is socially constructed has sparked a renewed interest in what it means to be White in the United States. Two aspects of the White race are useful to consider: the historical creation of Whiteness and how contemporary White people reflect on their racial identity.

When the English immigrants established themselves as the political founders of the United States, they also came to define what it meant to be White. Other groups that today are regarded as White—such as Irish, Germans, Norwegians, or Swedes—were not always considered White in the eyes of the English. Differences in language and religious worship as well as past allegiance to a king in Europe different from the English monarch meant these groups were seen not so much as Whites in the Western Hemisphere but more as nationals of their home country who happened to reside in North America.

The old distrust in Europe, where, for example, the English viewed the Irish as socially and culturally inferior, continued on this side of the Atlantic Ocean. Writing from England, Karl Marx reported that the average English worker looked down on the Irish the way poor Whites in the U.S. South looked down on Black people (Ignatiev 1994, 1995; Roediger 1994).

As European immigrants and their descendants assimilated to the English and distanced themselves from other oppressed groups such as American Indians and African Americans, they came to be viewed as White rather than as part of a particular culture. Writer Noel Ignatiev (1994:84), contrasting being White with being Polish, argues, "Whiteness is nothing but an expression of race privilege." This strong statement argues that being White, as opposed to being Black or Asian, is characterized by being a member of the dominant group. Whiteness, although it may often be invisible, is aggressively embraced and defended (Giroux 1997).

Read the Document on MySocLab: *How Did Jews Become White Folks?*

White people do not think of themselves as a race or have a conscious racial identity. A White racial identity emerges only when filling out a form asking for self-designation of race or when Whites are culturally or socially surrounded by people who are not White.

Many immigrants who were not "White on arrival" had to "become White" in a process long forgotten by today's White Americans. The long-documented transparent racial divide that engulfed the South during slavery let us ignore how Whiteness was constructed.

Therefore, contemporary White Americans give little thought to "being White." Consequently, there is little interest in studying "Whiteness" or considering "being White" except that it is "not being Black." Unlike non-Whites, who are much more likely to interact with Whites, take orders from Whites, and see Whites as leading figures in the mass media, Whites enjoy not being reminded of their Whiteness.

Unlike racial minorities, Whites downplay the importance of their racial identity, although they are willing to receive the advantages that come from being White. This means that advocating a "color-blind" or "race-neutral" outlook permits the privilege of Whiteness to prevail (Bonilla-Silva 2002; Feagin and Cobas 2008; Yancey 2003).

New scholarly interest seeks to view Whiteness but not from the vantage point of a White supremacist. Rather, focusing on White people as a race or on what it means today to be White goes beyond any definition that implies superiority over non-Whites. It also is recognized that "being White" is not the same experience for all Whites, any more than "being Asian American" or "being Black" is the same for all Asian Americans or all Blacks. Historian Noel Ignatiev observes that studying Whiteness is a necessary stage to the "abolition of whiteness"—just as, in Marxist analysis, class consciousness is a necessary stage to the abolition of class. By confronting Whiteness, society grasps the all-encompassing power that accompanies socially constructed race (Lewis 2004; McKinney 2003; Roediger 2006).

White privilege, introduced in Chapter 2, refers to the rights granted as a benefit or favor of being White and can be an element of Whiteness. However, of course, many Whites consciously minimize exercising this privilege. Admittedly, it is difficult when a White person is more likely than not to see national leaders, celebrities, and role models who also are White. For every Barack Obama, there are hundreds of movers and shakers who are White. For example, many White people champion the cause of the HBCUs (historically Black colleges and universities), conveniently ignoring that their presence is due to the existence of thousands of HWCUs (historically White colleges and universities) (Bonilla-Silva 2012).

When race is articulated or emphasized for Whites, it is more likely to be seen as threatening to Whites than allowing them to embrace their own race or national roots with pride. Behavioral economists Michael Norton and Samuel Sommers (2011) found that Whites view race as a zero-sum game—that is, decreases in bias against African Americans over the last 60 years are associated with increases in what they perceive as bias against Whites. While still seeing anti-Black bias as greater today than anti-White feeling in society, their analysis shows that, in the minds of the White respondents, the two biases are coming closer together. Black respondents also saw a marked decline in anti-Black bias during the same period but perceived only a modest increase in anti-White feelings. While Norton and Sommers's research deals only with perception of reality, it does suggest that race, and not just that of non-Whites, influences one's perception of society.

Rediscovering Ethnicity

Robert Park (1950:205), a prominent early sociologist, wrote in 1913, "A Pole, Lithuanian, or Norwegian cannot be distinguished, in the second generation, from an American, born of native parents." At one time, sociologists saw the end of ethnicity as nearly a foregone conclusion. W. Lloyd Warner and Leo Srole (1945) wrote in their often-cited *Yankee City* series that the future of ethnic groups seemed to be limited in the United States and that they would be quickly absorbed. Oscar Handlin's *The Uprooted* (1951) told of the destruction of immigrant values and their replacement by American culture. Although Handlin was among the pioneers in investigating ethnicity, assimilation was the dominant theme in his work.

Many writers have shown almost a fervent hope that ethnicity would vanish. For some time, sociologists treated the persistence of ethnicity as dysfunctional because it meant continuing old values that interfered with the allegedly superior new values. For example, holding on to one's language delayed entry into the larger labor market and the upward social mobility it afforded. Ethnicity was expected to disappear not only because of assimilation but also because aspirations to higher social class and status demanded that it vanish. It was assumed that one could not be ethnic and middle class, much less affluent.

The Third-Generation Principle

Historian Marcus Hansen's (1952) **principle of third-generation interest** was an early exception to the assimilationist approach to White ethnic groups. Simply stated, Hansen maintained that in the third generation—the grandchildren of the original immigrants—ethnic interest and awareness would increase. According to Hansen, "What the son wishes to forget, the grandson wishes to remember."

Hansen's principle has been tested several times since it was first put forth. John Goering (1971), in interviewing Irish and Italian Catholics, found that ethnicity was more important to members of the third generation than to the immigrants themselves. Similarly, Mary Waters (1990)—in her interviews of White ethnics living in suburban areas of San Jose, California, and Philadelphia, Pennsylvania—observed that many grandchildren wanted to study their ancestors' language, even though it would be a foreign language to them. They also expressed interest in learning more of their ethnic group's history and a desire to visit their homeland.

Social scientists in the past were quick to minimize the ethnic awareness of blue-collar workers. In fact, ethnicity was viewed as merely another aspect of White ethnics' alleged racist nature, an allegation examined later in this chapter. Curiously, the same intellectuals and journalists who bent over backward to understand the growing solidarity of Blacks, Hispanics, and Native Americans refused to give White ethnics the academic attention they deserved (Kivisto 2008; Wrong 1972).

The new assertiveness of ethnicity is not limited to Whites of European descent. Many members of third and successive generations of Asian and Latin American immigrants are showing renewed interest in their native languages. The very languages they avoided or even scorned themselves as children, they now want to learn as young adults. "*Heritage language*" programs have become increasingly common. Even when the descendants may easily communicate in their native language in everyday life, they often find they lack the language tools necessary for more sophisticated vocabulary or to be able to read easily (Nawa 2011).

Ethnic Paradox

While many nearly assimilated Whites are rediscovering their ethnicity (i.e., the principle of third-generation interest), others are at least publicly acknowledging their ethnicity from time to time (i.e., symbolic ethnicity). Yet research confirms that preserving elements of one's ethnicity may advance economic success and further societal acceptance.

Ethnic paradox refers to the maintenance of one's ethnic ties in a manner that can assist with assimilation with larger society. Immigrant youth as well as adults who maintain their ethnicity tend to have more success as indicated by health measures, educational attainment, and lower incidence of behavioral problems such as delinquency and truancy.

Researchers typically measure ethnic maintenance by facility in the mother language (not just conversational or "street" use) and living with others of the same ethnic background. These clear ethnic ties are not an automatic recipe for success. For example, residing with co-ethnics can lead to exploitation such as in neighborhoods where people steer those of their own ethnicity into dead-end, poor-paying, and even unhealthy working conditions. Yet for many ethnics, enclaves offer a refuge, sort of a halfway house, between two different cultures. Language maintenance, as noted in the previous chapter, is often critical to being literate and comfortable with English (Desmond and Kubrin 2009).

Symbolic Ethnicity

Observers comment on both the evidence of assimilation and the signs of ethnic identity that support a pluralistic view of society. How can both be possible?

First, the visible evidence of **symbolic ethnicity** might lead us to exaggerate the persistence of ethnic ties among White Americans. According to sociologist Herbert Gans (1979), ethnicity today increasingly involves symbols of ethnicity, such as eating ethnic food, acknowledging ceremonial holidays such as St. Patrick's Day, and supporting specific political issues or issues confronting the old country. One example was the push in 1998 by Irish Americans to convince state legislatures to make it compulsory that public schools teach about the Irish potato famine—a significant factor in immigration to the United States. This symbolic ethnicity may be more visible, but this type of ethnic heritage does not interfere with what people do, read, or say, or even whom they befriend or marry (Scully 2012).

The ethnicity of the twenty-first century, as embraced by English-speaking Whites, is largely symbolic. It does not include active involvement in ethnic activities or participation in ethnic-related organizations. In fact, sizable proportions of White ethnics have gained large-scale entry into almost all clubs, cliques, and fraternal groups. Such acceptance is a key indicator of assimilation. Ethnicity has become increasingly peripheral to the lives of members of the ethnic group. Although today's White ethnics may not relinquish their ethnic identity, other identities become more important.

Second, the ethnicity that exists may be more a result of living in the United States than importing practices from the past or the old country. Many so-called ethnic foods or celebrations, for example, began in the United States. The persistence of ethnic consciousness, then, may not depend on foreign birth, a distinctive language, and a unique way of life. Instead, it may reflect the experiences in the United States of a unique group that developed a cultural tradition distinct from that of the mainstream. For example, in Poland, the *szlachta*, or landed gentry, rarely mixed socially with the peasant class. In the United States, however, even with those associations still fresh, *szlachta* and peasants interacted together in social organizations as they settled in concentrated communities segregated physically and socially from others (Lopata 1994; Winter 2008).

Third, maintaining ethnicity can be a critical step toward successful assimilation. This ethnicity paradox facilitates full entry into the dominant culture. The ethnic community may give its members not only a useful financial boost but also the psychological strength and positive self-esteem that will allow them to compete effectively in a larger society. Thus, we may witness people participating actively in their ethnic enclave while trying to cross the bridge into the wider community (Lal 1995).

Therefore, ethnicity gives continuity with the past in the form of an effective or emotional tie. The significance of this sense of belonging cannot be emphasized enough. Whether reinforced by distinctive behavior or by what Milton Gordon (1964) called a sense of *peoplehood*, ethnicity is an effective, functional source of cohesion. Proximity to fellow ethnics is not necessary for a person to maintain social cohesion and in-group identity. Fraternal organizations or sports-related groups can preserve associations between ethnics who are separated geographically. Members of ethnic groups may even maintain feelings of in-group solidarity after leaving ethnic communities in the central cities for the suburban fringe.

Despite the diversity in the languages spoken among groups of Asian Americans and Asian Pacific Islanders, they have spent generations being treated as a monolithic group. Out of similar experiences have come panethnic identities in which people share a self-image, as do African Americans or Whites of European descent. As we noted in Chapter 1, **panethnicity** is the development of solidarity between ethnic subgroups. Are Asian Americans finding a panethnic identity? How does the Arab or Muslim American see himself or herself? In the Research Focus section, we consider the blending of ethnic and religious identities as young Americans seek to self-identify themselves.

Religious Pluralism

Religion plays a fundamental role in society and affects even those who do not practice or even believe in organized religion. **Religion** refers to a unified system of sacred beliefs and practices that encompass elements beyond everyday life that inspire awe, respect, and even fear (Durkheim [1912] 2001).

In popular speech, the term *pluralism* has often been used in the United States to refer explicitly to religion. Although certain faiths figure more prominently in the worship scene, the United States has a history of greater religious tolerance than most other nations. Today, religious bodies number more than 1,500 in the United States and range

Research Focus

Blended Identity and Self-Identifying as "Muslim American" and "Arab American"

An immigrant does not necessarily go through a process of shedding one identity for another or what is often described as assimilation. Immigrants and even their children and future generations may hold on to multiple identities. **Blended identity** is a self-image and worldview that combines religious faith, cultural background based on nationality, and the status of being a resident of the United States.

Consider the example of a Pakistani American. As shown in Figure 4.5, Muslims often find their daily activities defined by their faith, their nationality, and their status as Americans. Younger Muslims especially can move freely among the different identities. In Chicago, Muslim college students perform hip-hop in Arabic with lyrics like "La ilaha ila Allah" ("There is no God but Allah"). In Fremont, California, high school Muslim girls and some of their non-Muslim girlfriends hold an alternative prom, decked out in silken gowns, dancing to both 50 Cent and Arabic music, and dining on lasagna but pausing at sunset to face toward Mecca and pray.

How might this blended identity change over time? Sociologist Kristine Ajrouch and political scientist Amaney Jamal surveyed Arab Americans in the Detroit metropolitan area. Overall in the United States, 80 percent of Arab Americans select "White" because the government does not offer "Arab" as an option for race. Yet when given that choice, Ajrouch and Jamal found that many chose Arab American as a self-identifier but also considered themselves White.

Being Arab American does not mean that you do not see yourself as "American." Indeed, 94 percent of Arab Americans who are citizens describe themselves as very or quite proud to be American, compared to 98 percent of the general population.

It is interesting that younger Arab Americans seem more willing to use the label of "Arab American." Researchers wonder if the post-9/11 world has given new meaning to being Arab and/or Muslim American. Will younger people, as they become adults, embrace being "Arab American" in a sense of unity or seek to distance themselves in fear of being marginalized by society?

Sources: Abdo 2004a; Abdulrahim 2009; Ajrouch and Jamal 2007; Brittingham and de la Cruz 2005; Brown 2003; Mostofi 2003.

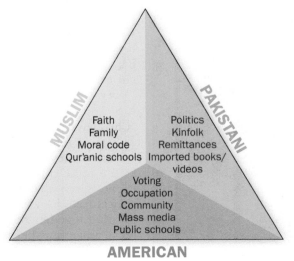

FIGURE 4.5
Blended Identity of Muslim Americans

from the more than 66 million members of the Roman Catholic Church to sects with fewer than 1,000 adherents. In every region of the country, religion is being expressed in greater variety, whether it be the Latinization of Catholicism and some Christian faiths or the de-Europeanizing of some established Protestant faiths, as with Asian Americans, or the de-Christianizing of the overall religious landscape with Muslims, Buddhists, Hindus, Sikhs, and others (Roof 2007).

How do we view the United States in terms of religion? Increasingly, the United States has a non-Christian presence. In 1900, an estimated 96 percent of the nation was Christian; slightly more than 1 percent was nonreligious, and approximately 3 percent held other faiths. In 2013, it was estimated that the nation was 74 percent Christian, 17 percent nonreligious, and another 9 percent all other faiths. The United States has a long Jewish tradition, and Muslims number close to 5 million. A smaller but also growing number of people adhere to such Eastern faiths as Hinduism, Buddhism, Confucianism, and Taoism (Newport 2011).

Sociologists use the word **denomination** for a large, organized religion that is not linked officially with the state or government. By far, the largest denomination in the United States is Catholicism; yet at least 26 other Christian religious denominations have 1 million or more members (Lindner 2012).

At least four non-Christian religious groups in the United States have numbers that are comparable to any of these large denominations: Jews, Muslims, Buddhists, and Hindus. In the United States, each numbers more than 1 million members. Within each of these groups are branches or sects that distinguish themselves from each other. For example, the Judaic faith embraces several factions such as Orthodox, Conservative, Reconstructionist, and Reform that are similar in their roots but marked by sharp distinctions. Continuing the examples, in the United States and the rest of the world, some Muslims are Sunni and others Shia. Further divisions are present within these groups, just as among Protestants and, in turn, among Baptists.

The United States has long been described as a Judeo-Christian nation, but with interest in other faiths and continuing immigration, this description, if it was ever accurate, is not now. This is especially true with the growth of Muslim Americans.

Islam in the United States has a long history stretching from Muslim Africans who came as slaves to today's Muslim community, which includes immigrants and native-born Americans. President Obama, the son of a practicing Muslim and who lived for years in Indonesia, the country with the largest Muslim population, never sought to hide his roots. However, reflecting the prejudices of many toward non-Christians, his Christian upbringing was stressed throughout his presidential campaigns. Little wonder that a national survey showed that 55 percent believe the U.S. Constitution establishes the country as a "Christian nation" (Cose 2008; Thomas 2007).

Even if religious faiths have broad representation, they tend to be fairly homogeneous at the local church level. This is especially ironic, given that many faiths have played critical roles in resisting racism and in trying to bring together the nation in the name of racial and ethnic harmony.

Broadly defined, faiths represent a variety of ethnic and racial groups. In Figure 4.6, we consider the interaction of White, Black, and

Religious faiths are often divided into many groups or denominations. Jewish worshippers in the United States may be Orthodox, Conservative, Reconstructionist, or Reform.

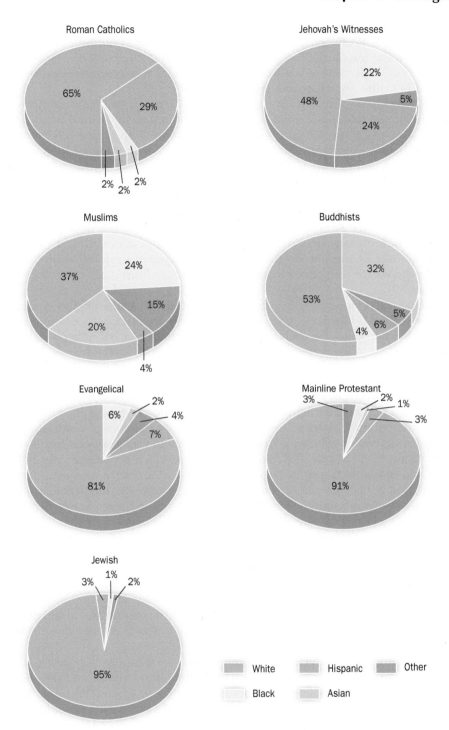

FIGURE 4.6
Racial and Ethnic Makeup of Selected Religions in the United States

Note: "Other" includes self-identified mixed races. Evangelical includes Baptist, Lutheran (Missouri and Wisconsin Synods), and Pentecostal, among others. Mainline Protestant includes Methodist, Lutheran (ELCA), Presbyterian, Episcopal, and United Church of Christ, among others, but excludes historically Black churches. Based on a national survey of 35,556 adults conducted in August 2007.

Source: Pew Forum on Religion and Public Life 2008b:120.

Hispanic races with religions. Muslims, Pentecostals, and Jehovah's Witnesses are much more diverse than Presbyterians or Lutherans. Religion plays an even more central role for Blacks and Latinos than Whites. A national survey indicated that 65 percent of African Americans and 51 percent of Latinos attend a religious service every week, compared to 44 percent of White non-Hispanics (Winseman 2004).

It would also be a mistake to focus only on older religious organizations when considering religion's role in society. Local churches that developed into national faiths in the 1990s, such as Calvary Chapel, Vineyard, and Hope Chapel, have a following among Pentecostal believers, who embrace a more charismatic form of worship devoid of many traditional ornaments, with pastors and congregations alike favoring informal attire. New faiths develop with increasing rapidity in what can only be called a very competitive market for individual religious faith. In addition, many people, with or without religious affiliation, become fascinated with spiritual concepts such as angels or become a part of loose-knit fellowships. Religion in the United States is an ever-changing social phenomenon. Other nonmainstream faiths emerge in new arenas, as evidenced by the successful campaign of Mitt Romney, a Mormon, to win the Republican nomination for president in 2012 or the visible role of celebrities promoting the Church of Scientology (Schaefer and Zellner 2011).

Divisive conflicts along religious lines are muted in the United States compared with those in, say, the Middle East. Although not entirely absent, conflicts about religion in the United States seem to be overshadowed by civil religion. **Civil religion** is the religious dimension in the United States that merges public life with sacred beliefs. It also reflects that no single faith is privileged over all others. Indeed, it even encompasses the conversation of nonbelievers regarding the human condition.

Sociologist Robert Bellah (1967) borrowed the phrase *civil religion* from eighteenth-century French philosopher Jean-Jacques Rousseau to describe a significant phenomenon in the contemporary United States. Civil religion exists alongside established religious faiths, and it embodies a belief system that incorporates all religions but is not associated specifically with any one. It is the type of faith to which presidents refer in inaugural speeches and to which American Legion posts and Girl Scout troops swear allegiance. In 1954, Congress added the phrase *under God* to the Pledge of Allegiance as a legislative recognition of religion's significance. Elected officials in the United States, beginning with Ronald Reagan, often conclude even their most straightforward speeches with "God bless the United States of America," which in effect evokes the civil religion of the nation.

Functionalists see civil religion as reinforcing central American values that may be more expressly patriotic than sacred in nature. Often, the mass media, following major societal upheavals, from the 1995 Oklahoma City bombing to the 2001 terrorist attacks, show church services with clergy praying and asking for national healing. Bellah (1967) sees no sign that the importance of civil religion has diminished in promoting collective identity, but he does acknowledge that it is more conservative than during the 1970s.

Beginning with the Clinton administration, the federal government has made explicit efforts to include religious organizations. The 1996 welfare reform act President Clinton signed provided that religious groups could compete for grants. President George W. Bush created a White House Office of Faith-Based and Community Initiatives to provide for a significant expansion of charitable choice. President Barack Obama has continued the office, naming a Pentecostal minister to oversee it (Gorski 2011; Jacoby 2009).

Conclusion

The immigrant presence in the United States can often be heard on the streets and the workplace as people speak in different languages. Check out your radio; as of 2011, radio stations broadcast in 35 languages other than English, including Albanian, Creole, Welsh, Yiddish, and Oji, a language spoken in Ghana (Keen 2011).

Throughout the history of the United States, as we have seen, there has been intense debate over the nation's policies that bring immigrants that speak these and other languages to the country. In a sense, this debate reflects the deep value conflicts in the U.S. culture and parallels the "American dilemma" identified by Swedish social economist Gunnar Myrdal (1944). But is this really a dilemma acknowledged by everyone? As we have seen, many do not recognize the privileges they have everyday by not being treated as a "minority," "an outsider," "them" rather than "us."

Despite this, what could be termed a "non-dilemma," one strand of our culture—epitomized by the words "Give us your tired, your poor, your huddled masses"—has emphasized egalitarian principles and a desire to help people in their time of need. At the time the Statue of Liberty was dedicated in 1886, one could hardly have anticipated that little more than a century later Barack Obama, the son of a Kenyan immigrant, would be elected president of the United States (Department of State 2013; DiTomaso 2012).

At the same time, however, hostility to potential immigrants and refugees—whether the Chinese in the 1880s, European Jews in the 1930s and 1940s, or Mexicans, Haitians, and Arabs today—reflects not only racial, ethnic, and religious prejudice but also a desire to maintain the dominant culture of the in group by keeping out those viewed as outsiders. The conflict between these cultural values is central to one of the American dilemmas of the twenty-first century.

The current debate about immigration is highly charged and emotional. Some people see it in economic terms, whereas others see new arrivals as a challenge to the very culture of our society. Today's

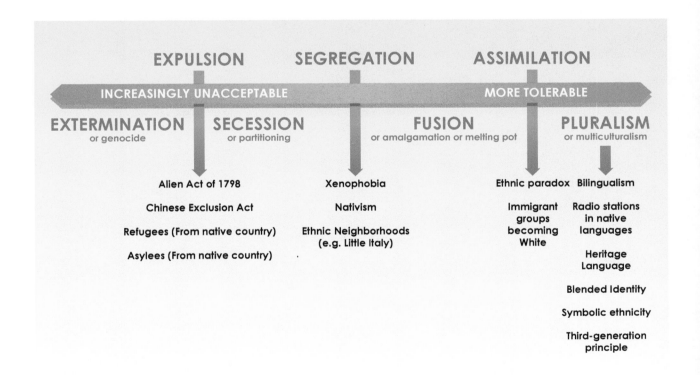

concern about immigrants follows generations of people coming to settle in the United States. Immigration in the past produced a diverse country in terms of both nationality and religion, even before the immigration of the last 60 years. Therefore, the majority of Americans today are not descended from the English, and Protestants are fewer than half of all worshipers.

Any study of life in the United States, especially one that focuses on dominant and subordinate groups, cannot ignore religion and ethnicity. The two are closely related because certain religious faiths predominate in certain nationalities. Religious activity and interest by White ethnics in their heritage continue to be prominent features of the contemporary scene. People have been and continue to be ridiculed or deprived of opportunities solely because of their ethnic or religious affiliation. To get a true picture of people's place in society, we must consider ethnicity and social class in association with their religious identification.

Religion is changing in the United States. In one commercial recognition of this fact, in 2003, Hallmark created its first greeting card for the Muslim holiday Eid-al-fitr, which marks the end of the month-long fast of Ramadan. The persistence of ethnicity is an intriguing issue. Some people may only casually exhibit their ethnicity and practice what has been called symbolic ethnicity. However, can people immerse themselves in their ethnic culture without society punishing them for their will to be different? The tendency to put down White ethnics through respectable bigotry continues. Despite this intolerance, ethnicity remains a viable source of identity for many citizens. There is also the ethnic paradox, which finds that practicing one's ethnic heritage often strengthens people and allows them to move successfully into the larger society.

The social significance of identity is a reoccurring theme in this chapter. We consider how identity may change as immigrants remain longer in the United States and how identity may differ between adult immigrants and their children born in the United States. Even among second- and third-generation immigrants, identity may not be straightforward because they employ multiple identities that others may not readily accept in the same manner.

Ethnicity and religion are a basic part of today's social reality and of each individual's identity. The emotions, disputes, and debate over religion and ethnicity in the United States are powerful indeed.

MySocLab   ✓ Study and Review on MySocLab

Summary

1. Immigration has long been regulated by the United States; the first significant restriction was the Chinese Exclusion Act in 1882.

2. Subsequent legislation through the national origins system favored northern and western Europeans. Not until 1965 were quotas by nation largely lifted.

3. Immigration policy is impacted by economic demands for workers who cannot be found among citizens. These workers may be professionals, but they also include large numbers of people who are prepared to do hard labor for wages deemed too low for most citizens but which are attractive to many people outside the United States.

4. Issues such as population growth, the environment, the brain drain, mixed-status households, English-language acquisition, and illegal immigration influence contemporary immigration policy.

5. Refugees present a special challenge to policymakers who balance humanitarian values against an unwillingness to accept all those who are fleeing poverty and political unrest.

6. While considering race and ethnicity in the United States, we often ignore how White people come to see themselves as a group and in relationship to others.

7. Feelings of ethnicity may be fading among the descendants of Europeans, but it may reemerge as reflected in either the third-generation principle or, in a more limited fashion, through symbolic ethnicity.

8. The ethnic diversity of the United States is matched by the many denominations among Christians as well as the sizable Jewish and Muslim presence.

Key Terms

asylees, p. 105

bilingual education, p. 101

bilingualism, p. 101

blended identity, p. 111

brain drain, p. 98

civil religion, p. 114

denomination, p. 112

ethnic paradox, p. 109

mixed status, p. 99

nativism, p. 91

panethnicity, p. 110

principle of third-generation interest, p. 108

refugees, p. 105

religion, p. 110

sinophobes, p. 92

symbolic ethnicity, p. 109

White privilege, p. 107

xenophobia, p. 91

Review Questions

1. What are the functions and dysfunctions of immigration?

2. What were the social and economic issues when public opinion mounted against Chinese immigration to the United States?

3. Ultimately, what do you think is the major concern people have about contemporary immigration to the United States: the numbers of immigrants, their legal status, or their nationality?

4. What principles appear to guide U.S. refugee policy?

Critical Thinking

1. What is your family's immigrant root story? Consider how your ancestors arrived in the United States and also how other immigrant groups have shaped your family's past.

2. What challenge does the presence of people in the United States speaking languages other than English present for them? For schools? For the workplace? For you?

3. When do you see ethnicity becoming more apparent? When does it appear to occur only in response to other people's advancing their own ethnicity? From these situations, how can ethnic identity be both positive and perhaps counterproductive or even destructive?

5 Native Americans

5-1 Examine the relationship between Native Americans and the first Europeans.

5-2 Identify how treaties and warfare impact Native Americans today.

5-3 Discuss how reservation life and federal policies affect Native Americans.

5-4 Describe the collective action of Native Americans.

5-5 List challenges that Native Americans face regarding economic development, education, healthcare, and environment.

Boozhoo might be the sign that welcomes you at the local coffee shop in this college town. On-campus restroom door signs say *Ikwewag* and *Ininiway*, but fortunately, each is followed by *Women* and *Men*, respectively. No, you're not attending a college in a foreign country: You are in Bemidji, Minnesota, checking out Bemidji State University. The town and college have made an effort to make Native Americans, and in particular members of the Ojibwe (or Chippewa) tribe, feel welcomed. Using the language also is an effort to keep it alive because fewer than 1,000 people in the United States speak it fluently.

The battle to keep language alive is fought throughout the United States, from Riverton, Wyoming, to Long Island, New York, to the Florida Everglades. Efforts are underway to significantly increase the numbers of the more than 370,000 native people who currently speak their native language at home.

In Wyoming, Ryan Wilson is teaching the Arapaho language in the Hinono' Eitinino' Oowuu', the Arapaho language Lodge, because no one under the age of 55 speaks it fluently and thus there are few surviving speakers. The Shinnecock native language on Long Island has not been spoken for nearly 200 years. Drawing on a historical vocabulary list made by Thomas Jefferson during a tribal visit in 1791, linguists are attempting to reintroduce the tribe of 1,700 people to their native language. In Florida, the Miccosukee Indian Schools' efforts to increase speaking their native language are having positive results, as are efforts around the country to increase the low population (only 14.8 percent) of native peoples who speak their native language at home.

The languages themselves are threatened because easily seventy of the 139 tribal languages could become extinct in a very few years. In Table 5.1, we highlight the ten most commonly spoken languages, although not necessarily fluently, by Native Americans (Cohen 2010; Frosch 2008; T. Lee 2011; National Congress of American Indians 2012; Siebens and Julian 2011; Sturtevant and Cattelino 2004).

Although this chapter focuses on the Native American experience in the United States, the pattern of land seizure, subjugation, assimilation, and resistance to domination has been repeated with indigenous people in nations throughout the world, including the tribal people in Mexico, Canada, and throughout Latin America. Hawaiians, another native people who fell under the political, economic, and cultural control of the United States, are considered in Chapter 8.

The common term *American Indians* tells us more about the Europeans who explored North America than it does about the native people. The label reflects the initial explorers' confusion in believing that they had arrived in "the Indies" of the Asian continent. However, reference to the diverse tribal groups either by *American Indians* or *Native Americans* is a result of the forced subordination to the dominant group. Today, most American Indians prefer to identify themselves using their tribal affiliation, such as Cherokee, or affiliations such as Cheyenne Arapaho if one has mixed ancestry. To collectively refer to all tribal people in this book, we use *Native Americans* and *American Indians* interchangeably.

An estimated 2.9 million Native Americans and Alaskan Natives lived in the United States in 2010. This represents an increase of about 18 percent over the year 2000, compared to a growth of about 1 percent among White non-Hispanics. In addition to the 2.9 million people who gave American Indian or Alaskan Native as their sole racial identification, another 2.3 million people listed

TABLE 5.1	
Major Tribal Languages	
1. Navajo	169,471
2. Yupik (Alaska)	18,950
3. Dakota (Sioux)	18,616
4. Apache	13,083
5. Keres (Pueblo)	12,945
6. Cherokee	11,610
7. Choctaw	10,343
8. Zuni	9,686
9. Ojibwa	8,371
10. Pima	7,270

Source: 2006–2010 American Community Survey in Siebens and Julian 2011: Table 1.

✳ Explore the Map on MySocLab: Land Controlled by Native Americans, 1784 to Today

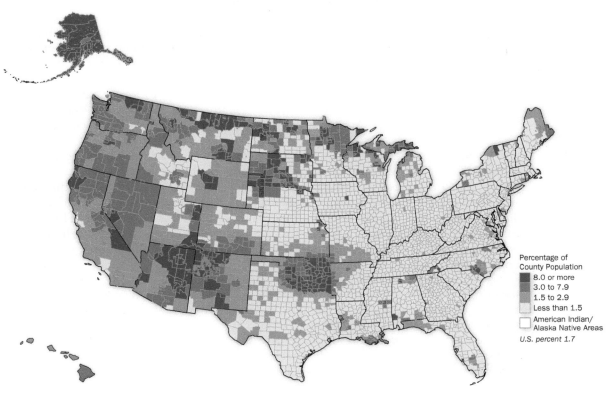

FIGURE 5.1
American Indian and Alaska Native Population

Source: Norris, Vines, and Hoeffel 2012: Figure 4 on p. 9.

multiple responses that included American Indian. As shown in Figure 5.1, Native Americans are located throughout the United States but are most present in the Southwest, Northwest, northern Great Plains, and Alaska (Norris, Vines, and Hoeffel 2012).

Early European Contacts

Native Americans have been misunderstood and ill treated by their conquerors for several centuries. Assuming that he had reached the Indies, Christopher Columbus called the native residents "people of India." The European immigrants who followed Columbus did not understand them any more than the Native Americans could have anticipated the destruction of their way of life. But the Europeans had superior weaponry, and the diseases they brought wiped out huge numbers of indigenous people throughout the Western hemisphere.

The first explorers of the Western hemisphere came long before Columbus and Leif Eriksson. The ancestors of today's Native Americans were hunters in search of wild game, including mammoths and long-horned bison. For thousands of years, these people spread through the Western hemisphere, adapting to its many physical environments. Hundreds of cultures evolved, including the complex societies of the Maya, Inca, and Aztec (Deloria 1995, 2004).

It is beyond the scope of this chapter to describe the many tribal cultures of North America, let alone the ways of life of Native Americans in Central and South America and the islands of the Caribbean. We must appreciate that the term *Indian culture* is a convenient way to gloss over the diversity of cultures, languages, religions, kinship systems, and political organizations that existed—and, in many instances, remain—among the peoples referred to collectively as *Native Americans* or *American Indians*. For example, in 1500, an estimated 700 distinct languages were spoken in the area north of Mexico. For simplicity, we refer to these many cultures as *Native American*, but we must be always mindful of the differences this term conceals. Similarly, we refer to non–Native Americans as non–Indians, recognizing in this context that this term encompasses many groups, including Whites, African Americans, and Hispanics in some instances (Schwartz 1994; Swagerty 1983).

The number of Native Americans north of the Rio Grande, estimated at about 10 million in 1500, gradually decreased as their food sources disappeared and they fell victim to diseases such as measles, smallpox, and influenza. By 1800, the Native American population was about 600,000; by 1900, it was reduced to fewer than 250,000. This loss of human life can only be described and judged as catastrophic. The United States does not bear total responsibility. The pattern had been well established by the early Spaniards in the Southwest and by the French and English colonists who sought control of the eastern seaboard.

Native Americans did have warfare between tribes, which presumably reduces the guilt for European-initiated warfare. However, their conflicts differed significantly from those of the conquerors. The Europeans launched large campaigns against the tribes, resulting in mass mortality. In contrast, in the Americas, the tribes limited warfare to specific campaigns designed for specific purposes such as recapturing a resource or avenging a loss.

Not all initial contacts led to deliberate loss of life. Some missionaries traveled well in advance of settlement in efforts to Christianize Native Americans before they came into contact with less-tolerant Europeans. Fur trappers, vastly outnumbered by Native Americans, were forced to learn their customs, but these trappers established routes of commerce that more and more non–Indians were to follow (Snipp 1989; Swagerty 1983; Thornton 1991).

Gradually, the policies directed from Europe toward the indigenous peoples of North America resembled the approach described in the world systems theory. As introduced in Chapter 1, the **world systems theory** takes the view that the global economic system is divided between nations that control wealth and those that provide natural resources and labor. The indigenous peoples and, more important to the Europeans, the land they occupied were targets of exploitation by Spain, England, France, Portugal, and other nations with experience as colonizers in Africa and Asia (Chase-Dunn and Hall 1998).

Treaties and Warfare

The United States formulated a policy toward Native Americans during the nineteenth century that followed the precedents established during the colonial period. The government policy was not to antagonize the Native Americans unnecessarily. Yet if the needs of tribes interfered with the needs, or even the whims, of non–Indians, then Whites were to have precedence.

Tribes were viewed as separate nations to be dealt with by treaties formed through negotiations with the federal government. Fair-minded as that policy might seem, it was clear from the beginning that the non–Indian government would deal harshly with tribal groups that refused to agree to treaties. Federal relations with the Native Americans were the responsibility of the secretary of war. Consequently, when the Bureau of Indian

Affairs (BIA) was created in 1824 to coordinate the government's relations with the tribes, it was part of the Department of War. The government's primary emphasis was to maintain peace and friendly relations along the frontier. Nevertheless, as settlers moved the frontier westward, they encroached more and more on land that Native Americans had inhabited for centuries.

The Indian Removal Act, passed in 1830, called for the relocation of all Eastern tribes across the Mississippi River. The Removal Act was popular with non–American Indians because it opened more land to settlement through annexation of tribal land. Almost all non–Indians felt that the Native Americans had no right to block progress—which was defined as

"NOT SO FAST! HOW DO WE KNOW YOU'RE NOT TERRORISTS WITH WEAPONS OF MASS DESTRUCTION?"

movement by White society. Among the largest groups relocated were the five tribes of the Creek, Choctaw, Chickasaw, Cherokee, and Seminole, who were resettled in what is now Oklahoma. The movement, lasting more than a decade, is called the Trail of Tears because the tribes left their ancestral lands under the harshest conditions. Poor planning, corrupt officials, little attention to those ill from a variety of epidemics, inadequate supplies, and the deaths of several thousand Native Americans characterized the forced migration (Hirsch 2009).

The Removal Act disrupted Native American cultures but didn't move the tribes far enough or fast enough to stay out of the path of the ever-advancing non-American Indian settlers. After the Civil War, settlers moved westward at an unprecedented pace. The federal government negotiated with the many tribes but primarily enacted legislation that affected them with minimal consultation. The government's first priority was almost always to allow the settlers to live and work regardless of Native American claims. Along with the military defeat of the tribes, the federal government tried to limit the functions of tribal leaders. If tribal institutions were weakened, it was felt, the Native Americans would assimilate more rapidly.

The more significant federal actions that continue up to the present are summarized in Table 5.2.

The Allotment Act

The Allotment Act of 1887 bypassed tribal leaders and proposed making individual landowners of tribal members. Each family was given as many as 160 acres under the government's assumption that, with land, Native Americans would become more like the White homesteaders who were flooding the not-yet-settled areas of the West.

The effect of the Allotment Act, however, was disastrous. To guarantee that they would remain homesteaders, the act prohibited the Native Americans from selling the land for 25 years. Yet no effort was made to acquaint them with the skills necessary to make the land productive. Many tribes were not accustomed to cultivating land and, if anything, considered such labor undignified, and they received no assistance in adapting to homesteading.

TABLE 5.2
Major Federal Policies

Year	Policy	Central Feature
1830	Removal Act	Relocated Eastern tribes westward
1887	Allotment Act	Subdivided tribal lands into individual household plots
1934	Reorganization Act	Required tribes to develop election-based governments and leaders
1934	Johnson-O'Malley Act	Aided public school districts with Native American enrollments
1946	Indian Claims Commission	Adjudicated litigation by tribes against the federal government
1952	Employment Assistance Program	Relocated reservation people to urban areas for jobs
1953	Termination Act	Closed reservations and their federal services
1971	Alaska Native Settlement Act	Recognized legally the lands of tribal people
1974	Indian Financing Act	Fostered economic development
1975	Indian Self-Determination and Education Assistance Act	Increased involvement by tribal people and governments
1986	Indian Gaming Regulation Act	Allowed states to negotiate gaming rights to reservations
1990	Native American Graves and Repatriation Act	Returned Native remains to tribes with authentic claims
1990	Indian Arts and Crafts Act	Monitored authenticity of crafts
1994	American Indian Religious Freedom Act	Sought to protect tribal spirituality, including use of peyote

Much of the land initially deeded under the Allotment Act eventually came into the possession of White landowners. The land could not be sold legally, but it could be leased with the BIA serving as the trustee. In this role, the federal government took legal title that included the duty to collect on behalf of the tribal members any revenues generated by non–Indians through mining, oil, timber operations, grazing, or similar activities. The failure of the government to carry out this duty has been an issue for well over a century.

Large parcels of land eventually fell into the possession of non–Indians. For Native Americans who managed to retain the land, the BIA required that, upon the death of the owner, the land be divided equally among all descendants, regardless of tribal inheritance customs. In documented cases, this division resulted in as many as 30 people trying to live off an 80-acre plot of worthless land. By 1934, Native Americans had lost approximately 90 million of the 138 million acres in their possession before the Allotment Act. The land left was generally considered worthless for farming and marginal even for ranching (Blackfeet Reservation Development Fund 2006; Deloria and Lytle 1983).

The Reorganization Act

The assumptions behind the Allotment Act and the missionary activities of the nineteenth century were that it was best for Native Americans to assimilate into White society, and an individual was best considered apart from his or her tribal identity. Gradually, in the twentieth century, government officials have accepted the importance of tribal identity. The Indian Reorganization Act of 1934, known as the Wheeler-Howard Act, recognized the need to use, rather than ignore, tribal identity. But assimilation, rather than movement toward a pluralistic society, was still the goal.

Many provisions of the Reorganization Act, including revocation of the Allotment Act, benefited Native Americans. Still, given the legacy of broken treaties, many tribes at first distrusted the new policy. Under the Reorganization Act, tribes could adopt a written constitution and elect a tribal council with a head. This system imposed foreign values and structures. Under it, the elected tribal leader represented an entire reservation, which might include several tribes, some hostile to one another. Furthermore, the leader had to be elected by majority rule, a concept alien to many tribes. Many full-blooded Native Americans resented the provision that mixed-bloods had full voting rights. The Indian Reorganization Act did facilitate tribal dealings with government agencies, but the dictation to Native Americans of certain procedures common to White society and alien to the tribes was another sign of forced assimilation.

As was true of earlier government reforms, the Reorganization Act sought to assimilate Native Americans into the dominant society on the dominant group's terms. In this case, the tribes were absorbed within the political and economic structure of the larger society. Apart from the provision that tribal chairmen were to oversee reservations with several tribes, the Reorganization Act solidified tribal identity. Unlike the Allotment Act, it recognized the right of Native Americans to approve or reject some actions taken on their behalf. The act still maintained substantial non–Native American control over the reservations. As institutions, the tribal governments owed their existence not to their people but to the BIA. These tribal governments rested at the bottom of a large administrative hierarchy (Cornell 1984; Deloria 1971; McNickle 1973; Washburn 1984; Wax and Buchanan 1975).

Reservation Life and Federal Policies

Today, more than one-third of Native Americans live on 557 reservations and trust lands in 33 states, which account for a bit more than 2 percent of the land throughout the United States. Even for those Native Americans who reside far away from the tribal lands, the reservations play a prominent role in their identities (Figure 5.2).

More than any other segment of the population, with the exception of the military, a Native American living on the reservation finds his or her life determined by the federal government. From the condition of the roads, to the level of fire protection, to the quality of the schools, the federal government through such agencies as the BIA and the Public Health Service effectively controls reservation life. Tribes and their leaders are now consulted more than in the past, but ultimate decisions rest in Washington, DC, to a degree that is not true for the rest of the civilian population.

Many of the policies instituted by the BIA in the twentieth century were designed with giving tribal people more autonomy but final control resting with the federal government. Most Native Americans and their organizations do not quarrel with this goal. They may only wish that the government and the White people had never gotten into the Indians' business in the first place. Disagreement between the BIA and the tribes and among Native Americans themselves has focused on *how* to reduce federal control and subsidies, not on whether they *should be* reduced. The government has taken three steps in this direction since World War II. Two of these measures have been the formation of the Indian Claims Commission and the passage of the Termination Act. The following section shows how the third step, the Employment Assistance Program, has created a new meeting place for Native Americans in cities, far from their native homelands and the reservations.

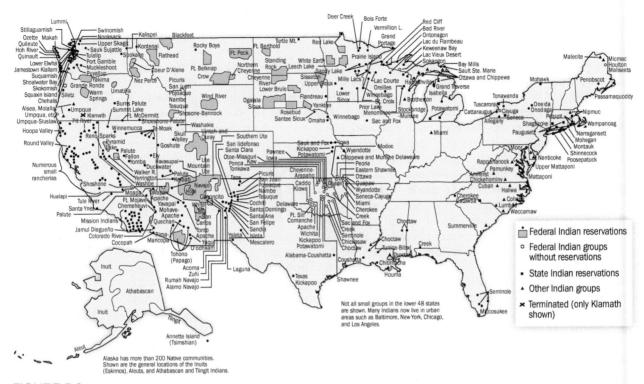

FIGURE 5.2
Native American Lands and Communities

Source: Bureau of Indian Affairs 1986:12–13.

Legal Claims

Native Americans have had a unique relationship with the federal government. As might be expected, little provision was ever made for them as individuals or tribes to bring grievances against the government. The U.S. Court of Federal Claims as well as Congress are now hearing cases and trying to resolve disputes.

In 1996, Elouise Cobell, a member of the Blackfeet tribe in Montana, brought a class-action lawsuit on behalf of a half-million American Indians, charging that the government had cheated them of billions of dollars in royalties under the trust arrangements created by the Allotment Act of 1887. The courts ruled that the BIA and other government agencies had extremely poor records even from recent times, much less going back in time. How difficult was the federal government defense in the *Cobell* case? The BIA shut down its website over fear that any information it gave out about almost anything could be wrong. The Department of Interior, by its own accounts, was spending more than $100 million annually in attempts to clean up the record keeping in a manner that will allow it to defend itself in court eventually. In late 2009, the federal government agreed to a settlement of $3.4 billion, including individual payments of at least $1,000 to 300,000 individual American Indians. Another similar case was settled in 2012 for just over $1 billion to 41 tribes for similar mismanagement (Hevesi 2011; T. Williams 2012a).

In specific land issues apart from the *Cobell* class action lawsuit, Native Americans often express a desire to recover their land rather than accept any financial settlements. After numerous legal decisions favoring the Sioux Indians, including a ruling of the U.S.

Watch the **Video** on **MySocLab**: *American Outrage*

Supreme Court, Congress finally agreed to pay $106 million for the land that was illegally seized in the aftermath of the Battle of the Little Big Horn. The Sioux rejected the money and lobbied for measures, such as the 1987 Black Hills Sioux Nation Act in Congress, to return the land to tribal authority. No positive action has yet been taken on these measures. In the meantime, however, the original settlement, the subsequent unaccepted payments, and the accrued interest brought the 2012 total of funds being held for the Sioux to more than $800 million. Despite the desperate need for housing, food, healthcare, and education, the Sioux would prefer to regain the land lost in the 1868 Fort Laramie Treaty and have not accepted payment (T. Williams 2012b).

The Termination Act

The Termination Act of 1953 initiated the most controversial government policy toward reservation Native Americans in the twentieth century. Like many such policies, the act originated in ideas that were meant to benefit Native Americans. The BIA commissioner, John Collier, had expressed concern in the 1930s over extensive government control of tribal affairs. In 1947, congressional hearings were held to determine which tribes had the economic resources to be relieved of federal control and assistance. The policy proposed at that time was an admirable attempt to give Native Americans greater autonomy while at the same time reducing federal expenditures, a goal popular among taxpayers.

The services the tribes received, such as subsidized medical care and college scholarships, should not have been viewed as special and deserving to be discontinued. These services were not the result of favoritism but merely fulfilled treaty obligations. The termination of the Native Americans' relationship to the government then came to be viewed by Native Americans as a threat to reduce services rather than a release from arbitrary authority. Native Americans might gain greater self-governance, but at a high price.

Unfortunately, the Termination Act as finally passed in 1953 emphasized reducing costs and ignored individual needs. Recommendations for a period of tax immunity were dropped. According to the act, federal services such as medical care, schools, and road equipment were supposed to be withdrawn gradually. Instead, when the Termination Act's provisions began to go into effect, federal services were stopped immediately, with minimal coordination between local government agencies and the tribes to determine whether the services could be continued by other means. The effect of the government orders on the Native Americans was disastrous, with major economic upheaval on the affected tribes, who could not establish some of the most basic services—such as road repair and fire protection—that the federal government had previously provided. The federal government resumed these services in 1975 with congressional action that signaled the end of another misguided policy intended to be good for tribal peoples (Deloria 1969; Ulrich 2010; Wax and Buchanan 1975).

Employment Assistance Program

The depressed economic conditions of reservation life might lead us to expect government initiatives to attract business and industry to locate on or near reservations. The government could provide tax incentives that would eventually pay for themselves. However, such proposals have not been advanced. Rather than take jobs to the Native Americans, the federal government decided to lead the more highly motivated away from the reservation. This policy has further devastated the reservations' economic potential.

In 1952, the BIA began programs to relocate young Native Americans to urban areas. One of these programs, after 1962, was called the Employment Assistance Program (EAP). The EAP's primary provision was for relocation, individually or in families, at government expense, to urban areas where job opportunities were greater than those on the reservations. The BIA stressed that the EAP was voluntary, but this was a fiction given the lack of viable economic alternatives open to American Indians. The program was not a success for the many Native Americans who found the urban experience unsuitable or unbearable. By 1965, one-fourth to one-third of the people in the EAP had returned to their home reservations. So great was the rate of return that in 1959 the BIA stopped releasing data on the percentage of returnees, fearing that they would give too much ammunition to critics of the EAP (Bahr 1972).

The movement of Native Americans into urban areas has had many unintended consequences. It has further reduced the labor force on the reservation. Those who leave tend to be better educated, creating the Native American version of the brain drain described in Chapter 4. Urbanization unquestionably contributed to the development of an intertribal network, or pan-Indian movement, which we describe later in this chapter. The city became the new meeting place of Native Americans, who learned of their common predicament both in the city and on the federally administered reservations. Government agencies also had to develop a policy of continued assistance to non-reservation Native Americans; despite such efforts, the problems of Native Americans in cities persist.

Collective Action

Native Americans have worked collectively through tribal or reservation government action and across tribal lines. As we noted in Chapter 1, the panethnic development of solidarity among ethnic subgroups has been reflected in the use of such terms as *Hispanic*, *Latino*, and *Asian American*. **Pan-Indianism** refers to intertribal social movements in which several tribes, joined by political goals but not by kinship, unite in a common identity. Today, these pan-Indian efforts are most vividly seen in cultural efforts and political protests of government policies (Cornell 1996; Jolivette 2008).

Proponents of these movements see the tribes as captive nations or even colonies. They generally see the enemy as the federal government. Until recently, pan-Indian efforts usually failed to overcome the cultural differences and distrust among tribal groups. However, some efforts to unite have succeeded. The Iroquois made up a six-tribe confederation dating back to the seventeenth century. The Ghost Dance briefly united the Plains tribes in the 1880s, some of which had earlier combined to resist the U.S. Army. But these were exceptions. It took nearly a century and a half of BIA policies to accomplish a significant level of unification.

The National Congress of American Indians (NCAI), founded in 1944 in Denver, Colorado, was the first national organization representing Native Americans. The NCAI registered itself as a lobby in Washington, DC, hoping to make the Native American perspective heard in the aftermath of the Reorganization Act described earlier. Concern about "White people's meddling" is reflected in the NCAI requirement that non–Indian members pay twice as much in dues. The NCAI has had its successes. Early in its history, it played an important role in creating the Indian Claims Commission, and it later pressured the BIA to abandon termination. It is still the most important civil rights organization for Native Americans and uses tactics similar to those of the NAACP, although the problems facing African Americans and Native Americans are legally and constitutionally different.

A later arrival was the more radical American Indian Movement (AIM), the most visible pan-Indian group. AIM was founded in 1968 by Clyde Bellecourt (of the White Earth Chippewa) and Dennis Banks (of the Pine Ridge Oglala Sioux), both of whom then lived in Minneapolis. Initially, AIM created a patrol to monitor police actions and document charges of police brutality. Eventually, it promoted programs for alcohol rehabilitation and school reform. By 1972, AIM was nationally known not for its neighborhood-based reforms but for its aggressive confrontations with the BIA and law enforcement agencies.

Protest Efforts

Fish-ins began in 1964 to protest interference by Washington State officials with Native Americans who were fishing, as they argued, in accordance with the 1854 Treaty of Medicine Creek, and were not subject to fine or imprisonment, even if they did violate White society's law. The fish-ins had protesters fishing en masse in restricted waterways. This protest was initially hampered by disunity and apathy, but several hundred Native Americans were convinced that civil disobedience was the only way to bring attention to their grievances with the government. Legal battles followed, and the U.S. Supreme Court confirmed the treaty rights in 1968. Other tribes continued to fight in the courts, but the fish-ins brought increased public awareness of the deprivations of Native Americans. These fishing rights battles continue today with the Chippewa in Wisconsin and Nez Perce in Idaho, among others (Bobo and Tuan 2006; D. Johnson 2005).

Most reservations today have a measure of self-government through an elected tribal. Pictured is the Navaho tribal council at work.

The fish-ins were only the beginning. After the favorable Supreme Court decision in 1968, other events followed in quick succession. In 1969, members of the San Francisco Indian Center seized Alcatraz Island in San Francisco Bay. The 13-acre island was an abandoned maximum-security federal prison, and the federal government was undecided about how to use it. The Native Americans claimed the "excess property" in exchange for $24 in glass beads and cloth, following the precedent set in the sale of Manhattan more than three centuries earlier. With no federal response and the loss of public interest in the demonstration, the protesters left the island more than a year later. The activists' desire to transform it into a Native American cultural center was ignored. Despite the outcome, the event gained international publicity for their cause. Red Power was born, and Native Americans who sympathized with the BIA were labeled *Uncle Tomahawks* or *apples* (red on the outside, white on the inside).

The most dramatic confrontation between Native Americans and the government happened in what came to be called the Battle of Wounded Knee II. In January 1973, AIM leader Russell Means led an unsuccessful drive to impeach Richard Wilson as tribal chairman of the Oglala Sioux tribe on the Pine Ridge Reservation. In the next month, Means, accompanied by some 300 supporters, started a 70-day occupation of Wounded Knee, South Dakota, site of the infamous cavalry assault in 1890 and now part of the Pine Ridge Reservation. The occupation received tremendous press coverage.

However, the coverage did not affect the outcome. Negotiations between AIM and the federal government on the occupation itself brought no tangible results. Federal prosecutions were initiated against most participants. AIM leaders Russell Means and Dennis Banks eventually faced prosecution on several felony charges, and both men were imprisoned. AIM had less visibility as an organization then. Russell Means wryly remarked in

1984, "We're not chic now. We're just Indians, and we have to help ourselves" (Hentoff 1984:23; see also Janisch 2008; Nagel 1988, 1996).

The most visible recent AIM activity has been its efforts to gain clemency for one of its leaders, Leonard Peltier. Imprisoned since 1976, Peltier was given two life sentences for murdering two FBI agents the year before on the embattled Sioux reservation of Pine Ridge, South Dakota. Fellow AIM leaders such as Dennis Banks organized a 1994 Walk for Justice to bring attention in Washington, DC, to the view that Peltier is innocent. This view was supported in two 1992 movie releases: the documentary *Incident at Oglala*, produced by Robert Redford; and the more entertaining but fictionalized *Thunderheart*. To date, clemency appeals to the president to lift the federal sentence have gone unheeded, but this issue remains the rallying point for today's remnants of AIM (Matthiessen 1991; Sandage 2008).

Collective Action: An Overview

Protest activities have created a greater solidarity among Native Americans as they seek solutions to common grievances with government agencies. Research shows that tribal people born since the collective action efforts of the 1960s are more likely to reject negative and stereotypic representations of American Indians than those born before the self-determination efforts. Whether through moderate groups such as the NCAI or the more activist AIM, these pan-Indian developments have awakened Whites to the real grievances of Native Americans and have garnered the begrudging acceptance of even the most conservative tribal members, who are more willing to cooperate with government action (Schulz 1998).

However, the results of collective action have not all been productive, even when viewed from a perspective sympathetic to Native American self-determination. Plains tribes dominate the national organizations, not only politically but also culturally. Powwow styles of dancing, singing, and costuming derived from the Plains tradition are

Powwows offer an opportunity for Native Americans from many tribes to gather for celebrations, competitive dancing and drumming, and selling goods and food.

spreading nationwide as common cultural traits (see Table 5.3 for the largest concentrations of Native Americans).

The growing visibility of **powwows** is symbolic of Native Americans in the 1990s. The phrase *pau wau* referred to the medicine man or spiritual leader of the Algonquian tribes, but Europeans who watched medicine men dance thought the word referred to entire events. Over the last hundred years, powwows have evolved into gatherings in which Native Americans of many tribes come to dance, sing, play music, and visit. More recently, they have become organized events featuring competitions and prizes at several thousand locations. The general public sees them as entertainment, but for Native Americans, they are a celebration of their cultures (Eschbach and Applebaum 2000).

American Indian Identity

Today, American Indian identity occurs on two levels: macro and micro. At the macro level is the recognition of tribes; at the micro level is how individuals view themselves as American Indian and how this perception is recognized.

Sovereignty

Sovereignty in this context refers to tribal self-rule. Supported by every U.S. president since the 1960s, sovereignty is recognition that tribes have vibrant economic and cultural lives. At the same time, numerous legal cases, including many at the Supreme Court level, continue to clarify to what extent a recognized tribe may rule itself and to what degree it is subject to state and federal laws. In 2004, the U.S. Supreme Court ruled 7–2 in *United States v. Lara* that a tribe has the inherent right to prosecute all American Indians, regardless of affiliation, for crimes that occur on the reservation. However, other cases in lower courts continue to chip away at tribal self-government.

This legal relationship can be quite complex. For example, tribal members always pay federal income, Social Security, unemployment, and property taxes but do not pay state income tax if they live and work only on the reservation. Whether tribal members on reservations pay sales, gasoline, cigarette, or motor vehicle taxes has been negotiated on a reservation-by-reservation basis in many states.

Focused on the tribal group, sovereignty remains linked to both the actions of the federal government and the actions of individual American Indians. The government ultimately determines which tribes are recognized, and although tribal groups may argue publicly for their recognition, self-declaration carries no legal recognition. This has always been an issue, but given the rise of casino gambling (discussed shortly), the determination of who constitutes a sovereign tribe and who does not may carry significant economic benefits.

The federal government takes this gatekeeping role of sovereignty very seriously— the irony of the conquering people determining who are "Indians" is not lost on many

TABLE 5.3	
Largest American Indian Groupings	
Reservations	
1. Navajo (AZ, NM, UT)	169,321
2. Pine Ridge (SO, NE)	16,906
3. Fort Apache (AZ)	13,014
4. Gila River (AZ)	11,251
5. Osage (OK)	9,920
6. San Carlos (AZ)	9,901
7. Rosebud (SD)	9,809
8. Tohono O'oodham (AZ)	9,278
9. Blackfeet (MT)	9,149
10. Flathead (MT)	9,138
Tribes	
1. Navajo	286,731
2. Cherokee	284,247
3. Ojibwa/Chippewa	112,757
4. Sioux	112,176
5. Choctaw	103,916
6. Apache	63,193
7. Lumbee	62,306
8. Pueblo	49,695
9. Creek	48,352
10. Iroquois	40,570
Cities	
1. New York City	111,749
2. Los Angeles	54, 236
3. Phoenix	43,724
4. Oklahoma City	36,572
5. Anchorage	36,062
6. Tulsa	35,990
7. Albuquerque	32,571
8. Chicago	26,933
9. Houston	25,521
10. San Antonio	20,137

Source: 2010 Census in Norris, Vines, and Hoeffel 2012: Tables 4, 6, 7.

Explore the Activity on MySocLab: *Native Americans*

tribal activists. In 1978, the Department of the Interior established what it called the *acknowledgment process* to decide whether any more tribes should have a government-to-government relationship. They must show that they were a distinct group and trace continuity since 1900 (Light and Rand 2007).

Individual Identity

Most people reflect on their ancestry to find roots or to self-identify themselves. For an individual who perceives himself or herself to be an American Indian, the process is defined by legalistic language. Recognized tribes establish a standard of ancestry, or what some tribes call "blood quantum," to determine who is a tribal member or "enrolled," as on the "tribal rolls." Understandably, there is some ambivalence about this procedure because it applies some racial purity measures. Still, tribes see it as an important way to guard against potential "wannabes" (Fitzgerald 2008).

This process may lead some individuals or entire extended families to be disenrolled. For these people, who perceive themselves as worthy of recognition by a tribe but are denied this coveted "enrollment" status, disputes have resulted that are rarely resolved satisfactorily for all parties. This has occurred for generations but has become more contentious recently for tribes that profit from casino gambling and must determine who is entitled to share in any profits that could be distributed to those on tribal rolls (Russell 2011).

Native Americans Today

Read the Document
on MySocLab: *Native American Mascots: What Social Science Tells Us*

The United States has taken most of the land originally occupied by or deeded to Native Americans, restricted their movement, unilaterally severed agreements, created a special legal status for them, and, after World War II, attempted to move them again. As a result of these efforts and generally poor economic conditions of most reservations, substantial numbers of Native Americans live in the nation's most populated urban areas. In Table 5.4, we provide some broad comparisons between the First Americans and the general population of the 50 states.

How are Native Americans treated today? A very public insult is the continuing use of American Indian names as mascots for athletic teams, including high schools, colleges,

TABLE 5.4 A Snapshot: Native Americans		
	Total Population	Native Americans
Average Family Size	3.17	3.62
Never Married	34.2%	44.2%
High School Graduates	85.0	76.6
College Graduates	27.9	13.0
Veterans	9.9	9.3
Born in United States	85.9%	93.0%
Unemployment Rate (2010)	5.1	12.9
Median Household Income	$51,914	$36,779
Families below Poverty Level	10.1%	22.1%

Source: Bureau of the Census, 2006–2010 American Community Survey American Indian and Alaska Native Tables DP02 and DP03.

and many professional sports teams in the United States. Almost all American Indian organizations, including AIM, have brought attention to the insulting use of Native Americans as the mascots of sports teams, such as the Washington Redskins, and to such spectator practices as the "Tomahawk chop" associated with the Atlanta Braves baseball team.

Many sports fans and college alumni find it difficult to understand why Native Americans take offense at a name such as "Braves" or even "Redskins" if it is meant to represent a team about which they have positive feelings. For Native Americans, however, the use of such mascots trivializes their past and their presence today. This at best puzzles if not infuriates most Native people, who already face several challenges today. The National Collegiate Athletic Association (NCAA), which oversees college athletics, has asked colleges to "explain" their use of mascot names, nicknames, or logos such as savages, braves, warriors, chieftains, redmen, and Indians, to name a few. In some cases, the NCAA has already banned the appearance of students dressed as such mascots in tournaments. Typically, college alumni and most students wonder what the fuss is about, while most Native people question why they should be so "honored" if they don't want to be (NCAA 2003a, 2003b; Wieberg 2006).

While it is easy and common to focus on problems with Native Americans, the vibrancy of native cultures should not be ignored. In "Speaking Out", film director and producer Chris Eyre (Cheyenne and Arapaho) speaks to the vibrancy of spirit he sees among Native Americans, especially among the youth.

Read the Document
on MySocLab: *Names,
Logos, Mascots, and
Flags: The Contradictory
Uses of Sport Symbols*

((🎙)) Speaking Out

Powwows and Karaoke

My daughter and I watch in fascination as an enormous grayish-purple cloud sweeps over the golden-brown rolling hills of the plains, cascades through the expansive sky and merges with the yellow horizon.

At that moment, I'm awe-struck by the power of the season changing from winter to spring, and I realize the spectacle would not be as beautiful without the dark gray cloud on the horizon.

I'm always inspired by the rebirth of the seasons. After I was born to my biological mother, Rose, of the Southern Cheyenne and Arapaho tribes, I was reborn within days to my adopted parents, Barb and Earl, in a white middle-class home in Klamath Falls, Oregon. As a dark-skinned 5-year-old, I would ask my mom what I was going to be when I grew up.

"Anything you want!" she said.

"A fireman?"

"Yes!"

"What about the president?"

Chris Eyre

"Yes!" she lied, lovingly. Or perhaps she had the foresight 30 years ago to think there would be a minority president.

As a Native American raised in a white environment, I have never seen things in black and white but always in many colors and shades of gray. I love singing country and western songs at karaoke, but I also love a good powwow and fry bread. Over the years, my work as an artist has always been about bridging the gap between the white world and the Native world. I then realized that it had already been done. There have been "Indian rednecks" for years.

I came to appreciate through my work that there are good people in both the Native and non-Native world. Though I also found that the American dream usually didn't include my people, the Natives. For example, religious freedom for Natives to practice their own traditions was not legally upheld until 1994.

(continued)

In the next 40 years, the greatest threat to Native tribal culture and tradition will be the American consumer ethic of personal economic gain at all costs. It runs deeply counter to the spirit of giving and codependence that is central to what we are as people.

As more Native Americans participate in the wider economy through business initiatives such as gaming, we will also struggle with assimilation, a force that we have fought over the years. It was only about 20 years ago that the public at large allowed Indian gaming as a way to give back to the Indians. Ten years ago, I remember seeing a Native kid at a Southern California powwow driving his parents' Hummer. A minority of tribes and their reservations have prospered from Indian gaming, but most still live in the same dire conditions.

Marginal cultures in the past have rightfully entered the mainstream through business, taking money from the majority and infusing it into their own tribes. It happened with Latinos, Asians and now Natives. It's the American way. My greatest fear is that after all these years largely as non-participants in the American dream, our inclusion will ultimately kill off tribal languages, traditions and our knowledge.

Today, it is inspiring to see the number of strong Native American youth eager to learn more of our ancient traditions and cultures from the elders, who are more than happy to share with those who respect them. The youth renaissance is rooted, I think, in the elders' tenacity, 1970s activism and a backlash against the mass media's depiction of Native Americans.

The dismal portrayal of Native reservations is inaccurate and harmful. The media focus solely on poverty and the cycle of oppression. What most outsiders don't see is the laughter, love, smiles, constant joking and humor and the unbreakable strength of the tribal spirit that is there. Some reservations are strongholds of community, serving the needs of their people without economic gain but with traditions leading the way. My hope is that Native evolution will be driven by a reinforced traditionalism passed down from one to another.

There is a calling not taught in religion or school; it is in one's heart. It is what the tribe is about: to give to the cycle; to provide for those older and younger. My daughter knows it, just as she knows the natural beauty of seeing the clouds coming in the spring.

I love the gray rain.

Source: Eyre 2010.

Any discussion of Native American socioeconomic status today must begin with emphasizing the diversity of the people. Besides the variety of tribal heritages already noted, the contemporary Native American population is split between those on and off reservations and those who live in small towns or central cities. Life in these contrasting social environments is quite different, but enough similarities exist to warrant some broad generalizations on the status of Native Americans in the United States.

The sections that follow summarize the status of contemporary Native Americans in economic development, education, healthcare, religious and spiritual expression, and the environment.

Economic Development

Native Americans are an impoverished people. Even to the most casual observer of a reservation, poverty is a living reality, not merely numbers and percentages. Some visitors seem unconcerned, arguing that because Native Americans are used to hardship and lived a simple life before the Europeans arrived, poverty is a familiar and traditional way of life. In an absolute sense of dollars earned or quality of housing, Native Americans are no worse off now. But in a relative sense that compares their position with that of non–Indians, they are dismally behind on all standards of income and occupational status. Bureau of Indian Affairs (2005) surveys show that overall unemployment is about 50 percent.

Given the lower incomes and higher poverty rates, it is not surprising that the occupational distribution of Native Americans is similarly bleak. Those who are employed are less likely to be managers, professionals, technicians, salespeople, or administrators. This pattern of low-wage employment is typical of many racial and ethnic minorities in the United States, but Native Americans differ in three areas: their roles in tourism, casino gambling, and government employment.

Tourism Tourism is an important source of employment for many reservation residents, who either serve the needs of visitors directly or sell souvenirs and craft items. Generally, such enterprises do not achieve the kind of success that improves the tribal economy significantly. Even if they did, sociologist Murray Wax (1971:69) argued, "It requires a special type of person to tolerate exposing himself and his family life to the gaze of tourists, who are often boorish and sometimes offensively condescending in their attitudes."

Tourism, in light of exploitation of tribal people, is a complex interaction of the outside with Native Americans. Interviews with tourists visiting museums and reservations found that, regardless of the presentation, many visitors interpreted their brief experiences to be consistent with their previously held stereotypes of and prejudices toward Native Americans. Yet, at the other extreme, some contemporary tourists conscious of the historical context are uncomfortable taking in Native foods and purchasing crafts at tribal settlements despite the large economic need many reservations have for such commerce (Laxson 1991; Padget 2004).

Craftwork rarely produces the profits that most Native Americans desire and need. The trading-post business has also taken its toll on Native American cultures. Many non–Indian craft workers have produced the items tourists want. Creativity and authenticity often are replaced by mechanical duplication of "genuine Indian" curios. Concern and controversy continue to surround art such as paintings and pottery that may not be produced by real Native Americans. In 1935, the federal government began to officially promote tribal arts. The influx of fraudulent crafts was so great that Congress added to its responsibilities the Indian Arts and Crafts Act in 1990, which severely punishes anyone who offers to sell an object as produced by a Native American artisan when it was not. The price of both economic and cultural survival is very high (Indian Arts and Crafts Board 2013).

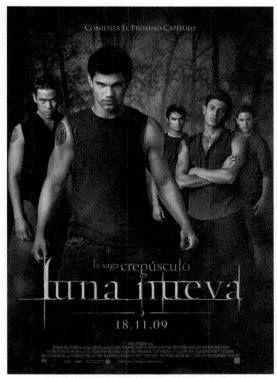

Shown here is the Spanish language version of a promotion for New Moon released in 2009. Perhaps one of the strangest tourist developments has been people trying to experience the four-book and movie series by seeking out the Quileute Nation in Washington State. Numbering only 750, this tribe is the subject of the fictionalized account of Native Americans who shapeshift into wolves as enemies of vampires. Tourists receive a hospitable welcome from tribal members who show off their picturesque rainforest location and a museum exhibit called "The Real Wolves of the Quileute."

Casino Gambling A recent source of significant income and some employment has been the introduction of gambling on reservations. Some forms of gambling, originally part of tribal ceremonies or celebrations, existed long before Europeans arrived in the Western hemisphere. Today, however, commercial gambling is the only viable source of employment and revenue available to several tribes.

Under the 1988 Indian Gaming Regulatory Act, states must negotiate gambling agreements with reservations and cannot prohibit any gambling already allowed under state law. By 2010, 239 tribal governments in 28 states were operating a variety of gambling operations, including off-track betting, casino tables such as blackjack and roulette, lotteries, sports betting, video games of chance, telephone betting, slot machines, and high-stakes bingo. The gamblers, almost all non–Native Americans, sometimes travel long distances for the opportunity to wager money. The actual casinos are a form of tribal government enterprise as opposed to private business operations.

The economic impact on some reservations has been enormous, and nationwide receipts amounted to $26.7 billion in 2010 from reservation casino operations—more than Las Vegas and Atlantic City combined. However, the wealth is uneven: About two-thirds of the

Read the Document on MySocLab: *Playing the Political Slots: American Indians and Casinos*

recognized Indian tribes have no gambling ventures. A few successful casinos have led to staggering windfalls, but reliance on a single industry can prove deadly as in the recent recession when the gaming industry in general, and on reservations, took a major hit (Meister 2012).

The more typical picture is of moderately successful gambling operations associated with tribes whose social and economic needs are overwhelming. Tribes that have opened casinos have experienced drops in unemployment and increases in household income not seen on nongaming reservations. However, three important factors must be considered:

1. The tribes do pay taxes. They pay $10 billion in gambling-generated taxes to local, state, and federal governments. That still leaves significant profits that can be paid to tribal members or reinvested in collective tribal operations.

2. Nationwide, the economic and social impact of this revenue is limited. The tribes that make substantial revenue from gambling are a small fraction of Native American people.

3. Even on the reservations that benefit from gambling enterprises, the levels of unemployment are substantially higher and the family income significantly lower than for the nation as a whole (Bartlett and Steele 2002; Katel 2006:365; Meister 2011; National Indian Gaming Association 2006; Sahagun 2004; Taylor and Kalt 2005).

Criticism is not hard to find, even among Native Americans, some of whom oppose gambling on moral grounds and because it is marketed in a form that is incompatible with Native American cultures. Opponents are concerned about the appearance of compulsive gambling among some tribal members. The majority of the gamblers are not Native Americans, and almost all of the reservation casinos, though owned by the tribes, are operated by non–Indian-owned businesses. Some tribal members feel that the casinos trivialize and cheapen their heritage. The issue of who shares in gambling profits also has led to heated debates in some tribal communities about who is a member of the tribe. In addition, established White gaming interests lobby Congress to restrict the tribes, which account for about 29 percent of total gaming revenue, so they do not compete with non-reservation casinos (Tensing 2011).

Native Americans' voting clout is very weak, even compared to that of African Americans and Latinos, but their lobbying power has become significant. Casino money fueled the 2006 scandal involving lobbyist Jack Abramoff, who cheated several tribes by pretending to lobby on their behalf. Although many of the political donations Native Americans make are aimed at protecting reservation casinos, tribes' political agendas include obtaining federal grants for education, roads, housing, and other projects. By the 2007–2008 election cycle, tribes with casinos accounted for four of the top donors nationwide (Capriccioso 2011b).

Although income from gambling has not dramatically changed the lifestyle of most Native Americans, it has been a magnet of criticism from outsiders. Critics question the special status afforded to Native Americans and contend that the playing field should be even. Tribal members certainly would endorse this view because most government policies over the last 200 years placed tribes at a major disadvantage. Attention is drawn to some tribes that made contributions to politicians involved in policies concerning gambling laws. Although some contributions may have been illegal, the national media attention was far more intense than was warranted in the messy area of campaign financing. In 2012, tribes made over $3.25 million in contributions to the presidential campaigns—ten times that just four years earlier. It is another example of how the notion that Native Americans are now playing the White man's game of capitalism "too well" becomes big news (Gold and Tanfani 2012).

We have examined sources of economic development such as tourism and legalized gambling, but the dominant feature of reservation life is, nevertheless, unemployment. A government report issued by the Full Employment Action Council opened with the statement that such words as *severe, massive,* and *horrendous* are appropriate to describe unemployment among Native Americans. Official unemployment figures for reservations range from 23 percent to 90 percent. It is little wonder that census data released in 2010 showed that the poorest county in the nation was wholly on tribal lands: Ziebach County, South Dakota, of the Cheyenne River Reservation, had a 62 percent poverty rate. Two of the other poorest six were defined by the Pine Ridge and Rosebud Reservations. The other poor counties were either in the devastated Gulf Coast area or defined largely by a prison facility (Joseph 2010).

The economic outlook for Native Americans need not be bleak. A single program is not the solution; the diversity of Native Americans and their problems demands a multifaceted approach. The solutions need not be unduly expensive; indeed, because the Native American population is very small compared with the total population, programs with major influence may be financed without significant federal expenditures. Murray Wax (1971) observed that reformers viewing the economically depressed position of Native Americans often seize on education as the key to success. As the next section shows, improving educational programs for Native Americans would be a good place to start.

Education

Government involvement in the education of Native Americans dates as far back as a 1794 treaty with the Oneida Indians. In the 1840s, the federal government and missionary groups combined to start the first school for American Indians. By 1860, the government was operating schools that were free of missionary involvement. Today, laws prohibit federal funds for Native American education from going to sectarian schools. Also, since the passage of the Johnson-O'Malley Act in 1934, the federal government has reimbursed public school districts that include Native American children.

Federal control of the education of Native American children has had mixed results from the beginning. Several tribes started their own school systems at the beginning of the nineteenth century, financing the schools themselves. The Cherokee tribe developed an extensive school system that taught both English and Cherokee, the latter using an alphabet developed by the famed leader Sequoyah. Literacy for the Cherokees was estimated by the mid-1800s at 90 percent, and they even published a bilingual newspaper. The Creek, Chickasaw, and Seminole also maintained school systems. But by the end of the nineteenth century, all these schools had been closed by federal order. Not until the 1930s did the federal government become committed to ensuring an education for Native American children. Despite the push for educational participation, by 1948 only one-quarter of the children on the Navajo reservation, the nation's largest, were attending school (Pewewardy 1998).

A serious problem in Native American education has been the unusually low level of enrollment. Nationwide, about 15 percent of 16- to 24-year-olds Native Americans were high school dropouts compared to 6.4 among Whites of a similar age. The term *dropout* is misleading because many tribal American schoolchildren have found their educational experience so hostile that they have no choice but to leave. In 2005, the South Dakota Supreme Court ruled that a school serving the Lakota Sioux tribe was routinely calling in the police to deal with the slightest misbehavior. The youth soon developed a juvenile record leading to what was termed a "school-to-discipline pipeline" (Dell'Angela 2005; DeVoe et al. 2008).

Rosalie Wax (1967) conducted a detailed study of the education among the Sioux on the Pine Ridge Reservation of South Dakota. She concluded that terms such as **kickout** or **pushout** are more appropriate than *dropout.* The children are not so much hostile toward school as they are set apart from it; they are socialized by their parents to be independent and not to embarrass their peers, but teachers reward docile acceptance and expect schoolchildren to correct one another in public. Socialization is not all that separates home from school. Teachers often are happy to find that Native American parents do not "interfere" with their job. Parents do not visit the school, and teachers avoid the homes, a pattern that furthers the isolation of school from home. This lack of interaction results partly from the predominance of non–Native American teachers, many of whom do not recognize the learning styles of American Indian students, although the situation is improving (Hilberg and Tharp 2002).

Do Native Americans see a curriculum that, at the very least, considers the unique aspects of their heritage? It is hoped things have changed since Charles Silberman (1971:173) visited a sixth-grade English class in a school on a Chippewa reservation. The students there were busy writing a composition for Thanksgiving: "Why We Are Happy the Pilgrims Came." Evidence of having Native cultures in the curriculum is uneven. Among teachers of eighth-graders, about one in four reports such presentations more than once a month in any subject among those attending schools that are at least one-fourth American (DeVoe et al. 2008). In Research Focus, we consider the importance of incorporating native teachings and cultures on the largest American Indian reservation.

The picture for Native Americans in higher education is decidedly mixed, with some progress and some promise. Enrollment in college increased steadily from the mid-1970s through the beginning of the twenty-first century, but degree completion, especially the completion of professional degrees, may be declining. The economic and educational backgrounds of Native American students, especially reservation residents, make the

Research Focus

Learning the Navajo Way

"Diné bizaad beeyashti!" Unfortunately, teachers do not commonly hear this declaration of "I speak Navajo!" So what leads to academic success? Often the answer is a supportive family, but this has not always been said about Native Americans. Educators rooted in the European education traditions often argue that American Indian families whose children are faithful to the traditional cultures cannot succeed in schools. This assimilationist view argues that to succeed in larger White-dominated society, it is important to start shedding the "old ways" as soon as possible. It is interesting that research done in the last 10 years has questioned the assimilationist view, concluding that American Indian students can improve their academic performance through educational programs that are less assimilationist and use curricula that build on what the Native American youth learn in their homes and communities.

Representative of this growing research is the study completed by sociologist Angela A. A. Willeto among her fellow Navajo tribal people. She studied a random sample of 451 Navajo high school students from 11 different Navajo Nation schools. She examined the impact of the students' orientation toward traditional Navajo culture on their performance. The prevailing view has been that all that is inherently Navajo in a child must be eliminated and replaced with mainstream White society beliefs and lifestyles.

The Navajo tradition was measured by a number of indicators, such as participating in Navajo dances, consulting a medicine man, entering a sweat bath to cleanse oneself spiritually, weaving rugs, living in a traditional hogan, and using the Navajo language. School performance was measured by grades, commitment to school, and aspirations to attend college. Willeto found that the students who lived a more traditional life among the Navajo succeeded in school just as well and were just as committed to success in school and college as high schoolers leading a more assimilated life.

Today, the Navajo Nation's Department of Dine' Education promotes embracing the past. For example, in 2012, Barboncito held a competition with students reading an 1868 speech. In his speech, the Navajo leader spoke boldly to General Tecumseh Sherman, whom President Andrew Johnson had dispatched to secure the Navajo's agreement to a treaty. Students were invited to write an essay or prepare a painting that indicated what the speech meant to them in 2012.

These results are important because many Native Americans accept an assimilationist view. Even within the Navajo Nation, where Navajo language instruction has been mandated in all reservation schools since 1984, many Navajos still equate learning only with the mastery of White society's subject matter.

Sources: Department of Dine' Education 2012; Reyhner 2001; Willeto 1999, 2007.

prospect of entering a predominantly White college very difficult. Native American students may soon feel isolated and discouraged, particularly if the college does not help them understand the alien world of American-style higher education. Even at campuses with large numbers of Native Americans in their student bodies, only a few Native American faculty members or advisors are present to serve as role models.

Another encouraging development in higher education in recent years has been the creation of tribally controlled colleges, usually two-year community colleges. The Navajo Community College (now called Diné College), the first such institution, was established in 1968, and by 2012 there were 37 tribal colleges in 14 states, with more than 16,000 students enrolled. Besides serving in some rural areas as the only educational institution for many miles, these colleges also provide services such as counseling and childcare. Tribal colleges enable students to maintain their cultural identity while training them to succeed, which means helping with job placement—a major challenge given the economic situation that most tribal colleges find in their immediate vicinity (American Indian Higher Education Consortium 2012; González 2012).

At higher levels, Native Americans largely disappear from the educational scene. In 2009, of the over 50,000 doctorates awarded to U.S. citizens, 332 went to Native Americans, compared with over 16,000 that went to citizens of foreign countries. This achievement of doctorates among Native Americans has not changed significantly since at least as far back as 1981 (National Center for Educational Statistics 2012).

Healthcare

For Native Americans, *healthcare* is a misnomer, another broken promise in the long line of unmet pledges the government has made. Compared to other groups, Native Americans are more likely to have poorer health and unmet medical needs and not be able to afford healthcare. They more likely have higher levels of diabetes, trouble hearing, and activity limitations and have experienced serious psychological distress (Frieden 2011).

In 1955, amidst criticism even then, the responsibility for healthcare through the Indian Health Service (IHS) transferred from the BIA to the Public Health Service. Although the health of Native Americans has improved markedly in absolute terms since the mid-1960s, their overall health is comparatively far behind all other segments of the population. With a new administration in 2009, yet another call was made for overhauling healthcare provided to Native Americans. With the pressure toward Native Americans to assimilate in all aspects of their lives, there has been little willingness to recognize their traditions of healing and treating illnesses. Native treatments tend to be noninvasive, with the patient encouraged to contribute actively to the healing benefits and prevent future recurrence. In the 1990s, a pluralistic effort was slowly emerging to recognize alternative forms of medicine, including those practiced by Native Americans. In addition, reservation healthcare workers began to accommodate traditional belief systems as they administered the White culture's medicine (Belluck 2009).

Read the Document on MySocLab: *Rape and the War against Native Women*

Contributing to the problems of healthcare and mortality on reservations are often high rates of crime, not all of which is reported. For tribal people along the Mexico–U.S. border, the rising amount and associated violence in the drug trade have only furthered their vulnerability. Poverty and few job opportunities offer a fertile environment for the growth of youth gangs and drug trafficking. All the issues associated with crime can be found on the nation's reservations. As with other minority communities dealing with poverty, Native Americans strongly support law enforcement but at the same time contend that the very individuals selected to protect them are abusing their people. As with efforts for improving healthcare, the isolation and vastness of some of the reservations make them uniquely vulnerable to crime (Eckholm 2010).

Religious and Spiritual Expression

Like other aspects of Native American cultures, religious expression is diverse, reflecting the variety of tribal traditions and the assimilationist pressure of the Europeans. Initially, missionaries and settlers expected Native Americans simply to forsake their traditions for European Christianity, and, as was the case in the repression of the Ghost Dance, sometimes force was used. Today, many Protestant churches and Roman Catholic parishes with large tribal congregations incorporate customs such as the sacred pipe ceremony, native incenses, sweat lodges, ceremonies affirming care for the Earth, and services and hymns in native languages.

Whether traditional in nature or reflecting the impact of Europeans, Native people typically embrace a broad world of spirituality. Whereas Christians, Jews, and Muslims adhere to a single deity and often confine spiritual expression to designated sites, traditional American Indian people see considerably more relevance in the whole of the world, including animals, water, and the wind.

After generations of formal and informal pressure to adopt Christian faiths and their rituals, in 1978, Congress enacted the American Indian Religious Freedom Act, which declares that it is the government's policy to "protect and preserve the inherent right of American Indians to believe, express, and practice their traditional religions." However, the act contains no penalties or enforcement mechanisms. For this reason, Hopi leader Vernon Masayesva (1994:93) calls it "the law with no teeth." Therefore, Native Americans are lobbying to strengthen this 1978 legislation. They are seeking protection for religious worship services for military personnel and incarcerated Native Americans, as well as better access to religious relics, such as eagle feathers, and better safeguards against the exploitation of sacred lands (Deloria 1992; Garroutte et al. 2009).

A major spiritual concern is the stockpiling of Native American relics, including burial remains. Contemporary Native Americans are increasingly seeking the return of their ancestors' remains and artifacts, a demand that alarms museums and archeologists. The Native American Graves Protection and Repatriation Act of 1990 requires an inventory of such collections and provides for the return of materials if a claim can be substantiated. In 2010, this was revised to cover all Native American remains—even those without identified ties to a tribe (J. Smith 2011).

In recent years, significant publicity has been given to a Native American expression of religion: the ritual use of peyote, which dates back thousands of years. The sacramental use of peyote was first noted by Europeans in the 1640s. In 1918, the religious use of peyote, a plant that creates mild psychedelic effects, was organized as the Native American Church (NAC). At first a Southwest-based religion, since World War II, the NAC has spread among northern tribes. The use of the substance is a small part of a long and moving ritual. The exact nature of NAC rituals varies widely. Clearly, the church maintains the tradition of ritual curing and seeking individual visions. However, practitioners also embrace elements of Christianity, representing a type of religious pluralism of Indian and European identities.

Peyote is a hallucinogen, however, and federal and state governments have been concerned about its use by NAC members. Several states passed laws in the 1920s and 1930s prohibiting the use of peyote. In the 1980s, several court cases involved the prosecution of Native Americans who were using peyote for religious purposes. Finally, in 1994, Congress amended the American Indian Religious Freedom Act to allow Native Americans the right to use, transport, and possess peyote for religious purposes (J. Martin 2001).

Today's Native Americans are asking that their traditions be recognized as an expression of pluralist rather than assimilationist coexistence. These traditions also are closely tied to religion. The sacred sites of Native Americans, as well as their religious practices, have been under attack. In the next section, we focus on aspects of environmental disputes that are anchored in the spiritualism of Native Americans (Kinzer 2000; Mihesuah 2000).

Environment

Environmental issues bring together many of the concerns we have previously considered for Native Americans: stereotyping, land rights, environmental justice, economic development, and spiritualism.

First, in some of today's environmental literature, we can find stereotypes of Native peoples as the last defense against the encroachment of "civilization." This image trivializes native cultures, making them into what one author called a "New Age savage" (Waller 1996).

Second, many environmental issues are rooted in continuing land disputes arising from treaties and agreements more than a century old. Reservations contain a wealth of natural resources and scenic beauty. In the past, Native Americans often lacked the technical knowledge to negotiate beneficial agreements with private corporations—and even when they had this ability, the federal government often stepped in and made the final agreements more beneficial to the non–Native Americans than to the residents of the reservations. The Native peoples have always been rooted in their land. It was their land that was the first source of tension and conflict with the Europeans. At the beginning of the twenty-first century, it is no surprise that land and the natural resources it holds continue to be major concerns. This does not mean that tribal governments are not willing to embrace new technologies. For example, some Plains American Indian tribes are starting to create wind farms that not only provide power for their own needs but also even allow them to sell extra power (Standen 2010).

Third, environmental issues reinforce the tendency to treat the first inhabitants of the Americas as inferior. This is manifested in **environmental justice**—a term introduced in Chapter 3 to describe efforts to ensure that hazardous substances are controlled so that all communities receive protection regardless of race or socioeconomic circumstances. Reservation representatives often express concern about how their lands are used as dumping grounds. For example, the Navajo reservation is home to hundreds of abandoned uranium mines—some are still contaminated. After legal action, the federal government finally provided assistance in 2000 to Navajos who had worked in the mines and showed ill effects from radiation exposure. Although compensation has been less than was felt necessary, the Navajos continue to monitor closely new proposals to use their land. Few reservations have escaped negative environmental impact, and some observers contend that Native American lands are targeted for nuclear waste storage. Critics see this as a de facto policy of nuclear colonialism, whereby reservations are forced to accept all the hazards of nuclear energy, but the Native American people have seen few of its benefits (Macmillan 2012).

Fourth, environmental concerns by American Indians often are balanced against economic development needs, just as they are in the larger society. On some reservations, authorizing timber companies access to hardwood forests led to conflicted feelings among American Indians. However, such arrangements often are the only realistic source of needed revenue, even if they mean entering into arrangements that more affluent people would never consider. The Skull Valley Goshute tribe of Utah has tried to attract a nuclear waste dump over state government objections.

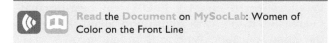

Read the Document on MySocLab: Women of Color on the Front Line

The Hualapai (WALL-uh-pie) in the remote Grand Canyon area outside the National Park have long suffered extreme economic poverty. In an effort to overcome this, they commissioned to build this for tourists over the canyon wall offering an amazing view. However, to some observers, it represents an assault on the environment. In response, Native Americans say they should be able to take advantage of the land at times, just like the White man has for centuries.

Eventually, the federal government rejected the tribe's plans. Even on the Navajo reservation, a proposed new uranium mine has its supporters—those who consider the promises of royalty payments coupled with alleged safety measures sufficient to offset the past half-century of radiation problems (Pasternak 2010).

Fifth, spiritual needs must be balanced against demands on the environment. For example, numerous sacred sites lie in such public areas as the Grand Canyon, Zion, and Canyonlands National Parks that, though not publicized, are accessible to outsiders. Tribal groups have in vain sought to restrict entry to such sites. The San Carlos Apaches unsuccessfully tried to block the University of Arizona from erecting an observatory on their sacred Mt. Graham. Similarly, Plains Indians have sought to ban tourists from climbing Devil's Tower, long the site of religious visions, where prayer bundles of tobacco and sage were left behind by Native peoples (Campbell 2008; Martin 2001).

Conclusion

Native Americans have to choose between assimilating to the dominant non–Indian culture and maintaining their identity. In the figure on the next page, we revisit the Spectrum of Intergroup Relations as it relates to Native Americans. Recently, some pluralism is evident, but the desire to improve themselves economically usually drives Native Americans toward assimilation.

Are Native Americans now receiving respect? People cheered on May 1, 2011 on hearing that Osama bin Laden was found and killed. However, the always-patriotic American Indian people were very troubled to learn that the military had assigned the code name *Geronimo* to the operation to capture the terrorist. The Chiricahua Apache of New Mexico were particularly disturbed to learn the name of their freedom fighter was being associated with a global terrorist. In response, the U.S. Defense Department said no disrespect was meant to Native Americans. But, of course, one can imagine that the operation never would have been named "Operation Lafayette" or "Operation Jefferson."

Maintaining one's tribal identity outside a reservation is not easy. One's cultural heritage must be consciously sought out while under the pressure to assimilate. Even on a reservation, it is not easy to integrate being Native American with elements of contemporary society. The dominant society needs innovative approaches to facilitate pluralism.

The reservations are economically depressed, but they also are the home of the Native American people spiritually and ideologically, if not always physically.

Furthermore, the reservation isolation means that the frustrations of reservation life and the violent outbursts regarding those frustrations do not alarm large numbers of Whites, as do disturbances in urban centers. Native Americans today, except in motion pictures, are out of sight and out of mind. Since the BIA's creation in 1824, the federal government has had much greater control over Native Americans than over any other civilian group in the nation. For Native Americans, the federal government and White people are synonymous. However, the typical non–Indian tends to be more sympathetic, if not paternalistic, toward Native Americans than toward African Americans.

Subordinate groups in the United States, including Native Americans, have made tremendous gains and will continue to do so in the years to come. But the rest of the population is not standing still. As Native American income rises, so does White income. As Native American children stay in school longer, so do White children. American Indian healthcare improves, but so does White healthcare. Advances have been made, but the gap remains between the descendants of the first Americans and those of later arrivals. Low incomes, inadequate education, and poor healthcare spurred relations between Native Americans and non–Indians to take a dramatic turn in the 1960s and 1970s, when Native Americans demanded a better life in America.

As the next chapter will show, African Americans have achieved a measure of recognition in Washington, DC, that Native Americans have not. Only 5 percent as numerous as the Black population, Native Americans

SPECTRUM OF INTERGROUP RELATIONS ABOUT HERE

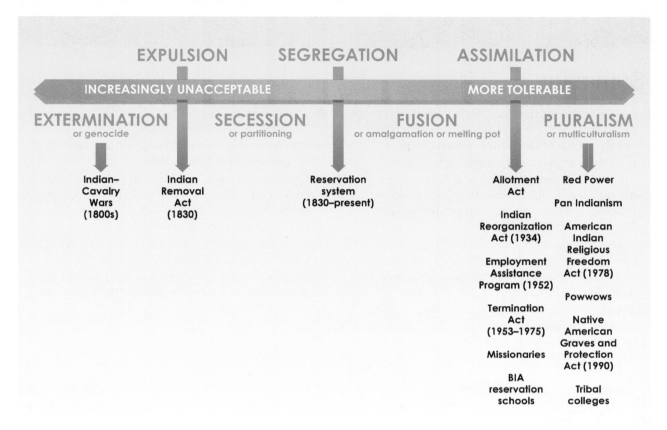

have a weaker collective voice, even with casino money fueling lobbying efforts. Only a handful of Native Americans have ever served in Congress, and many of the non–Indians representing states with large numbers of Native Americans have emerged as their biggest foes rather than their advocates.

The greatest challenge to and asset of the descendants of the first Americans is their land. More than 120 years after the Allotment Act, Native American peoples are still seeking what they feel is theirs. The land they still possess, although only a small slice of what they once occupied, is an important asset. It is barren and largely unproductive agriculturally, but some of it is unspoiled and rich in natural resources. It is no wonder that many large businesses, land developers, environmentalists, and casino managers covet Native American land for their own purposes. For Native Americans, the land they still occupy, as well as much of that occupied by other Americans, represents their roots, their homeland.

One Thanksgiving Day, a scholar noted that, according to tradition, at the first Thanksgiving in 1621 the Pilgrims and the Wampanoag ate together. The descendants of these celebrants increasingly sit at distant tables with equally distant thoughts of equality. Today's Native Americans are the "most undernourished, most short-lived, least educated, least healthy." For them, "that long-ago Thanksgiving was not a milestone, not a promise. It was the last full meal" (Dorris 1988:A23).

Summary

1. Early European Americans usually did not intend to antagonize the Native peoples unnecessarily, but the needs of the settlers always ruled.

2. Policies of the reservation era such as the Allotment, Reorganization, and Termination Acts and the Employment Assistance Program reflected a treatment of tribal people inferior to that of the White Europeans.

3. Native Americans have consistently resisted mistreatment through their tribes and reservation organizations and collectively across boundaries through pan-Indian efforts.

4. American Indians' identity issues emerge today through sovereignty questions at the macro level and self-identification and tribal enrollment at the micro level.

5. Despite gains over the last couple of generations, Native Americans trail the rest of the country in economic development, employment levels, and access to quality healthcare.

6. Quality education continues to be a challenge for American Indians. Efforts to bring native cultures to the curriculum and bolster tribal colleges seek to overcome a century of neglect.

7. Diversity of American Indian cultures is reflected in religious and spiritual expression.

8. Despite the loss of so much of their historical settlement areas, Native Americans struggle to achieve environmental justice

Key Terms

environmental justice, p. 141

fish-ins, p. 129

kickout or pushout, p. 137

pan-Indianism, p. 128

powwows, p. 131

sovereignty, p. 131

world systems theory, p. 122

Review Questions

1. Identify three policies or actions taken by the federal government that have significant impact today in the daily lives of Native Americans.

2. How have land rights been a continuing theme in White–Native American relations?

3. How much are Native Americans expected to shed their cultural heritage to become a part of contemporary society?

4. Do casinos and other gaming outlets represent a positive force for Native American tribes today?

5. What challenges do reservation residents face regarding receiving effective healthcare?

 Listen to **Chapter 6** on **MySocLab**

6 African Americans

6-1 Explain how slavery influences society today.

6-2 Address the challenges of Black leadership.

6-3 Discuss the reemergence of Black protest.

6-4 Summarize the outcome of the civil rights movement.

6-5 Examine the various acts of urban violence and oppression.

6-6 Define and explain the concept of Black Power.

6-7 Discuss the issues in education for African Americans.

6-8 Describe the current economic picture.

6-9 List the strengths and challenges of African American families.

6-10 Explain the housing gap and its impact on African Americans.

6-11 Identify the present concerns with the criminal justice system.

6-12 Explain the health care dilemma in the United States.

6-13 Address the current role of African Americans in politics.

The past is always reflected in the present. **Sundown towns** are communities from which non-Whites were systematically excluded from living. Let's consider the case of one sundown town. Back in 1816, Joseph Gee, a large landowner from North Carolina, settled along with his 18 slaves in a bend of the Alabama River to establish a cotton plantation. After slaves were freed, the Black workers largely remained as sharecroppers and tenant farmers up through the 1930s. People in the Alabama community, now called Gee's Bend, became so impoverished, the Red Cross arrived to prevent starvation.

Across the river from overwhelmingly Black Gee's Bend sits the Wilcox county seat, virtually all-White Camden. In 1962, Camden, like several communities in the South, was the site of civil rights protests. Camden was just one example of a sundown town.

The protesters came from Gee's Bend. They came by ferry, about a ten-minute trip. The people of predominantly White Camden did not like the marchers, so the county closed down the ferry. For over three decades, the ferry remained closed, requiring the 400 residents of all-Black Gee's Bend to drive more than 80 miles each way to get to their jobs, schools, or the hospital. Finally, in 1996, the isolation ended when ferry service was reinstated.

Two residents noted the significance of this event. "This is the first time there has been a concerted effort on the part of Blacks and Whites to do something positive," said Perry Hale, a Black high school teacher. Newspaper publisher Hollis Curl, who is White, remarked, "It's hard for people in other parts of the country to realize what a coming together this has been" (R. Tyson 1996).

Sundown towns like Camden emerged in the late nineteenth century and persisted for a hundred years into the late twentieth century. Although the precise number of sundown towns in the United States is unknown, it is estimated that there were several thousand such towns throughout the nation. The term *sundown town* comes from signs once posted at the city limits telling Black people to be out of town before sundown in no uncertain terms. In addition to excluding African Americans from many small towns, Chinese Americans, Japanese Americans, Mexican Americans, Jews, and Native Americans—citizens and noncitizens alike—also were subject to such exclusions. In some cases, the exclusion was official town policy. In other cases, the racism policy was enforced through intimidation. This intimidation could occur in several ways, including harassment by law enforcement officers and with the blessing of local citizens. At the time the Camden ferry service was terminated, not a single Black person was registered to vote in Wilcox County (Loewen 2005, 2012; Loewen and Schaefer 2008; K. Stevens 2012).

Relationships between Whites and Blacks in the United States have been marked by many episodes like those along the Alabama River—sometimes those relationships take a step backward and occasionally a step forward.

The United States, with more than 42 million Blacks (or African Americans), has the eighth-largest Black population in the world; only Brazil and six countries in Africa have larger Black populations. Despite their large numbers, Blacks in this country have had virtually no role in major national and political decisions and, therefore, captured the world's attention when Barack Obama was elected the first Black president in 2008 (Rastogi, Johnson, Hoeffel and Drewery 2011).

To a significant degree, the history of African Americans is the history of the United States. Black people accompanied the first explorers, and a Black man was among the first to die in the American Revolution. The enslavement of Africans was responsible for the South's wealth in the nineteenth century and led to the country's most violent domestic strife. After Blacks were freed from slavery, their continued subordination led to sporadic outbreaks of violence in the rural South and throughout urban America. This chapter begins with a brief history of African Americans into the beginning of the twenty-first century and also discusses their contemporary situation.

The Black experience in what came to be the United States began with them having something less than citizenship, but their experience was only slightly better than slavery. In 1619, twenty Africans arrived in Jamestown as indentured servants. Their children were born free people. Blacks in the British colonies were not the first in the New World, however; some Blacks had accompanied European explorers, perhaps even Columbus. But this information is a historical footnote only. By the 1660s, the British colonies passed laws making Africans slaves for life, forbidding interracial marriages, and making children of slaves bear the status of their mother regardless of their father's race. Slavery had begun in North America. More than three and a half centuries later, we still live with its legacy.

Slavery

Slavery seems far removed from the debates over issues that divide Whites and Blacks today. However, contemporary institutional and individual racism, which is central to today's conflicts, has its origins in the institution of slavery. Slavery was not merely a lone aspect of American society for three centuries; it has been an essential part of our country's life. For nearly half of this country's history, slavery was not only tolerated but also was legally protected by the U.S. Constitution as interpreted by the U.S. Supreme Court.

In sharp contrast to the basic rights and privileges enjoyed by White Americans, Black people in bondage lived under a system of repression and terror. For several decades, nearly one out of five people were Black and enslaved in the United States. Because the institution of slavery was so fundamental to our culture, it continues to influence Black–White relations in the twenty-first century.

Slave Codes

Slavery in the United States rested on five central conditions: slavery was for life, the status was inherited, slaves were considered mere property, slaves were denied rights, and coercion was used to maintain the system (Noel 1972). As slavery developed in colonial America and the United States, so did **slave codes**, laws that defined the low position of slaves in the United States. Although the rules varied from state to state and from time to time and were not always enforced, the more common features demonstrate how completely subjugated the Africans were:

1. A slave could not marry or even meet with a free Black.
2. Marriage between slaves was not legally recognized.
3. A slave could not legally buy or sell anything except by special arrangement.
4. A slave could not possess weapons or liquor.
5. A slave could not quarrel with or use abusive language toward Whites.
6. A slave could not possess property (including money) except as allowed by his or her owner.
7. A slave could neither make a will nor inherit anything.
8. A slave could not make a contract or hire him- or herself out.
9. A slave could not leave a plantation without a pass noting his or her destination and time of return.
10. No one, including Whites, was to teach a slave (in some areas, even a free Black) to read or write or to give a slave a book, including the Bible.
11. A slave could not gamble.
12. A slave had to obey established curfews.
13. A slave could not testify in court except against another slave.

Violations of these rules were dealt with in a variety of ways. Mutilation and branding were not unknown. Imprisonment was rare; most violators were whipped. An owner was largely immune from prosecution for any physical abuse of slaves. Because slaves could not testify in court, a White's actions toward enslaved African Americans were practically above the law (ACLU 1996; Elkins 1959; Franklin and Higginbotham 2011; Stampp 1956).

Slavery, as enforced through the slave codes, controlled and determined all facets of the lives of enslaved Africans. No exceptions were made for organization of family life and religious worship. Naturally, the Africans had brought their own cultural traditions to America. In Africa, they were accustomed to a closely regulated family life and a rigidly enforced moral code. Slavery rendered it impossible for them to retain family ties in the New World as kinfolk, including their children, were scattered among plantations.

Through the research of W. E. B. Du Bois and many others, we know that slave families had no standing in law. Marriages between slaves were not legally recognized, and masters rarely respected those unions when they sold adults or children. Slave breeding—a deliberate effort to maximize the number of offspring—was practiced with little attention to the emotional needs of the slaves. The slaveholder, not the parents, decided at what age children would begin working in the fields. The slave family could not offer its children shelter or security, rewards or punishments. The man's only recognized family role was to sire offspring—be the sex partner of a woman. In fact, slave men often were identified as a slave woman's possession, for example, "Nancy's Tom." Southern law consistently ruled that "the father of a slave is unknown to our law." However, the male slave did occupy an important economic role: Men held almost all managerial positions open to slaves (Du Bois 1970; Dunaway 2003).

Equating Black Africans with slavery reinforced blackness as a race, an inferior race. This process of **racial formation** was introduced in Chapter 1. Racial formation is a sociohistorical process by which racial categories are created, inhabited, transformed, and destroyed. The stigmatization of Black Africans during slavery and continuing after its end underscores how people socially construct race. So deeply constructed was this racial formation that it took generations before White people even began to question it.

The Attack on Slavery

Although the slave was vulnerable to his or her owner's wishes, slavery as an institution was vulnerable to outside opinion. For a generation after the American Revolution, restrictions on slaves increased even as Southerners accepted slavery as permanent. Slave revolts and antislavery propaganda only accelerated the intensity of oppression the slaves endured. This increase in restrictions led to the ironic situation that as slavery was attacked from within and without, conditions for the slaves became harsher and its defenders became more outspoken in asserting what they saw as its benefits.

Antislavery advocates, or **abolitionists**, included Whites and free Blacks. Many Whites who opposed slavery, such as Abraham Lincoln, did not believe in racial equality. In their minds, even though slavery was a moral evil, racial equality was unimaginable. This inconsistency did not lessen the emotional fervor of the efforts to end slavery. Antislavery societies had been founded even before the American Revolution, but the Constitution dealt the antislavery movement a blow. To appease the South, the framers of the Constitution recognized and legitimized slavery's existence. The Constitution even allowed slavery to increase Southern political power. A slave was counted as three-fifths of a person in determining population representation in the House of Representatives.

Abolitionists, both Black and White, continued to speak out against slavery and the harm it was doing not only to the slaves but also to the entire nation, which had become economically dependent on bondage. Frederick Douglass and Sojourner Truth, both freed slaves, became very visible in the fight against slavery through their eloquent speeches and publications. Harriet Tubman, along with other Blacks and sympathetic Whites, developed the Underground Railroad to transport escaping slaves to freedom in the North and Canada (Franklin and Higginbotham 2011).

Another aspect of Black enslavement was the slaves' own resistance to servitude. Slaves did revolt, and between 40,000 and 100,000 escaped from the South and slavery. Yet fugitive slave acts provided for the return of slaves even though they had reached free states. Enslaved Blacks who did not attempt escape, in part because failure often led to death, resisted slavery through such means as passive resistance. Slaves feigned clumsiness or illness; pretended not to understand, see, or hear; slaves ridiculed Whites with a mocking, subtle humor that their owners did not comprehend; and slaves destroyed farm implements and committed similar acts of sabotage. The most dramatic form of resistance was to flee enforced servitude by escaping through the Underground Railroad that linked safe houses and paths to freedom in the North and Canada (Kimmons 2008; Williams Jr. 2008).

Slavery's Aftermath

On January 1, 1863, President Lincoln issued the Emancipation Proclamation. The document created hope in slaves in the South, but many Union soldiers resigned rather than participate in a struggle to free slaves. The proclamation freed slaves only in the Confederacy, over which the president had no control. Six months after the surrender of the Confederacy in 1865, abolition became law when the Thirteenth Amendment abolished slavery throughout the nation.

From 1867 to 1877, during the period called Reconstruction, Black–White relations in the South were unlike anything they had ever been. The Reconstruction Act of 1867 put each Southern state under a military governor until a new state constitution could be written, with Blacks participating fully in the process. Whites and Blacks married each other, went to public schools and state universities together, and rode side by side on trains and streetcars. The most conspicuous evidence of the new position of Blacks was their presence in elected office (Du Bois 1969b; Foner 2006).

Reconstruction was ended as part of a political compromise in the election of 1876; consequently, segregation became entrenched in the South. Evidence of Jim Crow's reign was apparent by the close of the nineteenth century. The term **Jim Crow** has its origin in a dance tune, but by the 1890s it was synonymous with segregation and referred to statutes that kept African Americans in an inferior position. Segregation often preceded Jim Crow laws and in practice often went beyond their provisions. The institutionalization of segregation gave White supremacy its ultimate authority. In 1896, the U.S. Supreme Court ruled in *Plessy v. Ferguson* that state laws requiring "separate but equal" accommodations for Blacks were a "reasonable" use of state government power (Cheng 2008; Woodward 1974).

It was in the political sphere that Jim Crow exacted its price soonest. In 1898, the Court's decision in *Williams v. Mississippi* declared constitutional the use of poll taxes, literacy tests, and residential requirements to discourage Blacks from voting. In Louisiana that year, 130,000 Blacks were registered to vote. Eight years later, the number dropped to only 1,342 were. When all these measures failed to deprive every African American the right to vote, White supremacists erected a final obstacle: the **White primary** that forbade Black voting in election primaries. By the turn of the century, the South had a one-party system, making the primary the significant contest and the general election a mere rubber stamp. Beginning with South Carolina in 1896 and spreading to 12 other states within 20 years, statewide Democratic Party primaries were adopted. The party explicitly excluded Blacks from voting, an exclusion that was constitutional because the party was defined as a private organization that was free to define its own membership qualifications. The White primary brought an end to the political gains of Reconstruction (Lacy 1972; Lewinson 1965; Woodward 1974).

Reflecting on Slavery Today

The legacy of slavery continues more than 150 years after its end in the United States. We can see it in the nation's Capitol and the White House, which were built with slave labor, but we also can see it in the enduring poverty that grips a large proportion of the descendants of slavery.

Serious discussions have taken place for more than 30 years about granting reparations for slavery. **Slavery reparation** refers to the act of making amends for the injustice of slavery. Few people would argue that slavery was wrong and continues to be wrong where it is still practiced in parts of the world. However, what form should reparations take? Since 1989, Congressman John Conyers, a Black Democrat from Detroit, has annually introduced in Congress a bill to acknowledge the "fundamental injustice, cruelty, brutality, and inhumanity of slavery" and calls for the creation of a commission to examine the institution and to make recommendations on appropriate remedies. This bill has never made it out of committee, but the discussion continues outside the federal government. In 2009, Congress issued a joint resolution apologizing for slavery but it contained the specific "disclaimer" that nothing in the resolution authorized or supported any claim against the United States.

From every direction, the historical and social significance of slavery has been marginalized. Just prior to the 150th anniversary of the Civil War, various southern organizations and political leaders spoke of the need to *not* forget the Civil War and the bravery of the soldiers. However, many of the statements created a measure of controversy because they made no mention of slavery and suggested that the Confederacy was formed primarily because those states wanted the right to have more control over their affairs and not be subject to federal laws. In 2010, Virginia Governor Bob McDonnell designated April as Confederate History Month without mention of slavery. A 2011 national survey showed 25 percent of White people sympathize more with the Southern states than the Northern states looking back on the Civil War. Given the unease with which most people think of our nation's history of slavery, it is no surprise that national recognition of the Sesquicentennial (150th anniversary) of the Civil War was limited to the issuance of commemorative postage stamps (Blow 2013; Seelye 2010).

The year 2011 marked the sesquicentennial of the start of the Civil War. The United States still finds it difficult to come to terms with the power of slavery. Here, we see Confederate soldiers in a mock battle at a Civil War reenactment at a state park in Oregon.

The Challenge of Black Leadership

The institutionalization of White supremacy precipitated different responses from African Americans, just as slavery had. In the late 1800s and early 1900s, several articulate Blacks attempted to lead the first generation of freeborn Black Americans. Most prominent were Booker T. Washington and W. E. B. Du Bois. The personalities and ideas of these two men contrasted. Washington was born a slave in 1856 on a Virginia plantation. He worked in coal mines after emancipation and attended elementary school. Through hard work and driving ambition, Washington became the head of an educational institute for Blacks in Tuskegee, Alabama. Within 15 years, his leadership brought national recognition to the Tuskegee Institute and he became a national figure. Du Bois, on the other hand, was born in 1868 to a free family in Massachusetts. He attended Fisk University and the University of Berlin and became the first Black to receive a doctorate from Harvard. Washington died in 1915, and Du Bois died in self-imposed exile in Africa in 1963.

Explore the Activity on MySocLab: *Black Americans*

The Politics of Accommodation

Booker T. Washington's approach to White supremacy is called the *politics of accommodation*. He was willing to forgo social equality until White people saw Blacks as deserving of it. Perhaps his most famous speech was made in Atlanta on September 18, 1895, to an audience that was mostly White and mostly wealthy. Introduced by the governor of Georgia as "a representative of Negro enterprise and Negro civilization," Washington (1900) gave a five-minute speech in which he pledged the continued dedication of Blacks to Whites:

> *As we have proved our loyalty to you in the past, in nursing your children, watching by the sick-bed of your mothers and fathers, and often following them with tear-dimmed eyes to their graves, so in the future, in our humble way, we shall stand by you with a devotion that no foreigner can approach, ready to lay down our lives, if need be, in defense of yours.* (p. 221)

The speech catapulted Washington into the public forum, and he became the anointed spokesperson for Blacks for the next 20 years. President Grover Cleveland congratulated Washington for the "new hope" he gave Blacks. Washington's essential theme was compromise. Unlike Frederick Douglass, who had demanded the same rights for Blacks as for Whites, Washington asked that Blacks be educated because it would be a wise investment for Whites. He called racial hatred "the great and intricate problem which God has laid at the doors of the South." The Blacks' goal should be economic respectability. Washington's accommodating attitude ensured his popularity with Whites. His recognition by Whites contributed to his large following of Blacks, who were not used to seeing their leaders achieve fame among Whites.

It is easy in retrospect to be critical of Washington and to write him off as simply a product of his times. Booker T. Washington entered the public arena when the more militant proposals of Douglass had been buried. Black politicians were losing political contests and influence. To become influential as a Black, Washington reasoned, required White acceptance. His image as an accommodator allowed him to fight discrimination covertly. He assisted Presidents Roosevelt and Taft in appointing Blacks to patronage positions. Washington's goal was for African Americans eventually to have the same rights and opportunities as Whites. Just as people disagree with leaders today, some Blacks disagreed with the means Washington chose to reach that goal. No African American was more outspoken in his criticism of the politics of accommodation than W. E. B. Du Bois (Norrell 2009).

The Niagara Movement

The rivalry between Washington and Du Bois has been exaggerated. They enjoyed fairly cordial relations for some time. In 1900, Washington recommended Du Bois, at his request, for superintendent of Black schools in Washington, DC. By 1905, however, relations between the two had cooled. Du Bois spoke critically of Washington's influence, arguing that his power was being used to stifle African Americans who spoke out against the politics of accommodation. He also charged that Washington had caused the transfer of funds from academic programs to vocational education. Du Bois's greatest objection to Washington's statements was that they encouraged Whites to place the burden of the Blacks' problems on the Blacks themselves (Du Bois 1903).

As an alternative to Washington's program, Du Bois (1903) advocated the theory of the *talented tenth*, which reflected his atypical educational background. Unlike Washington, Du Bois was not at home with both intellectuals and sharecroppers. Although the very phrase *talented tenth* has an elitist ring, Du Bois argued that these privileged Blacks must serve the other nine-tenths. This argument was also Du Bois's way of criticizing Washington's emphasis on vocational education. Although he did not completely oppose the vocational approach, Du Bois thought education for African Americans should emphasize academics, which would be more likely to improve their position. Drawing on the talented tenth, Du Bois invited 29 Blacks to participate in a strategy session near Niagara Falls in 1905. Out of a series of meetings came several demands that unmistakably placed the responsibility for the problems facing African Americans on the shoulders of Whites.

The Niagara Movement, as it came to be called, was closely monitored by Booker T. Washington. Du Bois encountered difficulty gaining financial support and recruiting prominent people, and Du Bois (1968) himself wrote, "My leadership was solely of ideas. I never was, nor ever will be, personally popular" (p. 303). The movement's legacy was educating a new generation of African Americans in the politics of protest. After 1910, the Niagara Movement ceased to hold annual conventions. In 1909, however, the Niagara Movement leaders founded the National Association for the Advancement of Colored People (NAACP), with White and Black members. It was through the work of the NAACP that the Niagara Movement accomplished most of the goals set forth in 1905. The NAACP also marked the merging of White liberalism and Black militancy, a coalition unknown since the end of the abolition movement and Reconstruction (Rudwick 1957; Wortham 2008).

Remarkably, as Du Bois agitated for social change, he continued to conduct groundbreaking research into race relations. He oversaw the Atlanta Sociological Laboratory; its work at the time was generally ignored by the White-dominated academic institutions but is now gradually being rediscovered (Wright 2006).

In 1900, 90 percent of African Americans lived in the South. Blacks moved out of the South and into the West and North, especially the urban areas in those regions, during the post–Civil War period and continued to migrate through the 1950s and 1960s. By the 1980s and 1990s, a return to the South began as job opportunities grew in that part of the country and most vestiges of Jim Crow vanished in what had been the Confederacy states. By 2010, 55 percent of African Americans lived in the South, compared to 33 percent of the rest of the population (Figure 6.1).

A pattern of violence, with Blacks usually the victims, started in the South during Reconstruction and continued into the twentieth century, when it also spread northward. In 1917, a riot in East St. Louis, Illinois, claimed the lives of 39 Blacks and nine Whites. The several days of violence resulted from White fear of social and economic gains made

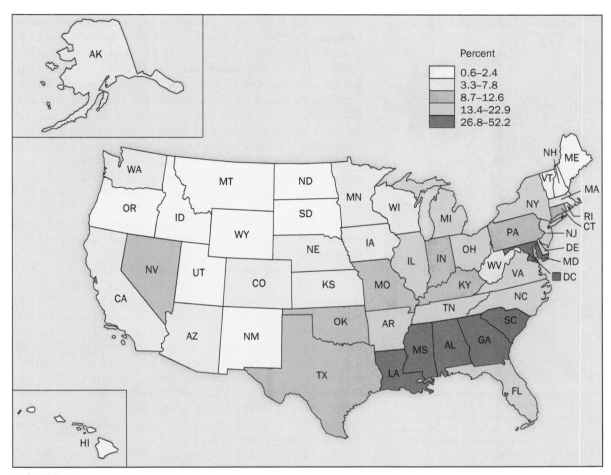

FIGURE 6.1
Black Population, 2010

Source: Rastogi, Johnson, Hoeffel and Drewery 2011: Table 5 on p. 8.

by Blacks. So much violence occurred in the summer of 1919 that it is commonly called the "red summer." Twenty-six riots broke out throughout the country as White soldiers who returned from World War I feared the new competition that Blacks represented. This period of violence against African Americans also saw a resurgence of the Ku Klux Klan, which at its height had nearly 9 million members (Berlin 2010; Grimshaw 1969; Schaefer 1971, 1980).

Reemergence of Black Protest

American involvement in World War II signaled improved economic conditions for both Whites and Blacks. Nearly a million African Americans served in the military in rigidly segregated units. Generally, more Blacks participated in the armed services in World War II than in previous military engagements, but efforts by Blacks to contribute to the war effort at home were hampered by discriminatory practices in defense plants.

Despite their second-class status until well after World War II, African Americans have contributed to every war effort. Notable were the Tuskegee Airmen, an all-Black unit of pilots who flew during World War II and received numerous decorations for valor. Surviving members continue to gather in celebratory reunions.

A. Philip Randolph, president of the Brotherhood of Sleeping Car Porters, threatened to lead 100,000 Blacks in a march on Washington in 1941 to ensure their employment and not have Black workers targeted for dismissal. Randolph's proposed tactic was nonviolent direct action, which he modeled on Mahatma Gandhi's practices in India. Randolph made it clear that he intended the march to be an all-Black event because he saw it as neither necessary nor desirable for Whites to lead Blacks to their own liberation. President Franklin Roosevelt responded to the pressure and agreed to issue an executive order prohibiting discrimination if Randolph would call off the march. The order and the Fair Employment Practices Commission it set up did not fulfill the original promises, but a precedent had been established for federal intervention in job discrimination (Garfinkel 1959).

Racial turmoil during World War II was not limited to threatened marches. Racial disturbances occurred in cities throughout the country, the worst riot occurring in Detroit in June 1943. In that case, President Roosevelt sent in 6,000 soldiers to quell the violence, which left 25 Blacks and nine Whites dead. The racial disorders were paralleled by a growth in civil disobedience as a means to achieve equality for Blacks. The Congress of Racial Equality (CORE) was founded in 1942 to fight discrimination with nonviolent direct action. This interracial group used sit-ins to open restaurants to Black patrons in Chicago, Baltimore, and Los Angeles (Grimshaw 1969).

The war years and the postwar period saw several U.S. Supreme Court decisions that suggested the Court was moving away from tolerating racial inequities. The White primary elections endorsed in Jim Crow's formative period were finally challenged in the 1944 *Smith v. Allwright* decision. The effectiveness of the victory was limited; many states simply passed statutes that used new devices to frustrate African American voters.

A particularly repugnant legal device for relegating African Americans to second-class status was the **restrictive covenant**, a private contract entered into by neighborhood property owners stipulating that property could not be sold or rented to certain minority groups, thus ensuring that they could not live in the area. In 1948, the Supreme Court finally declared in *Shelley v. Kramer* that restrictive covenants were not constitutional, although it did not actually attack their discriminatory nature. The victory was in many ways less substantial than it was symbolic of the new willingness by the Supreme Court to uphold the rights of Black citizens.

The Democratic administrations of the late 1940s and early 1950s made a number of promises to Black Americans. The party adopted a strong civil rights platform in 1948, but its provisions were not enacted. Once again, union president Randolph threatened Washington, DC, with a march. This time, he insisted that as long as Blacks were subjected to a peacetime draft, the military must be desegregated. President Truman responded by issuing an executive order on July 26, 1948, that desegregated the armed forces. The U.S. Army abolished its quota system in 1950, and training camps for the Korean War were integrated. Desegregation was not complete, however, especially in the reserves and the National Guard, and even today the armed forces face charges of racial favoritism. Whatever its shortcomings, the desegregation order offered African Americans an alternative to segregated civilian life (Moskos and Butler 1996).

The Civil Rights Movement

It is difficult to say exactly when a social movement begins or ends. Usually, a movement's ideas or tactics precede the actual mobilization of people and continue long after the movement's driving force has been replaced by new ideals and techniques. This description applies to the civil rights movement and its successor: the continuing struggle for African American freedom. Before 1954, there were some confrontations of White supremacy: the CORE sit-ins of 1942 and efforts to desegregate buses in Baton Rouge, Louisiana, in 1953. The civil rights movement gained momentum with a Supreme Court decision in 1954 that eventually desegregated the public schools, and it ended as a major force in Black America with the civil disorders of 1965 through 1968. However, beginning in 1954, toppling the traditional barriers to full rights for Blacks was the rule, not the exception.

Struggle to Desegregate the Schools

For the majority of Black children, public school education meant attending segregated schools. Southern school districts assigned children to school by race rather than by neighborhood, a practice that constituted **de jure segregation**, or segregation that results from children being assigned to schools specifically to maintain racially separate schools. It was this form of legal humiliation that was attacked in the landmark decree of *Linda Brown et al. v. Board of Education of Topeka, Kansas.*

Seven-year-old Linda Brown was not permitted to enroll in the grade school four blocks from her home in Topeka, Kansas. Rather, school board policy dictated that she attend the Black school almost two miles away. This denial led the NAACP Legal Defense and Educational Fund to bring suit on behalf of Linda Brown and 12 other Black children. The NAACP argued that the Fourteenth Amendment was intended to rule out segregation in public schools. Chief Justice Earl Warren of the Supreme Court wrote the unanimous opinion that "in the field of public education the doctrine of 'separate but equal' has no place. Separate educational facilities are inherently unequal."

The freedom that African Americans saw in their grasp at the time of the *Brown* decision amounted to a reaffirmation of American values. What Blacks sought was assimilation into White American society. The motivation for the *Brown* suit did not come merely because Black schools were inferior, although they were. Blacks were assigned to poorly ventilated and dilapidated buildings, with overcrowded classrooms and unqualified teachers. Less money was spent on Black schools than on White schools throughout the South in both rural and metropolitan areas. The issue was not such tangible factors, however, but the intangible effect of not being allowed to go to school with Whites. All-Black schools could not be equal to all-White schools. Even in this victory, Blacks reaffirmed White society and the importance of an integrated educational experience (Supreme Court of the United States 347 U.S. 483, August 17, 1954).

Although *Brown* marked the beginning of the civil rights movement, the reaction to it showed how deeply prejudice was rooted in the South. Resistance to court-ordered desegregation took many forms: Some people called for impeachment of all the Supreme Court justices. Others petitioned Congress to declare the Fourteenth Amendment unconstitutional.

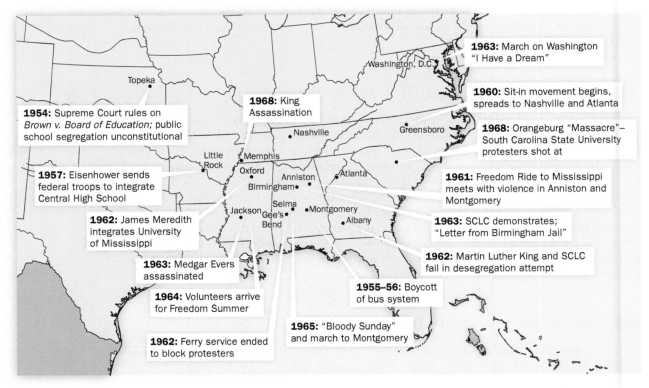

1963: March on Washington "I Have a Dream"

1960: Sit-in movement begins, spreads to Nashville and Atlanta

1954: Supreme Court rules on *Brown v. Board of Education;* public school segregation unconstitutional

1968: King Assassination

1968: Orangeburg "Massacre"– South Carolina State University protesters shot at

1957: Eisenhower sends federal troops to integrate Central High School

1961: Freedom Ride to Mississippi meets with violence in Anniston and Montgomery

1962: James Meredith integrates University of Mississippi

1963: SCLC demonstrates; "Letter from Birmingham Jail"

1963: Medgar Evers assassinated

1962: Martin Luther King and SCLC fail in desegregation attempt

1964: Volunteers arrive for Freedom Summer

1955–56: Boycott of bus system

1965: "Bloody Sunday" and march to Montgomery

1962: Ferry service ended to block protesters

FIGURE 6.2
Major Events of the Civil Rights Movement

Cities closed schools rather than comply. The governor of Arkansas used the state's National Guard to block Black students from entering a previously all-White high school in Little Rock (Figure 6.2).

The issue of school desegregation was extended to higher education, and Mississippi state troopers and the state's National Guard confronted each other over the 1962 admission of James Meredith, the first African American accepted by the University of Mississippi. Scores of people were injured and two were killed in this clash between segregationists and the law. A similar defiant stand was taken a year later by Governor George Wallace, who "stood in the schoolhouse door" to block two Blacks from enrolling in the University of Alabama. President Kennedy federalized the Alabama National Guard to guarantee admission of the students. *Brown* did not resolve the school controversy, and many questions remain unanswered. More recently, the issue of school segregation resulting from neighborhood segregation has been debated. Later, another form of segregation—*de facto segregation*— is examined more closely (Bell 2004, 2007; Pettigrew 2011).

Civil Disobedience

The success of a yearlong boycott of city buses in Montgomery, Alabama, dealt Jim Crow another setback. On December 1, 1955, Rosa Parks defied the law and refused to give her seat on a crowded bus to a White man. Her defiance led to the organization of the Montgomery Improvement Association, headed by 26-year-old Martin Luther King, Jr., a Baptist minister with a PhD from Boston University. The bus boycott was the first of many situations in which Blacks used nonviolent direct action to obtain the rights that Whites already enjoyed. The boycott eventually demanded the end of segregated seating. The *Brown* decision woke up all of America to racial injustice, but the Montgomery boycott marked a significant shift away from the historical reliance on NAACP court battles (Killian 1975).

Civil disobedience is based on the belief that people have the right to disobey the law under certain circumstances. This tactic was not new; Blacks in the United States had used it before and Gandhi also had urged its use in India. Under King's leadership, however, civil disobedience became a widely used technique and even gained a measure of acceptability among some prominent Whites. King distinguished between man-made laws that were unjust and should not be obeyed because they were not right, not in accordance with God's higher moral code (1963:82).

In disobeying unjust laws, King (1958: 101–107) developed this strategy:

- actively but nonviolently resisting evil,
- not seeking to defeat or humiliate opponents but to win their friendship and understanding,
- attacking the forces of evil rather than the people who happen to be doing the evil,
- being willing to accept suffering without retaliating,
- refusing to hate the opponent, and
- acting with the conviction that the universe is on the side of justice.

King, like other Blacks before him and since, made it clear that passive acceptance of injustice was intolerable. He hoped that by emphasizing nonviolence, Southern Blacks would display their hostility to racism in a way that would undercut violent reaction by Whites.

Congress had still failed to enact any sweeping federal barrier to discrimination. Following the example of A. Philip Randolph in 1941, Blacks organized the March on Washington for Jobs and Freedom on August 28, 1963. With more than 200,000 people participating, the march was the high point of the civil rights movement. The mass of people, middle-class Whites and Blacks looking to the federal government for support, symbolized the struggle. However, a public opinion poll conducted shortly before the march documented the continuing resentment of the majority of Whites: 63 percent were opposed to the rally (G. Gallup 1972).

King (1971:351) delivered his famous "I Have a Dream" speech before the large crowd; he looked forward to a time when all Americans will be able to unite together. Just eighteen days later, a bomb exploded in a Black church in Birmingham, Alabama, killing four little girls and injuring twenty other people.

Despair only increased as the November 1963 election results meant segregationists were successful in their bids for office. Most distressing was the assassination of President Kennedy on November 22. Blacks had found Kennedy to be an appealing president despite his previously mediocre legislative record in the U.S. Senate. His death left doubt as to the direction and pace of future actions on civil rights by the executive branch under President Lyndon Baines Johnson. Two months later, however, the

 Watch the Video on MySocLab: Martin Luther King, Jr. Speech 1963

Malcolm X and Martin Luther King, Jr., were the defining figures of the African American struggle for rights and dignity in the 1960s.

Twenty-Fourth Amendment was ratified, outlawing the poll tax that had long prevented Blacks from voting. The enactment of the Civil Rights Act on July 2, 1964, was hailed as a major victory and provided, at least for awhile, what historian John Hope Franklin called "the illusion of equality" (Franklin and Higginbotham 2011).

In the months that followed passage of the act, the pace of the movement to end racial injustice slowed. The violence continued, however, from the Bedford–Stuyvesant section of Brooklyn to Selma, Alabama. Southern state courts still found White murderers of Blacks innocent, and they had to be tried and convicted in federal, rather than criminal, court on the charge that by killing a person one violates that person's civil rights. Government records, which did not become public until 1973, revealed a systematic campaign by the FBI to infiltrate civil rights groups in an effort to discredit them in the belief that such activist groups were subversive. It was in such an atmosphere that the Voting Rights Act was passed in August 1965, but this significant, positive event was somewhat overshadowed by violence in the Watts section of Los Angeles that same week (Blackstock 1976).

Urban Violence and Oppression

Riots involving Whites and Blacks did not begin in the 1960s. As noted earlier in this chapter, urban violence occurred after World War I and even during World War II, and violence against Blacks in the United States is nearly 350 years old. But the urban riots of the 1960s affected Blacks and Whites in the United States and throughout the world so extensively that they deserve special attention. However, it is important to remember that most violence between Whites and Blacks has not been large-scale collective action but has involved only a small number of people.

The summers of 1963 and 1964 were a prelude to riots that gripped the country's attention. Although most people knew of the civil rights efforts in the South and legislative victories in Washington, everyone realized that the racial problem was national after several cities outside the South experienced violent disorder. In April 1968, after the assassination of Martin Luther King, Jr., more cities exploded than had in all of 1967. Even before the summer of 1968 began, there were 369 civil disorders. Communities of all sizes were hit (Oberschall 1968).

As the violence continued and embraced many ghettos, a popular explanation was that riot participants were mostly unemployed youths who had criminal records, often involving narcotics, and who were vastly outnumbered by the African Americans who repudiated the looting and arson. This explanation was called the **riff-raff theory** or the rotten-apple theory because it discredited the rioters and left the barrel of apples, White society, untouched. On the contrary, research shows that the Black community expressed sympathetic understanding toward the rioters and that the rioters were not merely the poor and uneducated but included middle-class, working-class, and educated residents (Sears and McConahay 1969, 1973; Tomlinson 1969; R. Turner 1994).

Several alternatives to the riff-raff theory explain why Black violent protest increased in the United States at a time when the nation was seemingly committed to civil rights for all. Two explanations stand out. One ascribes the problem to Black frustration with rising expectations in the face of continued deprivation relative to Whites.

The standard of living of African Americans improved remarkably after World War II, and it continued to do so during the civil rights movement. However, White income and occupation levels also improved, so the gap between the groups remained. Chapter 3 showed that feelings of relative deprivation often are the basis for perceived discrimination. **Relative deprivation** is the conscious feeling of a negative discrepancy between legitimate expectations and current actualities (W. Wilson 1973).

Explore the Concept on MySocLab: Relative Deprivation and Revolution

At the same time that African Americans were feeling relative deprivation, they also were experiencing growing discontent. **Rising expectations** refers to the increasing sense of frustration that legitimate needs are being blocked. Blacks felt that they had legitimate aspirations to equality, and the civil rights movement reaffirmed that discrimination had blocked upward mobility. As the horizons of African Americans broadened, they were more likely to make comparisons with Whites and feel discontented. The civil rights movement resulted in higher aspirations for Black America; yet for the majority, life remained unchanged. Not only were their lives unchanged but they also had a widespread feeling that the existing social structure held no prospect for improvement (Garner 1996; Sears and McConahay 1970; Thomas and Thomas 1984).

Black Power

The riots in the Northern ghettos captured the attention of Whites, and Black Power was what they heard. But Black Power was born *not* of Black but of White violence. On June 6, 1966, James Meredith was carrying out a one-person march from Memphis to Jackson, Mississippi, to encourage fellow African Americans to overcome their own fears and vote after the passage of the Voting Rights Act. During that march, an unidentified assailant shot and wounded Meredith. Blacks from throughout the country immediately continued the march. During the march, Stokely Carmichael of the Student Nonviolent Coordinating Committee proclaimed to a cheering Black crowd, "What we need is Black Power." King and others later urged "Freedom Now" as the slogan for the march. A compromise dictated that no slogan would be used, but the mood of Black America said otherwise (King 1967; Lomax 1971).

In retrospect, it may be puzzling that the phrase *Black Power* frightened Whites and offended so many Blacks. It was not really new. The National Advisory Commission on Civil Disorders (1968) correctly identified it as old wine in new bottles: Black consciousness was not new, even if the phrase was.

By advocating Black Power, Carmichael distanced himself from the assimilationism of King. Carmichael rejected the goal of assimilation into White middle-class society. Instead, he said, Blacks must create new institutions. To succeed in this endeavor, Carmichael argued that Blacks must follow the same path as the Italians, Irish, and other White ethnic groups. "Before a group can enter the open society, it must first close ranks....Group solidarity is necessary before a group can operate effectively from a bargaining position of strength in a pluralistic society" (Ture and Hamilton 1992:44). Prominent Black leaders opposed the concept; many feared that Whites would retaliate even more violently. King (1967) saw Black Power as a "cry of disappointment" but acknowledged that it had a "positive meaning."

Eventually, Black Power gained wide acceptance among Blacks and even many Whites. Although it came to be defined differently by nearly every new proponent,

 Explore the Map on MySocLab: Concentration of African Americans by County

Improved living conditions for Black people made the United States an attractive destination for Black people, as it had been for generations for people from Europe. The increase is dramatic with over 2 million in the 2010 Census having been born in Africa and the Caribbean and the majority of them having arrived in the previous ten years. Here, some Somali women are selling clothes in Minneapolis.

support of Black Power generally implied endorsing Black control of the political, economic, and social institutions in Black communities. One reason for its popularity among African Americans was that it gave them a viable option for surviving in a segregated society. The civil rights movement strove to end segregation, but the White response showed how committed White society was to maintaining it. Black Power presented restructuring society as the priority item on the Black agenda (Carmichael and Thelwell 2003).

In the wake of generations of struggle by African Americans allied with sympathetic Whites and members of other minority groups, we now consider how much progress has been made in such areas as education, the economy, family life, housing, criminal justice, healthcare, and politics.

Education

The African American population in the United States has placed special importance on acquiring education, beginning with its emphasis in the home of the slave family, even when the formal institution of marriage was prohibited, and continuing through the creation of separate schools for Black children because public schools were closed to them by custom or law. Today, long after the civil rights coalition has disbanded, education remains a controversial issue. Because racial and ethnic groups realize that formal schooling is the key to social mobility, they want to maximize this opportunity for upward mobility and, therefore, want better schooling. White Americans also appreciate the value of formal schooling and do not want to do anything that they perceive will jeopardize their own position.

Several measures document the inadequate education received by African Americans, starting with the quantity of formal education. Blacks as a group have always attained less education than Whites as a group. Despite programs such as Head Start, which are directed at all poor children, White children are still more likely to have formal prekindergarten education than are African American children. Later, Black children generally drop out of school sooner and, therefore, are less likely to receive high school diplomas, let alone college degrees. The gap in receiving college degrees has not been reduced in recent years, as shown in Figure 6.3. Presently, about 31 percent of non–Hispanic Whites 25 years and over have a bachelor's degree or higher compared to fewer than 18 percent

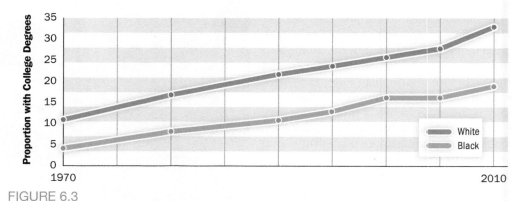

FIGURE 6.3

Percentage of Adults Receiving College Degrees

Blacks have made tremendous progress in terms of receiving college degrees, but so have Whites. Today's level of college completion among adult African Americans is about the level White Americans reached in the mid-1980s.

Note: Date since 2000 for non–Hispanic Whites. Proportion of population over age 25.

Source: Bureau of the Census 2010a: Table 145; 2011e.

of African Americans, who have fewer degrees than Ecuadorian Americans or Nicaraguan Americans. Despite this progress, however, the gap remains substantial, with the proportion of Blacks holding a college degree in 2010 about what it was for Whites in the early 1980s (Ogunwole, Drewery, and Rios-Vargas 2012).

Proposals to improve educational opportunities often argue for more adequate funding. Yet, there are disagreements over what changes would lead to the best outcome. For example, educators and African Americans in general have significant debates over the content of curriculum that is best for minority students. Some schools have developed academic programs that take an Afrocentric perspective and immerse students in African American history and culture. However, a few of these programs have been targeted as ignoring fundamentals. On other occasions, the Afrocentric curriculum has even been viewed as racist against Whites. The debates over a few controversial programs attract a lot of attention, clouding the widespread need to reassess the curriculum for racial and ethnic minorities.

Middle- and upper-class children occasionally face barriers to a high-quality education, but they are more likely than the poor to have a home environment that is favorable to learning. Even African American schoolchildren who stay in school are not guaranteed equal opportunities in life. Many high schools do not prepare students who are interested in college for advanced schooling. The problem is that schools are failing to meet the needs of students, not that students are failing in school. Therefore, the problems with schooling were properly noted as a part of the past discrimination component of total discrimination illustrated in Figure 3.1 on page 64.

School Segregation

It has been more than 50 years since the U.S. Supreme Court issued its unanimous ruling in *Brown v. Board of Education of Topeka, Kansas* that separate educational facilities are inherently unequal. What has been the legacy of that decision? Initially, the courts, with the support of the federal government, ordered Southern school districts to end racial separation. But as attention turned to larger school districts, especially in the North, the challenge was to have integrated schools even though the neighborhoods were segregated. In addition, some city school districts were predominantly African American and Hispanic and were surrounded by suburban school districts that were predominantly White. This type of school segregation, which results from residential patterns, is called **de facto segregation**.

Initially, courts sought to overcome de facto segregation just as they had de jure school segregation in the *Brown* case. Typically, students were bused within a school district to achieve racial balance, but in a few cases, Black students were bused to predominantly White suburban schools and White children were bused into the city. In 1974, however, the Supreme Court ruled in *Millikin v. Bradley* that it was improper to order Detroit and the suburbs to have a joint metropolitan busing solution. These and other Supreme Court decisions effectively ended initiatives to overcome residential segregation, once again creating racial isolation in the schools. Indeed, even in Topeka, one-third of the schools are segregated (Orfield et al. 1996).

School segregation has been so enduring that the term *apartheid schools* has been coined to refer to schools that are all Black. An analysis released in 2003 by the Civil Rights Project of Harvard University documented that one in six of the nation's Black students attends an **apartheid school**, and this proportion rose to one out of four in the Northeast and Midwest. If there has been any trend, it is that the typical African American student was less likely to have White classmates in 2010 than in 1970 (Frankenberg et al. 2003; Tefera et al. 2010).

Although studies have shown positive effects of integration, a diverse student population does not guarantee an integrated, equal schooling environment. For example, **tracking** in schools, especially middle and high schools, intensifies segregation at the classroom level.

Tracking is the practice of placing students in specific curriculum groups on the basis of test scores and other criteria. It also has the effect of decreasing White–Black classroom interaction because African American children are disproportionately assigned to general classes, and more White children are placed in college-preparatory classes. For example, in 2009, at an elementary school in suburban Montgomery County, Maryland, the school's faculty, which is nearly 75 percent White, identified the percentage of the student body, which is about 64 percent White, likely to be considered "gifted and talented": Forty-nine percent of White students and 67 percent of Asian students were so identified, compared to fewer than 8 percent of Latino students and fewer than 4 percent of African American children. Studies indicate that African American students are more likely than White students to be classified as learning disabled or emotionally disturbed. Although there are successes in public education, integration is not one of them (Ellison 2008; K. Thompson 2010).

Higher Education

Higher education for Blacks reflects the same pattern: The overall picture of African American higher education is not promising. Although strides were made in the period after the civil rights movement, a plateau was reached in the mid-1970s. African Americans are more likely than Whites to be part-time students and to need financial aid, which began to be severely cut in the 1980s. They also are finding the social climate on predominantly White campuses less than positive. As a result, the historically Black colleges and universities (HBCUs) are once again playing a significant role in educating African Americans. For a century, they were the only real source of college degrees for Blacks. Then, in the 1970s, predominantly White colleges began to recruit African Americans. As of 2010, however, the 105 HBCUs still accounted for about one-fifth of all Black college graduates (National Center for Educational Statistics 2011: Tables 250, 297).

As shown in Figure 6.3, although African Americans are more likely today to be college graduates, the upward trend in the 1970s and 1980s has moderated. Several factors account for this reversal in progress:

1. Reductions in financial aid and more reliance on loans than on grants-in-aid, coupled with rising costs, have discouraged students who would be the first members of their families to attend college.
2. Pushing for higher standards in educational achievement without providing remedial courses has locked out many minority students.
3. Employment opportunities, though slight for African Americans without some college, have continued to lure young people who must contribute to their family's income and who otherwise might have gone to college.
4. Negative publicity about affirmative action may have discouraged some African Americans from even considering college.
5. Attention to what appears to be a growing number of racial incidents on predominantly White college campuses also has been a discouraging factor.

Colleges and universities seem uneasy about these problems; publicly, the schools appear committed to addressing them.

There is little question that special challenges face the African American student at a college with an overwhelmingly White student body, faculty, advisors, coaches, and administrators. The campus culture may be neutral at best, and it is often hostile to members of racial minorities. The high attrition rate of African American students on predominantly White college campuses confirms the need for a positive environment.

The disparity in schooling becomes even more pronounced at the highest levels, and the gap is not closing. Only 6.1 percent of all doctorates awarded in 2008 were to native-born African Americans, reflecting a modest increase from 3.9 percent in 1981 (Bureau of the Census 2010a: Table 296).

In summary, the picture of education for Black Americans is uneven—marked progress in absolute terms (much better educated than a generation ago), but relative to Whites, the gap in educational attainment remains at all levels. Sixty years ago, the major issue appeared to be school desegregation, but the goal was to improve the quality of education received by Black schoolchildren. Today, the concerns of African American parents and most educators are similar—quality education. W. E. B. Du Bois advanced the same point in 1935—what a Black student needs "is neither segregated schools nor mixed schools. What he needs is Education" (p. 335).

The Economic Picture

The general economic picture for African Americans has gradually improved over the last 50 years, but this improvement is modest compared with that of Whites, whose standard of living also has increased. Therefore, in terms of absolute deprivation, African Americans are much better off today but have not experienced significant improvement with respect to their deprivation relative to Whites on almost all economic indicators. To better understand today's economic reality, we first focus on the middle class and then turn to a broader overview of the occupations that African American fill.

The Middle Class

Many characterizations of the African American community have been attacked because they overemphasize the poorest segment of that community. Also overemphasized and exaggerated is how much success African Americans have achieved. Social scientists face the challenge of avoiding a selective, one-sided picture of Black society. The problem is similar to viewing a partially filled glass of water. Does one describe it as half empty and emphasize the need for assistance? Or does one describe the glass as half full to give attention to what has been accomplished? The most complete description acknowledges both perspectives.

Read the Document on MySocLab: *Black Spaces, Black Places: Strategic Assimilation and Identity Construction in Middle-Class Suburbia*

A clearly defined African American middle class has emerged. In 2011, about 21 percent of African Americans earned more than the median income for White non-Hispanics. At least one-quarter of Blacks, then, are middle class or higher. Many observers have debated the character of this middle class. E. Franklin Frazier (1957), a Black sociologist, wrote an often-critical study of the African American middle class in which he identified its overriding goal as achieving petty social values and becoming acceptable to white society (DeNavas-Walt, Proctor, and Smith. 2012: Table PINC-03).

Directing attention to the Black middle class also requires that we consider the relative importance of race and social class. The degree to which affluent Blacks identify themselves in class terms or racial terms is an important ideological question. W. E. B. Du Bois (1952) argued that when racism decreases, class issues become more important. As Du Bois saw it, exploitation would remain, and many of the same people would continue to be subordinate. Black elites might become economically successful, either as entrepreneurs (Black capitalists) or professionals (Black white-collar workers), but they would continue to identify with and serve the dominant group's interest.

Social scientists have long recognized the importance of class. **Class** is a term used by sociologist Max Weber to refer to people who share a similar level of wealth and income. The significance of class in people's lives is apparent to all. This is not just in terms of the type of cars one drives or where one goes on vacation but also in the quality of public schools available and the healthcare one receives.

Besides class, two measures are useful to determine the overall economic situation of an individual or household: income and wealth. **Income** refers to salaries, wages, and other money received; **wealth** is a more inclusive term that encompasses all of a person's material assets, including land and other types of property. The Research Focus box, "Moving on Up, or Not," considers how African Americans are doing in terms of income and wealth.

 # Research Focus

Moving on Up, or Not

MOVING ON UP

Harvard political scientist Jennifer Hochschild (1995, 44) observed that, "One has not really succeeded in America unless one can pass on the chance for success to one's children." By this standard, how well is the Black American community doing?

To begin with, relative to White Americans, Blacks have much less income and wealth. According to a report released in 2012, the proportion of Blacks and Whites rising to the top and falling to (or starting from) the bottom of the income and wealth ladders differs dramatically. Just over two-thirds (65 percent) of Blacks grew up at the bottom of the income ladder compared with only 11 percent of Whites. In Table 6.1, we look at income and wealth spread across quartiles or fifths of the entire population. Clearly, Blacks are clustered toward the bottom quartile, while almost half of the Whites are in the top two-fifths. The same pattern exists for family wealth: 57 percent of blacks grew up at the bottom compared to only 14 percent of Whites. At the other end of the income and wealth pyramids, almost one-quarter (23 percent) of Whites were raised at the top versus only 2 percent of Blacks.

How do African Americans fare on matching or even enjoying greater economic success than their parents?

Admittedly, the current economic times are tough for all households, but even considering that, Blacks are less likely to rise above their parents' typically modest circumstances.

Black children are much less likely to end up in the middle class than White children. Not only is this true for the ones who grow up in poverty but also for those whose parents have made it to the middle class.

Only 23 percent of Blacks raised in the middle class exceed their parents' wealth, compared with 56 percent of Whites. Only at the very bottom do a majority of Blacks surpass their parents' wealth, but even there, White people below the poverty level do much better.

The American dream of upward mobility, while not being carried out as successfully by Black Americans, is certainly embraced by them. While only 52 percent of Whites believe their economic circumstances will be better in ten years, 73 percent of Blacks foresee improved personal finances ahead.

Sources: Economic Mobility Project 2012; Landry and Marsh 2011, Pew Charitable Trust 2011, 2012; Sawhill, Winship, and Grannis 2012.

TABLE 6.1
Percentage of Americans Raised in Each Quintile, by Race

	Family Income		Family Wealth	
	Black	White	Black	White
Raised in Top Quintile	2%	23%	2%	23%
Raised in Fourth Quintile	7%	23%	6%	22%
Raised in Middle Quintile	8%	22%	7%	23%
Raised in Second Quintile	18%	21%	28%	19%
Raised in Bottom Quintile	65%	11%	57%	14%

Notes: Numbers in each column may not sum to 100 percent due to rounding.

Source: Economic Mobility Project 2012: 18.

The complexity of the relative influence of race, income, and wealth was apparent in the controversy surrounding the publication of sociologist William J. Wilson's *The Declining Significance of Race* (1980). Pointing to the increasing affluence of African Americans, Wilson concluded, "...class has become more important than race in determining black life-chances in the modern world" (p. 150). The policy implications of his conclusion are that programs must be developed to confront class subordination rather than ethnic and racial discrimination. Wilson did not deny the legacy of discrimination reflected in the disproportionate number of African Americans who are poor, less educated, and living in inadequate and overcrowded housing. However, he pointed to "compelling evidence" that young Blacks were competing successfully with young Whites.

Early critics of Wilson commented that focusing attention on this small, educated elite ignores vast numbers of African Americans relegated to the lower class (Pinkney 1984; Willie 1978, 1979). Wilson himself was not guilty of such an oversimplification and indeed expressed concern over the plight of lower-class, inner-city African Americans as they seemingly fall even further behind. He pointed out that the poor are socially isolated and have shrinking economic opportunities (2011). However, it is easy for many people to conclude superficially that because educated Blacks are entering the middle class, race has ceased to be of concern.

Watch the Video on MySocLab: ABC 20/20: Colorism

Employment

This precarious situation for African Americans—the lack of dependable assets—is particularly relevant as we consider their employment picture. Higher unemployment rates for Blacks have persisted since the 1940s, when they were first documented. Even in the best economic times, the Black unemployment rate is still significantly higher than it is for Whites. In 2012, as the United States tried to emerge from a long recession, the Black unemployment rate stood at 14.4 percent compared to 7.0 percent for Whites. Considerable evidence exists that Blacks are the first fired as the business cycle weakens.

The employment picture is especially grim for African American workers aged 16 to 24. During the height of the recent recession, for Black youth aged 16–19, unemployment in 2012 hit just over 39 percent—equivalent to the national unemployment rate during the darkest period of the Great Depression (Bureau of Labor Statistics 2012b; Couch and Fairlie 2010).

Social scientists have cited many factors to explain why official unemployment rates for young African Americans are so high:

- Many African Americans live in the depressed economy of the central cities.
- Immigrants and illegal aliens present increased competition.
- White middle-class women have entered the labor force.
- Illegal activities whereby youths can make more money are increasingly prevalent.

None of these factors is likely to change soon, so depression-like levels of unemployment probably will persist (Haynes 2009).

The picture grows even more somber because we are considering only official unemployment. The federal government's Bureau of Labor Statistics counts as unemployed people only those who are actively seeking employment. Therefore, to be officially unemployed, a person must not hold a full-time job, must be registered with a government employment agency, and must be engaged in submitting job applications and seeking interviews. The official unemployment rate leaves out millions of Americans, Black and White, who are effectively unemployed. It does not count people who are so discouraged they have temporarily given up looking for employment. The problem of unemployment is further compounded by **underemployment**, or working at a job for

TABLE 6.2
Percentages of African American Employees in Selected Occupations, 1982–2010

Occupation	1982	1995	2010
Lawyers and judges	7.2	7.6	9.2
Physicians	2.3	3.6	4.3
Registered nurses	8.2	8.4	12.0
College professors	4.8	6.2	6.3
Librarians	7.2	7.6	9.2
Social workers	16.1	23.7	22.8
Managers	3.9	7.5	6.4
Sales workers	3.8	7.8	11.3
Cashiers	10.0	15.8	16.1
Police and detectives	9.3	11.2	12.1

Sources: Bureau of the Census *Statistical Abstract of the United States*: 1982 data in *1984* Table 616 on pp. 419–420; 1995 data in *1996* Table 637 on pp. 405–407; and 2010 data in *2012* Table 616 on pp. 393–396.

which one is overqualified, involuntarily working part-time instead of full-time, or being employed only intermittently.

Although a few African Americans have crashed through the glass ceiling and made it into the top echelons of business or government, more have entered a wider variety of jobs. As shown in Table 6.2, African Americans, who constitute 12.4 percent of the population, are underrepresented in high-status, high-paying occupations. The taboo against putting Blacks in jobs in which they would supervise Whites has weakened, and the percentage of African Americans in professional and managerial occupations has shown remarkable improvement. However, much improvement can still be made.

Family Life

In its role as a social institution providing for the socialization of children, the family is crucial to its members' life satisfaction. The family also reflects the influence, positive or negative, of income, housing, education, and other social factors. For African Americans, the family reflects both amazing stability and the legacy of racism and low income across many generations.

Challenges to Family Stability

More than one-third of African American children had both a father and a mother present in 2009 (see Figure 6.4). Although single-parent African American families are common, they are not universal. In comparison, such single-parent arrangements were also present in about one in five White families.

It is just as inaccurate to assume that a single-parent family is necessarily deprived as it is to assume that a two-parent family is always secure and happy. Nevertheless, life in a single-parent family can be extremely stressful for all single parents and their children, not just those who are members of subordinate groups. Because the absent parent is more often the father, the lack of a male presence almost always means the lack of a male income. This monetary impact on a single-parent household cannot be overstated.

Watch the Video on MySocLab: *Economics of the African-American Family*

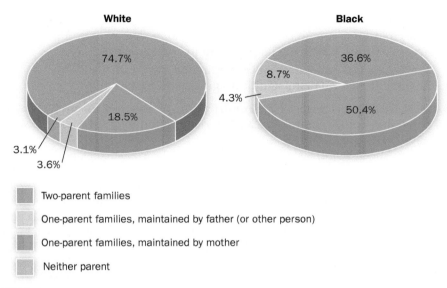

White

74.7%

18.5%

3.1%

3.6%

Black

36.6%

8.7%

4.3%

50,4%

■ Two-parent families

□ One-parent families, maintained by father (or other person)

■ One-parent families, maintained by mother

□ Neither parent

FIGURE 6.4

Living Arrangements for Children Younger Than 18

Note: Data reported in 2011 for 2009. White data are for White non-Hispanic and do not total to 100 percent due to rounding error.

Source: Kreider and Ellis 2011: 4–5.

For many single African American women living in poverty, having a child is an added burden. However, the tradition of extended family among African Americans eases this burden somewhat. The absence of a husband does not mean that no one shares in childcare: out-of-wedlock children born to Black teenage mothers often live with their grandparents and form three-generation households.

No single explanation accounts for the rise in single-parent households. Sociologists attribute the rapid expansion in the number of such households primarily to shifts in the economy that have kept Black men, especially in urban areas, out of work. The phenomenon certainly is not limited to African Americans. Increasingly, both White and Black unmarried women bear children. More and more parents, both White and Black, divorce, so even children born into a two-parent family might end up living with only one parent.

Strengths of African American Families

In the midst of ever-increasing single parenting, another picture of African American family life becomes visible: success despite discrimination and economic hardship. Robert Hill (1999), of the National Urban League and Morgan State University, listed the following five strengths of African American families that allow them to function effectively in a hostile (racist) society.

1. *Strong kinship bonds:* Blacks are more likely than Whites to care for children and the elderly in an extended family network.

2. *A strong work orientation:* Poor Blacks are more likely to be working, and poor Black families often include more than one wage earner.

3. *Adaptability of family roles:* In two-parent families, an egalitarian pattern of decision making is the most common. The self-reliance of Black women who are the primary wage earners best illustrates this adaptability.

4. *Strong achievement orientation*: Working-class Blacks indicate a greater desire for their children to attend college than do working-class Whites. A majority of low-income African American children want to attend college.

5. *A strong religious orientation*: Since the time of slavery, Black churches have been the impetus behind many significant grassroots organizations.

Read the Document
on MySocLab: *African American Families: A Legacy of Vulnerability and Resilience*

Social workers and sociologists have confirmed through social research the strengths that Hill noted first in 1972. In the African American community, these are the sources of family strength (Hudgins 1992).

Increasingly, social scientists are looking at both the weaknesses and the strengths of African American family life. Expressions of alarm about instability date back to 1965, when the Department of Labor issued the report *The Negro Family: The Case for National Action*. The document, commonly known as the Moynihan Report, after its principal author, sociologist Daniel Patrick Moynihan, outlined a "tangle of pathology" with the Black family at its core. More recently, two studies—the Stable Black Families Project and the National Survey of Black Americans—sought to learn how Black families encounter problems and resolve them successfully with internal resources such as those that Hill outlined in his highly regarded work (Department of Labor 1965; Massey and Sampson 2009).

The most consistently documented strength of African American families is the presence of an extended family household. The most common feature is having grandparents residing in the home. Extended living arrangements are much more common among Black households than among White ones. These arrangements are recognized as having the important economic benefit of pooling limited economic resources. Because of the generally lower earnings of African American heads of household, income from second, third, and even fourth wage earners is needed to achieve a desired standard of living or, in all too many cases, simply to meet daily needs (Haxton and Harknett 2009).

Housing

Housing plays a major role in determining the quality of a person's life. For African Americans, as for Whites, housing is the result of personal preferences and income. However, African Americans differ from Whites because their housing has been restricted through discrimination, which has not been the case for Whites. We devote significant attention to housing because, for most people, housing is critical to their quality of life and often represents their largest single asset.

Although Black housing has improved—as indicated by statistics on home ownership, new construction, density of living units, and quality as measured by plumbing facilities—African Americans remain behind Whites on all these standards. The quality of Black housing is inferior to that of Whites at all income levels, yet Blacks pay a larger proportion of their income for shelter.

Read the Document
on MySocLab: *Use of Black English and Racial Discrimination in Urban Housing Markets*

Typically in the United States, as noted, White children attend predominantly White schools, Black children attend predominantly Black schools, and Hispanic children attend predominantly Hispanic schools. This school segregation is not only the result of the failure to accept busing but also the effect of residential segregation. In their studies on segregation, Douglas Massey and Nancy Denton (1993) concluded that racial separation "continues to exist because white America has not had the political will or desire to dismantle it" (p. 8). In Chapter 1, we noted the pervasiveness of residential segregation as reflected in the most recent analysis of housing patterns (refer back to Table 1.2). Racial isolation in neighborhoods has only improved modestly over the last two generations.

What factors create residential segregation in the United States? Among the primary factors are the following:

- Because of private prejudice and discrimination, people refuse to sell or rent to people of the "wrong" race, ethnicity, or religion.
- The prejudicial policies of real estate companies steer people to the "correct" neighborhoods.
- Government policies do not effectively enforce anti-bias legislation.
- Public housing policies today, as well as past construction patterns, reinforce locating housing for the poor in inner-city neighborhoods.
- Policies of banks and other lenders create barriers based on race to financing home purchasing.

The issue of racial-based financing deserves further explanation. In the 1990s, new attention was focused on the persistence of **redlining**, the practice of discriminating against people trying to buy homes in minority and racially changing neighborhoods.

It is important to recall the implications of this discrimination in home financing for the African American community. Earlier in the chapter, we noted the great disparity between Black and White family wealth and the implications of this for the present and future generations. The key factor in this inequality was the failure of African Americans to accumulate wealth through home buying.

A dual housing market is part of today's reality, although attacks continue against the remaining legal barriers to fair housing. In theory, **zoning laws** are enacted to ensure that specific standards of housing construction will be satisfied. These regulations can also separate industrial and commercial enterprises from residential areas. However, some zoning laws in suburbs have curbed the development of low- and moderate-income housing that would attract African Americans who want to move out of the central cities.

For years, constructing low-income public housing in the ghetto has furthered racial segregation. The courts have not ruled consistently in this matter in recent years so, as with affirmative action, public officials lack clear guidance. Even if court decisions continue to dismantle exclusionary housing practices, the rapid growth of integrated neighborhoods is unlikely. In the future, African American housing probably will continue to improve and remain primarily in all-Black neighborhoods. This gap is greater than can be explained by differences in social class.

Criminal Justice

A complex, sensitive topic affecting African Americans is their role in criminal justice. It was reported in 2012 that Blacks constitute 4.3 percent of all lawyers, 12.1 percent of police officers, 10.6 percent of detectives, and 28.8 percent of security guards but 39 percent of jail and prison inmates.

Data collected annually in the FBI's Uniform Crime Report show that Blacks account for 28 percent of arrests, even though they represent only about 12 percent of the nation's population. Conflict theorists point out that the higher arrest rate is not surprising for a group that is disproportionately poor and, therefore, much less able to afford private attorneys, who might be able to prevent formal arrests from taking place. Even more significantly, the Uniform Crime Report focuses on index crimes (mainly property crimes), which are the type of crimes most often committed by low-income people.

These numbers are staggering but, as dramatic as they are, it is not unusual to hear exaggerations presented as facts, such as "more Black men are in prison than in college." The reality is sobering enough—581,000 in prison compared to 2,584,000 in college.

Read the Document on MySocLab: Navigating Public Places

While the number of African American judges is growing, they still are too few in number. For example, in Cook County, which includes Chicago, Black criminal court judges account for 21 percent of the total, which seems impressive, but Blacks are the defendants in 72 percent of the cases (Chaney 2009).

About one in 16 White males can expect to go to a state or federal prison during his life-time, yet for Black males, this lifetime probability is one out of three (Carson and Sabol 2012: Table 7; National Center for Educational Statistics 2011: Table a-39-1).

Most (actually 70 percent) of all the violent crimes against Whites are perpetrated by Whites, according to the FBI. In contrast to popular misconceptions about crime, African Americans and the poor are especially likely to be the victims of serious crimes. This fact is documented in **victimization surveys**, which are systematic interviews of ordinary peo-ple carried out annually to reveal how much crime occurs. These Department of Justice statistics show that African Americans are 35 percent more likely to be victims of violent crimes than are Whites (Truman 2011).

Central to the concerns of minorities regarding the criminal justice system is **differential justice**—that is, Whites are dealt with more leniently than are Blacks, whether at the time of investigation, arrest, indictment, conviction, sentencing, incarceration, or parole. Studies demonstrate that police often deal with African American youths more harshly than with White youngsters. Law is a public social institution and in many ways reproduces the inequality experienced in life (Peterson 2012).

In the "Speaking Out" box, legal scholar Michelle Alexandra considers how African Americans, especially males, are much more likely to be imprisoned and face lifetime consequences even after they have served their time. While Whites and Blacks equally engage in drug crimes (if anything, White youth more), Black men have been admitted to prison on drug offenses 20 to 50 times more often than White men.

It also has been accepted, albeit reluctantly, that the government cannot be counted on to address inner-city problems. In crimes involving African Americans, legal system scholars have observed **victim discounting**, or the tendency to view crime as less socially significant if the victim is viewed as less worthy. For example, the numerous killings of Black youth going to and from school attract much less attention than, for example, a

((𝕐)) Speaking Out

The New Jim Crow

Jarvious Cotton cannot vote. Like his father, his grandfather, great-grandfather, and great-great-grandfather, he has been denied the right to participate in our electoral democracy. Cotton's family tree tells the story of several generations of black men who were born in the United States but who were denied the most basic freedom that democracy promises—the freedom to vote for those who will make the rules and laws that govern one's life. Cotton's great-great-grandfather could not vote as a slave. His great-grandfather was beaten to death by the Ku Klux Klan for attempting to vote. His grandfather was prevented from voting by Klan intimidation. His father was barred from voting by poll taxes and literacy tests. Today, Jarvious Cotton cannot vote because he, like many black men in the United States, has been labeled a felon and is currently on parole.

Michelle Alexander

Cotton's story illustrates, in many respects, the adage, "The more things change, the more they remain the same." In each generation, new tactics have been used to achieve the same goals—goals shared by the Founding Fathers. Denying African Americans citizenship was deemed essential to the formation of the original union. Hundreds of years later, America is still not an egalitarian democracy. The arguments and rationalizations that have been trotted out in support of racial exclusion and discrimination in its various forms have changed and evolved, but the outcome has remained largely the same. An extraordinary percentage of black men in the United States are legally barred from voting today, just as they have been throughout most of American history. They are also subject to legalized discrimination in employment, housing, education, public benefits, and jury service, just as their parents, grandparents, and great-grandparents once were.

Since the collapse of Jim Crow, what has changed has less to do with the basic structure of society than with the language we use to justify it. In the era of colorblindness, it is no longer socially permissible to use race, explicitly, as a justification for discrimination, exclusion, and social contempt. So we don't. Rather than rely on race, we use our criminal justice system to label people of color "criminals" and then engage in all the practices we supposedly left behind. Today, it is perfectly legal to discriminate against criminals in nearly all the ways that it was once legal to discriminate against African Americans. Once you're labeled a felon, the old forms of discrimination—employment discrimination, housing discrimination, denial of the right to vote, denial of educational opportunity, denial of food stamps and other public benefits, and exclusion from jury service—are suddenly legal. As a criminal, you have scarcely more rights, and arguably less respect, than a Black man living in Alabama at the height of Jim Crow. We have not ended racial caste in America: We have merely redesigned it.

Source: Alexander 2012: 1–3.

---

shooting spree that takes five lives in a suburban school. When a schoolchild walks into a cafeteria or schoolyard with automatic weapons and kills a dozen children and teachers, it is a case of national alarm, as with Columbine. When children kill each other in drive-by shootings, it is viewed as a local concern, reflecting the need to clean up a dysfunctional neighborhood. Many African Americans note that the main difference between these two situations is not the death toll but who is being killed: middle-class Whites in the schoolyard shootings and Black ghetto youth in the drive-by shootings.

It is most important to remember that crime and victimization cannot be viewed in isolation but must be seen as interconnected with everything from education to employment, the quality of health care, to the homes to which one returns at the end of the day. W. E. B. Du Bois noted over a century ago that crime was difficult to address precisely because, "It is phenomenon that stands not alone, but rather as a symptom of countless wrong social conditions" (1996:242, originally 1899).

Healthcare

The price of being an African American took on new importance when a shocking study published in a prestigious medical journal revealed that two-thirds of boys in Harlem, a predominantly Black neighborhood in New York City, can expect to die young or in mid-adulthood—that is, before they reach age 65. In fact, they have less chance of surviving even to age 45 than their White counterparts nationwide have of reaching age 65. The medical researchers noted that it is not the stereotyped images of AIDS and violence that explain the staggering difference. Black men are much more likely to fall victim to unrelenting stress, heart disease, and cancer (Fing et al. 1996).

Morbidity and mortality rates for African Americans as a group, and not just Harlem men, are equally distressing. Compared with Whites, Blacks have higher death rates from diseases of the heart, pneumonia, diabetes, and cancer. Significant differences exist among segments of the population with Whites living longer than Blacks. So, for example, among those born in 1994, at one extreme a White female could anticipate living to 79.6 years, while a Black male could expect a lifespan of 64.9 years—that is, equivalent to what White females could reasonably expect who were born in 1935 (Arias 2010: Table 12; Bureau of the Census 2010a: Table 102).

Drawing on the conflict perspective, sociologist Howard Waitzkin (1986) suggests that racial tensions contribute to the medical problems of African Americans. In his view, the stress resulting from racial prejudice and discrimination helps explain the higher rates of hypertension found among African Americans (and Hispanics) than among Whites. Death resulting from hypertension is twice as common in Blacks as in Whites; it is believed to be a critical factor in Blacks' high mortality rates from heart disease, kidney disease, and strokes. Although medical experts disagree, some argue that the stress resulting from racism and suppressed hostility exacerbates hypertension among African Americans (Cooper et al. 1999; A. Green et al. 2007).

Related to the healthcare dilemma is the problem of environmental justice, which was introduced in Chapter 3 and again in Chapter 5 with reference to Native Americans.

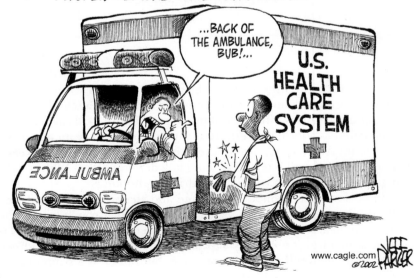

Problems associated with toxic pollution and hazardous garbage dumps are more likely to be faced by low-income Black communities than by their affluent counterparts. This disproportionate exposure to environmental hazards can be viewed as part of the complex cycle of discrimination faced by African Americans and other subordinate groups in the United States.

Just how significant is the impact of poorer health on the lives of the nation's less-educated people, less-affluent classes, and subordinate groups? Drawing on a variety of research studies, population specialist Evelyn Kitagawa (1972) estimated the "excess mortality rate" to be 20 percent. In other words, 20 percent more people were dying than otherwise might have because of poor health linked to race and class. Using Kitagawa's model, we can calculate that if every African American in the United States were White and had at least one year of college education, some 57,000 fewer Blacks would have died in 2012 and in each succeeding year (author's estimate based on Bureau of the Census 2011a: Table 1).

Politics

Despite Barack Obama entering the White House as president in 2009, African Americans have not received an equal share of the political pie. After Reconstruction, it was not until 1928 that a Black was again elected to Congress. With Obama's election to the presidency, once again, no African American serves in the U.S. Senate at the time of this writing. Recent years brought some improvement at local levels; the number of Black elected officials increased from fewer than 1,500 in 1970 to over 10,500 in 2011 (Joint Center for Political and Economic Studies 2011).

Obama's 2008 electoral victory was impressive and, while not a landside victory, his winning margin indicated widespread support. Expectedly, at least 93 percent of Blacks backed Obama in 2008 and again in 2012, but he also had 66 percent of all voters under 30, and 69 percent of first-time voters were prepared to vote for the first African American president (Connelly 2008; Edison Research 2012).

However, major problems confront the continued success of African American politicians. Locally elected Black officials find it difficult to make the jump to statewide office. Voters, particularly non-Black voters, have difficulty seeing Black politicians as anything other than representatives of the Black community and express concern that the views of Whites and other non-Blacks will not be represented by an African American.

The political gains by African Americans, as well as Hispanics, have been placed in jeopardy by legal actions that questioned race-based districts. Boundaries for elective office, ranging from city council positions to the U.S. House of Representatives, have been drawn in such a way so as to concentrate enough members of a racial or ethnic group to create a "safe majority" to make it likely that a member of that group will get elected. In Chapter 3, we noted how the push to require photo ID, regarded by many as a modern day example of institutional discrimination, by a growing number of states would have a greater negative impact on potential Black voters than the general electorate.

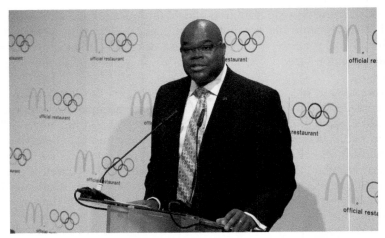

Thus far, few but now growing in numbers, African Americans are entering positions that few people of any color reach. Don Thompson was named CEO of McDonalds in 2012 having begun his career with the corporation in 1990 as an electrical engineer. In 2012, just five other African Americans were heads of Fortune 500 corporations.

The changing racial and ethnic landscape can be expected to have an impact on future strategies to elect African Americans to office, especially in urban areas. However, now that the number of Hispanics exceeds the number of Blacks nationwide, observers wonder how this might play out in the political world. A growing number of major cities, including Los Angeles and Chicago, are witnessing dramatic growth in the Hispanic population. Latinos often settle near Black neighborhoods or even displace Blacks who move into the suburbs, making it more difficult to develop African American districts. For example, South Central Los Angeles, the site of rioting in 1992 described earlier, is now two-thirds Latino. The full impact has not been felt yet because the Latino population tends to be younger, with many not yet reaching voting age. Nearly all elected officials who represent the area are Black. Yet resident concerns are nearly the same they were a generation earlier—quality schools, public safety, and economic development (Medina 2012).

Conclusion

While moving from slavery to freedom is dramatic, it took centuries and was opposed every step along the way. An example is the popular publication *The Negro Motorist Green Book*, which began publication in the 1930s by Harlem civic leader Victor Green and continued into the 1960s. The book offered African American travelers information on where they could be welcomed in diners, hotels, and even private residences. Even decades after end slavery ended, Blacks taking road trips found it useful to have guidance to avoid indignities, which ranged from disrespectful service to actual sundown towns (McGee 2010).

The dramatic events affecting African Americans today have their roots in the forcible bringing of their ancestors to the United States as slaves. In the South,

whether as slaves or later as victims of Jim Crow, Blacks were not a real threat to any but the poorest Whites, although even affluent Whites feared the perceived potential threat that Blacks posed. During their entire history here, Blacks have been criticized when they rebelled and praised when they went along with the system. During the time of slavery, revolts were met with increased suppression; after emancipation, leaders who called for accommodation were applauded.

Blacks, in their efforts to bring about change, have understandably differed in their willingness to form coalitions with Whites. African Americans who resisted in the days of either slavery or the civil rights movement (see the intergroup relations continuum in the figure on the following page) would have concurred with Du Bois's (1903) comment that a Black person "simply wishes to make it possible to be both a Negro and an American, without being cursed and spit upon by his fellows, without having the door of opportunity closed roughly in his face" (pp. 3–4). The object of Black protest seems simple enough, but for many people, including presidents, the point was lost.

How much progress has been made? When that progress covers several hundred years, beginning with slavery and ending with rights recognized constitutionally, it is easy to be impressed. However, let us consider Topeka, Kansas, the site of the 1954 *Brown v. Board of Education* case. Linda Brown, one of the original plaintiffs, also was touched by another segregation case. In 1992, the courts held that Oliver Brown, her grandchild, was victimized because the Topeka schools were still segregated, now for reasons of residential segregation. The remedy to separate schools in this Kansas city is still unresolved (Hays 1994).

Black and White Americans have dealt with the continued disparity between the two groups by endorsing several ideologies, as shown in the representation of the Spectrum of Intergroup Relations. Assimilation was the driving force behind the civil rights movement, which sought to integrate Whites and Blacks into one society. People who rejected contact with the other group endorsed separatism. As Chapter 2 showed, both Whites and Blacks generally lent little support to separatism. In the late 1960s, the government and various Black organizations began to recognize cultural pluralism as a goal, at least paying lip service to the desire of many African Americans to exercise cultural and economic autonomy. Perhaps on no other issue is this desire for control more evident than in the schools.

Substantial gains have been made, but will the momentum continue? Improvement has occurred in a generation inspired and spurred on to bring about change. If the resolve to continue toward that goal lessens in the United States, then the picture may become bleaker, and the rate of positive change may decline further.

SPECTRUM OF INTERGROUP RELATIONS

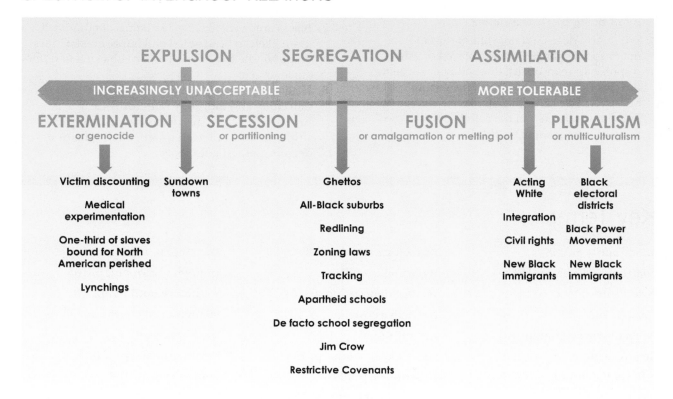

Looking Back

Summary

1. Slavery was a system that defined the people forcibly brought from Africa, and their descendants, as property of their masters, having no rights, yet governed by a series of slave codes. Despite the total restrictiveness of slavery as an institution, slaves often tried to resist the system while abolitionists worked for their freedom.

2. Throughout history, many individuals have emerged as leaders within the African American community. Particularly noteworthy were Booker T. Washington and W. E. B. Du Bois, both of whom, although they took different approaches, expressed dissatisfaction with the second-class status of being Black in America.

3. White Americans did not voluntarily embrace major social change. It was achieved only in response to years of civil disobedience through the civil rights movement and the example set by Martin Luther King, Jr. The pace of change was limited, as reflected in the calls for Black Power that came from some youthful members of the movement.

4. African Americans have made gains in all levels of formal schooling but still fall behind the gains made by others.

5. Income and wealth disparities persist between Black and White Americans, and African Americans continue to face the challenge of accumulating assets. Typically, Black Americans are underrepresented in high-wage, high-status occupations and overrepresented in low-wage, low-status occupations.

6. Family life among Black Americans has many identifiable strengths. A particular challenge faces the growing proportion of households that are moving into the middle class.

7. Blacks are more likely to be victims of crime and more likely to be arrested and imprisoned. Critics question whether minorities are subjected to differential justice.

8. Healthcare statistics reveal significantly higher morbidity and mortality rates for African Americans. Black Americans have made great strides in being elected to office but remain underrepresented nationally.

Key Terms

abolitionists, p. 148

apartheid schools, p. 161

civil disobedience, p. 157

class, p. 163

de facto segregation, p. 161

de jure segregation, p. 155

differential justice, p. 170

income, p. 164

Jim Crow, p. 149

racial formation, p. 148

redlining, p. 169

relative deprivation, p. 158

restrictive covenant, p. 154

riff-raff theory, p. 158

rising expectations, p. 159

slave codes, p. 147

slavery reparations, p. 150

sundown towns, p. 146

tracking, p. 161

underemployment, p. 165

victim discounting, p. 170

victimization surveys, p. 170

wealth, p. 164

White primary, p. 150

zoning laws, p. 169

Review Questions

1. In what ways were slaves defined as property?

2. To what degree have the civil rights movement initiatives in education been realized, or do they remain unmet?

3. What challenges face the African American middle class?

4. What are the biggest assets and problems facing African American families?

5. What are the similarities in the experiences of African Americans in the criminal justice and healthcare systems?

Critical Thinking

1. How much time do you recall spending in school thus far learning about the history of Europe? How about Africa? What do you think this says about the way education is delivered or what we choose to learn?

2. What would you consider the three most important achievements in civil rights for African Americans since 1950? What roles did Whites and Blacks play in making these events happen?

3. What was the ethnic and racial composition of the neighborhoods in which you have lived and the schools you have attended? Consider how the composition of one may have influenced the other. What steps would have been necessary to ensure more diversity?

4. How are the problems in crime, housing, and health interrelated?

Listen to Chapter 7 on MySocLab

7

Latinos

7-1 Discuss the characteristics of Latinos and explain pan-ethnicity.

7-2 Describe the current economic picture of Latinos.

7-3 Address the present role of Latinos in politics.

7-4 Explain the role of religion for Latinos.

7-5 Identify the contemporary roles of Mexican Americans and Puerto Ricans.

7-6 Summarize the issues surrounding statehood for Puerto Rico and its economy.

7-7 Examine and discuss the culture of Cuban Americans.

7-8 Describe the diversity among Central and South Americans and their immigration status in the U.S.

One would not be surprised to hear fellow citizens in Miami or El Paso speaking Spanish, but what about in a small town in Illinois, Kansas, or Alabama? Change can be unsettling in a small town, and when it comes to diversity in the United States, the pattern can vary from one community to the next.

Beardstown is an Illinois river town of about 6,000 people that serves the surrounding rich agriculture land. The major employer for over two decades is a meat-processing plant that offers decent wages for hard, often dangerous work. Immigrants directly from Mexico as well as Mexican Americans from elsewhere were lured to Beardstown by the low cost of living and the jobs that locals passed on. Today, the town founded by Germans is over a third Hispanic and its public schools are 44 percent Hispanic. While townspeople say the influx of Hispanic people has kept the local economy alive and culturally vibrant, the area was slow to mount bilingual programs not just for the schools but also for local businesses and public services from the hospital to the city hall.

The outlook for rural America is even more economically stressful in the Plains. In Ulysses, Kansas, which is similar in size and ethnic composition to Beardstown, Luz Gonzales opened The Down-Town Restaurant to serve the growing area Hispanic population. Initially, she mainly served Mexican food but found a clientele among long-term residents for diner food. So Gonzalez learned to prepare potato salad and other dishes that were exotic to her.

As noted at the outset, change is not easy. In Slocomb, Alabama, a town of 2,000 people that bills itself "Home of the Tomato," many of the local Latino workers who pick green beans, peaches, and strawberries fear seeking health care at the local clinic. The staff are friendly enough and speak Spanish, but on the way there, the workers may face roadblocks as part of immigration crackdowns. Even if the laborers are citizens, they fear exposing relatives and friends who are illegal immigrants. The quest for health care becomes an exercise in overcoming moral issues that most Americans would rarely consider.

In many rural areas, the population has declined steadily. By one estimate, more than a third of counties have lost population, but in 86 percent of these, the Hispanic population has increased, which serves to minimize overall population lost. While increases in the number of Spanish-speaking children is a challenge for schools, without their growing presence, districts would face an almost certain dramatic loss of school funding and massive spending cuts (Beardstown CUSD 15; Constantini 2011; Galewitz 2012; Jordan 2012; Mather and Pollard 2007; Sulzberger 2011; Wisniewski 2012).

According to Census Bureau projections, just over 57 million Americans will be of Spanish or Latin American origin by 2015. This will be more than one in six people in the United States. Collectively, this group is called *Hispanics* or *Latinos*, two terms that we use interchangeably in this book. Latinos accounted for over half the entire nation's population growth between 2000 and 2010. Just considering the public schools in larger cities, Latinos account for over 40 percent of first-graders in Chicago, New York City, San Diego, and Phoenix; over 60 percent in Dallas and Houston; over 70 percent in Los Angeles; and over 85 percent in San Antonio (Bureau of the Census 2012d: Table 4; Passel et al. 2011; Thomás Rivera Policy Institute 2009).

As of 2010, nearly 32 million Hispanics in the United States (two-thirds) are Mexican Americans, or Chicanos. The diversity of Latinos and their national distribution in the United States are shown in Figures 7.1 and 7.2. Except for Puerto Ricans, who are citizens by birth, legal status is

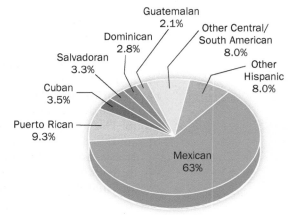

FIGURE 7.1
Hispanic Population of the United States by Origin

Note: "Other Hispanic" includes Spanish Americans and Latinos identified as mixed ancestry as well as other Central and South Americans not otherwise indicated by specific country. All nationalities with more than one million are indicated.

Source: 2010 census data in Ennis, Rios-Vargas, and Albert 2011:3.

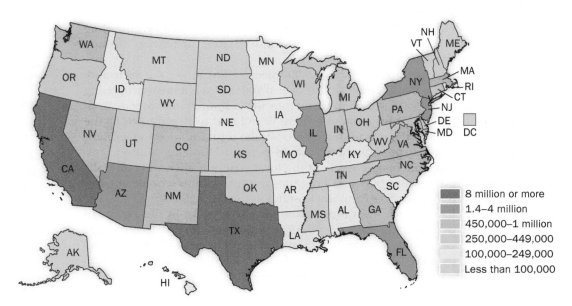

FIGURE 7.2
Where Most Hispanic Americans Live

Source: Ennis, Rios-Vargas, and Albert: Table 7.12.

a major issue within the Latino community. The specter of people questioning Latinos about their legal status even looms over legal residents. According to a national survey, the majority of Hispanic adults in the United States worry that they, a family member, or a close friend could be deported (Lopez et al. 2010).

Latino Identity

Is there a common identity among Latinos? Is a panethnic identity emerging? **Panethnicity** is the development of solidarity between ethnic subgroups. Hispanics do not share a common historical or cultural identity. We noted in Chapter 1 that ethnic identity is not self-evident in the United States and may lead to heated debates even among those who share the same ethnic heritage. Non-Hispanics often give a single label to the diverse group of native-born Latino Americans and immigrants. This labeling by the outgroup is similar to how the dominant group views American Indians or Asian Americans as one collective group. The treating of all Hispanics alike is an unfortunate lack of attention to their history and the history of the United States (C. Rodriquez 1994: 32).

Are Hispanics or Latinos themselves developing a common identity? While generally two-thirds of Latinos and Hispanics in the United State agree that they share a common culture, that does not mean they feel they share a common name. Overall, about half would prefer to use country of origin to identify themselves, such as *Mexican American*; the balance are split between *Hispanic* or *Latino* and *American*.

Among Hispanic youth aged 16–25, only a minority, about 20 percent, prefers to use panethnic names such as *Hispanic* or *Latino*. In Miami, Florida, bumper stickers proclaim "No soy Hispano, soy Cubano": "I am not Hispanic, I am Cuban." As might be expected, identity preferences vary according to whether one is an immigrant or is U.S.-born of U.S.-born Hispanics. About 72 percent of immigrant youth prefer country of origin compared to 32 percent of grandchildren (Pew Hispanic Center 2009, 2012a).

Explore the Map on MySocLab:
Second-Generation Latinos

An even trickier issue is how Latinos identify themselves in racial terms now and how they will in the future. Typically, the sharp White–Black divide is absent in their home countries, where race, if socially constructed, tends to be along a color gradient. A **color gradient** places people along a continuum from light to dark skin color rather than in two or three distinct racial groupings. The presence of color gradients is yet another reminder of the social construction of race. Terms such as *mestizo Hondurans*, *mulatto Colombians*, or *African Panamanians* reflect this continuum of color gradient. In the United States, Latinos tend to avoid taking on the label of being "White" or "Black," although lighter-skinned Hispanics generally distinguish themselves from Black Americans. Social scientists speculate whether in time, like the Irish almost a century ago, Latinos will come to be viewed as "White" rather than as a third collective group in addition to White and Black Americans (Bonilla-Silva 2004; Feagin and Cobas 2008; Pew Hispanic Center 2012a).

The Economic Picture

Among the many indicators of how well a group is doing economically in the United States, income is probably the best one. Table 7.1 summarizes several key measures broken down by the six largest Latino groups. The high rate of poverty is very troubling.

A study released in 2011 documented the continuing high rise in the poverty rate from 1977 through 2010 except for some decline during the relative prosperity the nation experienced in the late 1990s. The government has measured poverty for generations and while Blacks have a higher rate, the largest group of children below the poverty level had always been Whites. In the last two years, however, Hispanics as a group have far over-reached the number of White children in poverty. By 2010, 6.1 million Latino children were in poverty compared to 5 million Whites and 4.4 million Black children. Reflecting the low wages that Latinos often receive in the United States, poor Hispanic children are much more likely to have a working parent than either poor children in the White or Black communities (Lopez and Velasco 2011).

Income is just part of the picture. Low levels of wealth—total assets minus debt—are characteristic of Hispanic households. Although they appear to have slightly higher

Explore the Concept on MySocLab: Health Insurance Coverage Among Latino Subgroups

Explore the Concept on MySocLab: The Wage Gap, By Gender, Race/Hispanic Origin

TABLE 7.1
Hispanic Origin Groups

Group	Foreign Born	Bachelor's Degree	Proficient in English	Poverty Rate
Mexican Americans	36%	9%	64%	27%
Puerto Ricans	1	16	82	27
Cubans	59	24	58	18
Salvadorans	62	7	46	20
Dominicans	57	15	55	26
Guatemalans	67	8	41	26

Note: Include the six largest groups; all reporting at least one million.

Source: Motel and Patten 2012.

levels of median wealth than African American households, Hispanic households average less than 12 cents for every dollar in wealth owned by White non-Hispanic households. Also the trend is not encouraging with the Hispanic and non-Hispanic gap growing. Latinos not only are likely to continue to earn much less annually but also to have fewer financial resources to fall back on (Kent 2010).

By studying the income and poverty trends of Latino households, we can see how much—but also how little—has been accomplished to reduce social inequality among ethnic and racial groups. Although the income of Latinos has gradually increased over the last 30 years, so has White income. The gap between the two groups in both income and poverty level has remained relatively constant. Indeed, the $38,624 income of the typical Latino household in 2011 was more than $14,000 behind the typical *1987* White non-Hispanic household (DeNavas-Walt, Proctor, and Smith 2012: Tables H-16 and HINC-01).

Chapter 6 noted the growing proportion of poor African Americans who find it increasingly difficult to obtain meaningful work. This also has been said of today's poor Latinos, but their situation is much more difficult to predict. On the one hand, as a group, poor Latinos are more geographically mobile than poor African Americans, which increases their prospects of a brighter future. On the other hand, 54 percent of foreign-born Latinos and 17 percent of native-born Latinos send money abroad to help relatives, which puts a greater strain on supporting themselves in the United States (Lopez et al. 2009).

Explore the Concept on MySocLab: Uninsured Children by Poverty Status, Age, Race, and Hispanic Origin: 2009

The Political Presence

Until the late twentieth century, Latinos' political activity has been primarily outside conventional electoral activities. In the 1960s, urban Hispanics, especially Mexican Americans, developed activist groups aimed at what were regarded as especially unsympathetic policies of school administrators. About the same time, labor organizer César Chávez crusaded to organize migrant farmworkers. Efforts to organize agricultural laborers date back to the turn of the twentieth century, but Chávez was the first to enjoy any success. These laborers had never won collective bargaining rights, partly because their mobility and extreme poverty made it difficult for them to organize into a unified group.

Both major political parties have begun to acknowledge that Latinos form a force in the election process. Admittedly, for Puerto Ricans and Cuban Americans, as is discussed later, their central political issue has been the political future of their respective island homelands. Nonetheless, Republicans and Democrats have sought to gain support among Latinos. This recognition by establishment political parties has finally come primarily through the growth of the Hispanic population and also through policies that have facilitated non-English voters.

In 1975, Congress moved toward recognizing the multilingual background of the U.S. population. Federal law now requires bilingual or even multilingual ballots in voting districts where at least 5 percent of the voting-age population or 10,000 people do not speak English. The growing Latino presence documented in the 2010 Census has led Hispanic communities to anticipate that, following reapportionment, they will have even greater political representation, ranging from local council members to representatives and senators in Congress.

For a generation, political scholars spoke of the Latino power at the ballot box, but the Hispanic presence at the polls did not always live up to expectations. The turnout often has been poor because although Hispanics were interested in voting, many were ineligible to vote under the U.S. Constitution. They were noncitizens or, despite bilingual voting information, getting properly registered was a challenge.

This began to change with the 2010 Congressional elections and especially the 2012 presidential election. In the Obama–Romney race, Latinos nationwide constituted one out of every ten voters and their numbers were almost double that or even more in the key swing or battleground states of Colorado, Florida, Nevada, and Virginia. The potential for an even greater Latino political presence is strong.

Anticipating greater turnout, political parties are advancing more Hispanic candidates. Democrats have been decidedly more successful in garnering the Hispanic vote with ultimately 71 percent of Latinos backing Democrat candidate Obama in 2012. Even Cuban Americans, who have tended the favor the Republicans and their strong anti-Castro position, split their vote between Obama and Romney. While not all Latinos necessarily support easing immigration regulations, much of the tone in arguments for strict immigration laws alienates most Latinos. The Democrats promoted policies that allowed children who immigrated illegally as children or even infants with their parents a path to permanent residency following successful completion of their schooling. However, the Republicans officially opposed such steps and encouraged self-deportation for illegal immigrants and, if they did not comply with that, immediate deportation upon detection. The Hispanic community's rapidly growing population, higher proportions of voter registration, and higher participation in elections guarantee future efforts by politicians to gain their support. The Democrats have clearly garnered the allegiance of Hispanics, and the Republicans face a difficult challenge to sway them to their candidates (Campo-Flores 2012; Edison Research 2012; Lopez and Velasco 2011; Preston and Santos 2012).

Like African Americans, many Latinos resent that every four years the political movers and shakers rediscover that they exist. Latino community leaders derisively label candidates' fascination with Latino concerns near election time as either *fiesta politics* or *Hispandering*. Between major elections, modest efforts have been made to court their interest except by Latino elected officials; however, this may change as Latino presence at the ballot box is felt.

Religion

The most important formal organization in the Hispanic community is the Church. Most Puerto Ricans and Mexican Americans express a religious preference for the Catholic Church. In 2011, about 62 percent of Hispanics were Catholic. Figure 7.3 examines a more detailed background of specific religious affiliations indicated by Latinos.

Recently, the Roman Catholic Church has become more community oriented, seeking to identify Latino, or at least Spanish-speaking, clergy and staff to serve Latino parishes.

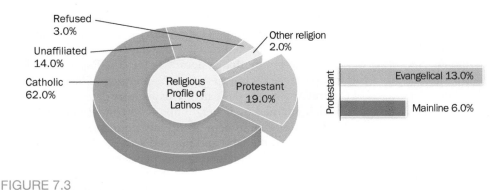

FIGURE 7.3
Religious Profile of Latinos

Source: Pew Hispanic Center 2012a.

The lack of Spanish-speaking priests has been complicated further because a smaller proportion of men are training for the priesthood, and even fewer of them speak Spanish (Ramirez 2000; Rosales 1996).

Not only is the Catholic Church important to Hispanics but Hispanics also play a significant role for the Church. The selection of Pope Frances from Argentina in 2013 was interpreted by many as an acknowledgment of the Latin American role in the global Roman Catholic Church. The population growth of Mexican Americans and other Hispanics has been responsible for the Catholic Church's continued growth in recent years, whereas mainstream Protestant faiths have declined in size. Hispanics account for more than a third of Roman Catholics in the United States. The Church is trying to adjust to Hispanics' more expressive manifestation of religious faith, which is reflected by frequent reliance on their own patron saints and the presence of special altars in their homes. Catholic churches in some parts of the United States are even starting to accommodate observances of the Mexican Día de los Muertos, or Day of the Dead. Such practices are a tradition from rural Mexico, where religion was followed without trained clergy. Yet in the United States today, Hispanics continue to be underrepresented among priests: only 4.4 percent nationwide are Hispanic (O'Connor 1998).

Although Latinos are predominantly Catholic, their membership in Protestant and other Christian faiths is growing. According to a national survey, first-generation Latinos (i.e., the immigrant generation) are 69 percent Catholic, but by the third generation (i.e., grandchildren of immigrants) only 40 percent are Catholic. As one pastor of the New Life Covenant Church in Chicago observed, when the young Latino parishioners leave his church saying, "Thank you for the Mass today," it is not hard to identify them as converts from Catholicism (Hagerty 2011; Pew Hispanic Center 2012a: 35).

Pentecostalism, a type of evangelical Christianity, is growing in Latin America and is clearly making a significant impact on Latinos in the United States. Adherents to Pentecostal faiths hold beliefs similar to those of evangelicals but also believe in the infusion of the Holy Spirit into services and in religious experiences such as faith healing. Pentecostalism and similar faiths are attractive to many Latinos because they offer followers the opportunity to express their religious fervor openly. Furthermore, many of the churches are small and, therefore, offer a sense of community, often with Spanish-speaking leadership. Gradually, the more established faiths are recognizing the desirability of offering Latino parishioners a greater sense of belonging (Hunt 1999).

Mexican Americans

Explore the Activity on MySocLab: *Mexican Americans*

Citizenship is the basic requirement for receiving one's legal rights and privileges in the United States. However, for Mexican Americans, citizenship has been an ambiguous concept at best. Mexican Americans (or Chicanos) have a long history in the United States that stretches back before the nation was even formed to the early days of European exploration. Santa Fe, New Mexico, was founded more than a decade before the Pilgrims landed at Plymouth. Mexican American people trace their ancestry to the merging of Spanish settlers with the Native Americans of Central America and Mexico. This ancestry dates to the brilliant Mayan and Aztec civilizations, which attained their height about 700 and 1500 CE, respectively. However, roots in the land do not guarantee a group any dominance over it. Over several centuries, the Spaniards conquered the land and merged with the Native Americans to form the Mexican people. In 1821, Mexico obtained its independence, but this independence was short-lived: Domination from the north began less than a generation later.

Today, Mexican Americans are creating their own destiny in the United States while functioning in a society that is often concerned about immigration, both legal and illegal. In the eyes of some, including a few in positions of authority, to be Mexican American is to be suspected of being in the country illegally or, at least, of knowingly harboring illegal aliens.

Wars play a prominent part in any nation's history. The United States was created as a result of the colonies' war with England to win their independence. In the 1800s, the United States acquired significant neighboring territory in two different wars. The legacy of these wars and the annexation that resulted were to create the two largest Hispanic minorities in the United States: Mexican Americans and Puerto Ricans.

A large number of Mexicans became aliens in the United States without ever crossing a border. These people first became Mexican Americans at the conclusion of the Mexican–American War. This two-year war culminated with a U.S. occupation of 11 months. Today, Mexicans visit the Museum of Interventions in Mexico City, which outlines the war and how Mexico permanently gave up half its country. The war is still spoken of today as "the Mutilation" (T. Weiner 2004).

In the war-ending Treaty of Guadalupe Hidalgo, signed February 2, 1848, Mexico acknowledged the annexation of Texas by the United States and ceded California and most of Arizona and New Mexico to the United States for $15 million. In exchange, the United States granted citizenship to the 75,000 Mexican nationals who remained on the annexed land after one year. With citizenship, the United States was to guarantee religious freedom, property rights, and cultural integrity—that is, the right to continue Mexican and Spanish cultural traditions and to use the Spanish language.

The beginnings of the Mexican experience in the United States were as varied as the people themselves. Some Mexican Americans were affluent, with large land holdings. Others were poor peasants barely able to survive. Along such rivers as the Rio Grande, commercial towns grew up around the increasing river traffic. In New Mexico and Arizona, many Mexican American people welcomed the protection that the U.S. government offered against several Native American tribes. In California, the gold miners quickly dominated life, and Anglos controlled the newfound wealth. One generalization can be made about the many segments of the Mexican American population in the nineteenth century: They were regarded as a conquered people. In fact, even before the war, many Whites who traveled into the West were already prejudiced against people of mixed blood (in this instance, against Mexicans). Whenever Mexican American and Anglo interests conflicted, Anglo interests won.

A pattern of second-class treatment for Mexican Americans emerged well before the twentieth century. Gradually, the Anglo system of property ownership replaced the Hispanic and Native American systems. Mexican Americans who inherited land proved no match for Anglo lawyers. Court battles provided no protection for poor Spanish-speaking landowners. Unscrupulous lawyers occasionally defended Mexican Americans successfully, only to demand half the land as their fee. Anglo cattle ranchers gradually pushed out Mexican American ranchers. By 1892, the federal government was granting grazing privileges on public grasslands and forests to anyone except Mexican Americans. Effectively, the people who became Mexican *Americans* had also become outsiders in their own homeland. The ground was laid for the twentieth century social structure of the Southwest, an area of growing productivity in which minority groups have increased in size but remain largely subordinate.

The Roman Catholic Church has a long history among Mexicans and Mexican Americans. The Mission San Xavier del Bac in Arizona was founded in 1700.

The Immigrant Experience

Nowhere else in the world do two countries with such different standards of living and wage scales share such an open border. Immigration from Mexico is unique in several respects. First, it has been a continuous large-scale movement for most of the last hundred years. The United States did not restrict immigration from Mexico through legislation until 1965. Second, the proximity of Mexico encourages past immigrants to maintain strong cultural and language ties with their homeland through friends and relatives. Return visits to the old country are only one- or two-day bus rides for Mexican Americans, not once-in-a-lifetime voyages, as they were for most European immigrants. The third point of uniqueness is the aura of illegality that has surrounded Mexican migrants. Throughout the twentieth century, the suspicion in which Anglos have held Mexican Americans has contributed to mutual distrust between the two groups.

The years before World War I brought large numbers of Mexicans into the expanding agricultural industry of the Southwest. The Mexican revolution of 1909–1922 thrust refugees into the United States, and World War I curtailed the flow of people from Europe, leaving the labor market open to Mexican Americans. After the war, continued political turmoil in Mexico and more prosperity in the Southwest brought still more Mexicans across the border.

Simultaneously, corporations in the United States, led by agribusiness, invested in Mexico in such a way as to maximize their profits but minimize the amount of money remaining in Mexico to provide needed employment. Conflict theorists view this investment as part of the continuing process in which American businesses, with the support and cooperation of affluent Mexicans, have used Mexican people when it has been in corporate leaders' best interests. Their fellow Mexicans use Mexican workers as cheap laborers in their own country, and Americans use them here as cheap labor or as undocumented workers and then dismiss them when they are no longer useful (Guerin-Gonzales 1994).

Beginning in the 1930s, the United States embarked on a series of measures aimed specifically at Mexicans. The Great Depression brought pressure on local governments to care for the growing number of unemployed and impoverished. Government officials developed a quick way to reduce welfare rolls and eliminate people seeking jobs: Ship Mexicans back to Mexico. This program of deporting Mexicans in the 1930s was called **repatriation**. As officially stated, the program was constitutional because only illegal aliens were to be repatriated. In reality, Mexicans and even people born in the United States of Mexican background were deported to relieve the economic pressure of the depression. The legal process of fighting a deportation order was overwhelming, however, especially for a poor Spanish-speaking family. The Anglo community largely ignored this outrage against the civil rights of those deported and showed no interest in helping repatriates ease the transition (Balderrama and Rodriguez 2006).

Watch the Video on MySocLab: *Latino Laborers*

When the depression ended, Mexican laborers again became attractive to industry. In 1942, when World War II depleted the labor pool, the United States and Mexico agreed to a program allowing migration across the border by contracted laborers, or **braceros**. Within a year of the initiation of the bracero program, more than 80,000 Mexican nationals had been brought in; they made up one-eleventh of the farmworkers on the Pacific Coast. The program continued with some interruptions until 1964. It was devised to recruit labor from poor Mexican areas for U.S. farms. In the program, which was supposed to be supervised jointly by Mexico and the United States, minimum standards were to be maintained for transportation, housing, wages, and health care of the braceros. Ironically, these safeguards placed the braceros in a better economic situation than Mexican Americans, who often worked alongside the protected Mexican nationals. Mexicans were still regarded as a positive presence by Anglos only when useful, and the Mexican American people were merely tolerated.

Like many policies of the past relating to disadvantaged racial and ethnic groups, the bracero program lives on. After decades of protests, the Mexican government finally issued checks of $3,500 to former braceros and their descendants. The payments were to resolve disputes over what happened to the money the U.S. government gave to the Mexican government to assist in resettlement. To say this has been regarded as too little, much too late is an understatement.

Another crackdown on illegal aliens was to be the third step in dealing with the perceived Mexican problem. Alternately called Operation Wetback and Special Force Operation, it was fully inaugurated by 1954. The term *wetbacks*, or **mojados**—derisive slang for Mexicans who enter illegally—refers to those who secretly swim across the Rio Grande. Like other roundups, this effort failed to stop the illegal flow of workers. For several years, some Mexicans were brought in under the bracero program while other Mexicans were being deported. With the end of the bracero program in 1964 and stricter immigration quotas for Mexicans, illegal border crossings increased because legal crossings became more difficult (J. Kim 2008).

More dramatic than the negative influence that continued immigration has had on employment conditions in the Southwest is the effect on the Mexican and Mexican American people themselves. Routinely, the rights of Mexicans, even the rights to which they are entitled as illegal aliens, are ignored. Of the illegal immigrants deported, few have been expelled through formal proceedings. The Mexican American Legal Defense and Education Fund (MALDEF) has repeatedly expressed concern over how the government handles illegal aliens.

Against this backdrop of legal maneuvers is the tie that the Mexican people have to the land both in today's Mexico and in the parts of the United States that formerly belonged to Mexico. *Assimilation* may be the key word in the history of many immigrant groups, but for Mexican Americans the key term is **La Raza**, literally *the people* or *the race.* Among contemporary Mexican Americans, however, the term connotes pride in a pluralistic Spanish, Native American, and Mexican heritage. Mexican Americans cherish their legacy and, as we shall see, strive to regain some of the economic and social glory that once was theirs (Delgado 2008a).

Despite the passage of various measures designed to prevent illegal immigration, neither the immigration nor the apprehension of illegal aliens is likely to end. Economic conditions are the major factor. For example, the prolonged recession beginning in 2008 leading to a weakened U.S. job market led to a significant decline in individuals seeking to enter the United States from Mexico either legally or illegally. Increased deportations might have contributed to a decline in the number of Mexican Americans in the United States if it were not for U.S.-born children of Mexican ancestry. Whether Mexican immigration returns to its historical levels of the 1990s, remains to be seen (Pew Hispanic Center 2012b).

Mexican Americans will continue to be more closely scrutinized by law enforcement officials because their Mexican descent makes them more suspect as potential illegal aliens. The Mexican American community is another group subject to racial profiling that renders their presence in the United States suspect in the eyes of many Anglos.

In the United States, Mexican Americans have mixed feelings toward the illegal Mexican immigrants. Many are their kin, and Mexican Americans realize that entry into the United States brings Mexicans better economic opportunities. However, numerous deportations only perpetuate the Anglo stereotype of Mexican and Mexican American alike as surplus labor. Mexican Americans, largely the product of past immigration, find that the continued controversy over illegal immigration places them in the conflicting role of citizen and relative. Mexican American organizations opposing illegal immigration must confront people to whom they are closely linked by culture and kinship, and they must cooperate with government agencies they deeply distrust.

Read the Document on MySocLab: *Mexican Americans and Immigrant Incorporation*

Family Life

The most important organization or social institution among Mexican Americans, or for that matter any group, is the family. The structure of the Mexican American family differs little from that of all families in the United States, a statement remarkable in itself, given the impoverished status of a significant number of Mexican Americans.

Latino households are described as laudably more familistic than others in the United States. **Familism** means pride and closeness in the family, which results in family obligation and loyalty coming before individual needs. The family is the primary source of both social interaction and caregiving. In Research Focus, we look at familism more closely.

Familism has been viewed as both a positive and a negative influence on individual Mexican Americans and Puerto Ricans. It has been argued that familism has had the negative effect of discouraging youths with a bright future from taking advantage of opportunities that would separate them from their family. Familism is generally regarded as good, however, because an extended family provides emotional strength in times of crisis. Close family ties maintain the mental and social well-being of the elderly. Most Latinos, therefore, see the intact, extended family as a norm and as a nurturing unit that provides support throughout a person's lifetime. The many significant aspects of familism include the importance of *campadrazgo* (the godparent–godchild relationship), the benefits of the financial dependency of kin, the availability of relatives as a source of advice, and the active involvement of the elderly in the family.

Read the Document
on MySocLab: *Care Options for Older Mexican Americans: Issues Affecting Health and Long-Term Service Needs*

⌕ Research Focus

The Latino Family Circle: Familism

Familism within the Mexican American and the entire Latino community is associated with a sense of obligation to fellow family members, the placement of family interests over individual desires, and exclusiveness of the family even over friends and work. Familism has been likened to a thick social network where one's family defines everyday social interaction.

Familism for the U.S.-born Latino is also associated with familiarity with Spanish so that one can truly relate to the older relatives for whom English may remain very much a foreign language. Being nominally Roman Catholic is another means of maintaining strong extended family ties. U.S. Hispanic families are undergoing transition with the simultaneous growth of more multigenerational families born in the United States as well family members from the homeland. This is all complicated by the mixed status present in so many Latino extended families (with the obvious exception of Puerto Ricans, for whom citizenship is automatic). As explained in Chapter 4, **mixed status** refers to families in which one or more is a citizen and one or more is a noncitizen. This especially becomes problematic when the noncitizens are illegal or undocumented immigrants. All the usual pressures

within a family become magnified when there is mixed status.

Although immigration makes generalizing about Latinos as a group very difficult at any one point in time, analysis of available data indicates that Hispanic households are taking on more of the characteristics of larger society. For example, cohabiting couples with or without children were relatively uncommon among Hispanic groups but now are coming to resemble the pattern of non-Hispanics. Similarly, Mexican-born women now living in the United States are more likely to enter marriage earlier, but later generations of women born in the United States are more likely to start marriage later. The same was true for Puerto Rican women born on the island, compared with those born on the mainland.

In the future, the greatest factor that may lead to a decline in familism is marriage across ethnic lines. Continuing immigration from Mexico has tended to slow outgroup marriage, but during periods of lessened migration, immigrants have been more likely to form unions with different Latino groups or with non-Hispanics.

Today, we begin to see a more individualistic orientation than a collective orientation or familism that is

more likely to encourage family members to move away from their relatives or, more dramatically, lead to desertion or divorce. Studies with other established, longer-term immigrant groups suggest that family members become more individualistic in their values and behavior. People both within and outside the Latino community are interested to see if Hispanics will follow this

pattern and whether the familism that has been so characteristic of much of the Latino community will fade.

Sources: Comeau 2012; Jacobson, England, and Barrus 2008; Landale and Oropesa 2002, 2007; Landale, Oropesa, and Bradatan 2006; Lichter, Brown, Qian, and Carmalt 2007; Sarkistan, Gerena, and Gerstel 2007; Zambrana 2011.

Puerto Ricans

As opposed to other minority groups, it seems that United States citizenship should be clear for Puerto Ricans. However, it continues to be ambiguous. Even Native Americans, who are subject to some unique laws and are exempt from others because of past treaties, have a future firmly dominated by the United States. This description does not necessarily fit Puerto Ricans. Their island home is the last major U.S. colonial territory and, for that matter, one of the few colonial areas remaining in the world. Besides assessing the situation of Puerto Ricans on the mainland, we also need to consider the relationship of the United States to Puerto Rico.

Explore the Activity on MySocLab: *Puerto Rican and Cuban Americans*

Puerto Ricans' current association with the United States, like that of the Mexican people, began as the result of the outcome of a war. The island of Borinquén, subsequently called Puerto Rico, was claimed by Spain in 1493. The native inhabitants, the Taíno Indians, were significantly reduced in number by conquest, slavery, and genocide. Although for generations the legacy of the Taíno was largely thought to be archaeological in nature, recent DNA tests revealed that more than 60 percent of Puerto Ricans today have a Taíno ancestor. About 20,000 identified themselves as Taíno in the 2010 census (Cockburn 2003:41; Kearns 2011).

After Spain ruled Puerto Rico for four centuries, the United States seized the island in 1898 during the Spanish–American War. Spain relinquished control of it in the Treaty of Paris. Puerto Rico's value for the United States, as it had been for Spain, was mainly its strategic location, which was advantageous for maritime trade.

The beginnings of rule by the United States quickly destroyed any hope that Puerto Ricans—or Boricua, as Puerto Ricans call themselves—had for self-rule. All power was given to officials appointed by the president, and Congress could overrule any act of the island's legislature. Even the spelling was changed briefly to Porto Rico to suit North

American pronunciation. English, previously unknown on the island, became the only language permitted in the school systems. The people were colonized—first politically, then culturally, and finally economically (Aran et al. 1973; Christopulos 1974).

The Jones Act of 1917 extended citizenship to Puerto Ricans, but Puerto Rico remained a colony. This political dependence altered in 1948, when Puerto Rico elected its own governor and became a commonwealth. This status, officially Estado Libre Asociado, or Associated Free State, extends to Puerto Rico and its people privileges and rights different from those of people on the mainland. Although Puerto Ricans are U.S. citizens and elect their own governor, they may not vote in presidential elections and have no voting representation in Congress. They are subject to military service, Selective Service registration, and all federal laws. Puerto Ricans have a homeland that is and at the same time is not a part of the United States.

The Bridge Between the Island and the Mainland

Despite their citizenship, immigration officials occasionally challenge Puerto Ricans. Because other Latin Americans attempt to enter the country posing as Puerto Ricans, Puerto Ricans find their papers scrutinized more closely than do other U.S. citizens.

Puerto Ricans came to the mainland in small numbers in the first half of the twentieth century, often encouraged by farm labor contracts similar to those extended to Mexican braceros. During World War II, the government recruited hundreds of Puerto Ricans to work on the railroads, in food-manufacturing plants, and in copper mines on the mainland. But migration has been largely a post–World War II phenomenon. The 1940 census showed fewer than 70,000 Puerto Ricans on the mainland. By 2010, more than 4.6 million Puerto Ricans lived on the mainland and 3.7 million residents lived on the island (Lopez and Velasco 2011).

Among the factors that have contributed to migration are the economic pull away from the underdeveloped and overpopulated island, the absence of legal restrictions against travel, and the increasingly cheap air transportation. As the migration continues, the mainland offers the added attraction of a large Puerto Rican community in New York City, which makes adjustment easier for new arrivals.

New York City still has a formidable population of Puerto Ricans (786,000), but significant changes have taken place. First, Puerto Ricans no longer dominate the Latino scene in New York City, making up only a little more than a third of the city's Hispanic population. Second, Puerto Ricans are now more dispersed throughout the mainland's cities.

As the U.S. economy underwent recessions in the 1970s and 1980s, unemployment among mainland Puerto Ricans, always high, increased dramatically. This increase is evident in migration. In the 1950s, half of the Latino arrivals were Puerto Rican. By the 1970s, they accounted for only 3 percent. Indeed, in some years of the 1980s, more Puerto Ricans went from the mainland to the island than the other way around.

Puerto Ricans returning to the island have become a significant force. Indeed, they now are given the name **Neoricans**, or *Nuyoricans*, a term the islanders also use for Puerto Ricans in New York. Longtime islanders direct a modest amount of hostility toward these Neoricans, numbering near 100,000, or about 2 percent of the population. They usually return from the mainland with more formal schooling, more money, and a better command of English than native Puerto Ricans. It is no surprise that Neoricans compete very well with islanders for jobs and land (Lopez and Velasco 2011).

The ethnic mix of the nation's largest city has gotten even more complex over the last 10 years as Mexican and Mexican American arrivals in New York City have far outpaced any growth among Puerto Ricans. New York City is now following the pattern of other cities such as Miami, where a single group no longer defines the Latino identity.

The Island of Puerto Rico

Puerto Rico, located about a thousand miles from Miami (see Figure 7.4), has never been the same since Columbus discovered it in 1493. The original inhabitants of the island succumbed in large proportions to death by disease, tribal warfare, hard labor, unsuccessful rebellions against the Spanish, and fusion with their conquerors.

Among the institutions Spain imported to Puerto Rico was slavery. Although slavery in Puerto Rico was not as harsh as in the southern United States, the legacy of the transfer of Africans is present in the appearance of Puerto Ricans today, many of whom are seen by people on the mainland as Black.

The commonwealth period that began in 1948 has been significant for Puerto Rico. Change has been dramatic, although it is debatable whether it has all been progress. On

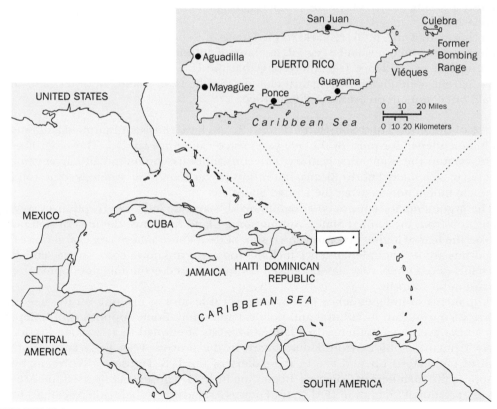

FIGURE 7.4
Puerto Rico

the positive side, Spanish was reintroduced as the language of classroom instruction, but the study of English also is required. The popularity in the 1980s of music groups such as Menudo shows that Puerto Rican young people want to maintain ties with their ethnicity. Such success is a challenge because Puerto Rican music is almost never aired on non-Hispanic radio stations. The Puerto Rican people have had a vibrant and distinctive cultural tradition, as seen clearly in their folk heroes, holidays, sports, and contemporary literature and drama. Dominance by the culture of the United States makes it difficult to maintain their culture on the mainland and even on the island itself.

Puerto Rico and its people reflect a phenomenon called **neocolonialism**, which refers to continuing dependence of former colonies on foreign countries. Initially, this term was introduced to refer to African nations that, even after gaining their political independence from Great Britain, France, and other European nations, continued to find their destiny in the hands of the former colonial powers. Although most Puerto Ricans today are staunchly proud of their American citizenship, they also want to have their own national identity independent of the United States. This has not been easy to achieve and likely will continue to be a challenge.

From 1902, English was the official language of the island, but Spanish was the language of the people, reaffirming the island's cultural identity independent of the United States. In 1992, however, Puerto Rico also established Spanish as an additional official language.

In reality, the language issue is related more to ideology than to substance. Although English is once again required in primary and secondary schools, textbooks might be written in English, although classes are conducted in Spanish. Indeed, Spanish remains the language of the island; 8 percent of the islanders speak only English, and among Spanish-speaking adults, only about 15 percent speak English "very well" (Bureau of the Census 2007d).

In "Speaking Out", in his remarks to the House of Representatives, Congressman Luis Gutierrez speaks about what he regards as abuse of authority by the Puerto Rican government against its residents. It is interesting that the U.S.-born representative of Puerto Rican parents defends himself against charges that he is an island "outsider" and thus should not comment on events in Puerto Rico.

Issues of Statehood and Self-Rule   Puerto Ricans have consistently argued and fought for independence for most of the 500 years since Columbus landed. They continue to do so, even in the twenty-first century. The contemporary commonwealth arrangement is popular with many Puerto Ricans, but others prefer statehood, whereas some call for complete independence from the United States.

The arguments for continued commonwealth status include a perception of special protection from the United States. Among some island residents, the idea of statehood invokes the fear of higher taxes and an erosion of their cultural heritage. Commonwealth supporters argue that independence includes too many unknown costs, so they embrace the status quo. Others view statehood as a key to increased economic development and expansion for tourism.

Proponents of independence have a long, vocal history of insisting on the need for Puerto Rico to regain its cultural and political autonomy. Some supporters of independence have even been militant. In 1950, nationalists attempted to assassinate President Harry Truman, killing a White House guard in the process. Four years later, another band of nationalists opened fire in the gallery of the U.S. House of Representatives, wounding five members of Congress. Beginning in 1974, a group calling itself the Armed Forces of National Liberation (FALN, for Fuerzas Armadas de Liberación Nacional) took responsibility for more than 100 explosions that continued through 1987. The FALN is not alone; at least four other militant groups advocating independence were identified

((◉)) Speaking Out

Puerto Ricans Cannot Be Silenced

Two weeks ago, I spoke about a serious problem in Puerto Rico.

The problem is a systemic effort by the ruling party to deny the right of the people to speak freely, to criticize their government openly, and to make their voices heard.

I talked about student protests that had been met with violent resistance by Puerto Rican police. I talked about closed meetings of the legislature, and about efforts to silence the local Bar Association.... [A recent report] details the complaints of students, legislators, the press, and the general public who were beaten and pepper sprayed by police. Female students who were treated with gross disrespect by the police.

The government's overreaction to demonstrations at the University and at the Capitol over the budget cuts and layoffs.

The images of police tactics and behavior explain why the Department of Justice is investigating the Puerto Rican police for "excessive force" and "unconstitutional searches."

How could you see these images and not speak out?

And I was hardly the first to speak out about these matters and will not be the last....

And what was the response to my speech defending the right of the Puerto Rican people to be heard?

It was to challenge my right to be heard....A leading member of the [Puerto Rican] ruling party even said, "Gutierrez was not born in Puerto Rico. His kids weren't born in Puerto Rico. Gutierrez doesn't plan on being buried in Puerto Rico....So Gutierrez doesn't

Luis Gutierrez

have the right to speak about Puerto Rico...."

If you see injustice anywhere, it is not only your right but your duty to speak out about it....

I may not be Puerto Rican enough for some people, but I know this: Nowhere on earth will you find a people harder to silence than Puerto Ricans.

You won't locate my love for Puerto Rico on my birth certificate or a driver's license, my children's birth certificate or any other piece of paper.

My love for Puerto Rico is right here—in my heart—a heart that beats with our history and our language and our heroes. A place where—when I moved there as a teenager—people talked and argued and debated because we care deeply about our island and our future.

That's still true today—and that freedom is still beating in the hearts of university students, workingmen and women, labor leaders, lawyers, and environmentalists and every person who believes in free speech. You will not silence them, and you will not silence me.

Abraham Lincoln, a leader who valued freedom above all else, said: "Those who deny freedom to others deserve it not for themselves."

It's good advice, and I hope Puerto Rican leaders take it.

Source: Spoken by Gutierrez in the House of Representatives, March 2, 2011. Gutierrez 2011.

as having been at work in the 1980s. The island itself is occasionally beset by violent demonstrations, often reacting to U.S. military installations there—a symbol of U.S. control (Santos-Hernández 2008).

The issue of Puerto Rico's political destiny is, in part, ideological. Independence is the easiest way for the island to retain and strengthen its cultural and political identity. Some nationalists express the desire that an autonomous Puerto Rico develop close political ties with communist Cuba. The crucial arguments for and against independence probably are economic. An independent Puerto Rico would no longer be required to use U.S. shipping lines, which are more expensive than those of foreign competitors. However, an independent Puerto Rico might be faced with a tariff wall when trading with its largest current customer, the mainland United States. Also, Puerto Rican migration to the mainland could be restricted.

Puerto Rico's future status most recently faced a vote in 2012. The latest nonbinding referendum had confusing wording in its two-part question. Observers of the results saw the voters split between statehood and continuation but with very few favoring independence. As it has for over a century, the political future of Puerto Rice remains in doubt (D. Patterson 2012).

The Social Construction of Race   The most significant difference between the meaning of race in Puerto Rico and on the mainland is that Puerto Rico, like so many other Caribbean societies, has a **color gradient**, a term that describes distinctions based on skin color made on a continuum rather than by sharp categorical separations. The presence of a color gradient reflects past fusion between different groups. Rather than seeing people as either black or white in skin color, Puerto Ricans perceive people as ranging from pale white to very black. Puerto Ricans are more sensitive to degrees of difference and make less effort to pigeonhole a person into one of two categories.

The presence of a color gradient rather than two or three racial categories does not necessarily mean less prejudice. Generally, however, societies with a color gradient permit more flexibility, and therefore, are less likely to impose specific sanctions against a group of people based on skin color alone. Puerto Rico has not suffered interracial conflict or violence; its people are conscious of different racial heritages. Studies disagree on the amount of prejudice in Puerto Rico, but all concur that race is not as clear-cut an issue on the island as it is on the mainland.

Racial identification in Puerto Rico depends a great deal on the attitude of the individual making the judgment. If one thinks highly of a person, then he or she may be seen as a member of a more acceptable racial group. Several terms are used in the color gradient to describe people racially: *blanco* (white), *trigueño* (bronze- or wheat-colored), *moreno* (dark-skinned), and *negro* (black) are a few. Factors such as social class and social position determine race, but on the mainland race is more likely to determine social class. This situation may puzzle people from the mainland, but racial etiquette on the mainland may be just as difficult for Puerto Ricans to comprehend and accept. Puerto Ricans arriving in the United States may find a new identity thrust on them by the dominant society (Denton and Villarrubia 2007; Landale and Oropesa 2002; Loveman and Muniz 2007; Sánchez 2007).

The Island Economy

The United States' role in Puerto Rico has produced an overall economy that, though strong by Caribbean standards, remains well below that of the poorest areas of the United States. For many years, the federal government exempted U.S. industries locating in Puerto Rico from taxes on profits for at least 10 years. In addition, the federal government's program of enterprise zones, which grants tax incentives to promote private investment in inner cities, has been extended to Puerto Rico. Unquestionably, Puerto Rico has become attractive to mainland-based corporations. Skeptics point out that as a result, the island's agriculture has been largely ignored. Furthermore, the economic benefits to the island are limited. Businesses have spent the profits gained on Puerto Rico back on the mainland.

Puerto Rico's economy is in severe trouble, even when compared with that of the mainland in a recession. Its unemployment rate in 2011 was 16.9 percent, compared with 8.8 percent for the mainland. In addition, the median household income is one-third of what it is in the United States. In 2011, 46 percent of the population was below the poverty rate, compared with 16 percent in the nation as a whole. Efforts to raise the wages of Puerto Rican workers only make the island less attractive to labor-intensive businesses—that is, those that employ larger numbers of unskilled people. Capital-intensive companies, such as the petrochemical industries, have found Puerto Rico attractive, but they have not created jobs for the semiskilled. A growing problem is that Puerto Rico has emerged as a major gateway to the United States for illegal drugs from South America. This, in turn, has led the island to experience waves of violence and the social ills associated with the drug trade (Bureau of the Census 2012e: Table S1701; Bureau of Labor Statistics 2011).

Puerto Rico is an example of the world systems theory initially presented in Chapter 1. **World systems theory** is the view of the global economic system as divided between certain industrialized nations that control wealth and developing countries that are controlled and exploited. Although Puerto Rico may be well off compared with many other Caribbean nations, it clearly is at the mercy of economic forces in the United States and, to a much lesser extent, other industrial nations. Puerto Rico continues to struggle with the advantages of citizenship and the detriment of playing a peripheral role in the economy of the United States.

Cuban Americans

Third in numbers only to Mexican Americans and Puerto Ricans, Cuban Americans are a significant ethnic Hispanic minority in the United States. Their presence in this country has a long history, with Cuban settlements in Florida dating back to as early as 1831. These settlements tended to be small, close-knit communities organized around a single enterprise such as a cigar-manufacturing firm.

Until recently, however, the number of Cuban Americans was very modest. The 1960 census showed that 79,000 people who had been born in Cuba lived in the United States. Fidel Castro's assumption of power after the 1959 Cuban Revolution led to sporadic movements to the United States and for generations defined the Cuban American political agenda in the United States. By 2010, more than 1.7 million people of Cuban birth or descent lived here.

Immigration

Cuban immigration to the United States since the 1959 revolution has been continuous, but there were three significant influxes of large numbers of immigrants through the 1980s. First, the initial exodus of about 200,000 Cubans after Castro's assumption of power lasted about three years. Regular commercial air traffic continued despite the United States' severing of diplomatic relations with Cuba. This first wave stopped with the missile crisis of October 1962, when all legal movement between the two nations was halted.

An agreement between the United States and Cuba in 1965 produced the second wave through a program of freedom flights—specially arranged charter flights from Havana to Miami. Through this program, more than 340,000 refugees arrived between 1965 and 1973. Despite efforts to encourage these arrivals to disperse into other parts of the United States, most settled in the Miami area (M. Abrahamson 1996).

The third major migration, the 1980 Mariel boatlift, has been the most controversial. In 1980, more than 124,000 refugees fled Cuba in the "freedom flotilla." In May of that year, a few boats from Cuba began to arrive in Key West, Florida, with people seeking asylum in the United States. President Carter (1978:1623), reflecting the nation's hostility toward Cuba's communist government, told the new arrivals and anyone else who might be listening in Cuba that they were welcome "with open arms and an open heart." As the number of arrivals escalated, it became apparent that Castro had used the invitation as an opportunity to send prison inmates, patients from mental hospitals, and drug addicts. However, the majority of the refugees were neither marginal to the Cuban economy nor social deviants.

Other Cubans soon began to call the refugees of this migration **Marielitos**. The word, which implies that these refugees were undesirable, refers to Mariel, the fishing port west of Havana from which the boats departed and where Cuban authorities herded people into boats. The term *Marielitos* remains a stigma in the media and in Florida. Because of their negative reception by longer-established Cuban immigrants and the group's modest skills and lack of formal education, these immigrants had a great deal of difficulty in adjusting to their new lives in the United States (Masud-Piloto 2008b).

The difficult transition for many members of this freedom flotilla also has other reasons. Unlike the earlier waves of immigrants, they grew up in a country bombarded with anti-American images. Despite these problems, their eventual acceptance by the Hispanic community has been impressive, and many members of this third significant wave have found employment. Most have applied for permanent resident status. Government assistance to these immigrants was limited, but help from some groups of Cuban Americans in the Miami area was substantial. However, for a small core group, adjustment was impossible. The legal status of a few of these detainees (e.g., arrivals who were held by the government pending clarification of their refugee or immigrant status) was ambiguous because of alleged offenses committed in Cuba or in the United States (Peréz 2001).

Since 1994, the United States has a **dry foot, wet foot** policy with respect to arrivals from Cuba. Government policy generally allows Cuban nationals who manage to actually reach the United States (dry foot) to remain, whereas those who are picked up at sea (wet foot) are sent back to Cuba. Furthermore, 20,000 visas are issued annually to immigrants who are seeking economic freedom and, for the most part, are not strongly anti-Castro. Unfortunately, other Cubans have taken great risks in crossing the Florida Straits, and an unknown number have perished before reaching the mainland or being intercepted by the Coast Guard. Through all these means, about 300,000 Cubans have come to the United States since 1964 (Economist 2009).

The Current Picture

Compared with other recent immigrant groups and with Latinos as a whole, Cuban Americans are doing well. As shown in Table 7.1, Cuban Americans have college completion rates that are significantly higher than other Latino groups. In this and all other social measures, the pattern is similar. Cuban Americans today compare favorably with other Hispanics, although recent arrivals as a group trail behind White Americans.

The presence of Cubans has been felt in urban centers throughout the United States but most notably in the Miami area. Throughout their various immigration phases, Cubans have been encouraged to move out of southern Florida, but many have returned to Dade County (metropolitan Miami), with its warm climate and proximity to other Cubans and Cuba itself. As of 2008, 49 percent of all Cuban Americans lived in the Miami area; another 20 percent lived elsewhere in Florida. Metropolitan Miami itself now has a Hispanic majority of 62 percent of the total population, compared with a Hispanic presence of only 4 percent in 1950 (American Community Survey 2009, Table B03001).

Probably no ethnic group has had more influence on the fortunes of a city in a short period of time than have the Cubans on Miami. Most people consider the Cubans' economic influence to be positive. With other Latin American immigrants, Cubans have transformed Miami from a quiet resort to a boomtown. To a large degree, they have re-created the Cuba they left behind. Today, the population of Miami is more than 59 percent foreign born—more than any other city. Residents like to joke that one of the reasons they like living in Miami is that it is close to the United States (N. Malone et al. 2003).

The relations between Miami's Cuban Americans and other groups have not been perfect. For example, other Hispanics—including Venezuelans, Ecuadorians, and

Colombians—resent being mistaken for Cubans and feel that their own distinctive nationalities are being submerged. Cubans now find that storefronts in Miami's Little Havana area advertise Salvadoran corn pancakes and that waitresses hail from El Salvador. Cuban Miamians are also slowly adjusting to sharing their influence with the growing diversity of Hispanics. One obvious symbol is the investment of the park district in building more and more soccer fields—Cubans traditionally play baseball (Dahlburg 2004a).

All Cuban immigrants have had much to adjust to, and they have not been able to immediately establish the kind of life they sought. Although some of those who fled Cuba were forced to give up their life's savings, the early immigrants of the first wave were generally well educated, had professional or managerial backgrounds, and therefore met with greater economic success than later immigrants. However, regardless of the occupations the immigrants were able to enter, their families had to make tremendous adjustments. Women who typically did not work outside the home often had to seek employment. Immigrant parents found their children being exposed to a foreign culture. All the challenges typically faced by immigrant households were complicated by the uncertain fates of those they left behind in Cuba.

The primary adjustment among South Florida's Cuban Americans has been more to each other than to Whites, African Americans, or other

Like all other immigrant groups, ethnic enclaves of shopping, restaurants, and just a place to converse emerge wherever people of the same nationality are concentrated. Pictured here is Little Havana in Miami.

Latinos. The prolonged immigration now stretching across two generations has led to differences between Cuban Americans in terms of ties to Cuba, social class, and age. There is no single Cuban American lifestyle.

The long-range prospects for Cubans in the United States depend on several factors. Of obvious importance are events in Cuba; many exiles have publicly proclaimed their desire to return to Cuba if the communist government is overturned. A powerful force in politics in Miami is the Cuban American National Foundation, which takes a strong anti-Castro position. The organization has actively opposed any proposals that the United States develop a more flexible policy toward Cuba. More-moderate voices in the Cuban exile community have not been encouraged to speak out. Indeed, sporadic violence has even occurred within the community over U.S.–Cuban relations. In addition, artists or speakers who come from Cuba receive a cold reception in Miami unless they are outspoken critics of Fidel Castro.

Cuban Americans have selectively accepted Anglo culture. Cuban culture itself has been tenacious; the Cuban immigrants do not feel they need to forget Spanish while establishing fluency in English, the way other immigrant children have shunned their linguistic past. Still, a split between the original exiles and their children is evident. Young people are more concerned about the Miami Dolphins football team than they are about what is happening in Havana. They are more open to reestablishing relations with a Castro-led Cuba. However, the more recent wave of immigrants, the *recién llegados* (recently arrived), have again introduced more openly anti-Castro feelings even as the presidency transferred from Fidel Castro to his brother Raúl in 2008 (Masud-Piloto 2008a).

Central and South Americans

Immigrants who have come from Central and South America are a diverse population that has not been closely studied. Indeed, most government statistics treat its members collectively as "other" and rarely differentiate among them by nationality. Yet people from Chile and Costa Rica have little in common other than their hemisphere of origin and the Spanish language, if that. Still others may come from indigenous populations, especially in Guatemala and Belize, and have a social identity apart from any national allegiance. Also, not all Central and South Americans even have Spanish as their native tongue; for example, immigrants from Brazil speak Portuguese, immigrants from French Guyana speak French, and those from Suriname speak Dutch.

Many of the nations of Central and South America have a complex system of placing people into myriad racial groups. Their experience with a color gradient necessitates an adjustment when they experience the Black–White racial formation of the United States.

Added to language diversity and the color gradient are social class distinctions, religious differences, urban-versus-rural backgrounds, and differences in dialect, even among those who speak the same language. Social relations among Central and South American groups with each other, Latinos, and non-Latinos defy generalization. Central and South Americans do not form, nor should they be expected to form, a cohesive group, nor do they naturally form coalitions with Cuban Americans, Mexican Americans, or Puerto Ricans (Orlov and Ueda 1980).

Immigration from countries such as El Salvador, whose capital San Salvador is pictured here, is heavily influenced by the economic and political conditions at any given time.

Immigration

Immigration from the various Central and South American nations has been sporadic, influenced by our immigration laws and social forces operating in the home countries. Perceived economic opportunities escalated the northward movement in the 1960s. By 1970, Panamanians and Hondurans represented the largest national groupings, most of them being identified in the census as "nonwhite." By 2010, El Salvador, Guatemala, and Columbia were the top countries of origin, each with at least a million present. Immigration often comes through Mexico, which may serve as a brief stop along the way or represent a point of settlement for six months to three years or even longer.

Since the mid-1970s, increasing numbers of Central and South Americans have fled unrest. Although Latinos as a whole are a fast-growing minority, the numbers of Central and South Americans increased even faster than the numbers of Mexicans or any other group in the 1980s. In particular, from about 1978, war and economic chaos in El Salvador, Nicaragua, and Guatemala prompted many to seek refuge in the United States. The impact of the turmoil cannot be exaggerated. Regarding the total populations of each country, it is estimated that anywhere from 13 percent in Guatemala to 32 percent in El Salvador left their respective countries. Not at all a homogeneous group, they range from Guatemalan Indian peasants to wealthy Nicaraguan exiles. These latest arrivals probably had some economic motivation for migration, but this concern was overshadowed or at least matched by their fear of being killed or hurt if they remained in their home country (Camarillo 1993; López 2004).

Watch the Video on MySocLab: Security, Railway Changes Slow Flow of Immigrants from Central America to U.S.

The Current Picture

Two issues have clouded the recent settlement of Central and South Americans. First, many of the arrivals are illegal immigrants. Among those uncovered as undocumented workers, citizens from El Salvador, Guatemala, and Colombia are outnumbered only by Mexican nationals. Second, significant numbers of highly trained and skilled people have left these countries, which are in great need of professional workers. We noted in Chapter 4 how immigration often produces a **brain drain**: immigration to the United States of skilled workers, professionals, and technicians.

The challenges to immigrants from Latin America are reflected in the experience of Colombians, who number more than a half million in the United States. The initial arrivals from this South American nation after World War I were educated middle-class people who quickly assimilated to life in the United States. Rural unrest in Colombia in the 1980s, however, triggered large-scale movement to the United States, where these newer Colombian immigrants had to adapt to a new culture and to urban life. The adaptation of this later group has been much more difficult. Some have found success by catering to other Colombians. For example, enterprising immigrants have opened bodegas (grocery stores) to supply traditional, familiar foodstuffs. Similarly, Colombians have established restaurants, travel agencies, and real estate firms that serve other Colombians. However, many immigrants are obliged to take menial jobs and to combine the income of several family members to meet the high cost of urban life. Colombians of mixed African descent face racial as well as ethnic and language barriers (Guzmán 2001).

Read the Document on MySocLab: *The Hispanic Dropout Mystery*

What is likely to be the future of Central and South Americans in the United States? Although much will depend on future immigration, they could assimilate over the course of generations. One less-positive alternative is that they will become trapped with Mexican Americans as a segment of the dual labor market for the urban areas where they live. A more encouraging possibility is that they will retain an independent identity, like the Cubans, while also establishing an economic base. For example, nearly 720,00 Dominicans (from the Dominican Republic) settled in the New York City area, where they make up a significant 6 percent of the population. In some neighborhoods, such as Washington Heights, one can easily engage in business, converse, and eat just as if one were in the Dominican Republic. People continue to remain attentive to events in Dominican politics, which often command greater attention than events in the United States. However, within their local neighborhoods, Dominicans here are focused on improving employment opportunities and public safety (American Community Survey 2009, Table B03001).

Conclusion

The signals are mixed today as they have been for the last two hundred years. Progress alternates with setbacks. Moves forward in one Latino group coincide with steps back among other groups. Social processes are highlighted in the Spectrum of Intergroup Relations that summarizes the experience of Latinos in the United States described throughout this chapter.

Latinos' role in the United States typically began with warfare resulting in the United States annexing territory or as a result of revolutions pushing refugees or immigrants here. In recent times, the Latino role in warfare has been to serve in uniform for the Untied States. "In World War II, more Latinos won Medals of Honor than any other ethnic group," said Democratic Representative Matthew Martinez, a former U.S. Marine who represented part of Los Angeles. "How much blood do you have to spill before you prove you are a part of something?" (Whitman 1987, 49). Many veterans of Iraq and Afghanistan are Latinos

who, even though legal residents of the United States, were not in a status that would make citizenship easy. Typically, Congress had to pass a resolution making fallen soldiers citizens after their death and on rare occasion would facilitate citizenship for a living veteran. Under a new rule, the families can now use their deceased as a sponsor for their own residency papers. In the twenty years from 1990 to 2010, the proportion of Latino ready reserve military personnel rose from 5 percent to 9.3 percent (Bureau of the Census Bureau of the Census 2011a: Table 514 on p. 337; P. Jonsson 2005; McKinley 2005).

While considering Latinos in an examination of American society, we constantly must also consider the impact of events in home countries, whether that be Cuba, El Salvador, or any of the many nations represented. Still, a contrasting image is offered by the refrain "Si usted no habla inglés puede quedarse rezagado": "If you don't speak English, you might be left behind."

SPECTRUM OF INTERGROUP RELATIONS

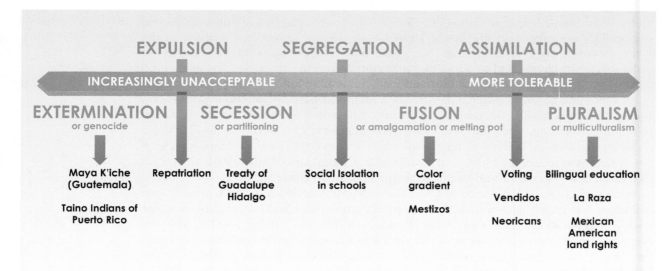

Summary

1. Latinos are a growing presence throughout the United States, and even though people of Mexican descent represent the majority, significant numbers of Latino immigrants come from throughout Latin America.

2. Latinos do not share a common cultural or single historical identity, yet a panethnic identity emerges in many aspects of life in the United States.

3. Economically, life for Latinos continues to improve—but relative to non-Hispanics, the gap has hardly changed over the last two generations.

4. A part of the assimilation as well as pluralism among Latinos has been growing involvement in electoral politics, which has been recognized by both the Democratic and Republican parties.

5. As a result of the 1848 Treaty of Guadalupe Hidalgo, which ended the Mexican–American War, the United States acquired a significant amount of Mexican territory, starting the long history of Latinos in the United States.

6. Federal policies such as repatriation, the bracero program, Operation Wetback, and Special Force Operation reflect that the United States regards Mexico and its people as a low-wage labor supply to be encouraged or shut off as dictated by U.S. economic needs.

7. Puerto Ricans have enjoyed citizenship by birth since 1917 but have commonwealth status on the island. The future status of Puerto Rico remains the key political issue within the Puerto Rican community.

8. Like much of the rest of the Caribbean and Latin America, Puerto Rico has more of a color gradient in terms of race than the sharp Black–White dichotomy of the mainland.

Key Terms

bracero, p. 186

brain drain, p. 199

color gradient, p. 181

dry foot, wet foot, p. 196

familism, p. 188

La Raza, p. 187

Marielitos, p. 196

mixed status, p. 188

mojados, p. 187

neocolonialism, p. 192

Neoricans, p. 190

panethnicity, p. 180

Pentecostalism, p. 184

repatriation, p. 186

world systems theory, p. 195

Review Questions

1. What different factors seem to unite and divide the Latino community in the United States?

2. How do Hispanics view themselves as a group? How do others view them?

3. Identify the factors that contribute to and limit the political power of Latinos as a group in the United States.

4. To what extent has the Cuban migration been positive, and to what degree do significant challenges remain?

5. How have Central and South Americans contributed to the diversity of the Hispanic peoples in the United States?

6. In what respects has Mexico been viewed as both a source of workers and as a place to leave unwanted laborers?

7. How does the case of Puerto Rico support the notion of race as a social concept?

Critical Thinking

1. Language and culture are almost inseparable. How do you imagine your life would change if you were not permitted to speak your native language? How has it been affected if you have been expected to speak some other language?

2. Observers often regard the family as a real strength in the Latino community. How can this strength be harnessed to address some of the challenges that Mexican Americans and Puerto Ricans face in the United States?

3. Consider what it means to be patriotic and loyal in terms of being a citizen of the United States. How do the concerns that Puerto Ricans have for the island's future and the Mexican concept of dual nationality affect those notions of patriotism and loyalty?

4. Are Mexican Americans assimilated, and are recent Mexican immigrants likely to assimilate over time?

Listen to Chapter 8 on MySocLab

8 Asian Americans

8-1 Identify the role of diversity among Asian Americans.

8-2 List and describe the characteristics of political activity and pan-Asian identity.

8-3 Examine and explain the culture of Chinese Americans.

8-4 Summarize the characteristics of Asian Indians.

8-5 Explain the four distinct periods of Filipino immigration.

8-6 Address the current picture of Korean Americans today.

8-7 Examine the various characteristics of Japanese American identity and explain the consequences of the wartime evacuation.

8-8 Identify the challenges for Southeast Asian Americans in the United States.

8-9 Discuss the embodiment of cultural diversity in Hawaii.

If the diversity of racial and ethnic groups is not yet apparent in this book, one need only look at the diversity among those collectively labeled *Asian Americans*. Consider Priscilla Chan, who at the age of 27 in May of 2012 was married and had sushi and Mexican food served at the reception. Both her parents, ethnic Chinese from Vietnam who arrived in the United States via refugee camps in the 1970s, worked such long hours in Boston restaurants that her grandmothers, who spoke no English, raised her. Born in the United States, Priscilla graduated from Harvard majoring in biology and later taught grade school while attending medical school. Of special interest is that she married a non-Asian (Facebook founder Mark Zuckerberg) and thus is an example of the 29 percent of recent Asian American newlyweds who marry non-Asians.

Then, one could look at football in Texas. Friday night lights is synonymous with Texas high school football, but at one school, many of the players were born on the Pacific island of Tonga. As 6-foot-2, 297-pound Trinity High offensive tackle Uatakini Cocker takes the line, he screams, "Mate ma'a Tonga," which means "I will die for Tonga." He is one of sixteen Tongan Americans playing for the school. The school has won the state football championship three of the last six years and was runner-up in another year. Trinity is located in Euless, which adjoins the Dallas-Fort Worth Airport, where Tongans in the early 1970s first started working. The success among some of these first immigrants initiated a pattern of **chain immigration**, whereby Tongan immigrants sponsor later immigrants. Euless boasts about 4,000 people either born in Tonga or their descendants.

Los Angeles's Little Tokyo is a happening place. Debbie Hazama, 35, a homemaker with three children, drove with her husband from the suburbs because not many Japanese Americans live where she does and she wants her children "to stay connected." Little Tokyo threw a day-long party of Asian hip-hop along with traditional martial arts demonstrations to gather Japanese Americans scattered across Southern California. During one festival, a 24-year-old South Pasadena woman grabbed a heavy mallet and took a swing at a drum, just as she had practiced for months. Nicole Miyako Cherry, the daughter of a Japanese American mother and a White American father, previously had little interest in her Japanese roots except for wearing a kimono for Halloween as a youngster. Yet in the last couple of years, she became interested in all things Japanese, including visiting Japan. Looking to her future as a social work therapist, she says she would like her own children to learn Japanese, go to Japanese festivals, play in Japanese sports leagues, and have Japanese first names.

Consider "The 100 Years Living Club," a group of elderly immigrants from India who gather at a mall in Fremont, California. These elders may talk about the latest community news, cheap flights to Delhi, or their latest run-in with their daughter-in-law.

Then there is Vietnamese American Tuan Nguyren, age 54, who tends to 80 areas in rural South Carolina overseeing 160,000 chickens. His wife lives 50 miles away where she operates a nail salon. They get together about once a week, and the main topic of conversation is how they are putting their four daughters through college. Making a poultry farm succeed is hard work and Nguyren has mentored other Vietnamese Americans who have struggled with the effort (Brown 2009; Copeland 2011; *Daily Mail* 2012; Euless Historical Preservation Committee 2011; Holson and Bilton 2012; Longman 2008; Pew Social and Demographic Trends 2012:5; Small 2011; Watanabe 2007: B13).

Immigration to the United States is more than quaint turn-of-the-century black-and-white photos taken at Ellis Island. Immigration, race, and ethnicity are being lived out among people of all ages, and for no collective group is this truer than for Asian Americans who live throughout the United States yet are not evenly distributed across the states (Figure 8.1).

Explore the Map on MySocLab: Concentration of Asian Americans by County

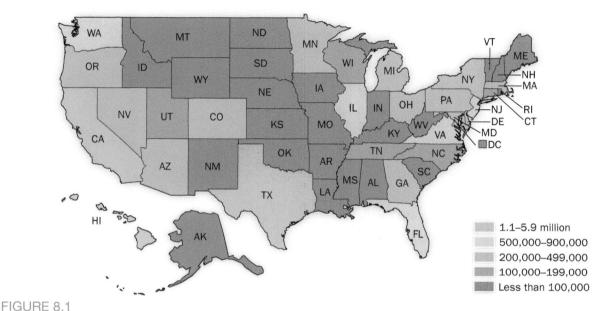

FIGURE 8.1
Where Most Asian Pacific Islanders Live

Sources: Census 2010 data in Hixson, Hepler, and Kim 2012: Tables 2.5; Hoeffel, Rastogi, Kim, and Shahid 2012: Tables 2, 3.

We first turn our attention in this chapter to the diversity of Asian Americans and then to the issue of Asian identity. We then consider in greater depth the major groups in order of size—Chinese, Asian Indians, Filipinos, Koreans, Southeast Asians, and Japanese. The chapter concludes by examining the coexistence of a uniquely mixed group of peoples— the people of Hawai'i—among whom Asian Americans and Pacific Islanders form the numerical majority.

Diversity Among Asian Americans

The successive waves of immigrants to the United States from the continent of Asia comprise a large number of nationalities and cultures. In addition to the seven groups listed in Figure 8.2, the U.S. Bureau of the Census enumerates 47 groups, including Iwo Jimian, Native Hawaiian, Pakistani, and Samoan. Asian Americans and Pacific Islanders, like other racial and ethnic groups, are not evenly distributed across the United States (Figure 8.2). Asian Americans also include ethnic groups, such as the Hmong, that do not correspond to any one nation. Collectively, Asian Americans in 2010 numbered about 15 million—a 43 percent increase over 2000, compared with an overall population increase of only 9.7 percent. This is a larger increase than Latinos experienced during the first decade of the twenty-first century (Hixson, Hepler, and Kim 2012; Hoeffel, Rastogi, Kim, and Shahid 2012).

Given this diversity among Asian Americans and Pacific Islanders, several generalizations made earlier about Native Americans also can apply to Asian Americans. Both groups are a collection of diverse peoples with distinct linguistic, social, and geographic

View the **Figure** on MySocLab: Country of Origin of Asian Americans

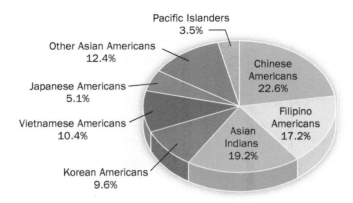

FIGURE 8.2
Asian Americans and Pacific Islanders

Note: Lists all specific groups with more than 750,000.

Source: See Figure 8.1.

backgrounds. As reflected in Table 8.1, even limiting the analysis to the six largest groups shows quite a range in the proportion of foreign born, attainment of a college degree, proficiency in English, and poverty rate.

Before we look in detail at the Asian American experience, we first need to deconstruct an image often held of Asian Americans as a group. They are viewed as the model minority— some kind of perfect, model minority. They constitute a **model minority** because, although they have experienced prejudice and discrimination, they seem to have succeeded economically, socially, and educationally without resorting to political or violent confrontations with Whites. We consider this view in greater detail in the next chapter when we consider how racism has changed, or not changed, in the United States. For now, we consider the complexity of social identity within the Asian American community.

Read the Document on MySocLab: Grouping All Asians Together Could Be Bad for Health

TABLE 8.1 Asian Origin Groups				
Group	Foreign Born	Bachelor's Degree	Proficient in English	Poverty Rate
Chinese Americans	76	51	52	14
Asian Indians	87	70	76	9
Filipino Americans	69	47	48	6
Vietnamese Americans	84	26	41	15
Korean Americans	78	53	64	15
Japanese Americans	32	46	82	8
General U.S. Population	16	28	90	13

Note: Based on 2012 national survey. Poverty rate based on 2010 income.

Source: Pew Social and Demographic Trends 2012: 13, 30, 33, 37, 41, 44, 47, 50.

Political Activity and Pan-Asian Identity

Against this backdrop of prejudice, discrimination, and a search for identity, it is no surprise to see Asian Americans seeking to recognize themselves. Historically, Asian Americans have followed the pattern of other immigrant groups: They bring social organizations, associations, and clubs from the homeland and later develop groups to respond to the special needs identified in the United States.

Rather than being docile, as Asian Americans are often labeled, they have organized in labor unions, played a significant role in campus protests, and been active in immigration rights issues. Recently, given a boost by anti-alien feelings after 9/11, Asian Americans staged demonstrations in several cities in an effort to persuade people to become citizens and register to vote (Chang 2007).

For newly arrived Asians, grassroots organizations and political parties are a new concept. With the exception of Asian Indians, the immigrants come from nations where political participation was unheard of or looked on with skepticism and sometimes fear. Using the sizable Chinese American community as an example, we can see why Asian Americans have been slow to achieve political mobilization. At least six factors have been identified that explain why Chinese Americans—and, to a large extent, Asian Americans in general—have not been more active in politics:

1. To become a candidate means to take risks, invite criticism, be assertive, and be willing to extol one's virtues. These traits are alien to Chinese culture.

2. Older people remember when discrimination was blatant, and they tell others to be quiet and not attract attention.

3. Many recent immigrants have no experience with democracy and arrive with a general distrust of government.

4. Like many new immigrant groups, Chinese Americans have concentrated on getting ahead economically and educating their children rather than thinking in terms of the larger community.

5. The brightest students tend to pursue careers in business and science rather than law or public administration and, therefore, are not prepared to enter politics.

6. Chinatowns notwithstanding, Chinese and other Asian American groups are dispersed and cannot control the election of even local candidates.

The Voting Rights Act requires Asian language materials in cities and counties where either 5 percent or 10,000 voting-age citizens speak the same native Asian language and have limited English proficiency. Following the release of the 2010 Census, that act now applies to cities in Alaska, California, Hawai'i, Illinois, Massachusetts, Michigan, Nevada, New Jersey, New York, Texas, and Washington (Pratt 2012).

Democrats and Republicans are increasingly regarding Asian Americans as a growing political force in the United States. For some time, the Republicans and Democrats seemed to evenly share the electorate. Yet increasingly, Asian American voters have backed the Democratic Party. In 2012, President Obama received a 73 percent backing in his bid for re-election. National survey data in 2012 showed that about 50 percent of Asian Americans lean toward the Democrats, compared to only 28 percent favoring the Republicans (Edison Research 2012; Pew Social and Demographic Trends 2012).

Despite the diversity among groups of Asian Americans and Asian Pacific Islanders, they have been treated as a monolithic group for generations. Out of similar experiences have come panethnic identities in which people share a self-image, as do African Americans or Whites of European descent. As noted in Chapter 1, **panethnicity** is the development of solidarity between ethnic subgroups. Are Asian Americans finding a panethnic identity?

It is true that in the United States, extremely different Asian nationalities have been lumped together in past discrimination and current stereotypes. The majority of research documents that Asian Americans identify by their own nationality group, but it also indicates that most *sometimes* think of themselves as Asian American. Some observers contend that a move toward pan-Asian identity represents a step in assimilation by downplaying cultural differences (Espiritu 1992; Wong, Ramakrishnan, Lee, and Junn 2011).

Pan-Asian identity often serves to solidify and strengthen organizing at the grassroots level when Asian Americans are trying to bring about change in neighborhoods and communities where they are outnumbered and underrepresented in the corridors of political power. From this perspective, pan-Asian unity is necessary and urgent for all Asian groups (Cheng and Yang 2000; Mitra 2008; Võ 2004).

Read the Document on MySocLab: *Asian and African Values: The Problem of Human Rights*

Chinese Americans

China, the most populous country in the world, has been a source of immigrants for centuries. Many nations have a sizable Chinese population whose history can be traced back more than five generations. The United States is such a nation. Even before the great migration from Europe began in the 1880s, more than 100,000 Chinese already lived in the United States. Today, Chinese Americans number more than 3.3 million.

Before and after the Chinese Exclusion Act, settlers attacked Chinese enclaves throughout the West on 183 separate occasions, driving the immigrants eastward, where they created Chinatowns, some of which still are thriving today. This engraving depicts the Denver riot of 1880, which culminated in one Chinese man being hanged. The lynchers were identified but released the next year. There was no restoration for the damage done by the estimated mob of 3,000 men (Ellis 2004; Pfaelzer 2007).

Early Settlement Patterns

From its beginning, Chinese immigration has aroused conflicting views among Americans. In one sense, Chinese immigration was welcome because it brought needed hardworking laborers to these shores. At the same time, it was unwelcome because the Chinese also brought an alien culture that the European settlers were unwilling to tolerate. People in the western United States also had a perception of economic competition, and the Chinese newcomers proved to be convenient and powerless scapegoats. As detailed in Chapter 4, the anti-Chinese mood led to the passage of the Chinese Exclusion Act in 1882, which was not repealed until 1943. Even then, the group that lobbied for repeal, the Citizens' Committee to Repeal Chinese Exclusion, encountered the old racist arguments against Chinese immigration (Pfaelzer 2007).

Gradually, the Chinese were permitted to enter the United States after 1943. In the beginning, the annual limit was 105. Then several thousand wives of servicemen were admitted, and college students were later allowed to remain after finishing their education. Not until after the 1965 Immigration Act did Chinese immigrants arrive again in large numbers, almost doubling the Chinese American community. Immigration continues to exert a major influence on the growth of the Chinese American population. It has approached 100,000 annually. The influx was so great in the 1990s that the number of new arrivals in that decade exceeded the total number of Chinese Americans present in 1980.

As the underside of immigration, illegal immigration is also functioning in the Chinese American community. The lure of perceived better jobs and a better life leads overseas Chinese to seek alternative routes to immigration if legal procedures are unavailable. The impact of illegal entry in some areas of the country can be significant. For example, every month in 2002, 340 illegal Chinese immigrants were apprehended at Chicago's O'Hare Airport and taken to a rural jail (Starks 2002).

A small but socially significant component of Chinese in the United States are those who have been adopted by American non–Chinese couples. Beginning in 1991, China loosened its adoption laws to address the growing number of children, particularly girls, who were abandoned under the country's one-child policy. This policy strongly encourages couples to have only one child; having more children can impede promotions and even force a household to accept a less-roomy dwelling. The numbers of adopted Chinese were small, but in recent years, about 7,000 have been adopted annually. This policy was tightened significantly in 2008 by the Chinese government, reducing the number of annual adoptions. Although most adoptees are still young, they and their adopting parents face the complex issues of cultural and social identity. Organized efforts now exist to reconnect these children with their roots in China, but for most of their lives, they are adjusting to being Chinese American in a non-Chinese American family (Department of State 2008b; Olemetson 2005).

It also is important to appreciate that even *Chinese American* is a collective term. There is diversity within this group represented by nationality (China versus Taiwan, for example), language, and region of origin. It is not unusual for a church serving a Chinese American community to have five separate services, each in a different dialect. These divisions can be quite sharply expressed. For example, near the traditional Chinatown of New York City, a small neighborhood has emerged of Chinese from China's Fujian Province. In this area, job postings include annotations in Chinese that translate as "no north," meaning people from the provinces north of Fujian are not welcome. Throughout the United States, some Chinese Americans also divide along pro-China and pro-Taiwan allegiances (Guest 2003; Lau 2008; Louie 2004; Sachs 2001).

Explore the Activity on MySocLab: *Chinese, Indian and Pacific Island Americans*

Occupational Profile of Chinese Americans

By many benchmarks, Chinese Americans are doing well. As a group, they have higher levels of formal schooling and household income compared to all Asian Americans and even to White non-Hispanics. Note, however, that the Chinese American poverty rate is high—an issue we return to later.

As we might expect, given the high income levels, half of all Chinese Americans serve in management, professional, and related occupations, compared to only a third of the general population. This reflects two patterns: first, entrepreneurial development by Chinese Americans who start their own businesses and, second, the immigration of skilled overseas Chinese as well as Chinese students who chose to remain in the United States following the completion of their advanced degrees (Bureau of the Census 2007a).

The background of the contemporary Chinese American labor force lies in Chinatown. For generations, Chinese Americans were largely barred from working elsewhere. The Chinese Exclusion Act was only one example of discriminatory legislation. Many laws were passed that made it difficult or more expensive for Chinese Americans to enter certain occupations. Whites did not object to Chinese in domestic service occupations or in the laundry trade because most White men were uninterested in such menial, low-paying work. When given the chance to enter better jobs, as they were in wartime, Chinese Americans jumped at the opportunities. Where such opportunities were absent, however, many Chinese Americans sought the relative safety of Chinatown. The tourist industry and the restaurants dependent on it grew out of the need to employ the growing numbers of idle workers in Chinatown.

Chinatowns Today

Chinatowns represent a paradox. The casual observer or tourist sees them as thriving areas of business and amusement, bright in color and lights, exotic in sounds and sights. Behind this facade, however, they have large poor populations and face the problems associated with all slums. Older Chinatowns were often located in deteriorating sections of cities, but increasingly they are springing up in new neighborhoods and even in the suburbs such as Monterey Park outside Los Angeles. In the older enclaves, the problems of Chinatowns include the entire range of social ills that affect low-income areas, but some have even greater difficulties because the glitter sometimes conceals the problems from outsiders and even social planners. A unique characteristic of Chinatowns, one that distinguishes them from other ethnic enclaves, is the variety of social organizations they encompass (Liu and Geron 2008).

Organizational Life   The Chinese in this country have a rich history of organizational membership, much of it carried over from China. Chief among such associations are the clans, or *tsu*; the benevolent associations, or *hui kuan*; and the secret societies, or *tongs*.

The clans, or **tsu**, that operate in Chinatown have their origins in the Chinese practice in which families with common ancestors unite. At first, immigrant Chinese continued to affiliate themselves with those sharing a family name, even if a blood relationship was absent. Social scientists agree that the influence of clans is declining as young Chinese become increasingly acculturated. The clans in the past provided mutual assistance, a function increasingly taken on by government agencies. The strength of the clans, although diminished today, still points to the extended family's important role for Chinese Americans. Social scientists have found parent–child relationships stronger and more harmonious than those among non–Chinese Americans. Just as the clans have become less significant, however, so has the family structure changed. The differences between family life in Chinese and non-Chinese homes are narrowing with each new generation.

The benevolent associations, or **hui kuan** (or *hui guan*), help their members adjust to a new life. Rather than being organized along kinship ties like the clans, hui kuan membership is based on the person's district of origin in China. Besides extending help with adjustment, the *hui kuan* lend money to and settle disputes between their members. They have thereby exercised wide control over their members. The various *hui kuan* are traditionally, in turn, part of an unofficial government in each city called the Chinese Six Companies, a name later changed to the Chinese Consolidated Benevolent Association (CCBA). The president of the CCBA is sometimes called the mayor of a Chinatown. The CCBA often protects newly arrived immigrants from the effects of racism. The organization works actively to promote political involvement among Chinese Americans and to support the democracy movement within the People's Republic of China. Some members of the Chinese community have resented, and still resent, the CCBA's authoritarian ways and its attempt to speak as the sole voice of Chinatown.

The Chinese have also organized in **tongs**, or secret societies. The secret societies' membership is determined not by family or locale but by interest. Some have been political, attempting to resolve the dispute over which China (the People's Republic of China or Taiwan) is the legitimate government, and others have protested the exploitation of Chinese workers. Other *tongs* provide illegal goods and services, such as drugs, gambling, and prostitution. Because they are secret, it is difficult to determine accurately the power of *tongs* today. Most observers concur that their influence has dwindled over the last 60 years and that their functions, even the illegal ones, have been taken over by elements less closely tied to Chinatown.

Some conclusions can be reached about these various social organizations. They serve as pillars of the Chinese American community but are less visible outside the traditional older Chinatowns. Metropolitan Chinese American communities see the increasing significance of nonprofit organizations that work between the ethnic community and the larger society, including the local, state, and federal government (Adams 2006; Soo 1999; Tong 2000; Zhao 2002; Zhou 2009).

Social Problems   It is a myth that Chinese Americans and Chinatowns have no problems. We saw some indication of that in the data in Table 8.1 Although overall household income levels ran 20 percent ahead of White non-Hispanics, the poverty of Chinese Americans as a group was 14 percent, compared to only 8.8 percent of Whites. Obviously, many Chinese Americans are doing well, but a significant group is doing poorly.

The false impression of Chinese American success grows out of our tendency to stereotype groups as being all one way or the other, as well as the Chinese people's tendency to keep their problems within their community. The false image is also reinforced by the desire to maintain tourism. The tourist industry is a double-edged sword. It provides needed jobs, even if some of them pay substandard wages. But it also forces Chinatown to keep its problems quiet and not seek outside assistance, lest tourists hear of social problems and stop coming. Slums do not attract tourists. This parallel between Chinese Americans and Native Americans finds both groups depending on the tourist industry even at the cost of hiding problems (Light, Sabagh, Bozorgmehr, and Der-Martirosian 1994).

In the late 1960s, White society became aware that all was not right in the Chinatowns. This awareness grew not because living conditions suddenly deteriorated in Chinese American settlements but because the various community organizations could no longer maintain the facade that hid Chinatowns' social ills. Despite Chinese Americans' remarkable achievements as a group, the inhabitants were suffering by most socioeconomic measures. Poor health, high suicide rates, rundown housing, rising crime rates, poor working conditions, inadequate care for the elderly, and the weak union representation of laborers were a few of the documented problems (Liu and Geron 2008).

Life in Chinatown may seem lively to an outsider, but beyond the neon signs, the picture can be quite different. Chinatown in New York City remained a prime site of sweatshops well into the 1990s. Dozens of women labor over sewing machines, often above restaurants. These small businesses, often in the garment industry, consist of workers sewing twelve hours a day, six or seven days a week, and earning about $200 weekly—well below minimum wage. The workers, most of whom are women, can be victimized because they are either illegal immigrants who may owe labor to the smugglers who brought them into the United States, or they are legal residents yet unable to find better employment (Finder 1994; Kwong 1994).

The attacks on the World Trade Center in 2001 made the marginal economy of New York's Chinatown even shakier. Although not located near the World Trade Center, the economy was close enough to the devastation to feel the drop in customary tourism and a significant decline in shipments to the garment industry. Initially, emergency relief groups ruled out assistance to Chinatown, but within a couple of months, agencies opened up offices in Chinatown. Within two months, 42,000 people had received relief because 60 percent of businesses had cut staff. Like many other minority neighborhoods, New York City's Chinatown may be economically viable, but it always is susceptible to severe economic setbacks that most other areas could withstand much more easily.

Festivals and events serve to focus the members of the Chinese American community, who now live often far apart from one another. Shown here is a dragon boat race in Seattle, Washington.

From 2000 to 2010, Chinatown's population in Manhattan dropped by 9 percent—the first decline ever. Notably, the proportion of foreign born also declined (Asian American Federation 2008; Lee 2001; Tsui 2011).

Increasingly, Chinese neither live nor work in Chinatowns; most have escaped them or have never experienced their social ills. Chinatown remains important for many of those who now live outside its borders, although less so than in the past. For many Chinese, movement out of Chinatown is a sign of success. Upon moving out, however, they soon encounter discriminatory real estate practices and White parents' fears about their children playing with Chinese American youths.

The movement of Chinese Americans out of Chinatowns parallels the movement of White ethnics out of similar enclaves. It signals the upward mobility of Chinese Americans, coupled with their growing acceptance by the rest of the population. This mobility and acceptance are especially evident in the presence of Chinese Americans in managerial and professional occupations.

Even with their problems and constant influx of new arrivals, we should not forget that first and foremost, Chinatowns are communities of people. Originally, in the nineteenth century, they emerged because the Chinese arriving in the United States had no other area in which they were allowed to settle. Today, Chinatowns represent cultural decompression chambers for new arrivals and an important symbolic focus for long-term residents. Even among many younger Chinese Americans, these ethnic enclaves serve as a source of identity.

Family Life

Family life is the major force that shapes all immigrant groups' experience in the United States. Generally, with assimilation, cultural behavior becomes less distinctive. Family life and religious practices are no exceptions. For Chinese Americans, the latest immigration wave has helped preserve some of the old ways, but traditional cultural patterns have undergone change even in the People's Republic of China, so the situation is very fluid.

The contemporary Chinese American family often is indistinguishable from its White counterpart except that it is victimized by prejudice and discrimination. Older Chinese Americans and new arrivals often are dismayed by the more American behavior patterns of Chinese American youths. Change in family life is one of the most difficult cultural changes to accept. Children questioning parental authority, which Americans grudgingly accept, is a painful experience for the tradition-oriented Chinese. The 2011 bestseller *Battle Hymn of the Tiger Mom* by legal scholar Amy Chua touched off heated discussions regarding her indictment of parents indulging their children and her focus on strong parental guidance in children's activities and interests.

Where acculturation has taken hold less strongly among Chinese Americans, the legacy of China remains. Parental authority, especially the father's, is more absolute, and the extended family is more important than is typical in White middle-class families. Divorce is rare, and attitudes about sexual behavior tend to be strict because the Chinese generally frown on public expressions of emotion. We noted earlier that Chinese immigrant women in Chinatown endure a harsh existence. A related problem beginning to surface is domestic violence. Although the available data do not indicate that Asian American men are any more abusive than men in other groups, their wives, as a rule, are less willing to talk about their plight and to seek help. The nation's first shelter for Asian women was established in Los Angeles in 1981, but the problem is increasingly being recognized in more cities (Banerjee 2000; Tong 2000).

Another problem for Chinese Americans is the rise in gang activity since the mid-1970s. Battles between opposing gangs have taken their toll, including the lives of some innocent bystanders. Some trace the gangs to the tongs and, thus, consider them an aspect, admittedly destructive, of the cultural traditions some groups are trying to maintain. However, a more realistic interpretation is that Chinese American youths from the lower classes are not part of the model minority. Upward mobility is not in their future. Alienated, angry, and with prospects of low-wage work in restaurants and laundries, they turn to gangs such as the Ghost Shadows and Flying Dragons and force Chinese American shopkeepers to give them extortion money (Chin 1996; Takaki 1998).

Asian Indians

The second-largest Asian American group (after Chinese Americans) is composed of immigrants from India and their descendants and numbers over 2.8 million. Sometimes immigrants from Pakistan, Bangladesh, and Sri Lanka also are included in this group.

Immigration

Like several other Asian immigrant groups, Asian Indians (or East Indians) are recent immigrants. Only 17,000 total came from 1820 to 1965, with the majority of those arriving before 1917. These pioneers were subjected to some of the same anti-Asian measures that restricted Chinese immigration. For example, the Supreme Court (1923) ruled that Asian Indians could not become naturalized citizens because they were not White and therefore were excluded under the 1917 law that applied to all natives of Asia. This prohibition continued until 1946.

Immigration law, although dropping nationality preferences, gave priority to the skilled, so the Asian Indians arriving in the 1960s through the 1980s tended to be urban, educated, and English-speaking. More than twice the proportion of Asian Indians aged 25 and older had a college degree, compared with the general population. These families experienced a smooth transition from life in India to life in the United States. They usually settled in urban areas or near universities or medical centers. Initially, they flocked to the Northeast, but by 1990, California had edged out New York as the state with the largest concentration of Asian Indians. The growth of Silicon Valley's information technology industry furthered the increase of Asian Indian professionals in Northern California (Bureau of the Census 2007a).

More recent immigrants, sponsored by earlier immigrant relatives, are displaying less facility with English, and the training they have tends to be less easily adapted to the U.S. workplace. They are more likely to work in service industries, usually with members of their extended families. They also often take positions that many Americans reject because of the long hours, the seven-day workweek, and vulnerability to crime. Consequently, Asian Indians are as likely to be cab drivers or managers of motels or convenience stores as they are to be physicians or college professors. Asian Indians see the service industries as transitional jobs to acclimatize them to the United States and to give them the money they need to become more economically self-reliant (Kalita 2003; Levitt 2004; Varadarajan 1999).

Watch the Video on MySocLab: *Dubai Labor*

The Current Picture

It is difficult to generalize about Asian Indians because, like all other Asian Americans, they reflect a diverse population. With more than 1.2 billion people in 2011, India will be the most populous nation in the world by 2025. Diversity governs every area. The Indian government recognizes 18 official languages, each with its own cultural heritage. Some can be written in more than one type of script. Hindus are the majority in India and also among the immigrants to the United States, but significant religious minorities include Sikhs, Muslims, Jains, and Zoroastrians.

Religion among Asian Indians presents an interesting picture. Among initial immigrants, religious orthodoxy often is stronger than it is in India. Immigrants try to practice the Hindu and Muslim faiths true to their practices in India rather than join the Caribbean versions of these major faiths already established in the United States by other immigrant groups. They also recognize local practices; 73 percent of the Hindus in the United States celebrate Christmas.

Although other Indian traditions are maintained, older immigrants see challenges not only from U.S. culture but also from pop culture from India, which is imported through motion pictures and magazines. It is a dynamic situation as the Asian Indian population moves into the twenty-first century (Kurien 2004, 2007; Pew Forum on Religion and Public Life 2012; Rangaswamy 2005).

Maintaining traditions within the family household is a major challenge for Asian Indian immigrants to the United States. These ties remain strong, and many Asian Indians see themselves as more connected to their relatives 10,000 miles away than Americans are to their kinfolk fewer than a hundred miles away. Parents are concerned about the erosion of traditional family authority among the desi. **Desi** (pronounced "DAY-see") is a colloquial name for people who trace their ancestry to South Asia, especially India.

Asian Indian children, dressed like their peers, go to fast-food restaurants and eat hamburgers while out on their own, yet Hindus and many Asian Indian Muslims are vegetarian by practice. Sons do not feel the responsibility to the family that tradition dictates. Daughters, whose occupation and marriage could, in India, be closely controlled by the family, assert their right to choose work and, in an even more dramatic break from tradition, select their husbands.

In Research Focus, we consider one cultural practice faced by Asian Indian and other immigrant groups that is not a part of American mainstream culture: arranged marriages.

Filipino Americans

Little has been written about the Filipinos, although they are the third-largest Asian American group in the United States, with 2.5 million people living here. Social science literature considers them Asians for geographic reasons, but physically and culturally, they also reflect centuries of Spanish colonial rule and the more recent U.S. colonial and occupation governments.

Immigration Patterns

Immigration from the Philippines has been documented since the eighteenth century; it was relatively small but significant enough to create a "Manila Village" along the Louisiana coast around 1750. Increasing numbers of Filipino immigrants came as American nationals when, in 1899, the United States gained possession of the Philippine Islands at the conclusion of the Spanish–American War. In 1934, the islands gained commonwealth

Research Focus

Arranged Marriages in America

The question becomes not does he or she love me, but who do my parents want me to marry? An **arranged marriage** is when others choose the marital partners not based on any preexisting mutual attraction. Indeed, typically in arranged marriages, the couple does not even know one another.

The idea of arranged marriages seems strange to most youth growing up in the United States culture that romanticizes finding Mr. or Ms. Right. In an arranged marriage, the bride and groom start off on neutral ground, with no expectations of each other. Then understanding develops between them as the relationship matures. The couple selected is assumed to be compatible because they are chosen from very similar social, economic, and cultural backgrounds.

Historically, arranged marriages are not unusual and even today are common in many parts of Asia and Africa. In cultures where arranged marriage is common, young people tend to be socialized to expect and look forward to such unions.

Even among young people who theoretically accepted parental mate selection, the rise of new technology has altered the playing field. Texting and Skype facilitate getting to know a potential mate even before being formally introduced. New Internet sites allow parents to create a profile for their child by drawing upon large databases to facilitate narrowing of potential brides or grooms.

But what happens in cultures that send very different messages? For example, immigrants from India, Pakistan, Bangladesh, and Nigeria may desire that their children enter an arranged union, but their children are growing up in a culture where most of their schoolmates are obsessed with dating as a prelude to marriage and endlessly discuss the latest episodes of The Bachelor and The Bachelorette.

Studies of young people, in countries such as Canada and the United States, whose parents still cling to the tradition of arranging their children's marriages, document the challenges this represents. Many young people do still embrace the tradition of their parents. As one first-year female Princeton student of Asian Indian ancestry puts it, "In a lot of ways, it's easier. I don't have pressure to look for a boyfriend" (Herschthal 2004). Young people like her will look to their parents and other relatives to finalize a mate or even accept a match with a partner who has been selected in the country of their parents. Change has brought with it some variations because the expectation for formally arranged marriages has been modified to assisted marriages in which parents identify a limited number of possible mates based on what is referred to as "bio-data"—screening for caste, family background, and geography. Children get final veto power but rarely head out on their own when seeking a mate. Young men and women may date on their own, but when it comes to marrying, they limit themselves to a narrow field of eligibles brought to them by their parents. The combination of arranged and assisted marriages has meant that Asian Indian immigrants have the highest rates of ethnic endogamy of any major immigrant group in the United States—about 90 percent ingroup marriage.

Sources: Bellafante 2005; Herschthal 2004; Talbani and Hasanali 2000; Tarabay 2008; Voo 2008; Zaidi and Shuraydi 2002.

 Listen to the **Audio** on **MySocLab:** *Defending and Attacking Polygamy in Saudi Arabia*

status. The Philippines gained their independence in 1948 and with it lost their unrestricted immigration rights. Despite the close ties that remained, immigration was sharply restricted to only 50-100 people annually until the 1965 Immigration Act lifted these quotas. Before the restrictions were removed, pineapple growers in Hawai'i lobbied successfully to import Filipino workers to the islands.

Besides serving as colonial subjects of the United States, Filipinos played another role in this country. The U.S. military accepted Filipinos in selected positions. In particular, the Navy put Filipino citizens to work in kitchens. Filipino veterans of World War II believed that their U.S. citizenship would be expedited. This proved untrue; the problem was only partially resolved by a 1994 federal court ruling. However, it was not until a special presidential action in 2009 that Filipino American veterans received compensation to partially acknowledge their service in World War II (Padilla 2008a; Perry and Simon 2009).

Filipino American World War II veterans protested in 1997 for full veterans' benefits for Filipinos who served in World War II.

Filipino immigration can be divided into four distinct periods:

1. The first generation, which immigrated in the 1920s, was mostly male and employed in agricultural labor.
2. A second group, which also arrived in the early twentieth century, immigrated to Hawai'i to serve as contract workers on Hawai'i's sugar plantations.
3. The post–World War II arrivals included many war veterans and wives of U.S. soldiers.
4. The newest immigrants, who include many professionals (physicians, nurses, and others), arrived under the 1965 Immigration Act. More than 40 percent of Filipino Americans have immigrated since 1990 (Bureau of the Census 2007a; Min 2006; Posadas 1999).

As in other Asian groups, the people are diverse. Besides these stages of immigration, the Filipinos also can be defined by various states of immigration (different languages, regions of origin, and religions), distinctions that sharply separate people in their homeland as well. In the Philippines and among Filipino immigrants to the United States, eight distinct languages with an estimated 200 dialects are spoken. Yet assimilation is under way; a 1995 survey showed that 47 percent of younger Filipino Americans speak only English and do not speak Tagalog, the primary language of the Philippine people (Bonus 2000; Kang 1996; Pido 1986).

The Current Picture

The Filipino population increased dramatically when restrictions on immigration were eased in 1965. More than two-thirds of the new arrivals qualified for entry as professional and technical workers, but like Koreans, they have often worked at jobs ranked below those they left in the Philippines. Surprisingly, U.S.-born Filipinos often have less formal schooling and lower job status than the newer arrivals. They come from poorer families that are unable to afford higher education, and they have been relegated to unskilled work, including migrant farmwork. Their poor economic background means that they have little start-up capital for businesses. Therefore, unlike other Asian American groups, Filipinos have not developed small business bases such as retail or service outlets that capitalize on their ethnic culture.

A significant segment of the immigration from the Philippines, however, constitutes a more professional educated class in the area of health professionals. Although a positive human resource for the United States, it has long been a brain drain on the medical establishment of the Philippines. This is apparent when we consider areas in the United States that reflect Filipino settlement in the last 40 years. For example, in metropolitan Chicago, Filipino Americans have household incomes 30 percent higher than the general population and higher than that of Asian Indians. When the United States ceased giving preference to physicians from abroad, doctors in the Philippines began to enter the United States retrained as nurses, which dramatically illustrates the incredible income differences between the United States and the Philippines. They also send significant money back as remittances to help members of the extended family (DeParle 2007; Espiritu and Wolf 2001; Lau 2006; Zarembro 2004).

Despite their numbers, no significant single national Filipino social organization has formed for several reasons. First, Filipinos' strong loyalty to family (*sa pamilya*) and church, particularly Roman Catholicism, works against time-consuming efforts to create organizations that include a broad spectrum of the Filipino community. Second, their diversity makes forming ties here problematic. Divisions along regional, religious, and linguistic lines present in the Philippines persist in the United States. Third, although Filipinos have organized many groups, they tend to be club-like or fraternal. They do not seek to represent the general Filipino population and, therefore, remain largely invisible to Anglos. Fourth, although Filipinos initially stayed close to events in their homeland, they show every sign of seeking involvement in broader non-Filipino organizations and avoiding group exclusiveness. Three-quarters of Filipino America are citizens, which is a larger proportion than most Asian American groups. The two political terms of Filipino American Benjamin Cayetano as governor of Hawai'i from 1994 to 2002 are an example of such involvement in mainstream political organizations (Bonus 2000; Kang 1996; Lau 2006; Padilla 2008a; Posadas 1999).

Korean Americans

The population of Korean Americans, with more than 1.4 million (see Figure 8.2), is now the fifth-largest Asian American group, yet Korean Americans often are overlooked in studies in favor of groups such as Chinese Americans and Japanese Americans, who have a longer historical tradition in the United States.

Historical Background

Today's Korean American community is the result of three waves of immigration. The initial wave of a little more than 7,000 immigrants came to the United States between 1903 and 1910, when laborers migrated to Hawai'i. Under Japanese colonial rule (1910–1945), Korean migration was halted except for a few hundred "picture brides" allowed to join their prospective husbands.

The second wave took place during and after the Korean War, accounting for about 14,000 immigrants from 1951 through 1964. Most of these immigrants were war orphans and wives of American servicemen. Little research has been done on these first two periods of immigration.

The third wave was initiated by the passage of the 1965 Immigration Act, which made it much easier for Koreans to immigrate. In the four years before the passage of the act, Koreans accounted for only seven of every 1,000 immigrants. In the first four years after the act's passage, 38 of every 1,000 immigrants to the United States were Korean. This third wave, which continues today, reflects the admission priorities set up in the 1965 immigration law. These immigrants have been well educated and have arrived in the United States with professional skills. More than 40 percent of Korean Americans have arrived in the United States since 1990, but by 2011 immigration had slowed to a trickle of fewer than 5,000 annually (Dolnick 2011; Kim and Yoo 2008; Min 2006).

In 1948, Sammy Lee, born of Korean immigrants, became the first Asian American to win a gold medal at the Olympics. It was not an easy path to victory because he faced prejudice and discrimination in Southern California. He was able to practice in the public pool only one day a week—the day on which the water was immediately drained and refilled. The rest of the time he was forced to dive into a pile of sand.

Korean Americans have established many Christian churches in the United States with 61 percent affiliated with Protestant denominations such as the Presbyterians and Methodists (Pew Forum on Religion and Public Life 2012).

However, many of the most recent immigrants must at least initially settle for positions of lower responsibility than those they held in Korea and must pass through a period of economic adjustment and even disenchantment for several years. These problems documented the pain of adjustment: stress, loneliness, alcoholism, family strife, and mental disorders. Korean American immigrants who accompanied their parents to the United States when young now occupy a middle, marginal position between the cultures of Korea and the United States. They have also been called the **ilchomose**, or "1.5 generation." Today, they are middle-aged, remain bilingual and bicultural, and tend to form the professional class in the Korean American community (Hurh 1998; K. Kim 2006).

The Current Picture

Read the Document on MySocLab: *Intimacy at a Distance, Korean American Style: Invited Korean Elderly and Their Married Children*

Today's young Korean Americans face many of the cultural conflicts common to any initial generation born in a new country. The parents may speak the native tongue, but the signs on the road to opportunity are in the English language, and the road itself runs through U.S. culture. It is difficult to maintain a sense of Korean culture in the United States; the host society is not particularly helpful. Although the United States fought a war there and U.S. troops remain in South Korea, Korean culture is foreign to contemporary Americans. In the few studies of attitudes toward Koreans, White Americans respond with vague, negative attitudes or simply lump Korean Americans with other Asian groups.

Studies by social scientists indicate that Korean Americans face many problems typical for immigrants, such as difficulties with language—79 percent of Korean Americans over age 5 do not speak English at home. In Los Angeles, home to the largest concentration, more than 100 churches have only Korean-language services, and local television stations feature several hours of Korean programs. The Korean immigrants' high level of education should help them cope with the challenge. Although Korean Americans stress conventional Western schooling as a means to success, Korean schools also have been established in major cities. Typically operated on Saturday afternoons, they offer classes in Korean history, customs, music, and language to help students maintain their cultural identity (Bureau of the Census 2007a; Hurh and Kim 1984; Johnson, Rios, Drewery, Ennis, and Kim 2010).

Korean American women commonly participate in the labor force, as do many other Asian American women. About 60 percent of U.S.-born Korean American women and half the women born abroad work in the labor force. These figures may not seem striking compared with the data for White women, but the cultural differences make the figures more significant. Korean women come here from a family system with established, well-defined marital roles: the woman is expected to serve as homemaker and mother only. Although these roles are carried over to the United States, because of their husbands' struggles to establish themselves, women are pressed to help support their families financially as well.

Many Korean American men begin small service or retail businesses and gradually involve their wives in the business. Wages do not matter because the household mobilizes to make a profitable enterprise out of a marginal business. Under economic pressure, Korean American women must move away from traditional cultural roles. However, the move is only partial; studies show that despite the high rate of participation in the labor force by Korean immigrant wives, first-generation immigrant couples continue in sharply divided gender roles in other aspects of daily living.

Korean American businesses are seldom major operations; most are small. They do benefit from a special form of development capital (or cash) used to subsidize businesses called a **kye** (pronounced "kay"). Korean Americans pool their money through the kye, an association that grants members money on a rotating basis to allow them to gain access to additional capital. Kyes depend on trust and are not protected by laws or insurance, as bank loans are. Kyes work as follows: Say, for example, that 12 people agree to contribute $500 a year. Then, once a year, one of these individuals receives $6,000. Few records are kept, because the entire system is built on trust and friendship. Rotating credit associations are not unique to Korean Americans; West Indians and Ethiopians have used them in the United States, for example. Not all Korean business entrepreneurs use the kye, but it does represent a significant source of capital. Ironically, these so-called mom-and-pop entrepreneurs, as they encounter success, feel competitive pressure from national chains that come into their areas after Korean American businesses have created a consumer market (Reckard 2007; Watanabe 2007).

In the early 1990s, nationwide attention was given to the friction between Korean Americans and other subordinate groups, primarily African Americans but also Hispanics. In New York City, Los Angeles, and Chicago, Korean American merchants confronted African Americans who were allegedly robbing them. The African American neighborhood groups sometimes responded with hostility to what they perceived as the disrespect and arrogance of the Korean American entrepreneurs toward their Black customers. Such friction is not new; earlier generations of Jewish, Italian, and Arab merchants encountered similar hostility from what to outsiders seems an unlikely source—another oppressed subordinate group. The contemporary conflict was dramatized in Spike Lee's 1989 movie *Do the Right Thing*, in which African Americans and Korean Americans clashed. The situation arose because Korean Americans are the latest immigrant group prepared to cater to the needs of the inner city and, as of 2011, own 70 percent of small grocery stores in New York City, which has been abandoned by business owners who have moved up the economic ladder (Dolnick 2011; Hurh 1998; N. Kim 2008; New American Media 2007).

Among Korean Americans, the church is the most visible organization holding the group together. Half of the immigrants were affiliated with Christian churches before immigrating. One study of Koreans in Chicago and Los Angeles found that 70 percent were affiliated with Korean ethnic churches, mostly Presbyterian, with small numbers of Catholics and Methodists. Korean ethnic churches are the fastest-growing segment of the

Presbyterian and Methodist faiths. The church performs an important function, apart from its religious one, in giving Korean Americans a sense of attachment and a practical way to meet other Korean Americans. The churches are much more than simply sites for religious services; they assume multiple secular roles for the Korean community. As the second generation seeks a church with which to affiliate as adults, they may find the ethnic church and its Korean-language services less attractive, but for now, the fellowship in which Korean Americans participate is both spiritual and ethnic (Kim and Pyle 2004; Kwon, Kem, and Warner 2001).

Japanese Americans

Explore the Activity on MySocLab: *Japanese Americans*

The nineteenth century was a period of sweeping social change for Japan: it brought the end of feudalism and the beginning of rapid urbanization and industrialization. Only a few pioneering Japanese came to the United States before 1885 because Japan prohibited emigration. After 1885, the numbers remained small relative to the great immigration from Europe at the time.

Early Japanese Immigration

With little consideration of the specific situation, the American government began to apply to Japan the same prohibitions it applied to China. The early feelings of anti-Asian prejudice were directed at the Japanese as well. The Japanese who immigrated into the United States in the 1890s took jobs as laborers at low wages under poor working conditions. Their industriousness in such circumstances made them popular with employers but unpopular with unions and other employees.

Japanese Americans distinguish sharply between themselves according to the number of generations a person's family has been in the United States. Generally, each succeeding generation is more acculturated, and each is successively less likely to know Japanese. The **Issei** (pronounced "EE-say") are the first generation, the immigrants born in Japan. Their children, the **Nisei** ("NEE-say"), are American born. The third generation, the **Sansei** ("SAHN-say"), must go back to their grandparents to reach their roots in Japan. The **Yonsei** ("YOHN-say") are the fourth generation. Because Japanese immigration is recent, these four terms describe almost the entire contemporary Japanese American population. Some Nisei are sent by their parents to Japan for schooling and to have marriages arranged, after which they return to the United States. Japanese Americans expect such people, called **Kibei** ("kee-bay"), to be less acculturated than other Nisei. These terms sometimes are used loosely, and occasionally Nisei is used to describe all Japanese Americans. However, we use them here as they were intended to differentiate the four generational groups (Yamashiro 2008).

The Japanese arrived just as bigotry toward the Chinese had been legislated in the harsh Chinese Exclusion Act of 1882. For a time after the act, powerful business interests on the West Coast welcomed the Issei. They replaced the dwindling number of Chinese laborers in some industries, especially agriculture. In time, however, anti-Japanese feelings grew out of the anti-Chinese movement. The same Whites who disliked the Chinese made the same charges about Japanese Americans. Eventually, a stereotype developed of Japanese Americans as lazy, dishonest, and untrustworthy.

The attack on Japanese Americans concentrated on limiting their ability to earn a living. In 1913, California enacted the Alien Land Act; amendments to the act in 1920 made it still stricter. The act prohibited anyone who was ineligible for citizenship from owning land and limited leases to three years. The anti-Japanese laws permanently influenced the form that Japanese American business enterprise was to take. In California, the land laws drove the Issei into cities. In the cities, however, government and union restrictions prevented large numbers from obtaining the available jobs, leaving self-employment as the only option. Japanese, more than other groups, ran hotels, grocery stores, and other medium-sized businesses. Although this specialty limited their opportunities to advance, it did give urban Japanese Americans a marginal position in the expanding economy of the cities (Robinson 2001).

The Wartime Evacuation

Japan's attack on Pearl Harbor on December 7, 1941, brought the United States into World War II and marked a painful tragedy for the Issei and Nisei. Almost immediately, public pressure mounted to "do something" about the Japanese Americans living on the West Coast. Many White Americans feared that if Japan attacked the mainland, Japanese Americans would fight on behalf of Japan, making a successful invasion a real possibility. Pearl Harbor was followed by successful Japanese invasions of one Pacific island after another, and a Japanese submarine attacked a California oil tank complex early in 1943.

Rumors mixed with racism rather than facts explain the events that followed. Japanese Americans in Hawai'i were alleged to have cooperated in the attack on Pearl Harbor by using signaling devices to assist the pilots from Japan. Front-page attention was given to pronouncements by the U.S. Navy secretary that Japanese Americans had the greatest responsibility for Pearl Harbor. Newspapers covered in detail FBI arrests of Japanese Americans allegedly engaging in sabotage to assist the attackers. They were accused of poisoning drinking water, cutting patterns in sugarcane fields to form arrows directing enemy pilots to targets, and blocking traffic along highways to the harbor. None of these charges were substantiated, despite thorough investigations. It made no difference. In the 1940s, the treachery of the Japanese Americans was a foregone conclusion regardless of evidence to the contrary (Kashima 2003; Kimura 1988; Lind 1946; ten Brock, Barnhart, and Matson 1954).

Executive Order 9066 On February 13, 1942, President Franklin Roosevelt signed Executive Order 9066. It defined strategic military areas in the United States and authorized the removal from those areas of any people considered threats to national security. The events that followed were tragically simple. All people on the West Coast of at least one-eighth Japanese ancestry were taken to assembly centers for transfer to evacuation camps. These camps are identified in Figure 8.3. This order covered 90 percent of the 126,000 Japanese Americans on the mainland. Of those evacuated, two-thirds were citizens, and three-fourths were under age 25. Ultimately, 120,000 Japanese Americans were in the camps. Of mainland Japanese Americans, 113,000 were evacuated, but to those were added 1,118 evacuated from Hawai'i, 219 voluntary residents (White spouses, typically), and, most poignantly of all, the 5,981 who were born in the camps (Robinson 2001; Takaki 1998).

The evacuation order did not arise from any court action. No trials took place. No indictments were issued. Merely having a Japanese great-grandparent was enough to mark a person for involuntary confinement. The evacuation was carried out with little difficulty. For Japanese Americans to have fled or militantly defied the order would only have confirmed the suspicions of their fellow Americans. There was little visible objection initially from the Japanese Americans. The Japanese American Citizens League (JACL), which had been founded by the Nisei as a self-help organization in 1924, even decided not to arrange a court test of the evacuation order. The JACL felt that cooperating with the military might lead to sympathetic consideration later when tensions subsided (Iwamasa 2008b).

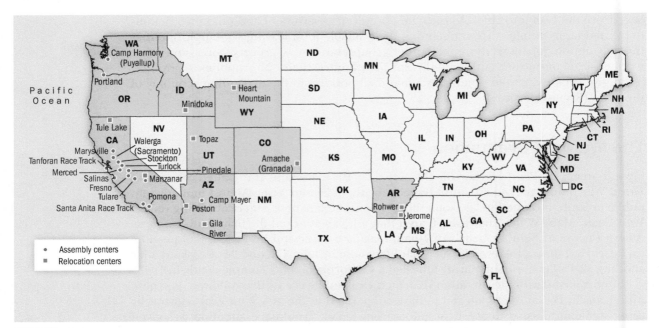

FIGURE 8.3
Japanese American Internment Camps

Japanese Americans were first ordered to report to assembly centers, from which, after a few
weeks or months, they were resettled in internment camps or relocation centers.

Source: National Park Service 2012.

Even before reaching the camps, the **evacuees**, as Japanese Americans being forced to resettle came to be called officially, paid a price for their ancestry. They were instructed to carry only personal items. No provision was made for shipping their household goods. The federal government took a few steps to safeguard the belongings they left behind, but the evacuees assumed all risks and agreed to turn over their property for an indeterminate length of time. These Japanese Americans were destroyed economically. Merchants, farmers, and business owners had to sell all their property at any price they could get. Precise figures of the loss in dollars are difficult to obtain, but after the war, the Federal Reserve Bank estimated it to be $400 million. To place this amount in perspective, in 2010 dollars, the economic damages sustained, excluding personal income, would be more than $3.6 billion (Bureau of the Census 2011a: 473; Commission on Wartime Relocation and Internment of Civilians 1982a, 1982b; Hosokawa 1969; Thomas and Nishimoto 1946).

The Camps   Ten camps were established in seven states. Were they actually concentration camps? Obviously, they were not concentration camps constructed for the murderous purposes of those in Nazi Germany, but such a positive comparison is no compliment to the United States. To refer to them by their official designation as *relocation centers* ignores these facts: The Japanese Americans did not go there voluntarily; they had been charged with no crime; and they could not leave without official approval.

Japanese Americans were able to work at wage labor in the camps. The maximum wage was set at $19 a month, which meant that camp work could not possibly recoup the losses incurred by evacuation. The evacuees had to depend on the government for food and shelter, a situation they had not experienced in prewar civilian life. More devastating than the economic damage of camp life was the psychological damage. Guilty of no crime, the Japanese Americans moved through a monotonous daily routine with no chance of changing the situation. Forced community life, with such shared activities as eating in mess halls, weakened the strong family ties that Japanese Americans, especially the Issei, took so seriously (Kitsuse and Broom 1956).

Amid the economic and psychological devastation, the camps began to take on some resemblance to U.S. cities of a similar size. High schools were established, complete with cheerleaders and yearbooks. Ironically, Fourth of July parades were held, with camp-organized Boy Scout and Girl Scout troops marching past proud parents. But the barbed wire remained, and the Japanese Americans were asked to prove their loyalty.

A loyalty test was administered in 1943 on a form all had to fill out: the Application for Leave Clearance. Many of the Japanese Americans were undecided on how to respond to two questions:

> *No. 27. Are you willing to serve in the armed forces of the United States on combat duty, wherever ordered?*
> *No. 28. Will you swear to abide by the laws of the United States and to take no action, which would in any way interfere with the war effort of the United States?* (Daniels 1972:113)

The ambiguity of the questions left many internees confused about how to respond. For example, if Issei said yes to the second question, would they then lose their Japanese citizenship and be left stateless? The Issei would be ending allegiance to Japan but were unable, at the time, to gain U.S. citizenship. Similarly, would Nisei who responded yes be suggesting that they had been supporters of Japan? For whatever reasons, 6,700 Issei and Nisei, many because of their unacceptable responses to these questions, were transferred to the high-security camp at Tule Lake for the duration of the war (Bigelow 1992).

Overwhelmingly, Japanese Americans showed loyalty to the government that had created the camps. In general, security in the camps was not a problem. The U.S. Army, which had overseen the removal of the Japanese Americans, recognized the value of the Japanese Americans as translators in the war ahead. About 6,000 Nisei were recruited to work as interpreters and translators, and by 1943, a special combat unit of 23,000 Nisei volunteers had been created to fight in Europe. The predominantly Nisei unit was unmatched, and it concluded the war as the most decorated of all American units.

Japanese American behavior in the concentration camps can be seen only as reaffirming their loyalty. True, some internees refused to sign an oath, but that was hardly a treasonous act. More typical were the tens of thousands of evacuees who contributed to the U.S. war effort.

A few Japanese Americans resisted the evacuation and internment. Several cases arising out of the evacuation and detention reached the U.S. Supreme Court during the war. Amazingly, the Court upheld lower court decisions on Japanese Americans without even raising the constitutionality of the whole plan. Essentially, the Court upheld the idea of an entire race's collective guilt. Finally, after hearing *Mitsuye Endo v. United States*, the Supreme Court ruled, on December 18, 1944, that the detainment was unconstitutional and consequently the defendant (and presumably all evacuees) must be granted freedom. Two weeks later, Japanese Americans were allowed to return to their homes for the first time in three years, and the camps were finally closed in 1946.

The immediate postwar climate was not pro–Japanese American. Whites terrorized returning evacuees in attacks similar to those against Blacks a generation earlier. Labor unions called for work stoppages when Japanese Americans reported for work.

Japanese Americans gather in an annual "Lest We Forget" ceremony at the Manzanar internment camp in northern California.

Fortunately, the most blatant expression of anti-Japanese feeling disappeared rather quickly. Japan stopped being a threat as the atomic bomb blasts destroyed Nagasaki and Hiroshima. For the many evacuees who lost relatives and friends in the bombings, however, it must have been a high price to pay for marginal acceptance (Iwamasa 2008a; Robinson 2001, 2009).

The Evacuation: What Does It Mean?

The social significance of the wartime evacuation has often been treated as a historical exercise, but in the wake of the stigmatizing of Arab and Muslim Americans after 9/11, singling out people of Japanese descent almost 70 years ago takes on new meaning. Japanese American playwright Chay Yew reflected recently, "You think you can walk away from history and it taps you on the back" (Boehm 2004:E2). We do not know yet the consequences of the current focus on identifying potential disloyal Americans, but we do have some perspective on stigmatizing Japanese Americans during and after World War II.

The evacuation policy cost the U.S. taxpayers a quarter of a billion dollars in construction, transportation, and military expenses. Japanese Americans, as already noted, effectively lost at least several billion dollars. These are only the tangible costs to the nation. The relocation was not justifiable on any security grounds. No verified act of espionage or sabotage by a Japanese American was recorded. How could it happen?

Racism cannot be ignored as an explanation. Japanese Americans were placed in camps, but German Americans and Italian Americans were largely ignored. Many of those whose decisions brought about the evacuation were of German and Italian ancestry. The fact was that the Japanese were expendable. Placing them in camps posed no hardship for the rest of society, and, in fact, other Americans profited by their misfortune. That Japanese Americans were evacuated because they were seen as expendable is evident from the decision not to evacuate Hawai'i's Japanese. In Hawai'i, the Japanese were an integral part of the society; removing them would have destroyed the islands economically (Kimura 1988; Robinson 2009).

Some people argue that the Japanese lack of resistance made internment possible. This seems a weak effort to transfer guilt—*to blame the victim*. In the 1960s, some Sansei and Yonsei were concerned about the alleged timidity of their parents and grandparents when faced with evacuation orders. However, many evacuees, if not most, probably did not really believe what was happening. "It just cannot be that bad," they may have thought. At worst, the evacuees can be accused of being naive. But even if they did see clearly how devastating the order would be, what alternatives were open to them? None.

The Commission on Wartime Relocation and Internment of Civilians in 1981 held hearings on whether additional reparations should be paid to evacuees or their heirs. The final commission recommendation in 1983 was that the government formally apologize and give $20,000 tax-free to each of the approximately 82,000 surviving internees. Congress began hearings in 1986 on the bill authorizing these steps, and President Ronald Reagan signed the Civil Liberties Act of 1988, which authorized the payments. The payments, however, were slow in coming because other federal expenditures had higher priority. Meanwhile, the aging internees were dying at a rate of 200 a month. In 1990, the first checks were finally issued, accompanied by President Bush's letter of apology. Many Japanese Americans were disappointed by and critical of the begrudging nature of the compensation and the length of time it had taken to receive it (Commission on Wartime Relocation and Internment of Civilians 1982a, 1982b; Department of Justice 2000; Haak 1970; Kitano 1976; Robinson 2012; Takezawa 1991).

Perhaps actor George Takei, of *Star Trek* fame in the role of Lieutenant Sulu, sums up best the wartime legacy of the evacuation of Japanese Americans. As a child, he had lived with his parents in the Tule Lake, California, camp. In 1996, on the fiftieth anniversary of the camp's closing and five years before 9/11 would turn the nation's attention elsewhere, he reflected on his arrival at the camp. "America betrayed American ideals at this camp. We must not have national amnesia; we must remember this" (Lin 1996:10).

The Economic Picture

The socioeconomic status of Japanese Americans as a group is different from that of other Asian Americans. Japanese Americans as a group are even more educated and enjoy even higher incomes than Chinese Americans as well as White Americans (refer to Table 8.1). In contrast to other Asian Americans, the Japanese American community is more settled and less affected by new arrivals from the home country.

The camps left a legacy with economic implications; the Japanese American community of the 1950s was very different from that of the 1930s. Japanese Americans were more widely scattered. In 1940, 89 percent lived on the West Coast. By 1950, only 58 percent of the population had returned to the West Coast. Another difference was that a smaller proportion than before was Issei. The Nisei and even later generations accounted for 63 percent of the Japanese population. By moving beyond the West Coast, Japanese Americans seemed less of a threat than if they had remained concentrated. Furthermore, by dispersing, Japanese American businesspeople had to develop ties to the larger economy rather than do business mostly with other Japanese Americans. Although ethnic businesses can be valuable initially, those who limit their dealings to those from the same country may limit their economic potential (Oliver and Shapiro 1996:46).

After the war, some Japanese Americans continued to experience hardship. Some remained on the West Coast and farmed as sharecroppers in a role similar to that of the freed slaves after the Civil War. Sharecropping involved working the land of others, who provided shelter, seeds, and equipment and who also shared any profits at the time of harvest. The Japanese Americans used the practice to gradually get back into farming after being stripped of their land during World War II (Parrish 1995).

However, perhaps the most dramatic development has been the upward mobility that Japanese Americans collectively and individually have accomplished. By occupational and academic standards, two indicators of success, Japanese Americans are doing very well. The educational attainment of Japanese Americans as a group, as well as their family earnings, is higher than that of Whites, but caution should be used in interpreting such group data. Obviously, large numbers of Asian Americans, as well as Whites, have little formal schooling and are employed in poor jobs. Furthermore, Japanese Americans are concentrated in areas of the United States such as Hawai'i, California, Washington, New York, and Illinois, where wages and the cost of living are far above the national average. Also, the proportion of Japanese American families with multiple wage earners is higher than that of White families. Nevertheless, the overall picture for Japanese Americans is remarkable, especially for a racial minority that had been discriminated against so openly and so recently (Inoue 1989; Kitano 1980; Nishi 1995).

The Japanese American story does not end with another account of oppression and hardship. Today, Japanese Americans have achieved success by almost any standard. However, we must qualify the progress that *Newsweek* (1971) once billed as their "Success Story: Outwhiting the Whites." First, it is easy to forget that several generations of Japanese Americans achieved what they did by overcoming barriers that U.S. society had created, not because they had been welcomed. However, many, if not most, have become acculturated. Nevertheless, successful Japanese Americans still are not wholeheartedly accepted into the dominant group's inner circle of social clubs and fraternal organizations. Second, Japanese Americans today may represent a stronger indictment of society than economically oppressed African Americans, Native Americans, and Hispanics. Whites can use few excuses apart from racism to explain why they continue to look on Japanese Americans as different—as "them."

Family Life

The contradictory pulls of tradition and rapid change that are characteristic of Chinese Americans are very strong among Japanese Americans today. Surviving Issei see their grandchildren as very nontraditional. Change in family life is one of the most difficult cultural changes for any immigrant to accept in the younger generations.

As cultural traditions fade, the contemporary Japanese American family seems to continue the success story. The divorce rate has been low, although it is probably rising. Similar conclusions apply to crime, delinquency, and reported mental illness. Data on all types of social disorganization show that Japanese Americans have a lower incidence of such behavior than all other minorities; it also is lower than that of Whites. Japanese Americans find it possible to be good Japanese and good Americans simultaneously. Japanese culture demands high ingroup unity, politeness, and respect for authority, and duty to community—all traits that are highly acceptable to middle-class Americans. Basically, psychological research has concluded that Japanese Americans share the high-achievement orientation held by many middle-class White Americans. However, one might expect that as Japanese Americans continue to acculturate, the

Asian Americans, like members of other racial and ethnic minorities, often express concerns about the indignities that other groups experience as well as themselves. Here, the Japanese American cartoonist Tak Toyoshima portrays this in his comic strip that he calls *Secret Asian Man*.

breakdown in traditional Japanese behavior will be accompanied by a rise in social deviance (Nishi 1995).

In the last 40 years, a somewhat different family pattern has emerged in what can almost be regarded as a second Japanese community forming. As Japan's economic engine took off in the latter part of the twentieth century, corporate Japan sought opportunities abroad. Because of its large automobile market, the United States economy became one destination. Top-level executives and their families were relocated to look after these enterprises. This has created a small but significant community of Japanese in the United States. Although they are unlikely to stay, they are creating a presence that is difficult to miss. Several private schools have been established since 1966 in the United States, in which children follow Japanese curriculum and retain their native language and culture. Saturday school is maintained for Japanese American parents whose children attend public school during the week. Although these private academies are removed from the broader culture, they help facilitate the nearby creation of authentic markets and Japanese bookstores. Researchers are interested to see what might be the lasting social implications of these households from Japan (Dolnick and Semple 2011; Lewis 2008; Twohey 2007).

Southeast Asian Americans

The people of Southeast Asia—Vietnamese, Cambodians, and Laotians—were part of the former French Indochinese Union. Southeast Asian is an umbrella term used for convenience; the peoples of these areas are ethnically and linguistically diverse. Ethnic Laotians constitute only half of the Laotian people, for example; a significant number of Mon-Khmer, Yao, and Hmong form minorities. Numbering more than 2.2 million in 2010, Vietnamese Americans are the largest group, with more than 1.5 million members, or about 15 percent of the total Asian American population (Hoeffel, Rastogi, Kim, and Shahid 2012).

The Refugees

The problem of U.S. involvement in Indochina did not end when all U.S. personnel were withdrawn from South Vietnam in 1975. The final tragedy was the reluctant welcome Americans and people of other nations gave to the refugees from Vietnam, Cambodia, and Laos. One week after the evacuation of Vietnam in April 1975, a Gallup poll reported that 54 percent of Americans were against giving sanctuary to the Asian refugees, with 36 percent in favor and 11 percent undecided. The primary objection to Vietnamese immigration was that it would further increase unemployment (Schaefer and Schaefer 1975).

Many Americans offered to house refugees in their homes, but others declared that the United States had too many Asians already and was in danger of losing its "national character." This attitude toward the Indochinese has been characteristic of the feeling that Harvard sociologist David Riesman called the **gook syndrome**. *Gook* is a derogatory term for an Asian, and the syndrome refers to the tendency to stereotype these people in the worst possible light. Riesman believed that the American news media created an unflattering image of the South Vietnamese and their government, leading the American people to believe they were not worth saving (Luce 1975).

The initial 135,000 Vietnamese refugees who fled in 1975 were joined by more than a million running from the later fighting and religious persecution that plagued Indochina. The United States accepted about half of the refugees, some of them the so-called boat people, primarily Vietnamese of ethnic Chinese background, who took to the ocean in overcrowded vessels, hoping that some ship would pick them up and offer sanctuary. Hundreds of thousands were placed in other nations or remain in overcrowded refugee camps administered by the United Nations.

The Current Picture

Like other immigrants, the refugees from Vietnam, Laos, and Cambodia face a difficult adjustment. Few expect to return to their homelands for visits, and fewer expect to return permanently. Therefore, many look to the United States as their permanent home and the home of their children. However, the adult immigrants still accept jobs well below their former occupational positions in Southeast Asia; geographic mobility has been accompanied by downward social mobility. For example, only a small fraction of refugees employed as managers in Vietnam have been employed in similar positions in the United States.

Language also is a factor in adjustment by the refugees; a person trained as a manager cannot hold that position in the United States until he or she is fairly fluent in English. The available data indicate that refugees from Vietnam have increased their earnings rapidly, often by working long hours. Partly because Southeast Asians comprise significantly different subgroups, assimilation and acceptance are not likely to occur at the same rate for all.

Although most refugee children spoke no English upon their arrival here, they have done extremely well in school. Studies indicate that immigrant parents place great emphasis on education and are pleased by the prospect of their children going to college—something rare in their homelands. It remains to be seen whether this motivation will decline as members of the next young generation look more to their American peers as role models.

The picture for young Southeast Asians in the United States is not completely pleasant. Crime is present in almost all ethnic groups, but some observers fear that in this group it has two very ugly aspects. Some of the crime may represent reprisals for the war: anti-Communists and Communist sympathizers who continue their conflicts here. At the same time, gangs are emerging as young people seek the support of close-knit groups even if they engage in illegal and violent activities. Of course, this pattern is similar to that followed by all groups in the United States. Indeed, defiance of authority can be regarded as a sign of assimilation. Another unpleasant but well-documented aspect of the current picture is the series of violent episodes directed at Southeast Asians by Whites and others expressing resentment over their employment or even their mere presence (Alvord 2000; K. Chu 2010; Zhou and Bankston 1998).

In 1995, the United States initiated normal diplomatic relations with Vietnam, which is leading to more movement between the nations. Gradually, Vietnamese Americans are returning to visit but generally not to take up permanent residence. **Viet Kieu**, Vietnamese living abroad, are making the return—some 500,000 in 2010 compared to 270,000 in 1996. Generational issues are also emerging as time passes. In Vietnamese communities from California to Virginia, splits emerge over a powerful symbol—under what flag to unite a nationality. Merchants, home residents, and college Vietnamese student organizations take a stand by whether they decide to display the yellow-with-red-bars flag of the now-defunct South Vietnam, sometimes called the "heritage flag," or the red-with-yellow-star flag of the current (and Communist) Vietnam (Tran 2008).

Meanwhile, for the more than 1.5 million Vietnamese Americans who remain, settlement patterns here vary. Little Saigons can be found in major cities in the United States long after the former South Vietnam capital of Saigon became Ho Chi Min City. Like many other immigrant groups in the second generation, some Vietnamese have moved into suburbs where residential patterns tend to be rather dispersed, but one can still spot mini-malls with Vietnamese restaurants and grocery stores—some even sporting a sloping red-tiled roof. Other Vietnamese Americans remain in rural areas— for example, the Gulf Coast fishermen who were rendered homeless by Hurricane Katrina in 2005. Perhaps one sign of how settled Vietnamese Americans have become is that some of the same organizations that helped the refugees learn English are now helping younger Vietnamese Americans learn Vietnamese (Anguilar-SanJuan 2009; Pfeifer 2008b; Triev 2009).

Case Study: A Hmong Community

Wausau (population 38,000) is a community in rural Wisconsin that is best known, perhaps, for the insurance company bearing its name. To sociologists, it is distinctive for its sizable Hmong (pronounced "Mong") population. The Hmong come from rural areas of Laos and Vietnam, where they were recruited to work for the CIA during the Vietnam War. This association made life difficult for them after the United States pulled out. Hence, many immigrated, and the United States has maintained a relatively open policy to their becoming permanent residents. Wausau finds itself with the greatest percentage of Hmong of any city in Wisconsin. Hmong and a few other Southeast Asians account for 11 percent of the city's population and about 18 percent of its public school students (Christensen 2012).

The Hmong, who numbered 248,000 as of 2010, immigrated to the United States from Laos and Vietnam after the end of the U.S. involvement in Vietnam in April 1975. The transition for the Hmong was difficult because they were typically farmers with little formal education. Poverty levels have been high and home ownership has been uncommon. Hmong have tended to form tight-knit groups organized around community leaders. Nationwide divisions exist along generational lines as well as dialect spoken and whether they are veterans of military service. Typically, Hmong Americans maintain strong cultural traditions surrounding marriage and funerals. Some are giving up Hmong traditional worship of spirits for Christian faiths. Perhaps reflecting their entry into mainstream culture, Hmong culture and the challenges faced by the Hmong in the United States were explored in Clint Eastwood's 2008 fictional film *Gran Torino* (Pfeifer 2008a).

Like other refugees from South Asia at the time, the first Hmong came to Wausau at the invitation of religious groups. Others followed as they found the surrounding agricultural lands were places they could find work. This created a pipeline of chain immigration to communities like Wausau. As introduced earlier, chain immigration refers to an immigrant who sponsors several other immigrants who, on their arrival, may sponsor still more. Even with sponsors or relatives, coming from a very rural peasant society, the immigrants faced dramatic adjustment upon arrival in the industrialized United States (Vang 2010).

In the 2008 motion picture *Gran Torino*, Clint Eastwood portrays a bitter retired autoworker. He is initially suspicious of his Hmong neighbors in Detroit but comes to appreciate their willingness to help and their strong family values.

Wausau school officials believed that progress in teaching the Hmong English was stymied because the newcomers continued to associate with each other and spoke only their native tongue. In the fall of 1993, the Wausau school board decided to distribute the Hmong and other poor students more evenly by restructuring its elementary schools in a scheme that required two-way busing.

Recalls of elected officials are rare in the United States, but in December 1993, opponents of the busing plan organized a special election that led to the removal of the five board members. This left the Wausau board with a majority who opposed the busing plan that had integrated Asian American youngsters into mostly White elementary schools. By 2011, neighborhood schools continued to play an important role in Wausau so that among elementary schools, the proportion of Hmong children ranged from less than 1 to 38 percent (School Digger 2011; Seibert 2002).

How events will unfold in Wausau is unclear. However, positive signs are identifiable in Wausau and other centers of Hmong life in the United States. Immigrants and their children are moving into nonagricultural occupations. Enrollment in citizenship classes is growing. Public healthcare programs directed at the Hmong community are widely publicized. The Wausau Area Hmong Mutual Association, funded by a federal grant and the local United Way, offers housing assistance. Although many of these immigrants struggle to make a go of it economically, large numbers have been able to move off public assistance. Language barriers and lack of formal schooling still are encountered by older Hmong residents, but the younger generation is emerging to face some of the same identity and assimilation questions experienced by other Asian American groups. To help facilitate the adjustment, some Wausau residents are learning Hmong through a special program at a local college (Dally 2011; Menchaca 2008; Peckham 2002).

Hawai'i and Its People

The entire state of Hawai'i appears to be the complete embodiment of cultural diversity. Nevertheless, despite a dramatic blending of different races living together, prejudice, discrimination, and pressure to assimilate are very much present in Hawai'i. As we will see, life on the island is much closer to that in the rest of the country than to the ideal of a pluralistic society. Hawai'i's population is unquestionably diverse, as shown in Figure 8.4.

To grasp contemporary social relationships, we must first understand the historical circumstances that brought the following races together on the islands: the native Hawaiians, the **kanaka maoli** (meaning "real or true people"), the various Asian peoples, and the **Haoles** (pronounced "hah-oh-lehs"), the term often used to refer to Whites in Hawai'i (Ledward 2008, Okamura 2008).

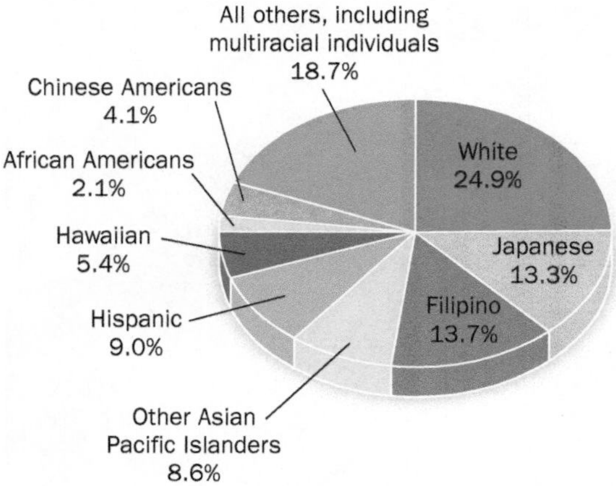

FIGURE 8.4
Hawai'i: Racial Composition

Source: American Community Survey 2010: Tables B02006, B03002, Cc02007.

All others, including multiracial individuals 18.7%
Chinese Americans 4.1%
African Americans 2.1%
Hawaiian 5.4%
Hispanic 9.0%
Other Asian Pacific Islanders 8.6%
White 24.9%
Japanese 13.3%
Filipino 13.7%

Historical Background

Geographically remote, Hawai'i was initially populated by Polynesian people who had their first contact with Europeans in 1778, when English explorer Captain James Cook arrived. The Hawaiians (who killed Cook) tolerated the subsequent arrival of plantation operators and missionaries. Fortunately, the Hawaiian people were united under a monarchy and received respect from the European immigrants, a respect that developed into a spirit of goodwill. Slavery was never introduced, even during the colonial period, as it was in so many areas of the Western hemisphere. Nevertheless, the effect of the White arrival on the Hawaiians themselves was disastrous. Civil warfare and disease reduced the number of full-blooded natives to fewer than 30,000 by 1900, and the number is probably well under 10,000 now. Meanwhile, large sugarcane plantations imported laborers from China, Portugal, Japan, and, in the early 1900s, the Philippines, Korea, and Puerto Rico.

In 1893, a revolution encouraged by foreign commercial interests overthrew the monarchy. During the revolution, the United States landed troops, and five years later, Hawai'i was annexed as a territory to the United States. The 1900 Organic Act guaranteed racial equality, but foreign rule dealt a devastating psychological blow to the proud Hawaiian people. American rule had mixed effects on relations between the races. Citizenship laws granted civil rights to all those born on the islands, not just the wealthy Haoles. However, the anti-Asian laws still applied, excluding the Chinese and Japanese from political participation.

The twentieth century witnessed Hawai'i's transition from a plantation frontier to the fiftieth state and an integral part of the national economy. During that transition, Hawai'i became a strategic military outpost, although that role has had only a limited effect on race relations. Even the attack on Pearl Harbor had little influence on Japanese Americans in Hawai'i.

The Current Picture

Hawai'i has achieved some fame for its good race relations. Tourists, who are predominantly White, have come from the mainland and have seen and generally accepted the racial harmony. Admittedly, Waikiki Beach, where large numbers of tourists congregate, is atypical of the islands, but even their tourists cannot ignore the differences in intergroup relations. If they look closely, they will see that the low-wage workers in the resorts and tourist industry tend to be disproportionately of Asian descent (Adler and Adler 2004).

One clear indication of the multicultural nature of the islands is the degree of exogamy: marrying outside one's own group. The outgroup marriage rate varies annually but seems to be stabilizing; about 40 percent of all marriages performed in the state involving residents are exogamous. The rate varies by group, from a low of 32 percent among Haoles to 66 percent among Chinese Americans with about half of Native Hawaiians outmarrying (Office of Hawaiian Affairs 2012).

Prejudice and discrimination are not alien to Hawai'i. Attitudinal surveys show definite racial preferences and sensitivity to color differences. Housing surveys taken before the passage of civil rights legislation showed that many people were committed to nondiscrimination, but racial preferences were still present. Certain groups sometimes dominate residential neighborhoods, but there are no racial ghettos. The various racial groups are not distributed uniformly among the islands, but they are clustered rather than sharply segregated.

The **sovereignty movement** is the effort by the indigenous people of Hawai'i, the kanala maoli, to secure a measure of self-government and restoration of their lands. The movement's roots and significance to the people are very similar to the sovereignty efforts by tribal people on the continental United States. The growing sovereignty movement also has sought restoration of the Native Hawaiian land that has been lost to Anglos over the last century, or at least compensation for it. Reaction to the movement has ranged from non-native Hawaiians seeing this as a big land grab and racist to those among the indigenous Hawaiians who see it as just not enough.

The Hawaiian term *kanaka maoli*, meaning "real or true people," is gaining use to reaffirm the indigenous people's special ties to the islands. Sometimes, the Native Hawaiians successfully form alliances with environmental groups that want to halt further commercial development on the islands. In 1996, a Native Hawaiian vote was held, seeking a response to the question, "Shall the Hawaiian people elect delegates to propose a Native Hawaiian government?" The results indicated that 73 percent voting were in favor of such a government structure. Since then, the state Office of Hawaiian Affairs has sought to create a registry of Hawaiians that is only about halfway to having all the estimated 200,000 people of significant Hawaiian descent on the islands come forward. In 2008, a Native Hawaiian independence group seized the historic royal palace in Honolulu to protest the U.S.-backed overthrow of the Hawaiian government more than a century ago. Although the occupation lasted barely a day, the political discontentment felt by many Native Hawaiians persists (Halualani 2002; Magin 2008; Okamura 2008; Staton 2004).

 Speaking Out

Recognizing Native Hawaiians

(The Native Hawaiian Government Reorganization Act)…allows us to take the necessary next step in the reconciliation process. The bill does three things. First, it authorizes an office in the Department of the Interior to serve as a liaison between Native Hawaiians and the United States. Second, it forms an interagency task force chaired by the Departments of Justice and Interior, and composed of officials from federal agencies that administer programs and services impacting Native Hawaiians. Third, it authorizes a process for the reorganization of the Native Hawaiian government for the purposes of a federally recognized government-to-government relationship. Once the Native Hawaiian government is recognized, an inclusive democratic negotiations process representing both Native Hawaiians and non-Native Hawaiians would be established. There are many checks and balances in this process. Any agreements reached would still require the legislative approval of the State and Federal governments.

Opponents have spread misinformation about the bill. Let me be clear on some things that this bill does not do. My bill will not allow for gaming. It does not allow for Hawaii to secede from the United States. It does not allow for private land to be taken. It does not create a reservation in Hawaii.

What this bill does do is allow the people of Hawaii to come together and address issues arising from the overthrow of the Kingdom of Hawaii more than 118 years ago.

Daniel Akaka

It is time to move forward with this legislation. To date, there have been a total of twelve Congressional hearings, including five joint hearings in Hawaii held by the Senate Committee on Indian Affairs and the House Natural Resources Committee. Our colleagues in the House have passed versions of this bill three times. We, however, have never had the opportunity to openly debate this bill on its merits in the Senate. We have a strong bill that is supported by Native communities across the United States, by the State of Hawaii, and by the Obama Administration.

Last week, I met with officials and community leaders in the state of Hawaii to share my intention to reintroduce this legislation. I received widespread support. This support was not surprising. A poll conducted by the Honolulu Advertiser in May of last year reported that 66 percent of the people of Hawaii support federal recognition for Native Hawaiians. And 82 percent of Native Hawaiians polled support federal recognition….

I encourage all of my colleagues to stand with me and support this legislation. I welcome any of my colleagues with concerns to speak with me so I can explain how important this bill is for the people of Hawaii. The people of Hawaii have waited for far too long. America has a history of righting past wrongs. The United States has federally recognized government-to-government relationships with 565 tribes across our country. It is time to extend this policy to the Native Hawaiians.

Source: Akaka 2011.

Much of the present discussion about sovereignty has focused over Hawai'i's congressional delegation seeking passage of the Native Hawaiian Government Reorganization Act, or the Akaka Bill, after U.S. Senator Daniel Akaka, the first U.S. Senator of Native Hawaiian ancestry. It would give people of Hawaiian ancestry more say over resources, provide affordable housing, take steps to preserve culture, and create a means by which they could better express their grievances. As of 2011, the measure had passed the House but was never discussed on the floor of the Senate (Akaka 2011). In "Speaking Out", Senator Akaka tries to set aside some of the criticism of the bill while calling for Congress to take the same step for the kanaka maoli as it has for American Indian tribes on the mainland.

Regardless of the outcome of the sovereignty movement, the multiracial character of the islands will not change quickly, but the identity of the Native Hawaiians has already been overwhelmed. Although they have a rich cultural heritage, they tend to be poor and often view the U.S. occupation as the beginning of their cultural and economic downfall. For centuries, they traditionally placed the earthly remains of their loved ones in isolated caves. However, as these archaeological sites were found by Haoles, the funeral remains made their way to the Bishop Museum, which is the national historical museum located in Honolulu. Now Native Hawaiians are using the Native American Graves and Protection Act to get the remains back and rebury them appropriately (LaDuke 2006).

"E Heluuelu Kaqkou," Nako'hlani Warrington tells her third graders ("Let's read together"). She has no need to translate because she is teaching at the public immersion school where all instruction is in the Hawaiian language. Not too long ago, it was assumed that only linguistic scholars would speak Hawaiian, but efforts to revive it in general conversation have resulted in its use well beyond "aloha." In 1983, only 1,500 people were considered native speakers; now native speakers number 68,000. This goes well beyond symbolic ethnicity. Language perpetuity is being combined with a solid grade school education, and a supportive doctoral program in the Hawaiian language was introduced in 2007 (*Indian Country Today* 2007; Kana'iaupuni 2008).

Conclusion

Who are the Asian Americans? Asian Americans are a rapidly growing group. Despite striking differences among them, they are often viewed as if they arrived all at once and from one culture. Also, they are often characterized as a successful or model minority. However, individual cases of success and some impressive group data suggest that the diverse group of peoples who make up the Asian American community are not uniformly successful. Indeed, despite high levels of formal schooling, Asian Americans earn far less than Whites with comparable education and continue to be victims of discriminatory employment practices.

As for other racial and ethnic minorities, assimilation seems to be the path most likely to lead to tolerance but not necessarily to acceptance. However, assimilation has a price that is well captured in the Chinese phrase "Zhancao zhugen": "To eliminate the weeds, one must pull out their roots." To work for acceptance means to uproot all traces of one's cultural heritage and former identity (Wang 1991).

The diversity within the Asian American community belies the similarity suggested by the pan-ethnic label *Asian American*. Chinese and Japanese Americans share a history of several generations in the United States. Native Hawaiians lost autonomy to over a century of rule by the United States. Filipinos are veterans of a half-century of direct U.S. colonization and a cooperative role with the military. In contrast, Vietnamese, Koreans, and Japanese are associated in a negative way with three wars. Korean Americans come from a nation that

SPECTRUM OF INTERGROUP RELATIONS

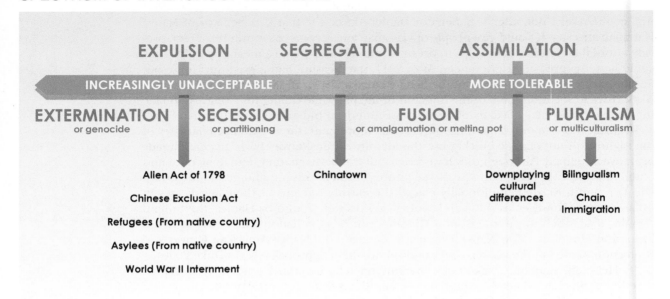

still has a major U.S. military presence and a persisting "cold war" mentality. Korean Americans and Chinese Americans have taken on middleman roles, whereas Filipinos, Asian Indians, and Japanese Americans tend to avoid the ethnic enclave pattern.

Not only is diversity central to describing the population of the United States but it also is central to describing who are Asian Americans.

This chapter has begun to answer that question by focusing on four of the larger groups: Asian Indians, Filipino Americans, Southeast Asian Americans, and Korean Americans. Hawai'i is a useful model because its harmonious social relationships cross racial lines. Although it is not an interracial paradise, Hawai'i does illustrate that, given proper historical and economic conditions, continuing conflict is not inevitable.

Looking Back

Summary

1. Asian Americans have been active politically through collective action and recently through seeking elected office. They embrace their unique identity but acknowledge their broader pan-Asian identity.

2. Although welcomed for their labor in the nineteenth century, Chinese immigrants were soon viewed as responsible for economic setbacks experienced by the nation, which culminated in the passage of the Chinese Exclusion Act.

3. Chinatowns are visible signs of continued growth of the Chinese American population and represent both promise and problems for the immigrants.

4. Asian Indians are a diverse group culturally and, although most are Hindu, embrace a number of faiths.

5. Filipino Americans have a long historical connection to the United States, with today's immigrants including both professionals as well as the descendants of those who have served in the U.S. military.

6. Southeast Asians' presence in the United States has typically resulted from waves of refugees. They have created significant settlements throughout the United States and often have dispersed throughout the larger population.

7. The Hmong, originally from Laos and Vietnam, are a distinctive ethnic group that took up residence in the United States following their loyal support of the war effort in Vietnam in the 1960s and 1970s.

8. Korean Americans have settled largely in urban areas, where many have become successful entrepreneurs.

9. Immigrants from Japan, like so many others, were permitted to come when they fulfilled an economic niche but were quickly marginalized socially and legally. The internment of people of Japanese ancestry during World War II is a clear instance of guilt by virtue of race.

10. The prosperity of Japanese Americans as a group reflects the willingness to endure post–World War II marginalization and continued investment in formal schooling for their children.

11. Hawai'i and its Native Hawaiians present a different multiracial pattern from that of the mainland but not one without both prejudice and discrimination.

Key Terms

arranged marriage, p. 215

chain immigration, p. 204

desi, p. 214

evacuees, p. 222

gook syndrome, p. 227

Haoles, p. 230

hui kuan, p. 210

ilchomose, p. 218

Issei, p. 220

kanaka maoli, p. 230

Kibei, p. 220

kye, p. 219

model minority, p. 206

Nisei, p. 220

panethnicity, p. 207

Sansei, p. 220

sovereignty movement, p. 231

tongs, p. 210

tsu, p. 210

Viet Kieu, p. 228

Yonsei, p. 220

Review Questions

1. What critical events or legislative acts increased each Asian American group's immigration into the United States?

2. What are the most significant similarities between the Chinese American and Japanese American experiences? What are the differences?

3. To what degree do race relations in Hawai'i offer both promise and a chilling dose of reality to the future of race and ethnicity on the mainland?

Critical Thinking

1. What stereotypical images of Asian Americans can you identify in the contemporary media?

2. What events can you imagine that might cause the United States to again identify an ethnic group for confinement in some type of internment camps?

3. Coming of age is difficult for anyone, given the ambiguities of adolescence in the United States. How is it doubly difficult for the children of immigrants? How do you think the immigrants themselves, such as those from Asia, view this process?

4. *American Indians, Hispanics,* and *Asian Americans* are all convenient terms to refer to diverse groups of people. Do you see these umbrella terms as being more appropriate for one group than for the others?

 Listen to Chapter 9 on MySocLab

9 Diversity: Today and Tomorrow

9-1 Explain the current idea of Post-Racialism.

9-2 Identify the present state of racial and ethnic diversity in the United States.

9-3 Discuss the origin and characteristics of the model minority image.

9-4 Address the concepts of "acting White" and "acting Black."

9-5 Examine the significance of social and cultural capital for minorities.

9-6 Summarize the frequency of cross-race, interethnic contact.

What metaphor do we use to describe a nation whose racial, ethnic, and religious minorities are becoming numerical majorities in cities coast to coast, as already seen in the California, Hawaii, New Mexico, Texas, and about one-tenth of all counties in the United States? By one scholarly analysis, Houston, not New York City or Miami, was found to be statistically the most racially diverse metropolitan area in the United States in 2012. The outpouring of statistical data and personal experience documents the racial and ethnic diversity of the entire nation. The mosaic might not be the same in different regions and communities; the tapestry of racial and ethnic groups is always close at hand wherever one is in the United States (Emerson, Brattner, Howell, Jeanty, and Cline 2012; Humes, Jones, and Ramirez 2011).

E Pluribus Unum, meaning "out of many, one" was adopted as the key phrase on the national seal approved in an Act of Congress in 1782. Although *E Pluribus Unum* may be reassuring to the diverse peoples of the United States, it does not describe what a visitor sees along the length of Fifth Avenue in Manhattan or in Monterey Park outside Los Angeles. It is apparent in the increasing numbers of Latinos in the rural river town of Beardstown, Illinois, and the emerging Somali immigrant population in Lewiston, Maine.

For several generations, the melting pot has been used as a convenient description of our culturally diverse nation. The analogy of an alchemist's cauldron was clever, even if a bit jingoistic; in the Middle Ages, the alchemist attempted to change less costly metals into gold and silver.

The phrase *melting pot* originated as the title of a 1908 play by Israel Zangwill. In the play, a young Russian Jewish immigrant to the United States composes a symphony that portrays a nation that serves as a crucible (or pot) where all ethnic and racial groups dissolve into a new, superior stock.

The belief that the United States was a melting pot became widespread in the first part of the twentieth century, particularly because it suggested that the United States had an almost divinely inspired mission to destroy artificial divisions and create a single humankind. However, the dominant group had indicated its unwillingness to welcome Native Americans, African Americans, Hispanics, Jews, and Asians, among many others, into the melting pot.

Read the Document on MySocLab: *Beyond the Melting Pot Reconsidered*

Although the metaphor of the melting pot is still used today, observers recognize that it hides as much about a multiethnic United States as it discloses. Therefore, the metaphor of the salad bowl emerged in the 1970s to portray a country that is ethnically diverse. As we can distinguish the lettuce from the tomatoes from the peppers in a tossed salad, we also can see the increasing availability of ethnic restaurants and the persistence of "foreign" language newspapers. The dressing over the ingredients is akin to the shared value system and culture covering, but not hiding, the different ingredients of the salad.

Yet even the notion of a salad bowl is wilting. Like its melting-pot predecessor, the picture of a salad is static—certainly not what we see in the United States. It also hardly calls to mind the myriad cultural pieces that make up the fabric or mosaic of our diverse nation.

The kaleidoscope offers another familiar, yet more useful, analogy. Patented in 1817 by Scottish scientist Sir David Brewster, the kaleidoscope is both a toy and increasingly a table artifact of upscale living rooms. Users of this optical device are aware that when they turn a set of mirrors, the colors and patterns reflected off pieces of glass, tinsel, or beads seem to be endless. The growing popularity of the phrase "people of color" aptly reflects the kaleidoscope that is the United States. The changing images correspond to the often-bewildering array of groups in the United States.

Explore the Activity on MySocLab: *Of Melting Pots, Mosaics, and Kaleidoscopes*

It is difficult to describe the image created by a kaleidoscope because it changes dramatically with little effort. As we can see in Figure 9.1, which focuses on the youth population, the last decade has seen a rapid increase in the number of racial and ethnic minorities and an actual decline in the number of White non-Hispanics. The old-time expression that "today's youth are tomorrow's leaders" takes on new meaning when viewed through the kaleidoscope of diversity. Similarly, in the kaleidoscope of the United States, we find it a challenge to describe the multiracial nature of this republic. Perhaps

Read the Document on MySocLab: Most Children Younger Than Age 1 Are Minorities, Census Bureau Reports

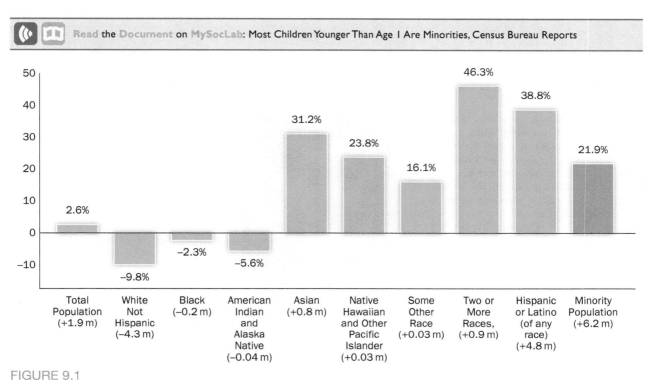

FIGURE 9.1

Youth and Diversity: Change 2000 to 2010 in Population Under Age 18

For the period from 2000 to 2010, the youth population among White non-Hispanics has dropped by almost 10 percent while increasing in the minority population by almost 22 percent.

Source: Bureau of the Census 2011d:slide 42.

in viewing the multiethnic, multiracial United States as a kaleidoscope, we may take comfort that the Greek word *kalos* means "beautiful" (Schaefer 1992).

How easy is it to describe the image to someone else as we gaze into the eyepiece of a kaleidoscope? That challenge is similar to that faced by educators who toil with what constitutes the ethnic history of the United States. We can forgive the faux pas by the *Washington Post* writer who described the lack of Hispanic-speaking (rather than Spanish-speaking) police as a factor contributing to the recent hostilities in the capital. Little wonder, given the bewildering ethnic patterns, that Chicago politicians, who sought to maintain the "safe" Hispanic congressional district after the results of the 2010 Census, found themselves scrutinized by Blacks fearful of losing their "safe" districts and critiqued by Latinos for not creating a second or even third safe seat. We can forgive Marlon Brando for sending a Native American woman to refuse his Oscar, thus protesting Hollywood's portrayal of Native Americans. Was he unaware of Italian Americans' disbelief when he won awards for his performance in *The Godfather*? We can understand why African Americans traumatized by Hurricane Katrina turned their antagonism from the White power structure that they perceived as ignoring their needs to the Latinos who took advantage of reconstruction projects in New Orleans.

As Galinna Espinoza, the editorial director of *Latina* magazine, points out in "Speaking Out" one cannot generalize about Latinos, much less all racial and ethnic minorities.

To develop a better understanding of the changing image through the kaleidoscope, we first try to learn what progress has taken place and why miscommunication among our diverse peoples seems to be the rule rather than the exception.

((🎙)) Speaking Out

That Latino "Wave" Is Very Much American

In 1990, I had just started my senior year at an Ivy League college when my political science professor asked me to come see her about the first paper I had turned in. While she complimented me on how much work I had put into it, she went on to explain that writing a college paper must be especially difficult for someone for whom English was not her first language.

I don't remember anything else she said after that, so consumed was I with trying to understand how she could have made this assumption. I was, after all an English major. Was it my accent I picked up during my childhood in Queens, NY? Or my last name?

Galina Espinoza

I find myself asking the same question now, with the release of the 2010 U.S. Census figures. Today, Hispanics number more than 50 million strong and account for 1 out of every 6 adults. Some politicians and pundits see our country besieged by a wave of non–English-speaking immigrants coming through a porous border.

Here's why they—like my professor—are wrong. What accounts for the dramatic rise in the Latino population are births: 1 out of every 4 children born in the United States today is Hispanic. In turn, that means most Latinos speak English as their first language. According to a 2007 analysis by the Pew Hispanic Center, "nearly all Hispanic adults born in the United

States of immigrant parents report they are fluent in English," a percentage that rises "among later generations of Hispanic adults."

Of course, like many Americans of different cultural backgrounds, Latinos identify strongly with their roots. But even if many of us are bilingual, or want our children to learn Spanish, our true link to Hispanic identity is not through language. It's through culture. We like to know how to cook the foods of our home countries and what our traditional holiday celebrations are. We like to see authentic portrayals of ourselves. Our favorite TV series, according to Advertising Age, are Grey's Anatomy and Desperate Housewives, which prominently feature Latino characters.

And when it comes to politics, we like leaders who understand that Cubans in Miami just might vote differently from Mexicans in Chicago. It is in the ways that our cultural identity begins to reshape the national one that the true social impact of Latinos will be felt. And so if you want to understand who your new Latino neighbors really are, know this: We want to eat our rice and beans. But our apple pie, too.

Source: Espinoza 2011:9A.

Has the Post-Racialism Era Arrived?

(🔊) **Listen** to the
Audio on
MySocLab:
*Inspired by
Obama*

At certain points in recent history, observers have declared that racism is for all intents and purposes gone. Many of the abolitionists were content to end slavery and cared relatively little about how the freed Negroes were treated following the Civil War. Certainly the legal end of de jure segregated schools in *Brown vs. Board of Education* proclaimed equality to many writers in the mid-1950s. But for even more, the election of an African American, the son of an immigrant no less, to the presidency in 2009 marked a new era.

Even the man he defeated implied we could take pride in entering some sort of era of post-racialism. Senator John McCain walked to the stage in Phoenix, Arizona, on election night to concede the election. In his opening remarks to his assembled supporters, he observed the following:

> *A century ago, President Theodore Roosevelt's invitation of Booker T. Washington to dine at the White House was taken as an outrage in many quarters.{{{8232}}}America today is a world away from the cruel and frightful bigotry of that time. There is no better evidence of this than the election of an African-American to the presidency of the United States.* (McCain 2008)

Have we moved on? The day after President Obama's re-election, a disturbance broke out on the campus of Hampden-Sydney in Virginia and at the University of Mississippi. White students hurled racial epithets and threatened violence at some of the Black students on the campus. Later, students gathered in vigils calling for racial harmony. Some have observed that the only thing left to do is simply stop talking about racism and, perhaps by extension, sexism. The sentiment is that if we don't focus on it or perhaps stop collecting data broken down by racial categories, then racism will disappear (Mitchell 2012; *Roanoke Times* 2012).

Does the evidence that an African American has been elected to the presidency mean "case closed" on intolerance and that everyone accepts diversity in the United States? Or was Obama able to grab the support of the majority of the electorate by speaking non-offensively about race and not being viewed as too "Black" (Dyson 2011; Touré 2011)? Obviously, few would endorse such a sweeping statement. Even the most casual reading of daily newspapers and Internet news bulletins recounts episodes of intolerance, hate crimes, and veiled racism in some of the opposition to immigration reform, affordable housing, and education reform.

Read the Document on MySocLab: *Race in the Era of President Obama*

The Glass Half Empty

A common expression makes reference to a glass half full or half empty. If one is thirsty, it is half empty and in need of being replenished. If one is attempting to clear dirty dishes, it is half full. For many people, especially Whites, the progress of subordinate groups or minorities makes it difficult to understand calls for more programs and new reforms and impossible to understand when minority neighborhoods erupt in violence.

In absolute terms, the glass has been filling up, but people in the early twenty-first century do not compare themselves with people in the 1960s. For example, Latinos and African Americans regard the appropriate reference group to be Whites today; compared with them, the glass is half empty at best.

Figure 9.2 shows the current picture and recent changes by comparing African Americans and Hispanics with Whites as well as contemporary data for Native Americans (American Indians). We see that the nation's largest minority groups—African Americans and Hispanics—have higher household income, complete more schooling, and enjoy longer life expectancy today than in 1975. White Americans have made similar strides in all three areas. The gap remains and, if one analyzes it closely, has actually increased in some instances. Both Blacks and Latinos in 2009 had just edged out the income level that Whites had exceeded back in 1975, more than three decades behind! Also, Black Americans today have barely matched the life expectancy that Whites had a generation earlier. Similarly, many minority Americans remain entrenched in poverty: nearly one out of four Hispanics and African Americans.

Read the Document on MySocLab: *Whites Account for Under Half of Births in U.S.*

Little has changed since 1975. We chose 1975 because that is a year for which we have comparable data for Latinos, Whites, and African Americans. However, the patterns would be no different if we considered 1950, 1960, or 1970. This does give us a starting point because, as Martin Luther King Jr. noted, "In order to answer the question, 'Where do we go from here?...we must first recognize where we are now" (Brooks 2012: 45).

Some people hearing of the current struggles of people of color seeking work observe, "Yes, we are in the midst of a very long recession; everyone is doing poorly." Yes that is true, but consider how Whites and Blacks have fared relative to one another. Let's consider unemployment rates. There are issues about how unemployment is measured, but if we use the most-used definition, we can get a fair general picture of economic well-being. In November 2011, the White unemployment rate peaked at 9.2 percent. At the same time, the Black unemployment rate was 16.1 percent.

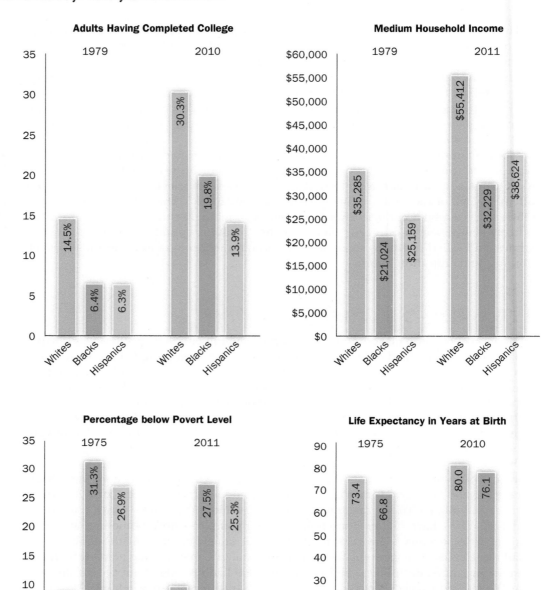

FIGURE 9.2

Changes in Schooling, Income, and Life Expectancy

Note: Education data are people age 25 and over. Data for 1975 Hispanic education estimated by author from data for 1970 and 1980. White data are for non-Hispanic (except in education and life expectancy).

Sources: Bureau of the Census 1988:167; Bureau of the Census 2011a: Tables 104, 229; DeNavas-Walt et al. 2011:Tables A-1, B-1.

If we turn to the good times six years earlier—November 2005—the unemployment rate for White America was only 4.3 percent. Yet, at the same time, the Black unemployment rate was 10.6 percent. In other words, the ability of African Americans to find work was as bad in the best recent economic times nationally as it was for Whites in the worst month of the recession (Bureau of Labor Statistics 2012b).

Is There a Model Minority?

"Asian Americans are a success! They achieve! They succeed! They have no protests, no demands. They just do it!" This is the general image people in the United States often hold of Asian Americans as a group. They constitute a model or ideal minority because, although they have experienced prejudice and discrimination, they seem to have succeeded economically, socially, and educationally without resorting to political or violent confrontations with Whites. Some observers point to the existence of a **model minority** as a reaffirmation that anyone can get ahead in the United States. Proponents of the model-minority view declare that because Asian Americans have achieved success, they have ceased to be subordinate and are no longer disadvantaged. This labeling is only a variation of **blaming the victim**: With Asian Americans, it is praising the victim. Examining aspects of the socioeconomic status of Asian Americans allows a more thorough exploration of this view.

Asian Americans, as a group, have impressive school enrollment rates in comparison to the total population. In 2010, half of Asian Americans 25 years old or older held bachelor's degrees, compared with 28 percent of the White population. These rates vary among Asian American groups: Asian Indians, Filipino Americans, Korean Americans, Chinese Americans, and Japanese Americans have higher levels of educational achievement than other Asian American groups. Yet other groups such as Vietnamese Americans and Pacific Islanders, including Native Hawaiians, fare much worse than White Americans (Bureau of the Census 2007a, 2011a).

This encouraging picture regarding some Asian Americans does have some qualifications, however, that question the optimistic model-minority view. According to a study of California's state university system, although Asian Americans often are viewed as successful overachievers, they have unrecognized and overlooked needs and experience discomfort and harassment on campus. As a group, they also lack Asian faculty and staff members to whom they can turn for support. They confront many identity issues and must do a "cultural balancing act" along with all the usual pressures faced by college students. The report noted that an "alarming number" of Asian American students appear to be experiencing intense stress and alienation, problems that have often been "exacerbated by racial harassment" (Ohnuma 1991; Teranishi 2010).

Another misleading sign of the apparent success of Asian Americans is their high incomes as a group. Like other elements of the image, however, this deserves closer inspection. Asian American family income approaches parity with that of Whites because of their greater achievement than Whites in formal schooling. If we look at specific educational levels, however, Whites earn more than their Asian counterparts of the same age. Asian Americans' average earnings increased by at least $2,300 for each additional year of schooling, whereas

Whites gained almost $3,000. Asian Americans as a group have significantly more formal schooling but have lower household family income. We should note that to some degree, some Asian Americans' education is from overseas and, therefore, may be devalued by U.S. employers. Yet in the end, educational attainment does pay off as much if one is of Asian descent as it does for White non-Hispanics (Kim and Sakamoto 2010; Zeng and Xie 2004).

So even with all the "tools" to succeed—supportive family, high achievement, and often attending prestigious schools—Asian Americans often hit what has been termed a bamboo ceiling. The **bamboo ceiling** refers to the barrier that talented Asian Americans face because of resentment and intolerance directed toward Asian Americans. The bamboo ceiling is clearly a nod to the term *glass ceiling*, a term that has historically been used to address barriers that women and minority group men have faced in the workplace. The presence of the bamboo ceiling reflects the cultural values and social norms that impact Asian professionals' interactions with others and cause others to make negative judgments about them (Hyun 2006, 2009).

Asian Americans are just over 5 percent of the U.S. population, but they account for 15 to 25 percent of Ivy League college enrollment. At the same time, as of 2011, they represented fewer than 2 percent of Fortune 500 CEOs and corporate officers. A national survey showed that Asian Americans who are successful in the corporate world must manage themselves so they don't seem too ambitious or have too many ideas. Only 28 percent of Asian Americans feel very comfortable "being themselves" at the workplace, compared to 45 percent of African Americans, 41 percent of Latinos, and 42 percent of White workers (Center for Work-Life [sic] Policy 2011).

Even the positive stereotype of Asian American students as academic stars or whiz kids can be burdensome to the people so labeled. Asian Americans who do only modestly well in school may face criticism from their parents or teachers for their failure to conform to the whiz kid image. Some Asian American youths disengage from school when faced with these expectations or receive little support for their interest in vocational pursuits or athletics (Kibria 2002; Maddux, Galinsky, Cuddy, and Polifroni 2008).

Striking contrasts are evident among Asian Americans. For every Asian American household in 2010 with an annual combined income of $250,000 or more, another earns fewer than $15,000 a year. Almost every Asian American group has a higher poverty rate than non–Hispanic Whites. The lone exception is Filipinos, who tend to live in the relatively high-income states of Hawaii and California (DeNavas-Walt, Proctor, and Smith 2011: Table HINC-01).

At first, one might be puzzled to see criticism of a positive generalization such as "model minority." Why should the stereotype of adjusting without problems be a disservice to Asian Americans? The answer is that this incorrect view helps exclude Asian Americans from social programs and conceals unemployment and other social ills. When representatives of Asian groups seek assistance for those in need, people who have accepted the model-minority stereotype resent them. This is especially troubling given that problems of substance abuse and juvenile delinquency need to be addressed within the Asian American community.

If a minority group becomes viewed as successful, its members no longer will be included in any program designed to alleviate any problems they encounter as minorities. The positive stereotype reaffirms the United States system of mobility: New immigrants as well as established subordinate groups ought to achieve more merely by working within the system. At the same time, viewed from the conflict perspective outlined in Chapter 1, this is yet another instance of blaming the victim: If Asian Americans have succeeded, then Blacks and Latinos must be responsible for their own low status rather than recognizing society's responsibility (Bascara 2008; Choi and Lahey 2006; Chou and Feagin 2008; Ryan 1976).

Acting White, Acting Black, or Neither

A common view advanced by some educators is that African Americans, especially males, do not succeed in school because they do not want to be caught acting White. That is, they avoid at all costs taking school seriously and do not accept the authority of teachers and administrators. Whatever the accuracy of such a generalization, acting White clearly shifts the responsibility of low school attainment from the school to the individual and, therefore, can be seen as yet another example of blaming the victim. **Acting White** is also is associated with speaking proper English or cultural preferences like listening to rock music rather than hip-hop (Ferguson 2007; Fordham and Ogbu 1986; Fryer 2006; Ogbu 2004; Ogbu with Davis 2003).

In the context of high achievers, to what extent do Blacks *not* want to act White? Many scholars have noted that individuals' efforts to avoid looking like they want an education has a long history and is hardly exclusive to any one race. Students of all colors may hold back for fear of being accused of being "too hardworking."

Back in the 1950s, one heard disparaging references to "teacher's pet" and "brown nosing." Does popularity come to high school debaters and National Honor Society students or to cheerleaders and athletes? Academic-oriented classmates are often viewed as social misfits, nerds, and geeks and are seen as socially inept even if their skill building will later make them more economically independent and often more socially desirable. For minority children, including African Americans, to take school seriously means they must overcome their White classmates' same desire to be cool and not a nerd. In addition, Black youth also must come to embrace a curriculum and respect teachers who are much less likely to look or sound like them (Chang and Demyan 2007; Ferguson 2007; Tyson et al. 2005).

The acting-White thesis overemphasizes personal responsibility rather than structural features such as quality of schools, curriculum, and teachers. Therefore, it locates the source of Black miseducation—and by implication, the remedy—in the African American household. As scholar Michael Dyson (2005) observes, "When you think the problems are personal, you think the solutions are the same." Often one may hear the comment, "If we could only get African American parents to encourage their children to work a little harder and act better (i.e., White), everything would be fine." As Dyson notes, "It's hard to argue against any of these things in the abstract; in principle, such suggestions sound just fine."

Of course, not all Whites act White. To equate acting White with high academic achievement has little empirical or cultural support. Although more Whites between ages 18 and 19 are in school, the differences are relatively small—69 percent of Whites compared to 65 percent of Blacks. Studies comparing attitudes and performance show that Black students have the same attitudes—good and bad—about achievement as their White counterparts. Too often, we tend to view White slackers who give a hard time to the advanced placement kids as "normal," but when low-performing African Americans do the same thing, it becomes a systemic pathology undermining everything good about schools. The primary stumbling block is not acting White or acting Black but being presented with similar educational opportunities (Buck 2011; Bureau of the Census 2011a: Table 224; Downey 2008; Tough 2004; Tyson et al. 2005).

Persistence of Inequality

Progress has occurred. Indignities and injustices have been eliminated, allowing us to focus on the remaining barriers to equity. But why do the gaps in income, living wages, education, and even life expectancy persist? Especially perplexing is whether the glass is half full or half empty, given the numerous civil rights laws, study commissions, favorable court decisions, and efforts by nonprofits, faith-based organizations, and the private sector.

In trying to comprehend the persistence of inequality among racial and ethnic groups, sociologists and other social scientists have found it useful to think in terms of the role played by social and cultural capital. Popularized by French sociologist Pierre Bourdieu, these concepts refer to assets that are not necessarily economic but do impact economic capital for one's family and future. Less cultural and social capital may be passed on from one generation to the next, especially when prejudice and discrimination make it difficult to overcome deficits. Racial and ethnic minorities reproduce disadvantage, while Whites are more likely to reproduce privilege (Bourdieu 1983; Bourdieu and Passeron 1990).

Cultural capital refers to noneconomic forces such as family background and past investments in education that is then reflected in knowledge about the arts and language. It is not necessarily book knowledge; it is the kind of education valued by the elites. African Americans and Native Americans have in the past faced significant restrictions in receiving a quality education. Immigrants have faced challenges due to English not being spoken at home. Muslim immigrants face an immediate challenge in functioning in a culture that gives advantages to a different form of spirituality and lifestyle. The general historical pattern has been for immigrants, especially those who came in large numbers and settled in ethnic enclaves, to take two or three generations to reach educational parity. Knowledge of hip-hop and familiarity with Polish cuisine is culture, but it is not the culture that is valued and prestigious. Society privileges or values some lifestyles over others. This is not good, but it is social reality. Differentiating between *pierogies* will not get you to the top of corporate America as fast as will differentiating among wines. This is, of course, not unique to the United States. Someone settling in Japan would have to deal with cultural capital that includes knowledge of Noh Theatre and tea ceremonies. In most countries, you are much better off following the run-up to the World Cup rather than the contenders for the next Super Bowl (DiMaggio 2005).

Social capital refers to the collective benefit of durable social networks and their patterns of reciprocal trust. Much has been written about the strength of family and friendship networks among all racial and ethnic minorities. Family reunions are major events. Family history and storytelling is rich and full. Kinfolk are not merely acquaintances but truly living assets upon whom one depends or, at the very least, feels comfortable to call on repeatedly. Networks outside the family are critical to coping in a society that often seems determined to keep anyone who looks different down. But given past as well as current discrimination and prejudice, these social networks may help you become a construction worker, but they are less likely to get you into a boardroom. Residential and school segregation make developing social capital more difficult. Immigrant professionals find that their skills or advanced degrees are devalued, and they are shut out of networks of the educated and influential. Working-class Latinos and Blacks have begun to develop informal social ties with their White coworkers and neighbors. Professional immigrants, in time, become accepted as equals, but racial and ethnic minority communities continue to resist institutional marginalization.

Social capital is tricky. If the networks include those who make hiring decisions and are influential, social contacts can be very beneficial. Bonding in this manner

Self-owned businesses are a way a minority community can create social capital. Pictured here is an African American woman in front of her beauty salon business.

Research Focus

Challenge to Pluralism: The Shark's Fin

Popular among the Chinese generally and also Chinese Americans is the delicacy of shark's fin soup. Generally viewed as a luxury food item, it is often served at special occasions such as wedding and anniversary banquets.

However, growing numbers feel that eating a soup using shark fins contributes to the global decline of certain species of sharks. They are not joining the celebration. It is puzzling because the fins themselves are virtually tasteless but are considered the critical ingredient to this delicacy, which typically includes mushrooms, diced ham, other seafood, and chicken for taste.

In 2011, California enacted a ban both on the sale and on the possession of shark fins, including shark's fin soup. Hawaii passed a similar law, as did Washington State and Oregon. Taken together, these four states account for 43 percent of the nation's Chinese American population.

These bans represent a frontal assault on their culture in the view of many in the Chinese American communities. Scholars would see this as a case for **cultural relativism**, where an action of a particular group is judged objectively within the context of a particular culture. However, even some Chinese Americans favor such a ban. California state legislator Paul Fong, who grew up with shark's fin soup, says he is "environmentally conscious" and takes "the scientists' side."

Cultural relativism often surfaces in the United States as a source of tension. Society and courts in particular refuse to recognize polygamous marriages, even if they are legal in the immigrants' country. Shark's fin soup is yet another battleground for how much society is willing to accommodate cultural differences (Brown 2011; Eilperin 2011; Forero 2006).

---

can a crucial bridge serving immigrants in their new homeland. However, if limited to one's own group, a network can serve the positive aspect of building self-confidence, as noted in the ethnic paradox in Chapter 4. **Ethnic paradox** refers to the maintenance of one's ethnic ties in a manner that can assist with assimilation with larger society. In Research Focus, we consider the intriguing case of shark fin soup and how that serves to bind many within the Chinese American community, but in the eyes of some Chinese Americans serves to unfairly make them stand out from mainstream American society (Coleman 1988; Cranford 2005; Lancee 2010; Portes 1998; Portes and Vickstrom 2011).

As the ranks of the powerful and important have been reached by all racial and ethnic groups, social capital is more widely shared, but this process has proven to be slower than advocates of social equality would prefer. Perhaps it will be accelerated by the tendency of successful minority members to be more likely to network with up-and-coming members of their own community. At the same time, Whites more likely will be more comfortable, even complacent, with the next generation making it on their own. We are increasingly appreciative of the importance of aspirations and motivations that are often much more present among people with poor or immigrant backgrounds than those born of affluence. We know that bilingualism is an asset, not a detriment. Children who have translated for their parents develop real-world skills at a much earlier age than their monolingual English counterparts (Bauder 2003; Monkman, Ronald, and Théraméne 2005; Portes 1998; Yosso 2005).

Considering cultural and social capital does leave room for measured optimism. Racial and ethnic groups have shared their cultural capital, whether it is the music we dance to or the food we eat. As the barriers to privilege weaken and eventually fall, people of all colors will be able to advance. The particular strength that African Americans, tribal people, Latinos, Asian Americans, and arriving immigrants bring to the table is that they also have the ability to resist and to refuse to accept second-class status. The role that cultural and social capital plays also points to the need to embrace strategies of intervention that will increasingly acknowledge the skills and talents found in a pluralistic society.

"They say we're not placing enough emphasis on diversity."

Talking Past One Another

In 1991, Los Angeles police beat up African American Rodney King, but a bystander videotaped this incident. Subsequently, the officers were acquitted of all wrongdoing in 1992, which touched off riots that left 55 dead. King, in an effort to stem the violence, pled to news cameras at the time "Can we all get along?"' (Medina 2012). Two decades and counting, we still ask this question, even in more tranquil situations such as in the workplace and the classroom. What do the data show?

First, do people really have close friends of different racial and ethnic backgrounds? Sociologists have attempted to gauge the amount of White–Black interaction. But unless the studies are done carefully, it is easy to overestimate just how much racial togetherness is taking place.

Take the case of sociologist Tom Smith, who heads up the respected General Social Survey. Smith noticed that a high proportion of Whites and African Americans indicate they have close friends of the other race. But is this, in fact, true? When Smith and his fellow researchers analyzed data from the survey, they found that response rates varied according to how the question was phrased.

For example, when asked whether any of their friends they feel close to were Black, 42.1 percent of Whites said, "Yes." Yet, when asked to give the names of friends to whom they feel close, only 6 percent of Whites listed a close friend of a different race or ethnicity.

Grace Kao and Kara Joyner looked at a national study of adolescents. Given that over a third of teens in the United States are non–White or Hispanic, one might expect a lot of cross-race friendships. Over 91 percent of non–Hispanic whites give non–Hispanic White as best same-sex friends—a margin close to what Smith found among all adults. Members of minorities, as one might expect, are a bit more open, with 85 percent of Blacks selecting only Blacks, and 62 percent of Mexican Americans naming only other Mexican Americans. Regardless of group, friendships that cross boundaries are less likely to involve visiting in each other's homes or sharing problems.

Overall, despite growing diversity in the social landscape, when research is conducted carefully, it shows that same diversity is not reflected in whom we regard as our own friends (Kao and Joyner 2004; Smith 1999; Vaquera and Kao 2008).

Second, do we at least listen to what others are saying if they come from a racial or ethnic background that differs from ours? As we have seen, despite diversity, we are not necessarily friends. African Americans, Italian Americans, Korean Americans, Puerto Ricans, Native Americans, Mexican Americans, and many others live in the United States and interact daily, sometimes face-to-face and constantly through the media. But communication does not mean we listen to, much less understand, one another. Sometimes we assume that, as we become an educated nation, we will set aside our prejudices. Yet, in recent years, our college campuses have been the scenes of tension, insults, and even violence. Fletcher Blanchard and his colleagues (1991) conducted an experiment at Smith College and found that even overheard statements can influence expressions of opinion on the issue of racism.

The researchers at Smith College asked a student who said she was conducting an opinion poll for a class to approach seventy-two White students as each was walking across

Watch the Video on MySocLab: *Sociology in Focus: Race and Ethnicity*

Read the Document on MySocLab: Talking Past Each Other: The Black and White Language of Race

the campus. Each time she did so, she also stopped a second White student—actually a confederate working with the researchers—and asked her to also participate in the survey. Both students were asked how Smith College should respond to anonymous racist notes that were sent to four African American students in 1989. However, the confederate was always instructed to answer first. In some cases, she condemned the notes; in others, she justified them. Blanchard and his colleagues (1991) concluded that "hearing at least one other person express strongly antiracist opinions produced dramatically more strongly antiracist public reactions to racism than hearing others express equivocal opinions or opinions more accepting of racism" (pp. 102–103). However, a second experiment demonstrated that when the confederate expressed sentiments justifying racism, the subjects were much less likely to express antiracist opinions than those who heard no opposing opinions. In this experiment, social control (through the process of conformity) influenced people's attitudes and the expression of those attitudes.

Third, are we even willing to discuss diversity? Or do we fear being seen as too politically correct or incorrect? Barack Obama as a candidate made speeches dedicated to revisiting the issue of race, but none of his White opponents did. There certainly was initial optimism about a new era of race; however, people today evoke a color-blind racism and see little evidence of intolerance except when confronted by a horrendous hate crime. Others contend that racism is often couched in a "backstage" manner through discussions of immigration, affirmative action, antipoverty programs, and profiling for national security (Kershaw 2009).

Barack Obama's two terms as president is historic, but little evidence suggests it has launched a nationwide discussion of race, much less a postracial nation of some type. With an African American elected president, were people more relaxed to openly discuss race? Even since he became president, Obama himself has seemed reluctant to discuss much less tackle policies related to race. As we noted in Chapter 3, he did weigh in on the shooting death of the Black youth Trayvon Martin, who was shot by a person on civilian patrol in what many have called a vicious case of racial profiling. Otherwise, Obama has been largely silent. His 2011 State of the Union address was the first by any president since 1948 to not mention poverty or the poor. One analysis of his public statements during his first two years in office found that he talked less about race than any Democratic president since 1961 (Gillion 2012; Harris 2012; White House 2012).

Listen to the **Audio** on **MySocLab**: *A Revealing History of a Multiracial America*

Fourth, even with an absence of cross-racial friendships and willingness to talk about race, realization is growing that people do not mean the same thing when they address problems of race, ethnicity, gender, or religion. A husband regularly does the dishes and feels he is an equal partner in doing the housework, not recognizing that he left the care of his infant daughter totally to his wife. A manager is delighted that he has hired a Puerto Rican salesperson but makes no effort to ensure the new employee will adjust to an all-White, non–Hispanic staff.

We talk, but do we talk past one another? Surveys regularly show that different ethnic and racial groups have different perceptions, whether on immigration policies, racial profiling, or whether discrimination occurs in the labor force. Sociologist Robert Blauner (1969, 1972) contends that Blacks and Whites see racism differently. Minorities see racism as central to society, as ever-present, whereas Whites regard it as a peripheral concern and a national concern only when accompanied by violence or involving a celebrity. African Americans and other minorities consider racist acts in a broader context: "It is racist if my college fails to have Blacks significantly present as advisers, teachers, and administrators." Whites would generally accept a racism charge if a job had been explicitly denied to an appropriately qualified minority member. Furthermore, Whites would apply the label *racist* only to the person or the few people who were actually responsible for the act. Members of minority groups would be more willing to call most of a college's members racist for allowing racist practices to persist. For many Whites, the word *racism* is a red flag, and they are reluctant to give it the wide use typically employed by minorities—that is, those who have been oppressed by racism (Lichtenberg 1992).

Is one view correct—the broader minority perspective or the more limited White outlook? No, but both are a part of the social reality in which we all live. We need to recognize both interpretations.

Read the **Document** on **MySocLab**: *A Different Mirror*

When we considered Whiteness in Chapter 4, we saw that the need to confront racism, however perceived, is not to make Whites guilty and absolve Blacks, Asians, Hispanics, and Native Americans of any responsibility for their present plight. Rather, to understand racism, past and present, is to understand how its impact has shaped both a single person's behavior and that of the entire society (Bonilla-Silva and Baiocchi 2001; Duke 1992).

Conclusion

As the United States promotes racial, ethnic, and religious diversity, it also strives to impose universal criteria on employers, educators, and realtors so that subordinate racial and ethnic groups can participate fully in the larger society. In some instances, to bring about equality of results—not just equality of opportunity— programs have been developed to give competitive advantages to women and minority men. These latest answers to social inequality have provoked much controversy over how to achieve the admirable goal of a multiracial, multiethnic society, undifferentiated in opportunity and rewards.

SPECTRUM OF INTERGROUP RELATIONS

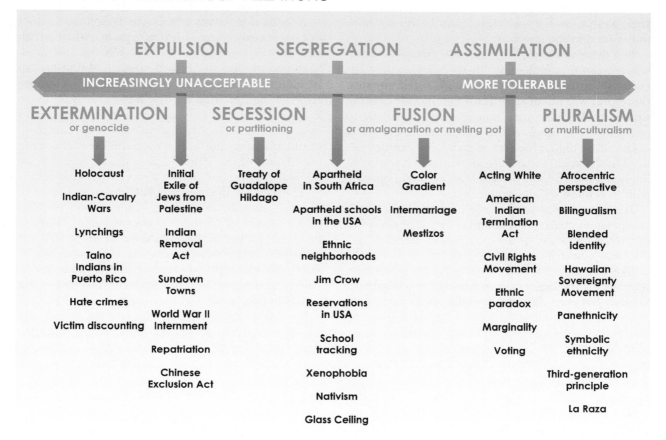

Relations between racial, ethnic, or religious groups take two broad forms: as situations characterized by either consensus or conflict. Consensus prevails where assimilation or fusion of groups has been completed. Consensus also prevails in a pluralistic society in the sense that members have agreed to respect differences among groups. By eliminating the contending group, extermination and expulsion also lead to a consensus society. In the study of intergroup relations, it is often easy to ignore conflict where a high degree of consensus is present because it is assumed that an orderly society has no problems. In some instances, however, this assumption is misleading. Through long periods of history, misery inflicted on a racial, ethnic, or religious group was judged to be appropriate, if not actually divinely inspired.

In recent history, achieving harmonious relations between all racial, ethnic, and religious groups has been widely accepted as a worthy goal. The struggle against oppression and inequality is not new. It dates back at least to the revolutions in England, France, and the American colonies in the seventeenth and eighteenth centuries. The twentieth century was unique in the extension of equality to the less-privileged classes, many of whose members are racial and ethnic minorities. Conflict along racial and ethnic lines is especially bitter now because it evokes memories of slavery, colonial oppression, and overt discrimination. Today's African Americans are much more aware of slavery than contemporary poor people are of seventeenth-century debtors' prisons.

Unquestionably, the goals of the struggle for justice among racial and ethnic groups have not completely been met. Many people are still committed to repression, although they may see it only as benign neglect of those less privileged. Such repression leads to the dehumanization of both the subordinated individual and the oppressor. Growth in equal rights movements and self-determination for developing countries largely populated by non–White people has moved the world onto a course that seems irreversible. The old ethnic battle lines now renewed in Iran, Kenya, Sudan, and Chechnya in Russia have only added to the tensions.

Self-determination, whether for groups or individuals, often is impossible in societies as they are currently structured. Bringing about social equality, therefore, will entail significant changes in existing situations. Because such changes are not likely to occur with everyone's willing cooperation, the social costs will be high. However, if racial and ethnic relations in the world today have any trend, it is the growing belief that the social costs, however high, must be paid to achieve self-determination.

It is naive to foresee a world of societies in which one person equals one vote and all are accepted without regard to race, ethnicity, religion, gender, age, disability status, or sexual orientation. It is equally unlikely to expect to see a society, let alone a world, that has no privileged class or prestigious jobholders. Contact between different peoples, as we have seen numerous times, precedes conflict. Contact also may initiate mutual understanding and appreciation.

Assimilation, even when strictly followed, does not necessarily bring with it acceptance as an equal, nor does it mean that one will also be tolerated. Segregation persists. Efforts toward pluralism can be identified, but we can also easily see the counter-efforts, whether they are the legal efforts to make English the official language or acts of intimidation by activists patrolling the nation's borders, Klansmen, skinheads, and others. However, the sheer changing population of the United States guarantees that we will learn, work, and play in a more diverse society.

The task of making this kaleidoscope image of diverse cultures, languages, colors, and religions into a picture of harmony is overwhelming. But the images of failure in this task, some of which we have witnessed in our news media, are even more frightening. We can applaud success and even take time to congratulate ourselves, but we must also review the unfinished agenda.

MySocLab   ✔ Study and Review on MySocLab

Summary

1. Like the image viewed in a kaleidoscope, the diversity of the American population is constantly changing with what has been often called minority groups accounting for increasing proportions of the population.

2. It is agreed that racial and ethnic minority groups have made great strides during the last two generations in the United States, but the gap between them and White men and women has remained the same.

3. Asian Americans are often labelled as a model minority, which overlooks the many problems they face and minimizes the challenges of succeeding despite prejudice and discrimination.

4. African Americans have made gains in all levels of formal schooling but still fall behind the gains made by others. Debate continues over the appropriateness of the notion that Black youths avoid the appearance of acting White.

5. Inequality persists despite visible improvement because most racial and ethnic groups are unable to accumulate social and cultural capital.

6. While interaction across racial and ethnic lines occurs with increasing significance, it is less clear whether we are all listening to what each other has to say.

7. White people generally apply the charge of racism when it is operating explicitly, whereas members of racial and ethnic groups are more likely to apply it more generally where disadvantages persist.

Key Terms

acting White, p. 245

bamboo ceiling, p. 244

blaming the victim, p. 243

cultural capital, p. 246

cultural relativism, p. 247

ethnic paradox, p. 247

model minority, p. 243

social capital, p. 246

Review Questions

1. What contributes to the changing image of diversity in the United States?

2. Pose views of an issue facing contemporary society that takes the position of half full and then half empty.

3. Why is it harmful to be viewed as a model minority?

4. Is one view of racism the correct one?

5. Why are White Americans less likely to be concerned with social and cultural capital?

Critical Thinking Questions

1. Considering the stereotypes that persist, how do stereotypes affect the people who are stereotyped as well as those who express them?

2. Consider conversations you have with people very different from yourself. Why do you feel those people are different? To what degree did you talk to them or past them? To what degree do they talk to you or past you?

3. How have places where you have worked, even part-time, differed from those of your parents or grandparents in terms of diversity of the workforce? What explains these changes?

Glossary

Parenthetical numbers refer to the pages on which the term is introduced

abolitionists Whites and free Blacks who favored the end of slavery. (180)

absolute deprivation The minimum level of subsistence below which families or individuals should not be expected to exist. (62)

acting White Taking school seriously and accepting the authority of teachers and administrators. (200)

affirmative action Positive efforts to recruit subordinate group members, including women, for jobs, promotions, and educational opportunities. (73)

Afrocentric perspective An emphasis on the customs of African cultures and how they have pervaded the history, culture, and behavior of Blacks in the United States and around the world. (27, 179)

amalgamation The process by which a dominant group and a subordinate group combine through intermarriage to form a new group. (24)

anti-Semitism Anti-Jewish prejudice or discrimination. (328)

apartheid The policy of the South African government intended to maintain separation of Blacks, Coloureds, and Asians from the dominant Whites. (385)

apartheid schools All-Black schools. (200)

arranged marriage When one's marital partner is chosen by others and the relationship is not based on any preexisting mutual attraction. (289)

assimilation The process by which a subordinate individual or group takes on the characteristics of the dominant group. (24)

asylees Foreigners who have already entered the United States and now seek protection because of persecution or a well-founded fear of persecution. (109)

authoritarian personality A psychological construct of a personality type likely to be prejudiced and to use others as scapegoats. (52)

bamboo ceiling A barrier to qualified Asian Americans in a business to experience upward mobility.

bilingual education A program designed to allow students to learn academic concepts in their native language while they learn a second language. (97)

bilingualism The use of two or more languages in places of work or education and the treatment of each language as legitimate. (97)

biological race The mistaken notion of a genetically isolated human group. (10)

blaming the victim Portraying the problems of racial and ethnic minorities as their fault rather than recognizing society's responsibilities. (17, 283)

blended identity Self-image and worldview that is a combination of religious faith, cultural background based on nationality, and current residency. (265)

Bogardus scale Technique to measure social distance toward different racial and ethnic groups. (70)

bracero Contracted Mexican laborer brought to the United States during World War II. (240)

brain drain Immigration to the United States of skilled workers, professionals, and technicians who are desperately needed in their home countries. (94, 230)

chain immigration When immigrants sponsor several other immigrants who, on their arrival, may sponsor still more. (88, 294)

civil disobedience A tactic promoted by Martin Luther King, Jr., based on the belief that people have the right to disobey unjust laws under certain circumstances. (187)

civil religion The religious dimension in American life that merges the state with sacred beliefs. (135)

class As defined by Max Weber, people who share similar levels of wealth. (15, 208)

colonialism A foreign power's maintenance of political, social, economic, and cultural dominance over people for an extended period. (20)

color-blind racism Use of race-neutral principles to defend the racially unequal status quo. (58)

color gradient The placement of people on a continuum from light to dark skin color rather than in distinct racial groupings by skin color. (221, 248, 374)

conflict perspective A sociological approach that assumes that the social structure is best understood in terms of conflict or tension between competing groups. (17)

contact hypothesis An interactionist perspective stating that intergroup contact between people of equal status in noncompetitive circumstances will reduce prejudice. (70, 388)

cultural capital Noneconomic forces such as family background and past investments in education that are then reflected in knowledge about the arts and language. (246)

cultural relativism An action of a particular group is judged objectively within the context of a particular culture. (146)

de facto segregation Segregation that is the result of residential patterns. (199)

de jure segregation Children assigned to schools specifically to maintain racially separated schools. (186)

denomination A large, organized religion not officially linked with the state or government. (134)

desi Colloquial name for people who trace their ancestry to South Asia, especially India and Pakistan. (288)

differential justice Whites being dealt with more leniently than Blacks, whether at the time of arrest, indictment, conviction, sentencing, or parole. (211)

discrimination The denial of opportunities and equal rights to individuals and groups because of prejudice or for other arbitrary reasons. (48, 61)

dry foot, wet foot Policy toward Cuban immigrants that allows those who manage to reach the United States (dry foot) to remain but sends those who are picked up at sea (wet foot) back to Cuba. (228)

dysfunction An element of society that may disrupt a social system or decrease its stability. (16)

emigration Leaving a country to settle in another. (19)

environmental justice Efforts to ensure that hazardous substances are controlled so that all communities receive protection regardless of race or socioeconomic circumstances. (72, 172)

ethnic cleansing Forced deportation of people accompanied by systematic violence. (22)

ethnic group A group set apart from others because of its national origin or distinctive cultural patterns. (8)

ethnic paradox The maintenance of one's ethnic ties in a way that can assist with assimilation in larger society. (139)

ethnocentrism The tendency to assume that one's culture and way of life are superior to all others. (45)

ethnophaulism Ethnic or racial slurs, including derisive nicknames. (36)

evacuees Japanese Americans interned in camps for the duration of World War II. (312)

exploitation theory A Marxist theory that views racial subordination in the United States as a manifestation of the class system inherent in capitalism. (52)

familism Pride and closeness in the family that result in placing family obligation and loyalty before individual needs. (252)

fish-ins Native American tribes' protests over government interference with their traditional rights to fish as they like. (158)

functionalist perspective A sociological approach emphasizing how parts of a society are structured to maintain its stability. (16)

fusion A minority and a majority group combining to form a new group. (24)

genocide The deliberate, systematic killing of an entire people or nation. (22)

glass ceiling The barrier that blocks the promotion of a qualified worker because of gender or minority membership. (78, 357)

glass escalator The male advantage experienced in occupations dominated by women. (80)

glass wall A barrier to moving laterally in a business to positions that are more likely to lead to upward mobility. (79)

globalization Worldwide integration of government policies, cultures, social movements, and financial markets through trade, movements of people, and the exchange of ideas. (20, 106)

gook syndrome David Riesman's phrase describing Americans' tendency to stereotype Asians and to regard them as all alike and undesirable. (292)

Haoles Native Hawaiians' term for Caucasians. (297)

hate crime Criminal offense committed because of the offender's bias against a race, religion, ethnic or national origin group, or sexual orientation group. (64)

Holocaust The state-sponsored systematic persecution and annihilation of European Jewry by Nazi Germany and its collaborators. (330)

homophobia The fear of and prejudice toward homosexuality. (403)

hui kuan Chinese American benevolent associations organized on the basis of the district of the immigrant's origin in China. (307)

ilchomose The 1.5 generation of Korean Americans—those who immigrated into the United States as children. (295)

immigration Coming into a new country as a permanent resident. (19)

income Salaries, wages, and other money received. (71, 202)

institutional discrimination A denial of opportunities and equal rights to individuals or groups resulting from the normal operations of a society. (65, 400)

intelligence quotient (IQ) The ratio of a person's mental age (as computed by an IQ test) to his or her chronological age, multiplied by 100. (11)

Islamophobia A range of negative feelings toward Muslims and their religion that ranges from generalized intolerance to hatred. (273)

Issei First-generation immigrants from Japan to the United States. (310)

Jim Crow Southern laws passed in the late nineteenth century that kept Blacks in their subordinate position. (180)

Kanaka maoli Hawaiian term to refer to Native Hawaiians. (230)

Kibei Japanese Americans of the Nisei generation sent back to Japan for schooling and to have marriages arranged. (310)

kickouts or pushouts Native American school dropouts who leave behind an unproductive academic environment. (165)

kye Rotating credit system used by Korean Americans to subsidize the start-up costs of businesses. (296)

labeling theory A sociological approach introduced by Howard Becker that attempts to explain why certain people are viewed as deviants and others engaging in the same behavior are not. (18)

marginality The status of being between two cultures at the same time, such as the status of Jewish immigrants in the United States. (15, 342)

Marielitos People who arrived from Cuba in the third wave of Cuban immigration, most specifically those forcibly deported by way of Mariel Harbor. The term is generally reserved for refugees who are seen as especially undesirable. (228)

melting pot Diverse racial or ethnic groups or both, forming a new creation, a new cultural entity. (24)

migration A general term that describes any transfer of population. (19)

minority group A subordinate group whose members have significantly less control or power over their own lives than do the members of a dominant or majority group. (6)

mixed status Families in which one or more members are citizens and one or more are noncitizens. (96, 253)

model minority A group that, despite past prejudice and discrimination, succeeds economically, socially, and educationally without resorting to political or violent confrontations with Whites. (281)

mojados Wetbacks; derisive slang for Mexicans who enter the United States illegally, supposedly by swimming the Rio Grande River. (240)

nativism Beliefs and policies favoring native-born citizens over immigrants. (90)

neocolonialism Continuing dependence of former colonies on foreign countries. (246)

Neoricans Puerto Ricans who return to the island to settle after living on the U.S. mainland (also called Nuyoricans). (245)

Nisei Children born of immigrants from Japan. (310)

normative approach The view that prejudice is influenced by societal norms and situations that encourage or discourage the tolerance of minorities. (53)

panethnicity The development of solidarity between ethnic subgroups as reflected in the terms Hispanic and Asian American. (13, 220, 285)

pan-Indianism Intertribal social movements in which several tribes, joined by political goals but not by kinship, unite in a common identity. (157)

Pentecostalism A religion similar in many respects to evangelical faiths that believes in the infusion of the Holy Spirit into services and in religious experiences such as faith healing. (255)

pluralism Mutual respect for one another's culture, a respect that allows minorities to express their own culture without suffering prejudice or discrimination. (25)

powwows Native American gatherings of dancing, singing, music playing, and visiting, accompanied by competitions. (157)

prejudice A negative attitude toward an entire category of people such as a racial or ethnic minority. (48)

principle of third-generation interest Marcus Hansen's contention that ethnic interest and awareness increase in the third generation, among the grandchildren of immigrants. (119)

racial formation A sociohistorical process by which racial categories are created, inhibited, transformed, and destroyed. (12, 178)

racial group A group that is socially set apart because of obvious physical differences. (7)

racial profiling Any arbitrary police-initiated action based on race, ethnicity, or national origin rather than a person's behavior. (57, 271, 284)

racism A doctrine that one race is superior. (12)

redlining The pattern of discrimination against people trying to buy homes in minority and racially changing neighborhoods. (69, 210)

refugees People living outside their country of citizenship for fear of political or religious persecution. (108)

relative deprivation The conscious experience of a negative discrepancy between legitimate expectations and present actualities. (62, 189)

religion A unified system of sacred beliefs and practices that encompasses elements beyond everyday life that inspire awe, respect, and even fear. (180)

remittances The monies that immigrants return to their countries of origin. (105, 223)

repatriation The 1930s program of deporting Mexicans. (239)

resegregation The physical separation of racial and ethnic groups reappearing after a period of relative integration. (23)

restrictive covenant Private contracts or agreements that discourage or prevent minority-group members from purchasing housing in a neighborhood. (184)

reverse discrimination Actions that cause better-qualified White men to be passed over for women and minority men. (76)

riff-raff theory Also called the rotten-apple theory; the belief that the riots of the 1960s were caused by discontented youths rather than by social and economic problems facing all African Americans. (189)

rising expectations The increasing sense of frustration that legitimate needs are being blocked. (190)

Sansei The children of the Nisei—that is, the grandchildren of the original immigrants from Japan. (310)

scapegoating theory A person or group blamed irrationally for another person's or group's problems or difficulties. (51, 329)

segregation The physical separation of two groups, often imposed on a subordinate group by the dominant group. (23)

self-fulfilling prophecy The tendency to respond to and act on the basis of stereotypes, a predisposition that can lead one to validate false definitions. (18)

sexism The ideology that one sex is superior to the other. (348)

sinophobes People with a fear of anything associated with China. (91)

slave codes Laws that defined the low position held by slaves in the United States. (177)

slavery reparations Act of making amends for the injustices of slavery. (187)

social capital Collective benefits of durable social networks and their patterns of reciprocal trust. (314)

social distance Tendency to approach or withdraw from a racial group. (70)

sociology The systematic study of social behavior and human groups. (15)

sovereignty Tribal self-rule. (160)

sovereignty movement Effort by the indigenous peoples of Hawai'i to secure a measure of self-government and restoration of their lands. (298)

stereotypes Unreliable, exaggerated generalizations about all members of a group that do not take individual differences into account. (18, 54)

stratification A structured ranking of entire groups of people that perpetuates unequal rewards and power in a society. (15)

sundown towns Communities in which non-Whites were systematically excluded from living. (185)

symbolic ethnicity Herbert Gans's term that describes emphasis on ethnic food and ethnically associated political issues rather than deeper ties to one's heritage. (121)

tongs Chinese American secret associations. (307)

tracking The practice of placing students in specific curriculum groups on the basis of test scores and other criteria. (200, 251)

tsu Clans established along family lines and forming a basis for social organization by Chinese Americans. (307)

underemployment Working at a job for which the worker is overqualified, involuntary working part-time instead of full-time, or being intermittently employed. (204)

victim discounting Tendency to view crime as less socially significant if the victim is viewed as less worthy. (211)

victimization surveys Annual attempts to measure crime rates by interviewing ordinary citizens who may or may not have been crime victims. (217)

Viet Kieu Vietnamese living abroad, such as in the United States. (293)

wealth An inclusive term encompassing all of a person's material assets, including land and other types of property. (71, 202)

White primary Legal provisions forbidding Black voting in election primaries; in one-party areas of the South, these laws effectively denied Blacks their right to select elected officials. (181)

White privilege Rights or immunities granted as a particular benefit or favor for being White. (38)

world systems theory A view of the global economic system as divided between nations that control wealth and those that provide natural resources and labor. (20, 150, 249, 372)

xenophobia The fear or hatred of strangers or foreigners. (90)

Yonsei The fourth generation of Japanese Americans in the United States; the children of the Sansei. (310)

zoning laws Legal provisions stipulating land use and the architectural design of housing, often used to keep racial minorities and low-income people out of suburban areas. (210)

References

Abdo, Geneive. 2004a. A Muslim Rap Finds Voice. *Chicago Tribune* (June 30): 1, 19.

Abdulrahim, Raja. 2009. UC urged to expand ethnic labels. *Los Angeles Times* (March 31): A4.

Abrahamson, Mark. 1996. *Urban Enclaves: Identity and Place in America.* New York: St. Martin's Press.

ACLU. 1996. *Racial Justice.* New York: American Civil Liberties Union.

Adams, Jane Meredith. 2006. Mystery Shrouds Slaying of Chinatown Businessman. *Washington Post* (March 31): 5.

Adler, Patricia A. and Peter Adler. 2004. *Paradise Laborers: Hotel Work in the Global Economy.* Ithaca, NY: Cornell University.

Adorno, T. W., Else Frenkel-Brunswik, Daniel J. Levinson, and R. Nevitt Sanford. 1950. *The Authoritarian Personality.* New York: Wiley.

Ajrouch, Kristine J. and Amancy Jamal. 2007. Assimilating to a White Identity: The Case of Arab Americans. *International Migration Review* (Winter): 860–879.

Akaka, Daniel. 2008. Akaka Bill. Accessed November 20, 2008 at http://Akaka.senate.gov/public/index.cfm?FuseAction=Issues .Home&issues=Akaka%20Bill&content_id=24#Akaka%20Bill.

Alexander, Michelle. 2012. The New Jim Crow: Mass Incarceration in the Age of Colorblindness. Rev. Ed. New York: The New Press.

Alliance for Board Diversity. 2009. *Women and Minorities on Fortune 100 Boards.* New York: Catalyst, the Executive Leadership Council, and the Hispanic Association on Corporate Responsibility.

Allport, Gordon W. 1979. *The Nature of Prejudice*, 25th anniversary ed. Reading, MA: Addison-Wesley.

Alvord, Valerie. 2000. Refugees' Success Breeds Pressure, Discrimination. *USA Today* (May 1): 74.

American Community Survey. 2009. *American Community Survey 2008.* Released August 2009 from www.census.gov.

————. 2010. *American Community Survey 2009.* Released August 2010 from www.census.gov.

American Indian Higher Education Consortium. 2012. "Home Page." Accessed July 11 at http://www.aihec.org.

Anderson, Elijah. 2011. *The Cosmopolitan Canopy: Race and Civility in Everyday Life.* New York: W. W. Norton and Company.

Anguilar-San Juan, Karin. 2009. Little Saigon: Staying Vietnamese in America. Minneapolis: University of Minnesota Press.

Ansell, Amy E. 2008. Color Blindness. pp. 320–322 in vol. 1, *Encyclopedia of Race, Ethnicity, and Society*, Richard T. Schaefer, ed. Thousand Oaks, CA: Sage.

Aran, Kenneth, Herman Arthur, Ramon Colon, and Harvey Goldenberg. 1973. *Puerto Rican History and Culture: A Study Guide and Curriculum Outline.* New York: United Federation of Teachers.

Archibold, Randal C. 2007. A City's Violence Feeds on Black-Hispanic Rivalry. *New York Times* (January 17): A1, A15.

Arias, Elizabeth. 2010. U.S. Life Tables by Hispanic Origin, *Vital and Health Statistics*, series 2, no. 152.

Ariel/Hewitt. 2009. *401(K) Plans in Living Color.* Chicago, IL: Ariel Education Institute and Ariel Investments/Hewitt Associates.

Asante, Molefi Kete. 2007. *An Afrocentric Manifesto: Toward an African Renaissance.* Cambridge, UK: Polity.

————. 2008. Afrocentricity. pp. 41–42 in vol. 1, *Encyclopedia of Race, Ethnicity, and Society*, Richard T. Schaefer, ed. Thousand Oaks, CA: Sage.

Asian American Federation. 2008. *Revitalizing Chinatown Businesses: Challenges and Opportunities.* New York: Asian American Federation.

Bahr, Howard M. 1972. An End to Invisibility. pp. 404–412 in *Native Americans Today: Sociological Perspectives*, Howard M. Bahr, Bruce A. Chadwick, and Robert C. Day, eds. New York: Harper & Row.

Balderrama, Francisco E. and Raymond Rodriguez. 2006. *Decade of Betrayal: Mexican Repatriation in the 1930s.* Revised. Albuquerque: University of New Mexico Press.

Bamshad, Michael J. and Steve E. Olson. 2003. Does Race Exist? *Scientific American* (December): 78–85.

Banerjee, Neela. 2000. Fighting Back against Domestic Violence: Asian American Women Organize to Break the Silence. *AsianWeek* (November 30), 22: 13–15.

Banton, Michael 2008. The Sociology of Ethnic Relations. *Ethnic and Racial Studies* (May): 1–19.

Bartlett, Donald L. and James B. Steele. 2002. Casinos: Wheel of Misfortune. *Time* (December 10), 160: 44–53, 56–58.

Bascara, Victor. 2008. Model Minority. pp. 910–912 in vol. 2, *Encyclopedia of Race, Ethnicity, and Society*, Richard T. Schaefer, ed. Thousand Oaks, CA: Sage.

Bash, Harry M. 2001. If I'm So White, Why Ain't I Right? Some Methodological Misgivings on Taking Identity Ascriptions at Face Value. Paper presented at the annual meeting of the Midwest Sociological Society, St. Louis.

Bauder, Harald. 2003. Brain Abuse, or the Devaluation of Immigrant Labour in Canada. *Antipode* (September), 35: 699–717.

Beardstown CUSD 15. 2012. 2011 Illinois District Report Card. Beardstown, IL.

Bell, Derrick. 1994. The Freedom of Employment Act. *The Nation* 258 (May 23): 708, 710–714.

————. 2004. *Silent Covenants: Brown v. Board of Education and the Unfulfilled Hopes for Racial Reform.* Cambridge, MA: Oxford University Press.

Bell, Wendell. 1991. Colonialism and Internal Colonialism. pp. 52–53 in 4th ed., *The Encyclopedic Dictionary of Sociology*, Richard Lachmann, ed. Guilford, CT: Dushkin Publishing Group.

Bellafante, Ginia. 2005. Young South Asians in America Embrace "Assisted" Marriages. *New York Times* (August 23): A1, A15.

Bellah, Robert. 1967. Civil Religion in America. *Daedalus* 96 (Winter): 1–21.

Belluck, Pam. 2009. New Hopes for Reform in Indian Health Care. *New York Times* (December 2): A1, A28.

Belton, Danielle C. 2009. Blacks in Space. *American Prospect* (June): 47–49.

Berlin, Ira. 2010. *The Making of African America: The Four Great Migrations.* New York: Viking Press.

Bernard, Tara Siegel. 2012. Blacks Face Bias in Bankruptcy, Study Suggests. *New York Times* (January 21): A1.

Bertrand, Marianne and Sendhi Mullainatham. 2004. Are Emily and Greg More Employable that Lakisha and Jamal? A Field Experiment on Labor Market Discrimination. *American Economic Review* 94 (September): 991–1013.

Best, Joel. 2001. Social Progress and Social Problems: Toward a Sociology of Gloom. *Sociological Quarterly* 42 (1): 1–12.

Bigelow, Rebecca. 1992. Certain Inalienable Rights. *Friends Journal* (November), 38: 6–8.

Bjerk, David. 2008. Glass Ceilings or Sticky Floors? Statistical Discrimination in a Dynamic Model of Hiring and Promotion. *The Economic Journal* 118 (530): 961–982.

Blackfeet Reservation Development Fund. 2006. *The Facts v. the Brochure.* Blackfeet Restoration.

Blackstock, Nelson. 1976. *COINTELPRO: The FBI's Secret War on Political Freedom.* New York: Vintage Press.

Blanchard, Fletcher A., Teri Lilly, and Leigh Ann Vaughn. 1991. Reducing the Expression of Racial Prejudice. *Psychological Science* 2 (March): 101–105.

Blauner, Robert. 1969. Internal Colonialism and Ghetto Revolt. *Social Problems* 16 (Spring): 393–408.

———. 1972. *Racial Oppression in America.* New York: Harper & Row.

Blazak, Randy. 2011. Isn't Every Crime a Hate Crime? The Case for Hate Crime Laws. *Sociology Compass* 5 (4): 244–255.

Bloom, Leonard. 1971. *The Social Psychology of Race Relations.* Cambridge, MA: Schenkman Publishing.

Blow, Charles M. 2013. Escaping Slavery. *New York Times* (January 4): A15. Accessible at http://www.nytimes.com/2013/01/05/opinion/blow-escaping-slavery.html?_r=0.

Bobo, Lawrence and Mia Tuan. 2006. *Prejudices in Politics: Group Position, Public Opinion, and the Wisconsin Treaty Rights Dispute.* Cambridge, MA: Harvard University Press.

Boehm, Mike. 2004. Repeating the History. *Los Angeles Times* (February 20): E2.

Bogardus, Emory. 1968. Comparing Racial Distance in Ethiopia, South Africa, and the United States. *Sociology and Social Research* 52 (January): 149–156.

Bohmer, Susanne and Kayleen V. Oka. 2007. Teaching Affirmative Action: An Opportunity to Apply, Segregate, and Reinforce Sociological Concepts. *Teaching Sociology* 35 (October): 334–349.

Bonilla-Silva, Eduardo. 1996. Rethinking Racism: Toward a Structural Interpretation. *American Sociological Review* 62 (June): 465–480.

———. 2002. The Linguistics of Color Blind Racism: How to Talk Nasty about Blacks without Sounding Racist. *Critical Sociology* 28 (1 -2): 41–64.

———. 2004. From Bi-Racial to Tri-Racial: Towards a New System of Racial Stratification in the USA. *Ethnic and Racial Studies* 27 (November): 931–950.

———. 2006. *Racism without Racists*, 2nd ed. Lanham, MD: Rowman & Littlefield.

———. 2012. "The Invisible Weight of Whiteness: The Racial Grammar of Everyday Life in Contemporary America." *Ethnic and Racial Studies* 35 (February): 173–194.

——— and David Dietrich 2011. The Sweet Enchantment of Color-Blind Racism in Obamerica. *The ANNALS of the American Academy of Political and Social Science* 2011 634 (March): 190–206.

——— and David G. Embrick. 2007. "Every Place Has a Ghetto...": The Significance of Whites' Social and Residential Segregation. *Symbolic Interaction* 30 (3): 323–345.

——— and Gianpaolo Baiocchi. 2001. Anything but Racism: How Sociologists Limit the Significance of Racism. *Race and Society* 4: 117–131.

Bonus, Rick. 2000. *Locating Filipino Americans: Ethnicity and the Cultural Politics of Space.* Philadelphia, PA: Temple University Press.

Bourdieu, Pierre. 1983. The Forms of Capital. pp. 241–258 in *Handbook of Theory and Research for the Sociology of Education*, J. G. Richardson, ed. Westport, CT: Greenwood.

——— and Jean-Claude Passeron. 1990. *Reproduction in Education, Society, and Culture*, 2nd ed. London: Sage. (Originally published as La Reproduction (1970).

Bowles, Scott. 2000. Bans on Racial Profiling Gain Steam. *USA Today* 2 (June): 3A.

Bowman, Scott W. 2011. Multigenerational Interactions in Black Middle Class Wealth and Asset Decision Making. *Journal of Family and Economic Issues* 32: 15–26.

Bowser, Benjamin and Raymond G. Hunt, eds. 1996. *Impacts of Racism on White Americans.* Beverly Hills, CA: Sage Publications.

Braxton, Gregory. 2009. "Reality Television" in More Ways Than One. *Los Angeles Times* (February 17): A1, A15.

——— and Louise Seamster. 2011. The Sweet Enchantment of Color Blindness in Black Face: "Explaining the 'Miracle," Debating the Politics, and Suggesting A Way for Hope to be "For Real" in America. *Political Power and Social Theory* 22:139–175.

Brennan Center. 2006. *Citizens without Proof.* November. New York: Brennan Center for Justice at NYU School of Law.

———. 2013. Election 2012: Voting Laws Roundup. Accessed January 13, 2013, at www.brennancenter.org.

Brittingham, Angela and G. Patricia de la Cruz. 2005. *We the People of Arab Ancestry in the United States.* CENSR-21. Accessible at www.census.gov/prod/2005pubs/censr-21.pdf.

Buchanan, Angela B., Nora G. Albert, and Daniel Beaulieu. 2010. *The Population with Haitian Ancestry in the United States: 2009.* ACSR/09-18. Accessible at www.census.gov.

Brooks, Rakim. 2012. A Linked Fate: Barack Obama and Black America. *Dissent* (Summer): 42–45.

Brooks-Gunn, Jeanne, Pamela K. Klebanov, and Greg J. Duncan. 1996. Ethnic Differences in Children's Intelligence Test Scores: Role of Economic Deprivation, Home Environment, and Maternal Characteristics. *Child Development* 67 (April): 396–408.

Brown, Patricia Leigh. 2003. For the Muslim Prom Queen, There are No Kings Allowed. *New York Times* 9 (June): A1, A24.

———. 2009. "Invisible Immigrants, Old and Left with 'Nobody to Talk To.'" *New York Times* (April 3): A1, A10.

———. 2011. Soup without Fins? Some Californians Simmer. *New York Times* (March 5).

Brulliard, Karin. 2006. A Proper Goodbye: Funeral Homes Learn Immigrants' Traditions. *Washington Post National Weekly Edition* (May 7): 31.

Buchanan, Angela B., Nora G. Albert, and Daniel Beaulieu. 2010. *The Population with Haitian Ancestry in the United States: 2009.* ACSR/09-18. Accessible at www.census.gov.

Buck, Stuart. 2010. *Acting White: The Ironic Legacy of Desegregation.* New Haven: Yale University Press.

Budig, Michelle J. 2002. Male Advantage and the Gender Composition of Jobs: Who Rides the Glass Escalator? *Social Problems* 49 (2): 258–277.

Bureau of Indian Affairs. 2005. *American Indian Population and Labor Force Report.* Washington, DC: BIA, Office of Indian Services.

Bureau of Labor Statistics 2011b. *Economy at a Glance: Puerto Rico.* Washington DC: U.S. Department of Labor.

———. 2012a. Employment Status of the Civilian Population. June 2012. Accessed July 26 at http://bls.gov/news.release/empsit.t02.htm.

———. 2012b. Databases, Tables and Calculators by Subject. White and Black Unemployment Rates From Current Population Survey 2002–2012. Accessible at www.bls.gov.

Bureau of the Census. 2007a. *The American Community Survey-Asians: 2004.* ACS-05. Washington, DC: U.S. Government Printing Office.

———. 2007c. *The American Community-Pacific Islanders: 2004.* ACS-06. Washington, DC: U.S. Government Printing Office.

———. 2007h. *2006 American Community Survey. Selected Economic Characteristics: Puerto Rico and the United States.* Accessed August 16, 2008, at HYPERLINK "http://www.census.gov"www.census.gov.

———. 2010a. *Statistical Abstract of the United States, 2011.* Washington, DC: U.S. Government Printing Office.

———. 2010b. *U.S. Population Projections.* Accessible at http://www.census.gov/population/www/projections/2009projections.html.

———. 2011a. *The Statistical Abstract of the United States 2012.* Accessible at www.census.gov/compedia/statab/.

———. 2011b. 2006–2010 American Community Survey American Indian and Alaska Native Tables. Accessible at www.census.gov.

———. 2011d. *2010 Center of Population.* Accessible at http://2010.census.gov/news/pdf/03242011_pressbrf_slides230pm.pdf. http://www.census.gov/population/www/projections/2009projections. html.

_____. 2011k. *Foreign Born*. Current Population Survey – March 2012. Detailed Tables. Accessed at http://www.census.gov/ population/ foreign/data/cps2010.html.

_____. 2012b. Selected Economic Characteristics. 2006–2010 American Community Survey. American Indian and Alaska Native Tables. Table DP03. Accessible at http://factfinder2.census.gov.

_____. 2012d. "Most Children Younger Than Age 1 are Minorities, Census Bureau Reports." May 17. Accessible at http://www.census. gov/newsroom/releases/archives/population/cb12-90.html.

_____. 2012e. Poverty Status in the Past 12 Months. 2011 American Community Survey. 1-Year Estimates. Table S1701. United States and Puerto Rico. Accessible at www.census.gov.

_____. 2012p. U.S. Census Bureau Projections Show a Slower Growing , Older, More Diverse Nation a Half Century from Now. News Release December 12. Accessible at HYPERLINK "http://www.census.gov"www.census.gov.

Calavita, Kitty. 2007. Immigration Law, Race, and Identity. *Annual Reviews of Law and Social Sciences* 3: 1–20.

Camarillo, Albert. 1993. Latin Americans: Mexican Americans and Central Americans. pp. 855–872 in *Encyclopedia of American Social History*, Mary Koplec Coyton, Elliot J. Gorn, and Peter W. Williams, eds. New York: Charles Scribner.

Camarota, Steven A. and Karen Jensnenus. 2009. *A Shifting Tide: Recent Trends in the Illegal Immigrant Population*. Washington, DC: Center for Immigration Studies.

Campbell, Gregory R. 2008. Sacred Sites, Native American. pp. 1179–1182 in vol. 3, *Encyclopedia of Race, Ethnicity, and Society*, Richard T. Schaefer, ed. Thousand Oaks, CA: Sage.

Campo-Flores, Arena. 2012. Cuban-Americans Move Left. *The Wall Street Journal* (November 9): A6.

Canfield, Clarke. 2012. Maine major: Somalis should leave culture at door. *Twin City Times* (Lewiston-Auburn, ME) October 4. Accessed November 12 at http://www.twincitytimes.com/columns/enough-is-enough-extremist-liberals-widen-the-divide-with-somalis.

Capriccioso, Rob. 2011. The Donor Party. *Indian Country Today* (March 23): 43–49.

Carmichael, Stokely, with Ekwueme Michael Thelwell. 2003. *The Life and Struggles of Stokely Carmichael (Kwame Ture)*. New York: Scribner.

Carpusor, Adrian G. and William E. Loges. 2006. Rental Discrimination and Ethnicity in Names. *Journal of Applied Social Psychology* 36 (4): 934–952.

Carr, James H. and Nandinee K. Kutty, eds. 2008. *Segregation: The Rising Costs for America*. New York: Routledge.

Carroll, Joseph. 2006. Public National Anthem Should Be Sung in English. *The Gallup Poll* (May): 3.

Carson, E. Ann and William J. Sabol. 2012. *Prisoners in 2011*. December. Washington, DC: Bureau of Justice Statistics.

Carter, Jimmy. 1978. Public Papers of the President of the United States. Book Two: June 30 to December 31, 1978. Washington, DC: National Archives and Records Service.

Catalyst. 2001. Women Satisfied with Current Job in Financial Industry but Barriers Still Exist. Press release July 25, 2001. Accessed January 31, 2002, at www. catalystwomen.org.

Cave, Damien. 2011. Crossing Over, and Over. *New York Times* (October 3): A1, A6.

Center for Constitutional Rights. 2011. *Stop-and-Frisks of New Yorkers in 2010 Hit All-Time High at 600, 601; 87 percent of Those Stopped Black and Latino*. Accessed March 2, 2011, at http://ccrjustice.org.

Center for Work-Life Policy. 2011. Asian-Americans Still Feel Like Outsiders in Corporate America, New Study from the Center for Work-Life Policy Finds. July 20. New York: Center for Work-Life Policy.

Chaney, Kathy. 2009. Are there too few Black Criminal Court Judges? *Chicago Defender* (March 11). Accessible at http://www.chicago defender.com/ article3442-are-there-too-few-black-criminal-court-judges.html.

Chang, Cindy. 2007. Asians Flex Muscles in California Politics. *New York Times* (February 27): A11.

Chang, Doris F. and Amy Demyan. 2007. Teachers' Stereotypes of Asian, Black and White Students. *School Psychology Quarterly* 22 (2): 91–114.

Chase-Dunn, Christopher and Thomas D. Hall. 1998. World-Systems in North America: Networks, Rise and Fall and Pulsations of Trade in Stateless Systems. *American Indian Culture and Research Journal*, 22(1): 23–72.

Cheng, Lucie, and Philip Q. Yang. 2000. The "Model Minority" Deconstructed. pp. 459–482 in Min Zhou and James V. Gatewood, *Contemporary Asian American: A Multidisciplinary Reader*, Min Zhou and James V. Gatewood, eds. New York: New York University Press.

Cheng, Shu-Ju Ada. 2008. Jim Crow. p. 795 in vol. 2, *Encyclopedia of Race, Ethnicity, and Society*, Richard T. Schaefer, ed. Thousand Oaks, CA: Sage.

Chin, Ko-lin. 1996. *Chinatown Gangs: Extortion, Enterprise, and Ethnicity*. New York: Oxford University Press.

Chirot, Daniel and Jennifer Edwards. 2003. Making Sense of the Senseless: Understanding Genocide. *Contexts* 2 (Spring): 12–19.

Choi, Yoonsun and Benjamin B. Lahey. 2006. Testing the Model Minority Stereotype: Youth Behaviors across Racial and Ethnic Groups. *Social Science Review* (September): 419–452.

Chou, Roslaind S. and Joe R. Feagin. 2008. *The Myth of the Model Minority: Asian Americans Facing Racism*. Boulder: Paradigm Publishers.

Christensen, Kim. 2012. Interview. Wisconsin School District. November 8.

Christopulos, Diana. 1974. Puerto Rico in the Twentieth Century: A Historical Survey. pp. 123–163 in *Puerto Rico and Puerto Ricans: Studies in History and Society*, Adalberto López and James Petras, eds. New York: Wiley.

Chu, Judy. 2011. Chinese Exclusion Act of 1882. June 1. Congressional Record, U.S. House of Representatives. June 1, 2011. Accessible at http://www.gpo.gov/fdsys/pkg/CREC-2011-06-01-pt1-PgH3809-4. pdf.

Chu, Kathy. 2010. Vietnam: A New Land of Opportunity. *USA Today* (August 18): A1, A2.

Citrin, Jack, Amy Lerman, Michael Murakami, and Kathryn Pearson. 2007. Testing Huntington: Is Hispanic Immigration a Threat to American Identity? *Perspectives on Politics* 5 (March): 31–48.

Clark, Kenneth B. and Mamie P. Clark. 1947. Racial Identification and Preferences in Negro Children. pp. 169–178 in *Readings in Social Psychology*, Theodore M. Newcomb and Eugene L. Hartley, eds. New York: Holt, Rinehart & Winston.

Cockburn, Andrew. 2003. True Colors: Divided Loyalty in Puerto Rico. *National Geographic Magazine* (March), 203: 34–55.

Cognard-Black, Andrew J. 2004. Will They Stay, or Will They Go? Sex—Atypical among Token Men Who Teach. *Sociological Quarterly* 45 (1): 113–139.

Coker, Tumaini, et al. 2009. Perceived Racial/Ethnic Discrimination among Fifth-Grade Students and Its Association with Mental Health. *American Journal of Public Health* 99 (5): 878–884.

Coleman, James S. 1988. Social Capital in the Creation of Human Capital. *American Journal of Sociology* 94 (Suppl.): S95–S120.

Comeau, Joseph A. 2012. Race/Ethnicity and Family Contact: Toward a Behavioral Measure of Familism. *Hispanic Journal of Behavioral Sciences* 34 (2): 251–268.

Commission on Civil Rights. 1976. *Fulfilling the Letter and Spirit of the Law: Desegregation of the Nation's Public Schools*. Washington, DC: U.S. Government Printing Office.

_____. 1981. *Affirmative Action in the 1980s: Dismantling the Process of Discrimination*. Washington, DC: U.S. Government Printing Office.

Commission on Wartime Relocation and Internment of Civilians. 1982a. *Recommendations*. Washington, DC: U.S. Government Printing Office.

_____. 1982b. Report. Washington, DC: U.S. Government Printing Office.

Conley, Dalton. 2011. When Roommates were Random. *New York Times* (August 29). Accessible at http://www.nytimes.com/2011/08/29/opinion/when-roommates-were-random.html.

Connelly, Marjorie. 2008. Dissecting the Changing Electorate. *New York Times* (November 8): section WK.

Constantini, Cristina. 2011. Beardstown, Small Midwestern Meatpacking Town, Wrestles With Immigration Issue. Huffington Post (December). Accessible at http://www.huffingtonpost.com/2011/12/07/beardstown-illinois-small-town-wrestles-with-immigration-issues_n_1134797.html.

Conyers, James L., Jr. 2004. The Evolution of Africology: An Afrocentric Appraisal. *Journal of Black Studies* 34 (May): 640–652.

Cooper, Richard S., Charles N. Rotimi, and Ryk Ward. 1999. The Puzzle of Hypertension in African Americans. *Scientific American* (February): 56–63.

Copeland, Larry. 2011. Asian Farmers Crop up in Southeast. *USA Today* (February 9): 3A.

Cornell, Stephen. 1984. Crisis and Response in Indian–White Relations: 1960–1984. *Social Problems* (October), 32: 44–59.

_____. 1996. The Variable Ties that Bind: Content and Circumstance in Ethnic Processes. *Ethnic and Racial Studies* (April), 19: 265–289.

Correll, Joshua, Bernadette Park, Charles M. Judd, Bernd Wittenbrink, Melody S. Sadler, and Tracie Keesee. 2007a. Across the Thin Blue Line: Police Officers and Racial Bias in the Decision to Shoot. *Journal of Personality and Social Psychology* 92 (6): 1006–1023.

_____, _____, _____, _____, _____, and _____. 2007b. The Influence of Stereotypes and Decisions to Shoot. *European Journal of Social Psychology* 37: 1102-117.

Cose, Ellis. 1993. *The Rage of a Privileged Class.* New York: HarperCollins.

Couch, Kenneth A., and Robert Fairlie 2010. Last Hired, Fast Fired? Black–White Unemployment and the Business Cycle. *Demography* 47 (February): 227–247.

Cox, Oliver C. 1942. The Modern Caste School of Social Relations. *Social Forces* (December), 21: 218–226.

Cranford, Cynthia J. 2005. Networks of Exploitation: Immigrant Labor and the Restructuring of the Los Angeles Janitorial Industry. *Social Problems* 52 (3): 379–397.

Cullen, Andrew. 2011. Struggle and progress: 10 years of Somalis in Lewiston. December 18 *Lewiston-Auburn Sun Journal.* Accessed April 16, 2012, at http://www.sunjournal.com/news/city/2011/12/18/struggle-and-progress-10-years-somalis-lewiston/1127846.

DaCosta, Kimberly McClain. 2007. *Making Multiracials: State, Family, and Market in the Redrawing of the Color Line.* Standford, CA: Stanford University Press.

Dade, Corey. 2012a. Census Bureau Rethinks The Best Way to Measure Race. Accessed December 29 at www.wbur.org.

_____. 2012b. The Fight Over Voter ID Laws Goes to the United Nations. March 9. Accessible at www.npr.org.

Dahlburg, John-Thor. 2004. The Spanish-Speaking Heritage of the State Now Reflects All of Latin America, Not Just Cuba. *Los Angeles Times* (June 28): A1, A12.

Daily Mail. 2012. How £12 billion Facebook bride embodies the American dream. Mail Online May 26. Accessed July 17.

Dally, Chad. 2011. Hmong Heritage Month Refocuses on Health. *Wausau Daily Herald* (April 3): A3.

Daniels, Roger. 1972. *Concentration Camps, USA.* New York: Holt, Rinehart & Winston.

Davidson, James D. and Ralph E. Pyle. 2011. *Ranking Faiths: Religious Stratification in America.* Lanham MD: Rowman and Littlefield.

Davis, Michelle R. 2008. Checking Sources: Evaluating Web Sites Requires Careful Eye. *Education Week* (March 6). Accessed June 20, 2008, at www.edweek.org.

de la Garza, Rodolfo O., Louis DeSipio, F. Chris Garcia, John Garcia, and Angelo Falcon. 1992. *Latino Voices: Mexican, Puerto Rican, and Cuban Perspectives on American Politics.* Boulder, CO: Westview Press.

Del Olmo, Frank. 2003. Slow Motion Carnage at the Border. *Los Angeles Times* (May 18): M5.

Delgado, Héctor L. 2008a. La Raza. pp. 830–831 in vol. 2, *Encyclopedia of Race, Ethnicity, and Society,* Richard T. Schaefer, ed. Thousand Oaks, CA: Sage.

DellaPergola, Sergio. 2007. World Jewish Population, 2007. pp. 551–600 in *American Jewish Yearbook 2007,* David Singer and Lawrence Grossman, eds. New York: American Jewish Committee.

Dell'Angela, Tracy. 2005. Dakota Indians Say Kids Trapped in "School-to-Prison" Pipeline. *Chicago Tribune* (November 29): 1, 12.

Deloria, Vine, Jr. 1969. *Custer Died for Your Sins: An Indian Manifesto.* New York: Avon.

_____. 1971. *Of Utmost Good Faith.* New York: Bantam.

_____. 1992. Secularism, Civil Religion, and the Religious Freedom of American Indians. *American Indian Culture and Research Journal,* 16 (2): 9–20.

_____. 1995. *Red Earth, White Lies.* New York: Scribner's.

_____. 2004. Promises Made, Promises Broken. pp. 143–159 in *Native Universe: Voices of Indian America,* Gerald McMaster and Clifford E. Trofzer, eds. Washington, DC: National Geographic.

_____ and Clifford M. Lytle. 1983. *American Indians, American Justice.* Austin: University of Texas Press.

DeNavas-Walt, Carmen, Bernadette D. Proctor, and Jessica C. Smith. 2012. *Income, Poverty, and Health Insurance Converge in the United States: 2011.* Washington, DC: U.S. Government Printing Office.

Denton, Nancy A. and Jacqueline Villarrubia. 2007. Residential Segregation on the Island: The Role of Race and Class in Puerto Rican Neighborhoods. *Sociological Forum* 22 (March): 1573–1586.

DeParle, Jason. 2007. A Good Provider Is One Who Leaves. *New York Times* (April 22): 50–57, 72, 122–123.

Department of Diné Education 2012. Navaho Nation Department of Diné Education. Accessed December 10 at http://www.navajonationdode.org.

Department of Justice. 2000. *The Civil Liberties Act of 1988: Redress for Japanese Americans.* Accessed June 29, 2000, at www.usdoj.gov/crt/ora/main.html.

_____. 2011. *Hate Crime Statistics, 2010.* Accessed at www.fbi.gov.

_____. 1965. *The Negro Family: The Case for National Action.* Washington, DC: U.S. Government Printing Office.

Department of State. 2008b. *Immigrant Visas Issued to Orphans Coming to U.S.* Accessed September 3, 2008, at www.travel.state.gov/family/adoption/stats/stats_451.html.

_____. 2013. Statue of Liberty. Accessible at http://infousa.state.gov/life/symbceleb/new_colossus.html.

Desmond, Scott A. and Charise E. Kubrin. 2009. The Power of Place: Immigrant Communities and Adolescent Violence. *Sociological Quarterly* 50 (2009): 581–607.

Deutscher, Irwin, Fred P. Pestello, and H. Frances Pestello. 1993. *Sentiments and Acts.* New York: Aldine de Gruyter.

DeVoe, Jill Fleury, Kristen E. Darling-Church, and Thomas D. Snyde. 2008 *Status and Trends in the Education of American Indians and Alaska Natives: 2008.* Washington, DC: National Center for Education Statistics.

Dey, Judy Goldberg and Catherine Hill. 2007. *Behind the Pay Gap.* Washington, DC: American Association of University Women.

DiMaggio, Paul. 2005. Cultural Capital. pp. 167–170 in *Encyclopedia of Social Theory,* George Ritzer, ed. Thousand Oaks, CA: Sage Publications.

DiTomaso, Nancy. 2012. *The American Non-Dilemma: Racial Inequality Without Racism.* New York: Russell Sage.

_____ Corinne Post, and Rochelle Parks-Yancy. 2007. Workforce Diversity and Inequality: Power, Status, and Numbers. *Annual Review of Sociology* 33: 473–501.

Divine, Robert A., T. H. Breen, R. Hal Williams, Ariela J. Gross, and H. W. Brands. 2013. *America: Past and Present.* Upper Saddle River, NJ: Pearson.

Dobbin, Frank, Alexandra Kalev, and Erin Kelly. 2007. *Diversity Management in Corporate America. Contexts* 6 (4): 21–27.

Dolnick, Sam. 2011. Many Korean Grocers, a New York Staple, Are Closing Down. *New York Times* (June 2): A19.

_____ and Kirk Semple. 2011. Scattered Across New York, with Disaster at Home. *New York Times.* (March 16): A25–26.

Dorris, Michael. 1988. For the Indians, No Thanksgiving. *New York Times* (November 24): A23.

Downey, Douglas B. 2008. Black/White Differences in School Performance: The Oppositional Culture Explanation. *Annual Review of Sociology* 34: 107–126.

Du Bois, W. E. B. 1903. *The Souls of Black Folks: Essays and Sketches* (reprint). New York: Facade Publications, 1961.

_____. 1969a. *An ABC of Color* [1900]. New York: International Publications.

_____. 1969b. *The Suppression of the African Slave-Trade to the United States of America, 1638–1870.* New York: Schocken.

_____. 1970. *The Negro American Family.* Cambridge, MA: MIT Press.

_____. 1996. *The Philadelphia Negro: A Social Study.* Philadelphia: University of Pennsylvania Press (originally published in 1899).

Duke, Lynne. 1992. You See Color-Blindness, I See Discrimination. *Washington Post National Weekly Edition* 9 (June 15): 33.

Durkheim, Émile. 2001. *The Elementary Forms of Religious Life* [1912]. New Translation by Carol Cosman. New York: Oxford University Press.

Dyson, Michael Eric. 2005. *Is Bill Cosby Right?* New York: Basic Civitas, Perseus Books.

_____. 2011. *"Tour(é)ing Blackness."* Foreword in *Who'd Afraid of Post-Blackness?* pp. xiii–xx. New York: Free Press.

Eckholm, Erik. 2010. In Drug War, Tribe Feels Invaded by Both Sides. *New York Times* (January 25): A1, A10.

Economic Mobility Project. 2007. *Economic Mobility of Black and White Families.* Washington, DC: Pew Charitable Trust.

_____. 2012. Pursuing the American Dream: Economic Mobility Across Generations. Washington, DC: Pew Charitable Trusts.

The Economist. 2009. Cuba and America: Gently Does It. *Economist* (May 9): 32–33.

Edison Research. 2012. Voters and Issues: National Election Poll. Reproduced in *New York Times* (November 7) and (November 8): 1, 4.

Eilperin, Juliet. 2011. Hunting Sharks to Save Humans. *The Guardian Weekly* (November 11, 2011): 32–33.

El-Haj, Nadia Abu. 2007. The Genetic Reinscription of Race. *Annual Review of Anthropology* 16: 283–300.

Elkins, Stanley. 1959. *Slavery: A Problem in American Institutional and Intellectual Life.* Chicago: University of Chicago Press.

Ellis, Mark R. 2004. Denver's Anti-Chinese Riot. pp. 142–143 in *Encyclopedia of the Great Plains,* David J. Wishart, ed. Lincoln: University of Nebraska Press.

Ellison, Brandy J. 2008. Tracking. pp. 1316–1318 in vol. 3, *Encyclopedia of Race, Ethnicity, and Society,* Richard T. Schaefer, ed. Thousand Oaks, CA: Sage.

Emerson, Michael O., Jenifer Bratter, Junia Howeel, P. Wilner Jeanty, and Mike Cline. 2012. *Houston Region Grows More Racially/Ethnically Diverse, With Small Declines in Segregation.* A Joint Report Analyzing Census Data from 1990, 2000, and 2010. Houston, TX: Kinder Institute for Urban Research & the Hobby Center for the Study of Texas.

Ennis, Sharon R., Merarys Rios-Vargas, and Nora G. Albert. 2011. *The Hispanic Population: 2010.* C2010BR-404. Accessible at http://www.census.gov/prod/cen2010/briefs/c2010br-04.pdf.

Eschbach, Karl and Kalman Applebaum. 2000. Who Goes to Powwows? Evidence from the Survey of American Indians and Alaskan Natives. *American Indian Culture and Research Journal* 24(2): 65–83.

Espiritu, Yen Le. 1992. *Asian American Panethnicity: Bridging Institutions and Identities.* Philadelphia, PA: Temple University Press.

_____ and Diane Wolf. 2001. pp. 157–186 in *Ethnicities: Children of Immigrants in America,* Ruben G. Rumbaut and Alejandro Portes, eds. Berkeley: University of California Press.

Euless Historical Preservation Committee. 2011. Halatono Netane with Chris Jones. Accessed at www.eulesstx.gov/history/narratives/HalatonoNetane.htm.

Eyre, Chris. 2010. Powwows and Karaoke. *Smithsonian* (July/August): 102–103.

FBI. 2012. "Hate Crime Statistics, 2011." Accessible at www.Fbi.gov/ucr/ucr.htm.

_____ and José A. Cobas. 2008. Latinos/as and White Racial Frame: The Procrustean Bed of Assimilation. *Sociological Inquiry* 78 (February): 39–53.

_____ and Eileen O'Brien. 2003. *White Men on Race, Power, Privilege, and the Shaping of Cultural Consciousness.* Boston, MA: Beacon Press.

_____ and Karyn D. McKinney. 2003. *The Many Costs of Racism.* Lanham, MD: Rowan and Littlefield.

_____ and Sean Elias. 2012. Rethinking Racial Formation Theory: a Systematic Racism Critique. *Ethnic and Racial Studies* (April): 1–30.

_____ Hernán Vera, and Pinar Batur. 2000. *White Racism,* 2nd ed. New York: Routledge.

Feldman, Marcus W. 2010. The Biology of Race. pp. 136–159 in *Doing Race,* Hazel Rose Markus and Paula M. L. Moya, eds. New York: W. W. Norton.

Felsenthal, Carol. 2009. The Making of a First Lady. *Chicago Magazine* (February). Accessible at http://www.chicagomag.com/Chicago-Magazine/?February-2009/The-Making-of-a-First-Lady/.

Ferber, Abby L. 2008. Privilege. pp. 1073–1074 in vol. 3, *Encyclopedia of Race, Ethnicity, and Society,* Richard T. Schaefer, ed. Thousand Oaks, CA: Sage.

Ferguson, Ronald. 2007. Parenting Practices, Teenage Lifestyles, and Academic Achievement among African-American Children. *Focus* 25 (Spring–Summer): 18–26.

Fernandez, Manny and Kareem Fahim. 2006. Five on Plane Are Detained at Newark but Later Freed. *New York Times* (May 5): 29.

Finder, Alan. 1994. Muslim Gave Racist Speech, Jackson Says. *New York Times* (January 23): 21.

Fine, Gary. 2008. Robber's Cave. pp. 1163–1164 in vol. 3, *Encyclopedia of Race, Ethnicity, and Society,* Richard T. Schaefer, ed. Thousand Oaks, CA: Sage.

Fing, Jing, Shantha Madhavan, and Michael H. Alderman. 1996. The Association between Birthplace and Mortality from Cardiovascular Causes among Black and White Residents of New York City. *New England Journal of Medicine* (November 21), 335: 1545–1551.

Fitzgerald, Kathleen J. 2008. Native American Identity. pp. 954–956 in vol. 2, *Encyclopedia of Race, Ethnicity, and Society,* Richard T. Schaefer, ed. Thousand Oaks, CA: Sage.

Foerstrer, Amy. 2004. Race, Identity, and Belonging: "Blackness" and the Struggle for Solidarity in a Multiethnic Labor Union. *Social Problems* 51 (3): 386–409.

Foner, Eric. 2006. *Forever Free: The Story of Emancipation and Reconstruction.* New York: Knopf.

Fordham, Signithia and John U. Ogbu. 1986. Black Students' School Success: Coping with the Burden of "Acting White." *Urban Review* 18 (3): 176–206.

Frank, Reanne, Ilana Redstone, A. Krech, and Bob Lu. 2010. Latino Immigrants and the U.S. Racial Order: How and Where Do They Fit In? *American Sociological Review* 75 (3): 378–401.

Frankenberg, Erica, Chungmei Lee, and Gary Orfield. 2003. *A Multiracial Society with Segregated Schools: Are We Losing the Dream?* Cambridge, MA: Civil Rights Project, Harvard University.

Franklin, John Hope and Evelyn Brooks Higginbotham. 2011. *From Slavery to Freedom: A History of African Americans,* 9th ed. New York: McGraw-Hill.

Frazier, E. Franklin. 1957. *Black Bourgeois: The Rise of a New Middle Class.* New York: Free Press.

Frey, William H. 2011. *Census Data: Blacks and Hispanics Take Different Segregation Paths* (February 24). Accessible at http://www.brookings.edu.

Frieden, Thomas R. 2011. CDC Health Disparities and Inequities Report – United States, 2011. *Morbidity and Mortality Weekly Report* (January 14).

Frosch, Dan. 2008. Its Native Tongue Facing Extinction, Arapaho Tribe Teaches the Young. *New York Times* (October 17): A14.

Fryer Law Firm. 2012. The Fryer Law Firm: Profiles. Accessed April 8 at http://www.fryerclosings.com/Profiles.htm.

Fryer, Roland G. 2006. Acting White. *Education Next* (Winter): 53–59.

_____, Lisa Kahn, Steven D. Levitt, and Jörg L. Spenkuch. 2012. The Plight of Mixed Race Adolescents. *Review of Economics and Statistics* 94 (3):621-634.

Fuller, Chevon. 1998. Service Redlining. *Civil Rights Journal* 3 (Fall): 33–36.

Galewitz, Phil. 2012. Many Migrants Get Care in Field. *USA Today* (June 7): 3A.

Gallup, George H. 1972. *The Gallup Poll, Public Opinion, 1935–1971.* New York: Random House.

Gallup. 2012. *Religion* Accessed April 7, at www.gallup.com/poll/1690/Religion.aspx.

Gans, Herbert J. 1979. Symbolic Ethnicity: The Future of Ethnic Groups and Cultures in America. *Ethnic and Racial Studies* 2 (January): 1–20.

Garner, Roberta. 1996. *Contemporary Movements and Ideologies.* New York: McGraw-Hill.

Garroutte, Era M., J. Beals, E.M. Keane, C. Kaufman, P. Spicer, J. Henderson, P.N. Henderson, C.M. Mitchell, S.M. Manson, and The Al-SUPERPFP Team. (Sept. 2009). Religiosity and Spirituality in Two American Indian Populations. *Journal for the Scientific Study of Religion* 48(3): 480–500.

Gerth, H. H. and C. Wright Mills. 1958. *From Max Weber: Essays in Sociology.* New York: Galaxy Books.

Ghosh, Bobby. 2010. Islam in America. *Time* (August 30): 20–26.

Giago, Tim. 2001. National Media Should Stop Using Obscene Words. *The Denver Post* (January 21).

Gillion, Daniel Q. 2012. The Paradox of Descriptive Representation in the Executive Office: Racial Rhetoric and Presidential Approval. Unpub. paper. Revision of 2011 annual meeting paper American Political Science Association.

Giroux, Henry A. 1997. Rewriting the Discourse of Racial Identity: Towards a Pedagogy and Politics of Whiteness. *Harvard Educational Review* 67 (Summer): 285–320.

Gittell, Marilyn and Bill McKinney. 2007. *The Economic Status of Working Women in New York.* New York: Howard Samuels Center.

Gleason, Philip. 1980. American Identity and Americanization. pp. 31–58 in *Harvard Encyclopedia of American Ethnic Groups,* Stephen Therstromm, ed. Cambridge, MA: Belknap Press of Harvard University Press.

Goering, John M. 1971. The Emergence of Ethnic Interests: A Case of Serendipity. *Social Forces* 48 (March): 379–384.

Gold, Matea and Joseph Tanfani. 2012. Tribal leaders bet on Obama. *Chicago Tribune* (September 27): 19.

Gomez, Alan. 2010. Rise Seen in Births to Illegal Dwellers. *USA Today* (August 12): A1.

Gonzalez, David. 2009. A Family Divided by 2 Worlds, Legal and Illegal. *New York Times* (April 26): 1, 20–21.

Gonzalez, Jennifer. 2012. Tribal Colleges Offer Basic Education to Students "Not Prepared for College." *Chronicle of Higher Education* (April 13): A25.

Gordon, Milton M. 1964. *Assimilation in American Life: The Role of Race, Religion, and National Origins.* New York: Oxford University Press.

Gorski, Philip S. 2011. Barack Obama and Civil Religion. *Political Power and Social Theory* 22: 179–214.

Gray-Little, Bernadette and Hafdahl, Adam R. 2000. Factors Influencing Racial Comparisons of Self-Esteem: A Qualitative Review. *Psychological Bulletin* 126 (1): 26–54.

Green, Alexander R., et al. 2007. Implicit Bias among Physicians and Its Prediction of Thrombolysis Decisions for Black and White Patients. *Journal of General Internal Medicine* (September), 22: 1231–1238.

Greenhouse, Steven. 2012. Equal Opportunity Panel Updates Hiring Policy. *New York Times* (April 26): B3.

Grieco, Elizabeth M. and Rachel C. Cassidy. 2001. Overview of Race and Hispanic Origin. *Current Population Reports.* Ser. CENBR/01-1. Washington, DC: U.S. Government Printing Office.

Grieco, Elizabeth M., Yesenia D. Acosta, G. Patricia de la Cruz, Christine Gambino, Thomas Gryn, Luke J. Larsen, Edward N. Trevelyan, and Nathan P. Watters. 2012. *The Foreign-Born Population in the United States: 2010. May 2012 ACS-19.* Accessible at www.census.gov.

Grimshaw, Allen D. 1969. *Racial Violence in the United States.* Chicago: Aldine.

Ground. *Village Voice* (October), 29: 19–23.

Guerin-Gonzales, Camille. 1994. *Mexican Workers and American Dreams.* New Brunswick, NJ: Rutgers University Press.

Guest, Kenneth J. 2003. *God in Chinatown: Religion and Survival in New York's Evolving Immigrant Community.* New York: University Press.

Gupta, Sanjay. 2012. Interview of Dr. Alfredo Quinones-Hinojosa. CNN Interview. May 18.

Guzmán, Betsy. 2001. *The Hispanic Population.* Census 2000 Brief Series C2kBR/01-3. Washington, DC: U.S. Government Printing Office.

Haak, Gerald O. 1970. Co-Opting the Oppressors: The Case of the Japanese-Americans. *Society* (October), 7: 23–31.

Halualani, Rona Tamiko. 2002. *In the Name of Hawaiians: Native Identities and Cultural Politics.* Minneapolis: University of Minnesota Press.

Hammond, Laura. 2010. Obliged to Give: Remittances and the Maintenance of Transitional Networks Between Somalis at Home and Abroad. *Bildhaan: An International Journal of Somali Studies* 10 (Article 11) at http://digitalcommons.macalester.edu/bildhaan/.

Handlin, Oscar. 1951. *The Uprooted: The Epic Story of the Great Migrations That Made the American People.* New York: Grossett and Dunlap.

Hansen, Marcus Lee. 1952. The Third Generation in America. *Commentary* (November 14): 493–500.

Harlow, Caroline Wolf. 2005. *Hate Crime Reported by Victims and Police.* Bureau of Justice Statistics Special Report (November). Accessed May 8, 2008, at http://www.ojp.usdoj.gov/bjs/pub/pdf/hcrvp.pdf.

Harris, Fredrick C. 2012. The Price of a Black President. *New York Times* (October 28): 1, 9.

Haxton, Charrisse and Kristen Harknett. 2009. Racial and Gender Differences in Kin Support. *Journal of Family Issues* 30 (August): 1019–1040.

Haynes, V. Dio. 2009. Blacks Hit Hard by Economy's Punch. *Washington Post* (November 24). Accessed July 27, 2011, at http://www.washingtonpost.com/wp-dyn/content/article/2009/11/23/AR2009112304092.html.

Hays, Kristen L. 1994. Topeka Comes Full Circle. *Modern Maturity* (April–May): 34.

Hentoff, Nicholas. 1984. Dennis Banks and the Road Block to Indian Ground. *Village Voice* (October), 29: 19–23.

Herbert, Bob. 2010. Jim Crow Policy. *New York Times* (February 2): A27.

Herrnstein, Richard J. and Charles Murray. 1994. *The Bell Curve: Intelligence and Class Structure in American Life.* New York: Free Press.

Herschthal, Eric. 2004. Indian Students Discuss Pros, Cons of Arranged Marriages. *Daily Princetonian* (October 20).

Hevesi, Dennis. 2011. Elouise Cobell, 65, Sued for Indian Funds. *New York Times* (October 18): A19.

Hilberg, Soleste and Ronald G. Tharp. 2002. *Theoretical Perspectives, Research Findings, and Classroom Implications of the Learning Styles of American Indian and Alaska Native Students.* Washington, DC: Eric Digest.

Hill, Robert B. 1999. *The Strengths of African American Families: Twenty-Five Years Later.* Lanham, MD: University Press of America.

Hirsch, Mark. 2009. Thomas Jefferson: Founding Father of Indian Removal. *Smithsonian Institution* (Summer): 54–58.

Hisnanick, John J. and Katherine G. Giefer. 2011. *Dynamics of Economic Well-Being: Fluctuations in the U.S. Income Distribution 2004–2007.* Washington, DC: U.S. Government Printing Office.

Hixson, Lindsay, Bradford B. Hepler, and Myoung Ouk Kim. 2012. *Islander Population: 2010.* May 2012. C2010BR-12. Washington DC: U.S. Government Printing Office.

Hochschild, Jennifer. 1995. *Facing Up to the American Dream: Race, Class, and the Soul of the Nation.* Princeton, NJ: Princeton University Press.

Holson, Laura M. and Nick Bilton. 2012. Facebook's Royal Wedding. *New York Times* (May 25).

Hosokawa, Bill. 1969. *Nisei: The Quiet Americans.* New York: Morrow.

Hudgins, John L. 1992. The Strengths of Black Families Revisited. *The Urban League Review* (Winter), 15: 9–20.

Hughlett, Mike. 2006. Judge: Craigslist Not Liable for Ad Content. *Chicago Tribune* (November 16), section 3: 1.

Huisman, Kimberly A., Mazie Hough, Kristin M. Langellier, and Carol Nordstrom Toner. 2011. *Somalis in Maine: Crossing Cultural Currents.* Berkeley, CA: North Atlantic Books.

Humes, Karen R., Nicholas A. Jones, and Roberto R. Ramirez. 2011. Overview of Race and Hispanic Organization. *2010 Census Briefs.* C2010 BR-02.

Hunt, Larry L. 1999. Hispanic Protestantism in the United States: Trends by Decade and Generation. *Social Forces* 77 (4): 1601–1624.

Huntington, Samuel P. 1993. The Clash of Civilizations? *Foreign Affairs* 73 (no. 3, Summer): 22–49.

———. 1996. *The Clash of Civilizations and the Remaking of World Order.* New York: Simon & Schuster.

Hurh, Won Moo. 1998. *The Korean Americans.* Westport, CT: Greenwood Press.

_____ and Kwang Chung Kim. 1984. *Korean Immigrants in America: A Structural Analysis of Ethnic Confinement and Adhesive Adaptation.* Cranbury, NJ: Farleigh Dickinson University Press.

Hyun, Jane. 2006. Breaking the Bamboo Ceiling: Career Strategies for Asians. New York: HarperBuisness.

Ignatiev, Noel. 1994. Treason to Whiteness Is Loyalty to Humanity. Interview with Noel Ignatiev. *Utne Reader* (November–December): 83–86.

Indian Arts and Crafts Board 2013. Indian Arts and Crafts Act: Know the Law. Accessed January 20 at http://www.iacb.doi.gov.

Inoue, Miyako. 1989. Japanese Americans in St. Louis: From Internees to Professionals. *City and Society* (December), 3: 142–152.

Institute for Jewish and Community Research 2008. How Many Jews Are in World Today? Accessed September 7, 2008, at bechollashon.org/population/today.php.

Iwamasa, Gayle Y. 2008a. Internment Camps. pp. 745–747 in vol. 2, *Encyclopedia of Race, Ethnicity, and Society,* Richard T. Schaefer, ed. Thousand Oaks, CA: Sage.

_____. 2008b. Japanese American Citizens League. pp. 781–782 in vol. 2, *Encyclopedia of Race, Ethnicity, and Society,* Richard T. Schaefer, ed. Thousand Oaks, CA: Sage.

Jacobs, Sally. 2008. Learning to be Michelle Obama. *Boston Globe* (June 15). Accessible at http://www.boston.com/news/nation/articles/2008/06/15/learning_to_be_michelle_obama/.

Jacobs, Tom. 2008. Patriarchy and Paychecks. *Miller-McCune* 1 (2): 18–19.

Jacobson, Cardell, J. Lynn England and Robyn J. Barrus. 2008. Familism. pp. 477–478 in vol. 1, *Encyclopedia of Race, Ethnicity, and Society,* Richard T. Schaefer, ed. Thousand Oaks, CA: Sage.

Jacoby, Susan. 2009. Keeping the Faith, Ignoring the History. *New York Times* (March 1): 11.

Janisch, Roy F. 2008. Wounded Knee 1890 and 1973. pp. 1415–1417 in vol. 3, *Encyclopedia of Race, Ethnicity, and Society,* Richard T. Schaefer, ed. Thousand Oaks, CA: Sage.

Jefferies, Sierra M. 2007. Environmental Justice and the Skull Valley Goshute Indians' Proposal to Store Nuclear Waste. *Journal of Land, Resources, and Environmental Law* 27 (2): 409–429.

Johnson, David. 2005. Uncertain Progress 25 Years After Defying State. *News from Indian County* (June 27), 19: 1, 5.

Johnson, Tallese D., Merarys Rios, Malcolm P. Drewery, Sharon R. Ennis, and Myoung Ouk Kim. 2010. People Who Spoke a Language Other Than English at Home by Hispanic Origin and Race: 2009. *American Community Survey Brief* ACSBR/09-19. Accessible at www.census.gov.

Johnston, Tim. 2008. Australia to Apologize to Aborigines for Past Mistreatment. *New York Times* (January 31).

Joint Center for Political and Economic Studies, 2011. National Roster of Black Elected Officials: Fact Sheet. Washington, DC: JCPES.

Jolivette, Andrew. 2008. Pan-Indianism. pp. 1022–1028 in vol. 2, *Encyclopedia of Race, Ethnicity, and Society,* Richard T. Schaefer, ed. Thousand Oaks, CA: Sage.

Jones, Jeffrey M. 2012. Americans More Positive About Immigration. June 16. Accessible at http://www.gallup.com/poll/155210/Americans-Positive-Immigratoin.aspx.

Jones, Nicholas and Amy Symens Smith. 2001. *The Two or More Races Population: 2000.* Series C2KBR/01-6. Washington, DC: U.S. Government Printing Office.

Jonsson, Patrik. 2005. Noncitizen Soldiers: The Quandaries of Foreign-Born Troops. *Christian Science Monitor,* (July 5): 1.

Jordan, Miriam. 2012. Heartland Draws Hispanics To Help Revive Small Towns. *New York Times* (November 9): A1, A8.

Joseph, Dan. 2010. *America's 10 Poorest Counties are in Gulf Coast States, Kentucky and on Indian Reservations.* December 17. Accessed April 27, 2011, at http://www.cnsnews.com.

Kagan, Jerome. 1971. The Magical Aura of the IQ. *Saturday Review of Literature* 4 (December 4): 92–93.

Kahlenberg, Richard D. 2010. 10 Myths about Legacy Preference in College Admissions. *Chronicle of Higher Education* (October 1): A23–A25.

Kalev, Alexandria, Frank Dobbin, and Erin Kelly. 2006. Best Practices or Best Guesses? Diversity Management and the Remediation of Inequality. *American Sociological Review* 71: 589–617.

Kalita, S. Mitra. 2003. *Suburban Sahibs: Three Immigrant Families and Their Passage from India to America.* New Brunswick, NJ: Rutgers University Press.

Kana'iaupuni, Shawn Malia. 2008. Hawaiians. pp. 599–602 in vol. 1, *Encyclopedia of Race, Ethnicity, and Society,* Richard T. Schaefer, ed. Thousand Oaks, CA: Sage.

Kang, Jerry and Kristen Lane. 2010. Seeing Through Colorblindness: Implicit Bias and the Law. *UCLA Law Review* 58: 465–520.

Kang, K. Connie. 1996. Filipinos Happy with Life in U.S. but Lack United Voice. *Los Angeles Times* (January 26): A1, A20.

Kao, Grace and Kara Joyner. 2004. Do Race and Ethnicity Matter among Friends? *Sociological Quarterly* 45 (3): 557–573.

Kashima, Tetsuden. 2003. *Judgment Without Trial: Japanese Americans Imprisonment During World War II.* Seattle: University of Washington Press.

Katel, Peter. 2006. American Indians. *CQ Researcher* (April 28): 16.

Katz, Jeffrey. 2012. Google's Monopoly and Internet Freedom. *Wall Street Journal* (June 8): A15.

Kearns, Rick. 2011. On the Rise. *Indian County Today* (May 18): 10.

Keen, Judy. 2011. Transmitting the Immigrant Life. *USA Today* (June 16): 3A.

Kennedy, Randall. 2010. The Enduring Relevance of Affirmative Action. *American Prospect* (September): 31–33.

Kent, Mary Mederios. 2010. *Large Wealth Gap Among U.S. Racial and Ethnic Groups.* Accessed September 9, 2010, at http://www.prb.org/Articles/2010/usnetworth.aspx?p=1.

Kershaw, Sarah. 2009. Talk About Race? Relax, It's O.K. *New York Times* (January 15), section E: 1.

Kibria, Nazli. 2002. *Becoming Asian American: Second-Generation Chinese and Korean American Identities.* Baltimore, MD: Johns Hopkins Press.

Killian, Lewis M. 1975. *The Impossible Revolution, Phase 2: Black Power and the American Dream.* New York: Random House.

Kim, Barbara and Grace J. Yoo. 2008. Korean Americans. pp. 811–814 in vol. 2, *Encyclopedia of Race, Ethnicity, and Society,* Richard T. Schaefer, ed. Thousand Oaks, CA: Sage.

Kim, ChangHwan and Arthur Sakamoto. 2010. Have Asian American Men Achieved Labor Market Parity with White Men? *American Sociological Review* 73 (6): 934–957.

Kim, Henry H. and Ralph E. Pyle. 2004. An Exception to the Exception: Second-Generation Korean American Church Participation. *Social Compass* 3: 321–333.

Kim, Joon K. 2008. Wetbacks. pp. 1393–1395 in vol. 3, *Encyclopedia of Race, Ethnicity, and Society,* Richard T. Schaefer, ed. Thousand Oaks, CA: Sage.

Kim, Kiljoong. 2006. The Korean Presence in Chicago. In *The New Chicago,* John Koval et al., eds. Philadelphia: Temple University Press.

Kim, Nadia U. 2008. *Imperial Citizens: Koreans and Race from Seoul to LA.* Stanford, CA: Stanford University Press.

Kimura, Yukiko. 1988. *Issei: Japanese Immigrants in Hawaii.* Honolulu: University of Hawaii Press.

King, Martin Luther, Jr. 1958. *Stride Towards Freedom: The Montgomery Story.* New York: Harper.

_____. 1963. *Why We Can't Wait.* New York: Mentor.

_____. 1967. *Where Do We Go from Here: Chaos or Community?* New York: Harper & Row.

_____. 1971. I Have a Dream. pp. 346–351 in *Black Protest Thought in the Twentieth Century,* August Lacy, Dan. 1972. *The White Use of Blacks in America.* New York: McGraw-Hill.

Kinloch, Graham C. 1974. *The Dynamics of Race Relations: A Sociological Analysis.* New York: McGraw-Hill.

Kinzer, Stephen. 2000. Museums and Tribes: A Tricky Truce. *New York Times* (December 24), section 2: 1, 39.

Kitagawa, Evelyn. 1972. Socioeconomic Differences in the United States and Some Implications for Population Policy. pp. 87–110 in *Demographic and Social Aspects of Population Growth,* Charles F. Westoff and Robert Parke, Jr., eds. Washington, DC: U.S. Government Printing Office.

Kitano, Harry H. L. 1976. *Japanese Americans: The Evolution of a Subculture,* 2nd ed. Englewood Cliffs, NJ: Prentice Hall.

———. 1980. Japanese. In *Harvard Encyclopedia of American Ethnic Groups,* Stephen Thernstrom, ed. Cambridge, MA: Belknap Press of Harvard University Press.

Kitsuse, John I. and Leonard Broom. 1956. *The Managed Casualty: The Japanese American Family in World War II.* Berkeley: University of California Press.

Kivisto, Peter. 2008. *Third Generation Principle.* pp. 1302–1304 in vol. 3, *Encyclopedia of Race, Ethnicity, and Society,* Richard T. Schaefer, ed. Thousand Oaks, CA: Sage.

Koch, Wendy. 2006. Push for "Official" English Heats up. *USA Today* (October 9): 1A.

Kochhar, Rakesh, Richard Fry, and Paul Taylor. 2011. Twenty-to-One: Wealth Gaps Rise to Record Highs Between Whites, Blacks and Hispanics. Washington, DC: Pew Social and Demographic Trends.

Kotkin, Joel. 2010. Ready Set Grow. *Smithsonian* (July/August): 61–73.

Kreider, Rose M. and Renee Ellis. 2011. Living Arrangements of Children: 2009: 70–126. Washington, DC: O.S. Government Printing Office.

Kristof, Nicholas D. 2010. America's History of Fear. *New York Times* (September 5): A10.

Kroeger, Brooke. 2004. When a Dissertation Makes a Difference. *New York Times* (March 20). Accessed January 15, 2005, at www.racematters.org/devahpager.htm.

Kucsera, John, and Genevieve Siegel-Hawley. 2012. *E Pluribus… Separation: Deepening Double Segregation for More Students.* Los Angeles: The Civil Rights Project, UCLA.

Kurien, Prena. 2004. Multiculturalism, Immigrant Religion, and Diasporic Nationalism: The Development of an American Hinduism. *Social Problems* 51 (3): 362–385

Kwong, Peter. 1994. The Wages of Fear. *Village Voice* (April 26), 39: 25–29.

LaDuke, Winona. 2006. Hui Na Iwa—The Bones Lives: Hawaiians and NAGPRA. *News from Indian Country* (April 3): 17.

Lal, Barbara Ballis. 1995. Symbolic Interaction Theories. *American Behavioral Scientist* 38 (January): 421–441.

Lancee, Bram. 2010. The Economic Returns of Immigrants' Bonding and Bridging Social Capital: The Case of the Netherlands. *International Migration Review* 44 (Spring): 202–226.

Landale, Nancy S., R. S. Oropesa, and C. Bradatan. 2006. Hispanic Families in the United States: Family Structure and Process in an Era of Family Change. pp. 138–178, in *Multiple Origins, Uncertain Destinies: Hispanics and the American Future.* Washington, DC: National Academic Press.

Landry, Bart and Kris Marsh. 2011. The Evolution of the New Black Middle Class. *Annual Review of Sociology* 37: 373–394.

LaPiere, Richard T. 1934. Attitudes vs. Actions. *Social Forces* (October 13): 230–237.

———. 1969. Comment of Irwin Deutscher's Looking Backward. *American Sociologist* 4 (February): 41–42.

Lau, Yvonne M. 2006. Re-Envisioning Filipino American Communities: Evolving Identities, Issues, and Organizations. pp. 141–153 in *The New Chicago,* John Koval et al., eds. Philadelphia: Temple University Press.

———. 2008. Chinatowns. pp. 201–205 in vol. 1, *Encyclopedia of Race, Ethnicity, and Society,* Richard T. Schaefer, ed. Thousand Oaks, CA: Sage.

Lautz, Jessica. 2011. *Race/Ethnicity of Home Buyers, 2003–2010.* Accessed at economistoutlookblogs.realtor.org/2011/03/16/race-ethnicity-of-home-buyers-2003-2010.

Laxson, Joan D. 1991. "We" See "Them": Tourism and Native Americans. *Annals of Tourism Research,* 18(3): 365–391.

Leavitt, Paul. 2002. Bush Calls Agent Kicked Off Flight Honorable Fellow. *USA Today* (January 8).

Ledward, Brandon C. 2008. Haole. pp. 579–581 in vol. 2, *Encyclopedia of Race, Ethnicity, and Society,* Richard T. Schaefer, ed. Thousand Oaks, CA: Sage.

Lee, Jennifer. 2001. Manhattan's Chinatown Reeling from the Effects of September 11. *New York Times* (November 21): B1, B9.

Lee, Tanya. 2011. A Sign of Hope. *Indian County Today* (April 6): 25–27.

Leehotz, Robert. 1995. Is Concept of Race a Relic? *Los Angeles Times* (April 15): A1, A14.

Levin, Jack and Jim Nolan. 2011. *The Violence of Hate: Confronting Racism, Anti-Semitism, and Other Forms of Bigotry.* 3rd ed. Upper Saddle River, NJ: Pearson.

Levitt, Peggy. 2004. Salsa and Ketchup: Transnational Migrants Struggle Two Worlds. *Contexts* (Spring): 20–26.

Lewin, Tamar. 2006. Campaign to End Race Preferences Splits Michigan. *New York Times* (October 31): A1, A19.

Lewinson, Paul. 1965. *Race, Class, and Party: A History of Negro Suffrage and White Politics in the South.* New York: Universal Library.

Lewis, Amanda E. 2004. "What Group?" Studying Whites and Whiteness in the Era of "Color-Blindness." *Sociological Theory* 22 (December): 623–646.

Lewis, Shawn D. 2008. Pressuring Culture: Japanese-Style Private School Thrives with U.S. Transplants. *Detroit News* (July 17).

Lichtenberg, Judith. 1992. Racism in the Head, Racism in the World. *Report from the Institute for Philosophy and Public Policy* 12 (Spring–Summer): 3–5.

Lichter, Daniel T., J. Brian Brown, Zhenchao Qian, and Julie H. Carmalt. 2007. Marital Assimilation among Hispanics: Evidence of Declining Cultural and Economic Incorporation? *Social Science Quarterly* 88 (3): 745–765.

Light, Ivan H., Georges Sabagh, Mendi Bozorgmehr, and Claudia Der-Martirosian. 1994. Beyond the Ethnic Enclave Economy. *Social Problems* (February), 41: 65–80.

Light, Steven Andrew and Kathryn R. L. Rand. 2007. *Indian Gaming and Tribal Sovereignty: The Casino Compromise.* Lawrence: University of Kansas Press.

Lin, Sam Chu. 1996. Painful Memories. *AsianWeek* (July 12), 17: 10.

Lind, Andrew W. 1946. *Hawaii's Japanese: An Experiment in Democracy.* Princeton, NJ: Princeton University Press.

Lindner, Eileen. 2012. *Yearbook of American and Canadian Churches.* Nashville, TN: Abingdon Press.

Liu, Michael and Kim Geron. 2008. Changing Neighborhood: Ethnic Enclaves and the Struggle for Social Justice. *Social Justice* 35 (2): 18–35.

Livingston, Gretchen and D'Vera Cohn. 2012. *U.S. Birth Rate Falls to a Record Low; Decline Is Greatest Among Immigrants.* Washington, DC: Pew Research Center.

Loewen, James. 2005. *Sundown Towns: A Hidden Dimension of American Racism.* New York: Free Press.

——— and Richard Schaefer. 2008. Sundown Towns. pp. 301–304 in vol. 2, *Encyclopedia of Race, Ethnicity, and Society,* Richard T. Schaefer, ed. Thousand Oaks, CA: Sage.

Lofquist, Daphne, Terry Lugaila, Martin O'Connell, and Sarah Feliz. 2012. *Households and Families: 2010.* C2012BR-14. Accessible at http://www.census.gov/newsroom/releases/archives/2012_census/cb12-68.html.

Logan, John R. and Brian J. Stults. 2011. *The Persistence of Segregation in the Metropolis: New Findings from the 2010 Census.* Providence RI: US 2010 Project.

Lomax, Louis E. 1971. *The Negro Revolt,* rev. ed. New York: Harper & Row.

Longman, Jeré. 2008. Polynesian Pipeline Feeds a Football Titan. *New York Times* (October 8): A1, A20.

Lopata, Helena Znaniecki. 1994. *Polish Americans,* 2nd ed. New Brunswick, NJ: Transaction Books.

López, Ana Alicia Peña. 2004. Central American Labor Migration, 1980–2000. *Diálgo* (Spring): 3–14.

López, David and Yen Espiritu. 1990. Panethnicity in the United States: A Theoretical Framework. *Ethnic and Racial Studies* (April 13): 198–224.

López, Julie Amparano. 1992. Women Face Glass Walls as Well as Ceilings. *Wall Street Journal* (March 3).

López, Mark Hugo, Gretchen Livingston, and Rakeshhan. 2009. *Hispanics and the Economic Downturn: Housing Woes and Remittance Cuts.* Washington, DC: Pew Hispanic Center.

——— Rich Moran, and Paul Taylor. 2010. *Illegal Immigration Backlash Worries, Divides Latinos.* Washington, DC: Pew Research Center.

_____ and Gabriel Velasco. 2011. A Demographic of Puerto Ricans, 2009. Washington, DC: Pew Hispanic Center.

Louie, Andrea. 2004. *Chineseness across Borders: Renegotiation Chinese Identities in China and the United States.* Durham, NC: Duke University Press.

Loveman, Mora and Jeronimo O. Muniz. 2007. How Puerto Rico Became White: Boundary Dynamics and Intercensus Racial Reclassification. *American Sociological Review* (December), 72: 915–939.

Luce, Clare Boothe. 1975. Refugees and Guilt. *New York Times* (May 11): E19.

Lugo, Luis, et al. 2010. *Public Remains Conflicted Over Islam.* Washington, DC: Pew Forum on Religion and Public Life.

Mack, Raymond W. 1996. Whose Affirmative Action? *Society* 33 (March–April): 41–43.

Macmillan, Leslie. 2012. Uranium Mines Dot Navajo Land, Neglected and Still Perilous. *New York Times* (April 1): 16.

Maddux, William W., Adam D. Galinsky, Amy J. C. Cuddy, and Mark Polifroni. 2008. When Being a Model Minority Is Good...and Bad: Realistic Threat Explains Negativity Toward Asian Americans. *Personality and Social Psychology Bulletin* 34 (January): 74–89.

Magin, Janis L. 2008. Occupation of Royal Palace Invigorates Native Hawaiian Movement. *New York Times* (May 3): A14.

Malhotra, Nei and Yotam Margalit. 2009. State of the Nation: Anti-Semitism and the Economic Crisis. *Boston Review* (May/June). Accessed at http://bostonreview.net/BR34.3/malhotra_margalit.php.

Malone, Nolan, Kaari F. Baruja, Jospeh M. Costanzo, and Cynthia J. Davis. 2003. *The Foreign-Born Population: 2000.* C2KBR-34. Accessible at http://www.census.gov/prod/2003pubs/c2kbr-34.pdf.

Maning, Anita. 1997. Troubled Waters: Environmental Racism Suit Makes Waves. *USA Today* (July 31): A1.

Manning, Robert D. 1995. Multiculturalism in the United States: Clashing Concepts, Changing Demographics, and Competing Cultures. *International Journal of Group Tensions* (Summer): 117–168.

Martin, Daniel C. and James E. Yankay. 2012. Refugees and Asylees: 2011. *Annual Flow Report* (May). Office of Immigration Statistics, Department of Homeland Security. Accessible at http://www.dhs.gov/xlibrary/assets/statistics/publications/ois_rfa_fr_2011.pdf.

_____. 2012. Refugees and Asylees 2011. Washington, DC: *Department of Homeland Security, Office of Immigration Statistics.*

Martin, Joel W. 2001. *The Land Looks After Us: A History of Native American Religion.* New York: Oxford University Press.

Martin, Timothy W., Josh Dawsey, and Betsy McKay. 2012. The Gender Barrier Falls at Augusta. *Wall Street Journal* (August 21): B1.

Marx, Karl and Frederick Engels. 1955. *Selected Works in Two Volumes.* Moscow: Foreign Languages Publishing House.

Masayesva, Vernon. 1994. The Problem of American Indian Religious Freedom: A Hopi Perspective. *American Indian Religions: An Interdisciplinary Journal* 1 (Winter): 93–96.

Massey, Douglas S. 2011. The Past and Future of American Civil Rights. *Daedalus* 140 (Spring): 37–54.

_____ and Nancy A. Denton. 1993. *American Apartheid: Segregation and the Making of the Underclass.* Cambridge, MA: Harvard University Press.

_____ and Margarita Mooney. 2007. The Effects of America's Three Affirmative Action Programs on Academic Performance. *Social Problems* 54 (1): 99–117.

_____ and Robert J. Sampson. 2009. The Moynihan Report Revisited: Lessons and Reflections after Four Decades. *Annuals* 621 (January).

Masud-Piloto, Felix. 2008a. Cuban Americans. pp. 357–359 in vol. 1, *Encyclopedia of Race, Ethnicity, and Society,* Richard T. Schaefer, ed. Thousand Oaks, CA: Sage.

_____. 2008b. Marielitos. pp. 872–874 in vol. 2, *Encyclopedia of Race, Ethnicity, and Society,* Richard T. Schaefer, ed. Thousand Oaks, CA: Sage.

Mather, Mark and Kelvin Pollard. 2007. Hispanic Gains Minimize Population Losses in Rural and Small-Town America. Population Reference Bureau. Accessible at http://www.prb.org/Articles/2007/HispanicGains.aspx.

Matthiessen, Peter. 1991. *In the Spirit of Crazy Horse.* New York: Peking.

Mazzocco, Philip J., Timothy C. Brock, Gregory J. Brock, Kristen R. Olson, and Mahzarin, R. Banaji. 2006. The Cost of Being Black: White Americans' Perceptions and the Question of Reparations. *DuBois Review* 3 (2): 261–297.

McCabe, Kristen. 2012. Foreign-Born Health Care Workers in the United States. June. Accessible at www.migrationinformation.org/USfocus/display.cfm?id=898.

McGee, Celia. 2010. The Open Road Wasn't Quite Open to All. *New York Times* (August 23): C1, C2.

McIntosh, Peggy. 1988. *White Privilege: Unpacking the Invisible Knapsack.* Wellesley, MA: Wellesley College Center for Research on Women.

McKinley, James C., Jr. 2005. Mexican Pride and Death in U.S. Service. *New York Times* (March 22): A6.

McKinney, Karyn D. 2003. I Feel "Whiteness" When I Hear People Blaming Whites: Whiteness as Cultural Victimization. *Race and Society* 6: 39–55.

_____. 1976. *Sociological Ambivalence and Other Essays.* New York: Free Press.

_____. 2008. Confronting Young People's Perceptions of Whiteness: Privilege or Liability? Race and Society 6: 39–55.

McNickle, D'Arcy. 1973. *Native American Tribalism: Indian Survivals and Renewals.* New York: Oxford University Press.

Medina, Jennifer. 2012. In Years Since the Riots, a Changed Complexion in South Central. *New York Times* (April 25): A1, A14.

Meister, Alan. 2011. *Indian Gaming Industry Report.* Newton, MA: Casino City Press.

_____. 2012. *Indian Gaming Industry Report.* Newton, MA: Casino City Press.

Merton, Robert K. 1949. Discrimination and the American Creed. pp. 99–126 in *Discrimination and National Welfare,* Robert M. MacIver, ed. New York: Harper & Row.

Menchaca, Charles. 2008. Scholars Learn Hmong Basics. *Wausau Daily Herald* (August 14).

Meyers, Dowell. 2007. *Immigrants and Boomers: Forging a New Social Contract for the Future of America.* New York: Russell Sage.

Michigan State University. 2012. I have Concerns with My Roommate's Social Media Web Profile. Accessed April 18 at http://liveon.msu.edu/node/139.

Migration News. 2012. DHS: Border, Interior, USCIS. April 19 (2). Accessible at http://migration.ucdavis.edu/mn/comments.php?id-3745_0_2_0.

Mihesuah, Devon A., ed. 2000. *Reparation Reader: Who Owns American Indian Remains?* Lincoln: University of Nebraska Press.

Miller, Norman. 2002. Personalization and the Promise of Contact Theory. *Journal of Social Issues* 58 (Summer): 387–410.

Min, Pyong Gap. 2006. *Asian Americans: Contemporary Trends and Issues,* 2nd ed. Thousand Oaks, CA: Sage.

Mitchell, W. J. T. 2012. Seeing Through Race. Cambridge: Harvard University Press.

Mitra, Diditi. 2008. Pan-Asian Identity. pp. 1016–1019 in vol. 2, *Encyclopedia of Race, Ethnicity, and Society,* Richard T. Schaefer, ed. Thousand Oaks, CA: Sage.

Mohamed, Besheer and John O'Brien. 2011. Ground Zero of Misunderstanding. *Contexts* (Winter): 62–64.

Monkman, Karen, Margaret Ronald, and Florence Délimon Thérámene. 2005. Social and Cultural Capital in an Urban Latino School Community. *Urban Education* 40 (January): 4–33.

Montagu, Ashley. 1972. *Statement on Race.* New York: Oxford University Press.

Mostofi, Nilou. 2003. Who We Are: The Perplexity of Iranian-American Identity. *Sociological Quarterly* 44 (Fall): 681–703.

Motel, Seth and Eileen Patten. 2012. The 10 Largest Hispanic Origin Groups: Characteristics, Rankings, Top Counties. Washington, DC: Pew Hispanic Center.

Moulder, Frances V. 1996. *Teaching about Race and Ethnicity: A Message of Despair or a Message of Hope?* Paper presented at annual meeting of the American Sociological Association, New York.

Murray, Sara. 2013. What Senate Bill Means for Different Immigrants. *Wall Street Journal* (April 13). Accessible at http://blogs.wsj.com/

washwire/2013/04/16/what-senate-bill-means-for-different-immigrants/.

Myrdal, Gunnar. 1944. *An American Dilemma: The Negro Problem and Modern Democracy.* New York: Harper & Row.

NAACP. 2008. *Out of Focus—Out of Sync Take 4.* Baltimore MD: NAACP.

Nagel, Joane. 1988. *The Roots of Red Power: Demographic and Organizational Bases of American Indian Activism 1950–1990.* Paper presented at annual meeting of the American Sociological Association, Atlanta, GA.

———. 1996. *American Indian Ethnic Renewal: Red Power and the Resurgence of Identity and Culture.* New York: Oxford University Press.

Nahm, H. Y. 2012. 23 Big Milestones in Asian American History. Accessed November 9 at http://goldsea.com/AAD/Milestones/milestones.html.

Naimark, Norman M. 2004. Ethnic Cleansing, History of. pp. 4799–4802 in *International Encyclopedia of Social and Behavioral Sciences,* N. J. Smelser and P. B. Baltes, eds. New York: Elsevier.

Nash, Manning. 1962. Race and the Ideology of Race. *Current Anthropology* 3 (June): 285–288.

National Advisory Commission on Civil Disorders. 1968. *Report.* New York: Bantam.

National Center for Education Statistics. 2009. *Digest of Education Statistics 2008.* Accessible at nces.ed.gov.

———. 2011a. *Digest of Education Statistics 2010.* Accessible at nces. ed.gov.

———. 2011b. The Condition of Education 2010. Accessible at www.nces.gov.

———. 2012. Percentage of Degrees Conferred by Sex and Race. Accessed July 11 at *New York Times.* 2005b. Warnings Raised About Exodus of Philippine Doctors and Nurses (November 27): 13.

———. 2013. *Digest of Education Statistics 2012.* Accessible at nces.ed.gov.

National Conference of Christians and Jews (NCCJ). 1994. *Taking America's Pulse.* New York: NCCJ.

National Congress of American Indians. 2012. Toward a New Era. *Annual Report 2010–2011.* Washington, DC: NCAI.

National Indian Gaming Association. 2006. Indian Gaming Facts. Accessed September 27, 2006, at www.indiangaming.org.

National Park Service. 2012. The War Relocation Camps of World War II: When Fear Was Stronger than Justice – Supplementary Resources. Accessed July 16 at http://www.nps.gov/history/nr/twhp/wwwlps/lessons/89nanzanar/89lrnmore.htm.

Nawa, Fariba. 2011. Struggling to Stay Bilingual. *Christian Science Monitor* (October 17): 38–39.

NCAA (National Collegiate Athletic Association). 2003a. Executive Committee Reviews American Indian Mascot Input. Press release (April 25).

———. 2003b. NCAA Executive Committee Passes Recommendations Regarding American Indian Mascots, Confederate Flag and NCAA Budget. Press release (August 11).

New America Media. 2007. *Deep Divisions, Shared Destiny.* San Francisco, CA: New America Media.

Newman, William M. 1973. *American Pluralism: A Study of Minority Groups and Social Theory.* New York: Harper & Row.

Newport, Frank. 2011. Christianity Remains Dominant Religion in the United States. December 23. Accessible at http://www.gallup.com/poll/151760/Christianity-Remains-Dominant-Religion-United-States.aspx.

Newsweek. 1971. Success Story: Outwhiting the White. 77 (June 121): 24–25.

New York Times. 1991. For Two, an Answer to Years of Doubt on Use of Peyote in Religious Rite (July 9): A14.

———. 2005a. U.S. Panel Backs Nuclear Dump on Indian Reservation in Utah (September 10): A10.

———. 2005b. Warnings Raised About Exodus of Philippine Doctors and Nurses (November 27): 13.

Nishi, Setsuko Matsunaga. 1995. Japanese Americans. pp. 95–133 in *Asian Americans: Contemporary Trends and Issues,* Pyong Gap Min, ed. Thousand Oaks, CA: Sage Publications.

Noel, Donald L. 1972. *The Origins of American Slavery and Racism.* Columbus, OH: Charles Merrill.

Norrell, Robert J. 2009. *Up From History: The Life of Booker T. Washington.* Cambridge, MA: Harvard University Press.

Norris, Tina, Paula L. Vines, and Elizabeth M. Hoeffel. 2012. The American Indian and Alaska Native Population: 2010. C2010BR-10. Accessible at www.census.gov.

Norton, Michael I. and Samuel R. Sommers. 2011. Whites See Racism as a Zero-Sum Game That They Are Now Losing. *Perspectives on Psychological Science* 6 (3): 215.

Oberschall, Anthony. 1968. The Los Angeles Riot of August 1965. *Social Problems* (Winter), 15: 322–341.

Office of Hawaiian Affairs. 2012. Native Hawaiian Data Book 2011. Accessible at http://www.ohadatabook.com/fr_statlinks.11.html.

Office of Immigration Statistics. 2011. *Yearbook of Immigration Statistics: 2010.* Accessible at http://www.dhs.gov/files/statistics/publications/LPR10.shtm.

Ogbu, John U. 2004. Collective Identity and the Burden of "Acting White" in Black History, Community, and Education. *Urban Review* 36 (March): 1–35.

——— and Astrid Davis. 2003. *Black American Students in an Affluent Suburb: A Study of Academic Disengagement.* Mahwah, NJ: Lawrence Erlbaum Associates.

Ogunwole Stella U., Malcolm P. Drewery, Jr., and Merarys Rios-Vargas. 2012. *The Population with a Bachelor's Degree or Higher by Race and Hispanic Origin: 2006–2010.* May: ACSBR/10-19. Washington, DC: U.S. Government Printing Office.

Ohnuma, Keiko. 1991. Study Finds Asians Unhappy at CSU. *AsianWeek* 12 (August 8): 5.

Okamura, Jonathan Y. 2008. *Ethnicity and Inequality in Hawaii.* Philadelphia, PA: Temple University Press.

Olemetson, Lynette. 2005. Adopted in China, Seeking Identity in America. *New York Times* (March 23): A1.

Oliver, Melvin L., and Thomas M. Shapiro. 1996. *Black Wealth/White Wealth: New Perspective on Racial Inequality.* New York: Routledge.

——— and ———. 2006. *Black Wealth/White Wealth.* 10th anniversary ed. New York: Routledge.

Oregon State University 2006. Name can Lead to Housing Discrimination. Public release date 24-May-2006. Accessible at http://www.eurekalert.org/pub_releases/2006-05/osu-ncl052306.php.

Orlov, Ann and Reed Ueda. 1980. Central and South Americans. pp. 210–217 in *Harvard Encyclopedia of American Ethnic Groups,* Stephan Thernstrom, ed. Cambridge, MA: Belknap Press of Harvard University Press.

O'Connor, Anne-Marie. 1998. Church's New Wave of Change. *Los Angeles Times* (March 25): A1, A16.

O'Neill, William. 1969. *Everyone Was Brave: The Rise and Fall of Feminism in America.* Chicago: Quadrangle.

Padget, Martin. 2004. *Indian Country: Travels in the American Southwest, 1840–1935.* Albuquerque: University of New Mexico Press.

Padilla, Efren N. 2008. Filipino Americans. pp. 493–497 in vol. 1, *Encyclopedia of Race, Ethnicity, and Society,* Richard T. Schaefer, ed. Thousand Oaks, CA: Sage.

Pager, Devah. 2003. The Mark of a Criminal. *American Journal of Sociology* 108: 937–975.

——— and Bruce Western. 2006. Race at Work: Realities of Race and Criminal Record in the NYC Job Market. *Report prepared for 50th anniversary of the New York City Museum on Human Rights.* Accessed June 3, 2008, at www.princeton.edu/~pager/race_at_work.pdf.

———, ———, and Bart Bonikowski. 2009. Discrimination in a Low-Wage Labor Market: A Field Experiment. *American Sociological Review* 74 (October): 777–799.

Paluck, Elizabeth Levy and Donald P. Green. 2009. Prejudice Reduction: What Works? A Review and Assessment of Research and Practice. *Annual Review of Psychology* 60: 339–367.

Pariser, Eli. 2011a. *The Filter Bubble. What the Internet Is Hiding from You.* New York: Penguin Press.

———. 2011b. In our own little Internet bubbles. *The Guardian Weekly* (June 24): 32–33.

Parrish, Michael. 1995. Betting on Hard Labour and a Plot of Land. *Los Angeles Times* (July 7): A1, A20.

Passel, Jeffery S. and D'Vera Cohn. 2009. *A Portrait of Unauthorized Immigrants in the United States.* Washington, DC: Pew Hispanic Center.

_____. 2011. *Unauthorized Immigrant Population National and State Trends, 2010.* Washington, DC: Pew Research Center.

_____, and Mark Hugo López. 2011. *Census 2010: 50 Million Latinos.* Washington, DC: Pew Hispanic Center.

Pasternak, Judy. 2010. *Yellow Dirt: An American Story of a Poisoned Land and a people Betrayed.* New York: Simon and Schuster.

Pastor, Jr., Manuel, Rachel Morello-Frosch, and James L. Saad. 2005. The Air Is Always Cleaner on the Other Side: Race, Space, and Ambient Air Toxics Exposure in California. *Journal of Urban Affairs* 27 (2): 127–148.

Patterson, David Royston. 2012. Will Puerto Rico Be America's 51st State? *New York Times* (November 25): section SR BW: 4.

Pearson, Bryan. 2006. Brain Drain Human Resource Crisis. *The Africa Report* (October): 95–98.

Peckham, Pat. 2002. Hmong's Resettlement Changes Agency's Focus. *Wausau Daily Herald* (February 10): 1A, 2A.

Pellow, David Naguib and Robert J. Brulle. 2007. Poisoning the Planet: The Struggle for Environmental Justice. *Contexts* 6 (Winter): 37–41.

Perry, Barbara, ed. 2003. *Hate and Bias Crime: A Reader.* New York: Routledge.

Perry, Tony and Richard Simon. 2009. Filipino Veterans of WWII to Get Long-Overdue Funds. *Los Angeles Times* (February 18): B1, B7.

Peréz, Linsandro. 2001. Growing Up in Cuban Miami: Immigrants, the Enclave, and New Generations. pp. 91–125 in *Ethnicities,* Ruben G. Rumbaut and Alejandro Portes, eds. Berkeley: University of California Press.

Peterson, Ruth D. 2012. The Central Place of Race in Crime and Justice. *Criminology* 50 (No. 2): 303–327.

Pettigrew, Thomas F. 2011. Did Brown Fail. *Du Bois Review* 8 (No. 2): 511–516.

Pew Charitable Trust. 2011. Downward Mobility from the Middle Class. Waking Up from the American Dream. September 6. Accessible at http://www.pewstates.org/uploadedFiles/PCS_Assets/2011/MiddleClassReport.pdf.

_____. 2012. Weathering the Great Recession: Did High-Poverty Neighborhoods Fare Worse? Accessible at http://www.pewstates.org/uploadedFiles/PCS_Assets/2012/Pew_urban_neighborhoods_report.pdf.

Pew Forum on Religion and Public Life. 2008. *U.S. Religious Landscape Survey: Religious Beliefs and Practices: Diverse and Political Relevant.* Washington, DC: Pew Forum on Religion and Public Life.

_____. 2010. *Growing Number of Americans Say Obama Is a Muslim.* Washington, DC: Pew Forum.

_____. 2011. *The Future of the Global Muslim Population.* Washington, DC: Pew Forum.

_____. 2012. *Latinos, Religion and Campaign 2012: Catholics Favor Obama, Evangelicals Divided.* Accessible at http://www.pewforum.org/Race/Latinos-Religionand-Campaign-2012.aspx.

Pew Hispanic Center. 2011a. Mapping the Latino Electorate. Accessible at http://pewhispanic.org/docs/?DocID=26.

_____. 2011b. Unauthorized Immigrants: Length of Residency, Patterns of Parenthood. December 1. Washington, DC: Pew Hispanic Center.

_____. 2011c. The Mexican-American Boom: Births Overtake Immigration. July 14. Washington, DC: Pew Hispanic Center.

_____. 2011d. Unauthorized Immigrants: Length of Residency, Patterns of Parenthood. December 1, Washington: Pew Hispanic Center.

_____. 2012a. When Labels Don't Fit: Hispanics and Their Views of Identity. April 4. Washington, DC: Pew Hispanic Center.

_____. 2012b. Net Migration from Mexico Falls to Zero – and Perhaps Less. Washington, DC: Pew Hispanic Center.

_____. 2013. A Nation of Immigrants. A Portrait of the 40 Million, Including 11 Million Unauthorized. January 29. Washington DC: Pew Hispanic Center.

Pew Research Center. 2010. Blacks Upbeat about Black Progress, Prospects. Accessible at http://pewsocialtrends.org/2010/01/12/blacks-upbeat-about-black-progress-prospects.

Pew Social and Demographic Trends. 2012. *The Rise of Asian Americans.* Washington, DC: Pew Social and Demographic Trends.

Pewewardy, Cornel. 1998. Our Children Can't Wait: Recapturing the Essence of Indigenous Schools in the United States. *Cultural Survival Quarterly* (Spring): 29–34.

Pfaelzer, Jean. 2007. *Driven Out: The Forgotten War Against Chinese Americans.* New York: Random House.

Pfeifer, Mark. 2008b. Vietnamese Americans. pp. 1365–1368 in vol. 3, *Encyclopedia of Race, Ethnicity, and Society.* Richard T. Schaefer, ed. Thousand Oaks, CA: Sage.

Pido, Antonio J. A. 1986. *The Filipinos in America.* New York: Center for Migration Studies.

Pincus, Fred L. 2003. *Reverse Discrimination: Dismantling the Myth.* Boulder, CO: Lynne Rienner.

_____. 2008. Reverse Discrimination. pp. 1159–1161 in vol. 3, *Encyclopedia of Race, Ethnicity, and Society,* Richard T. Schaefer, ed. Thousand Oaks, CA: Sage.

Pinkney, Alphonso. 1984. *The Myth of Black Progress.* New York: Cambridge University Press.

Portes, Alejandro. 1998. Social Capital: Its Origins and Applications in Modern Society. *Annual Review of Sociology* 24: 1–24.

_____, and Erik Vickstrom. 2011. Diversity, Social Capital, and Cohesion. *Annual Review of Sociology* 37: 461–479.

Posadas, Barbara M. 1999. *The Filipino Americans.* Westport, CT: Greenwood Press.

Powell-Hopson, Darlene and Derek Hopson. 1988. Implications of Doll Color Preferences among Black Preschool Children and White Preschool Children. *Journal of Black Psychology* 14 (February): 57–63.

Pratt, Tomothy. 2012. More Asian Immigrants Find Options on Ballots. *New York Times* (October 19): A14.

Preston, Julia. 2007. Polls Surveys Ethnic Views among Chief Minorities. *New York Times* (December 13).

_____. 2010. On Gangs, Asylum Law Offers Little. *New York Times* (June 30): A15, A19.

_____ and Fernanda Santos. 2012. A Record Latino Turnout, Solidly Backing Obama. *New York Times* (November 8): 13.

Pryor, John H., Laura Palucki Blake, Sylvia Hurtado, Linda DeAngelo, and Serge Tran. 2010. *The American Freshman: National Norms for Fall 2010.* Los Angeles, CA: Higher Education Research Institute, UCLA.

_____, Kevin Eagan, Laura Palucki Blake, Sylvia Hurtado, Jennifer Berdan, Matthew H. Case. 2012. *The American Freshman: National Norms Fall 2012.* Los Angeles: Higher Education Research Institute, UCLA.

Purdy, Matthew. 2001. Ignoring and Then Embracing the Truth about Racial Profiling. *New York Times* (March 11).

Quillian, Lincoln. 2006. New Approaches to Understanding Racial Prejudice and Discrimination. pp. 299–328 in *Annual Reviews of Sociology 2006,* Karen S. Cook, ed. Palo Alto, CA: Annual Reviews Inc.

Quiñones-Hinojosa, Alfredo with Mim Eichler Rivas. 2011. *Becoming Dr. Q: My Journey from Migrant Farm Worker to Brain Surgeon.* Berkeley: University of California Press.

Ramirez, Margaret. 2000. Study Finds Segregation of Latinos in Catholic Church. *Los Angeles Times* (March 1): A1, A24.

Ramos, Jorge. 2010. *A Country for All.* New York: Vintage Books.

Rangaswamy, Padma. 2005. Asian Indians in Chicago. In *The New Chicago,* John Koval et al., eds. Philadelphia: Temple University Press.

Rastogi, Sonya, Tallese D. Johnson, Elizabeth M. Hoeffel, and Malcolm P. Drewery, Jr. 2011. The Black Population: 2010. C2010BR-06. September 2011. Accessible at www.census.gov.

Ratledge, Ingela. 2012. Is the Bachelor Racist? *TV Guide* (May 6): 6.

Reckard, E. Scott. 2007. A Power Shift in Koreatown. *Los Angeles Times* (May 25): C1, C4.

Reskin, Barbara F. 2012. The Race Discrimination System. *Annual Review of Sociology:* 38.

Reyhner, Jon. 2001. *Family, Community, and School Impacts on American Indian and Alaskan Native Students Success.* Paper presented at annual meeting of the National Indian Education Association (October 29).

Richmond, Anthony H. 2012. Globalization: Implications for Immigrants and Refugees. *Ethnic and Racial Studies* 25 (September): 707–727.

Richter, Paul. 2012. Clinton Declares Affirmative Action Is "Good for America." *Los Angeles Times* (July 20). Accessed at http://articles.latimes.com/1995-07-20/news/mn-26049_1_affirmative-action-programs.

Roanoke Times. 2012. Hampton-Sydney College reports post-election unrest. November 9. Accessible at http://www.roanoke.com/news/breaking/ws/316446.

Robinson, Greg. 2001. *By Order of the President: FDR and the Internment of Japanese Americans.* Cambridge: Harvard University Press.

———. 2009. *A Tragedy of Democracy: Japanese Confinement in North America.* New York: Columbia University Press.

———. 2012. *After Camp: Portraits in Midcentury Japanese Americans Life and Politics.* Berkeley: University of California Press.

Robinson, Michelle. 1985. *Princeton-Educated Blacks and the Black Community.* Senior Honors Thesis. Accessible at www.politico.com/news/stories/0208/8642.html.

Robnett, Belinda and Cynthia Feliciano. 2011. Patterns of Racial-Ethnic Exclusion by Internet Daters. *Social Forces* 80 (No. 3, March): 807, 828.

Rodríguez, Clara E. 1989. *Puerto Ricans: Born in the USA.* Boston: Unwin Hyman.

Roediger, David R. 1994. *Towards the Abolition of Whiteness: Essays on Race, Politics, and Working Class History (Haymarket).* New York: Verso Books.

———. 2006. Whiteness and Its Complications. *Chronicle of Higher Education* 52 (July 14): B6–B8.

Roof, Wade Clark. 2007. Introduction. *The Annals* 612 (July): 6–12.

Rose, Arnold. 1951. *The Roots of Prejudice.* Paris: UNESCO.

Rudwick, Elliott. 1957. The Niagara Movement. *Journal of Negro History* (July), 42: 177–200.

Rusk, David. 2001. *The "Segregation Tax": The Cost of Racial Segregation to Black Homeowners.* Washington, DC: Brookings Institution.

Russell, Steve. 2011. Of Blood and Citizenship. *Indian County Today* (July 27): 22–29.

Ryan, William. 1976. *Blaming the Victim,* rev. ed. New York: Random House.

Saad, Lydia. 2006. Anti-Muslim Sentiments Fairly Commonplace. *The Gallup Poll* (August 10).

Sachs, Susan. 2001. For Newcomers, a Homey New Chinatown. *New York Times* (July 22): A1, A44.

Sahagun, Louis. 2004. Tribes Fear Backlash to Prosperity. *Los Angeles Times* (May 3): B1, B6.

Sandage, Diane. 2008. Peltier, Leonard. pp. 1033–1035 in vol. 2, *Encyclopedia of Race, Ethnicity, and Society,* Richard T. Schaefer, ed. Thousand Oaks, CA: Sage.

Santos-Hernández, Jenniffer M. 2008. Puerto Rican Armed Forces of National Liberation. pp. 1084–1085 in vol. 2, *Encyclopedia of Race, Ethnicity, and Society,* Richard T. Schaefer, ed. Thousand Oaks, CA: Sage.

Sarkisian, Natalia, Mariana Gerena, and Naomi Gerstel. 2007. Extended Family Integration among Euro and Mexican Americans: Ethnicity, Gender, and Class. *Journal of Marriage and Family* (February), 69: 40–54.

Saulny, Susan. 2011. Black? White? Asian? More Young Americans Choose All of the Above. *New York Times* (January 29): A1, A17–A18.

Sawhill, Isabel V., Scott Winship, and Kerry Searle Grannis. 2012. *Pathways to the Middle Class" Balancing Personal and Public Responsibilities.* Washington, DC: Brookings.

Schaefer, Richard T. 1970. Racial Socialization, Comparison Levels, and the Watts Riot. *Journal of Social Issues* (Winter), 26: 121–140.

———. 1971. The Ku Klux Klan: Continuity and Change. *Phylon* (Summer), 32: 143–157.

———. 1973. *The Politics of Violence: The New Urban Blacks and the Watts Riots.* Boston: Houghton-Mifflin.

———. 1976. *The Extent and Content of Racial Prejudice in Great Britain.* San Francisco, CA: R&E Research Associates.

———. 1980. The Management of Secrecy: The Ku Klux Klan's Successful Secret. pp. 161–177 in *Secrecy: A Cross-Cultural Perspective,* Stanton K. Sears, David O., and J. B. McConahay. 1969. Participation in the Los Angeles Riot. *Social Problems* (Summer), 17: 3–20.

———. 1986. Racial Prejudice in a Capitalist State: What Has Happened to the American Creed? *Phylon* 47 (September): 192–198.

———. 1992. People of Color: The "Kaleidoscope" May Be a Better Way to Describe America than "the Melting Pot." *Peoria Journal Star* (January 19): A7.

———. 1996. Education and Prejudice: Unraveling the Relationship. *Sociological Quarterly* 37 (January): 1–16.

———. 2008. Nativism. pp. 611–612 in vol. 1, *Encyclopedia of Social Problems,* Vincent N. Parrillo, ed. Thousand Oaks, CA: Sage.

———. and Sandra L. Schaefer. 1975. Reluctant Welcome: U.S. Responses to the South Vietnamese Refugees. *New Community* (Autumn), 4: 366–370.

——— and William Zellner. 2011. *Extraordinary Groups,* 9th ed. New York: Worth.

School Digger. 2011. *Wausan School District.* Accessed June 1, 2011, at www.schooldigger.com.

Schulz, Amy J. 1998. Navajo Women and the Politics of Identity. *Social Problems* (August), 45: 336–352.

Schwartz, John. 1994. Preserving Endangered Speeches. *Washington Post National Weekly Edition* (March 21), 11: 38.

Scott, Janny. 2003. Debating Which Private Clubs Are Acceptable and Private. *New York Times* 7 (December 8): 5.

Scully, Marc. 2012. Whose Day Is It Anyway? St. Patrick's Day as a Contested Performance of National And Diasporic Irishness. *Studies in Ethnicity and Nationalism* 12 (No. 1) 118–135.

Seibert, Deborah. 2002. Interview with Author. *Wausau Daily Herald,* Staff Member (March 27).

Semple, Kirk. 2012. Many U.S. Immigrants' Children Seek American Dream Abroad. *New York Times* (April 16). Accessed April 21, 2013 at http://www.nytimes.com/2012/04/16/us/more-us-children-of-immigrants-are-leaving-us.html?ref=kirksemple.

Shanklin, Eugenia. 1994. *Anthropology and Race.* Belmont, CA: Wadsworth.

Shapiro, Thomas M. 2004. *The Hidden Cost of Being African American: How Wealth Perpetuates Inequality.* New York: Oxford University Press.

———. 2010. *New Study Finds Racial Wealth Gap Quadrupled Sing Mid-1980s.* Boston, MA: Institute on Assets and Social Policy.

———, Tatjana Meschede, and Laura Sullivan. 2010. The Racial Wealth Gap Increases Fourfold. *Research and Policy Brief* (May) *of Institute on Assets and Social Policy.* University of Michigan. MA: Institute on Assets and Social Policy.

Sherwood, Jessica Holden. 2010. *Wealth, Whiteness, and the Matrix of Privilege: The View from the Country Clubs.* Lanham, MD: Rowman and Littlefield.

Shin, Hyon B. and Robert A. Kominski. 2010. Language Use in the United States 2007. *Census Brief ACS-12.* Washington, DC: U.S. Government Printing Office.

Siebens, Julie and Tiffany Julian. 2011. Native North American Languages Spoken at Home in the United States and Puerto Rico: 2006-2010. ACSBF/10-10. Accessible at www.census.gov.

Sigelman, Lee and Steven A. Tuch. 1997. Metastereotypes: Blacks' Perception of Whites' Stereotypes of Blacks. *Public Opinion Quarterly* 61 (Spring): 87–101.

Silberman, Charles E. 1971. *Crisis in the Classroom: The Remaking of American Education.* New York: Random House.

Simon Wiesenthal Center. 2008. *iReport: Online Terror + Hate: The First Decade.* Los Angeles, CA: Simon Wisenthal Center.

Simpson, Cam. 2009. Obama Hones Immigration Policy. *Wall Street Journal* (July 29): A6.

Simpson, Jacqueline C. 1995. Pluralism: The Evolution of a Nebulous Concept. *American Behavioral Scientist* 38 (January): 459–477.

Skrentny, John D. 2008. Culture and Race/Ethnicity: Bolder, Deeper, and Broader. *Annals* 619 (September): 59–77.

Slavin, Robert E. and Alan Cheung. 2003. *Effective Reading Programs for English Language Learners.* Baltimore, MD: Johns Hopkins University, Center for Research on the Education of Students Placed at Risk.

Small, Cathy A. 2011. *Voyages: From Tongan Villages to American Suburbs.* 2nd ed. Ithaca NY: Cornell University Press.

Smith, Julian. 2011. Insider: Who Owns the Dead? *Archaeology* 64 (January/February).

Smith, Tom W. 1999. *Measuring Inter-Racial Friendships: Experimental Comparisons.* GSS Methodological Report No. 91. Chicago: NORC.

_____. 2006. *Taking America's Pulse III. Intergroup Relations in Contemporary America.* Chicago: National Opinion Research Center, University of Chicago.

Snipp, C. Matthew. 1989. *American Indians: The First of This Land.* New York: Sage.

Society for Human Resource Management. 2008. *2007 State of Workplace Diversity Management.* Alexandria, VA: SHRM.

Soltero, Sonia White. 2008. *Bilingual Education.* pp. 142–146 in vol. 1, *Encyclopedia of Race, Ethnicity, and Society,* Richard T. Schaefer, ed. Thousand Oaks, CA: Sage.

Song, Tae-Hyon. 1991. *Social Contact and Ethnic Distance between Koreans and the U.S. Whites in the United States.* MA thesis, Western Illinois University, Macomb.

Soo, Julie D. 1999. Strained Relations: Why Chinatown's Venerable Associations Are Ending Up in Court. *AsianWeek* (January 14): 15–18.

Soohan Kim, and Alexandra Kalev. 2011. "You Can't Always Get What You Need: Organizational Determinants of Diversity Programs." American Sociological Review 76 (3): 386.

Southern Poverty Law Center. 2010. *Ten Ways to Fight Hate: A Community Response Guide.* Montgomery, AL: SPLC.

Stampp, Kenneth M. 1956. *The Peculiar Institution: Slavery in the Ante-Bellum South.* New York: Random House.

Standen, Amy. 2010. *Tribal Lands Struggle to Bring Clean Power Online.* Accessed at www.wbur.org/npr.

Starks, Carolyn. 2002. Sitting Here in Limbo. *Chicago Tribune* (March 26).

Staton, Ron. 2004a. Still Fighting for National Hawaiian Recognition. *AsianWeek* (January 22): 8.

Steinberg, Stephen. 2007. *Race Relations: A Critique.* Stanford, CT: Stanford University Press.

Steinhauer, Jennifer. 2006. An Unwelcome Light on Club Where Legends Teed Off. *New York Times* (September 23): A8.

Stonequist, Everett V. 1937. *The Marginal Man: A Study in Personality and Culture Conflict.* New York: Scribner's.

Stretesky, Paul and Michael Lynch. 2002. Environmental Hazards and School Segregation in Hillsborough County, Florida, 1987–1999. *Sociological Quarterly* 43: 553–573.

Sturtevant, William C. and Jessica R. Cattelino. 2004. *"Florida Seminole and Miccosukee." In Handbook of North American Indians (Southeast).* R. D. Fogelson, ed. pp. 429–449, Vol. 14. Washington, DC: Smithsonian Institution Press.

Sullivan, Keith. 2005. Desperate Moves. *Washington Post National Weekly Edition* (March 14): 9–10.

Sulzberger, A.G. 2011. Hispanics Reviving Faded Towns on the Plains. *New York Times* (November 14): A1, A20.

Supreme Court of the United States 347 U.S. 483, August 17, 1954.

Swagerty, William R. 1983. Native Peoples and Early European Contacts. pp. 15–16 in *Encyclopedia of American Social History,* Mary Kupiec Clayton, Elliot J. Gorn, and Peter W. Williams, eds. New York: Scribner's.

Sze, Julie and Jonathan K. London. 2008. Environmental Justice at the Crossroads. *Sociology Compass* (4): 1331–1354.

Sánchez, José Ramón. 2007. *Boricua Power: A Political History of Puerto Ricans in the United States.* New York: New York University Press.

Takaki, Ronald. 1998. *Strangers from a Different Shore: A History of Asian Americans.* Updated and revised. Boston, MA: Little, Brown, Back Bay edition.

Takezawa, Yasuko I. 1991. Children of Inmates: The Effects of the Redress Movement among Third Generation Japanese Americans. *Qualitative Sociology* (Spring), 14: 39–56.

Talbani, Aziz and Parveen Hasanali. 2000. Adolescent Females between Tradition and Modernity: Gender Role Socialization in South Asian Immigrant Culture. *Journal of Adolescence* 23: 615–627.

Taylor, Jonathan B. and Joseph P. Kalt. 2005. *American Indians on Reservations: A Databook of Socioeconomic Change between the 1990 and 2000 Censuses.* Cambridge, MA: The Harvard Project on American Indian Development.

Taylor, Paul, et al. 2010. *Marrying Out: One-in-Seven New U.S. Marriages is Interracial or Interethnic.* Washington, DC: Pew Research Center.

Taylor, Stuart, Jr. 1987. High Court Backs Basing Promotion on a Racial Quota. *New York Times* (February 26): 1, 14.

_____. 1988. Justices Back New York Law Ending Sex Bias by Big Clubs. *New York Times* (June 21): A1, A18.

Tefera, Adai, Genevieve Seigel-Hawley, and Erica Frankenberg. 2010. *School Integration Efforts Three Years after Parents Involved.* Los Angeles: The Civil Rights Project, UCLA.

ten Brock, Jacobus, Edward N. Barnhart, and Floyd W. Matson. 1954. *Prejudice, War and the Constitution.* Berkeley: University of California Press.

Teranishi, Robert T. 2010. *Asians in the Ivory Tower: Dilemmas of Racial Inequity in American Higher Education.* New York: Teachers College Press.

The Economist. 2009. Cuba and America: Gently Does It. *Economist* (May 9): 32–33.

Thomas, Curlew O. and Barbara Boston Thomas. 1984. Blacks' Socioeconomic Status and the Civil Rights Movement's Decline, 1970–1979: An Examination of Some Hypotheses. *Phylon* (March), 45: 40–51.

Thomas, Dorothy S. and Richard S. Nishimoto. 1946. *The Spoilage: Japanese-American Evacuation and Resettlement.* Berkeley: University of California Press.

Thomas, Oliver. 2007. So What Does the Constitution Say about Religion? *USA Today* (October 15): 15A.

Thomas, William Isaac. 1923. *The Unadjusted Girl.* Boston, MA: Little, Brown.

Thompson, Krissah. 2010. Montgomery Parents' "Study Circles" Aim to Close the Gap on Student Achievement." *Washington Post* (November 9).

Thomás Riviera Policy Institute. 2009. *Majority/Near-Majority of First Graders in Top Ten U.S. Cities are Latino.* Release March 5.

Thornton, Russell. 1991. *North American Indians and the Demography of Contact.* Paper presented at annual meeting of the American Sociological Association, Cincinnati, OH.

Tice, Lindsay. 2007. Another side of Brent Matthews. *Lewiston-Auburn Sun Journal.* (April 29). Accessed April 16, 2012, at http://www.sunjournal.com/node/239728.

Toensing, Gale Courey. 2011. Recession-Proof Is in the Pudding. *Indian Country Today* (April 13): 28–31.

Tomaskovic-Devey, Donald and Patricia Warren. 2009. Explaining and Eliminating Racial Profiling. *Contexts* 8 (Spring): 34–39.

Tomlinson, T. M. 1969. The Development of a Riot Ideology among Urban Negroes. pp. 226–235 in *Racial Violence in the United States,* Allen D. Grimshaw, ed. Chicago: Aldine.

Tong, Benson. 2000. *The Chinese Americans.* Westport, CT: Greenwood Press.

Tough, Paul. 2004. The "Acting White" Myth. *New York Times* (December 12).

Touré. 2011. Who's Afraid of Post-Blackness? New York: Free Press.

Townsend, Sarah S. M., Hazel R. Markos, and Hilary Bergsieker. 2009. My Choice, Your Categories: The Denial of Multiracial Identities. *Journal of Social Issues* 65 (1): 185–204.

Tran, My-Thuan. 2008. Their Nation Lives On. *Los Angeles Times* (April 30): B1, B8–B9.

Triev, Monica M. 2009. *Identity Construction Among Chinese-Vietnamese Americans Being, Becoming, and Belonging.* El Paso, TX: LFB Scholarly Publishing LLC.

Truman, Jennifer L. 2011. Criminal Victimization Survey. *BJS Bulletin* (September).

Tsui, Bonnie. 2011. The End of Chinatown. *The Atlantic* (December): 17–18.

Ture, Kwame and Charles Hamilton. 1992. *Black Power: The Politics of Liberation.* New York: Vintage Books.

Turner, Margery Austin, Fred Freiburg, Erin Godfrey, Clark Herbig, Diane K. Levy, and Robin R. Smith. 2002. *All Other Things Being Equal: A Paired Testing Study of Mortgage Lending Institutions.* Washington, DC: Urban Institute.

Turner, Ralph H. 1994. Race Riots Past and Present: A Cultural-Collective Approach. *Symbolic Interaction,* 17(3): 309–324.

Twohey, Megan. 2007. Outside, It's Suburban; Inside, It's Japan. *Chicago Tribune* (December 29): 1, 2.

Tyson, Ann Scott. 1996. Alabama Ferry to Bridge Racial Divide. *USA Today* (February 13), Sect. 4: 4.

Tyson, Karolyn, William Darity, Jr., and Domini R. Castellino. 2005. It's Not "a Black Thing": Understanding the Burden of Acting White and Other Dilemmas of High Achievement. *American Sociological Review* 70 (August): 582–605.

U.S. Court of Appeals. 2008. *Chicago Lawyers' Committee for Civil Rights Under Law, Inc. v. Craigslist, Inc. For the Seventh Circuit.* No. 06 C 657 (February 15).

United Nations High Commission on Refugees. 2008. *2007 Global Trends: Refugees, Asylum-seekers, Returnees, Internally Displaced and Stateless Persons.* Geneva: UNHCR.

University of North Dakota. 2008. *B.R.I.D.G.E.S.* Accessed July 8, 2008, at www.und.edu/org/bridges/index2.html.

Vang, Chia Youyee. 2010. *Hmong America: Reconstructing Community in America.* Champaign: University of Illinois Press.

Vaquera, Elizabeth and Gace Kao. 2008. Do you like me as much as I like you? Friendship reciprocity and its effects on school outcomes among adolescents. *Social Science Research* 37: 55–72.

Varadarajan, Tunko. 1999. A Patel Motel Cartel? *New York Times Magazine* (July 4): 36–39.

Voo, Jocelyn, 2008. "Arranged marriage gets high-tech twist." Accessed July 16, 2012 at http://articles.cnn.com/2008-04-23/living/web.arranged.marriages_1_cell-phones-marriage-profile?_s=PM:LIVING.

Võ, Linda Trinh. 2004. *Mobilizing an Asian American Community.* Philadelphia: Temple University Press.

Waitzkin, Howard. 1986. *The Second Sickness: Contradictions of Capitalistic Health Care,* rev. ed. New York: Free Press.

Waller, David. 1996. Friendly Fire: When Environmentalists Dehumanize American Indians. *American Indian Culture and Research Journal* 20 (2): 107–126.

Wallerstein, Immanuel. 1974. *The Modern World System.* New York: Academic Press.

Wang, L. Ling-Chi. 1991. Roots and Changing Identity of the Chinese in the United States. *Daedalus* (Spring), 120: 181–206.

Wark, Colin and John F. Galliher. 2007. Emory Bogardus and the Origins of the Social Distance Scale. *American Sociologist* 38: 383–395.

Warner, W. Lloyd and Leo Srole. 1945. *The Social Systems of American Ethnic Groups.* New Haven, CT: Yale University.

Washburn, Wilcomb E. 1984. A Fifty-Year Perspective on the Indian Reorganization Act. *American Anthropologist* (June), 86: 279–289.

Washington, Booker T. 1900. *Up from Slavery: An Autobiography.* New York: A. L. Burt.

Watanabe, Teresa. 2007. Reclaiming Cultural Ties. *Los Angeles Times* (May 13): B1, B13.

Waters, Mary. 1990. *Ethnic Options. Choosing Identities in America.* Berkeley, CA: University of California Press.

Wax, Murray L. 1971. *Indian Americans: Unity and Diversity.* Englewood Cliffs, NJ: Prentice Hall.

_____ and Robert W. Buchanan. 1975. *Solving "the Indian Problem": The White Man's Burdensome Business.* New York: New York Times Book Company.

Wax, Rosalie. 1967. The Warrior Drop-Outs. *Trans-Action* (May), 4: 40–46.

Weber, Max. 1947. *The Theory of Social and Economic Organization* [1913–1922], Henderson and T. Parsons, trans. New York: Free Press.

Weinberg, Daniel H. 2007. Earnings by Gender: Evidence from Census 2000. *Monthly Labor Review* (July–August): 26–34.

Weiner, Tim. 2004. Of Gringos and Old Grudges: This Land Is Their Land. *New York Times* (January 9): A4.

Welch, William M. 2011. More Hawaii Resident Identify as Mixed Race. *USA Today* (February 28).

Wessel, David. 2001. Hidden Costs of Brain Drain. *Wall Street Journal* (March 1): 1.

West, Darrel M. 2010. *Brain Gain: Rethinking U.S. Immigration Policy.* Washington, DC: Brookings Institution Press.

White House. 2012. Remarks by the President on the Nomination of Dr. Jim Kim for World Bank President. March 23. Accessible athttp://www.whitehouse.gov/photos-and-video/video/2012/03/23/president-obama-nominated-jim-yong-kim-world-bank-president#transcript.

Whitman, David. 1987. For Latinos, a Growing Divide. *U.S. News and World Report* (August 10), 103: 47–49.

Wickham, De Wayne. 1993. Subtle Racism Thrives. *USA Today* (October 25): 2A, 15, A1, A26.

Wieberg, Steve. 2006 NCAA to rename college football subdivision's. *USA Today* (August 3).

Wilkes, Rima and John Iceland. 2004. Hypersegregation in the Twenty-First Century. *Demography* 41 (February): 23–36.

Willeto, Angela A. 1999. Navajo Culture and Female Influences on Academic Success: Traditional Is Not a Significant Predictor of Achievement among Young Navajos. *Journal of American Indian Education* (Winter), 38: 1–24.

_____. 2007. Native American Kids: American Indian Children's Well- Being Indicators for the Nation and Two States. *Social Indicators Research* (August), 83: 149–176.

Williams, Kim M. 2005. Multiculturalism and the Civil Rights Future. *Daedalus* 134 (1): 53–60.

Williams, Timothy. 2012a. U.S. Will Pay A Settlement of $1 Billion To 41 Tribes. New York Times (April 14): A10.

_____. 2012b. Sioux Racing to Find Billions to Buy Sacred Land in Black Hills. *New York Times* (October 4): A1, A20.

Willie, Charles V. 1978. The Inclining Significance of Race. *Society* (July–August), 15: 10, 12–13.

_____. 1979. *The Caste and Class Controversy.* Bayside, NY: General Hall.

Willoughby, Brian. 2004. *10 Ways to Fight Hate on Campus.* Montgomery, AL: Southern Poverty Law Center.

Wilson, William Julius. 1973. *Power, Racism and Privilege: Race Relations in Theoretical and Sociohistorical Perspectives.* New York: Macmillan.

_____. 1980. *The Declining Significance of Race: Blacks and Changing American Institutions,* 2nd ed. Chicago: University of Chicago Press.

_____. 2011. "The Declining Significance of Race: Revisited and Revised." Annals of the American Academy of Arts and Sciences 140 (Spring): 55–69.

Winant, Howard. 1994. *Racial Conditions: Politics, Theory, Comparisons.* Minneapolis, MN: University of Minnesota Press.

_____. 2004. *The New Politics of Race: Globalism, Difference, Justice.* Minneapolis, MN: University of Minnesota Press.

Winerip, Michael. 2011. New Influx of Haitians, But Not Who Was Expected. *New York Times* (January 16): 15, 22.

Winseman, Albert L. 2004. *U.S. Churches Looking for a Few White Men.* Accessed July 27, 2004, at www.gallup.com.

Winter, S. Alan. 2008. Symbolic Ethnicity. pp. 1288–1290 in vol. 3, *Encyclopedia of Race, Ethnicity, and Society,* Richard T. Schaefer, ed. Thousand Oaks, CA: Sage.

Wisniewski, Mary. 2012. *Transformed by immigration, and Illinois farm town thrives.* Chicago Tribune (July 15). Accessible at www.chicago-tribune.com.

Withrow, Brian L. 2006. *Racial Profiling: From Rhetoric to Reason.* Upper Saddle River, NJ: Prentice Hall.

Wong, Janelle, S. Karthick Ramakrishnan, Taeku Lee, and Jane Junn. 2011. *Asian American Political Participation: Emerging Constituents and Their Political Identities.* New York: Russell Sage Foundation.

Woodward, C. Vann. 1974. *The Strange Career of Jim Crow,* 3rd ed. New York: Oxford University Press.

Working, Russell. 2007. Illegal Abroad, Hate Web Sites Thrive Here. *Chicago Tribune* (November 13): A1, A15.

Wortham, Robert A. 2008. Du Bois, William Edward Burghardt. pp. 423–427 in vol. 1, *Encyclopedia of Race, Ethnicity, and Society,* Richard T. Schaefer, ed. Thousand Oaks, CA: Sage.

Wright II, Earl. 2006. W. E. B. Du Bois and the Atlantic University Studies on the Negro Revisited. *Journal of African American Studies,* 9 (4): 3–17.

Wrong, Dennis H. 1972. How Important Is Social Class? *Dissent* 19 (Winter): 278–285.

Wyatt, Edward. 2009. No Smooth Ride on TV Networks' Road to Diversity. *New York Times* (March 18): 1, 5.

Wyman, Mark. 1993. *Round-Trip to America. The Immigrants Return to Europe, 1830–1930*. Ithaca, NY: Cornell University Press.

Yamashiro, Jane H. 2008. Nisei. pp. 985–988 in vol. 2, *Encyclopedia of Race, Ethnicity, and Society*, Richard T. Schaefer, ed. Thousand Oaks, CA: Sage.

Yancey, George. 2003. *Who Is White? Latinos, Asians, and the New Black–Nonblack Divide*. Boulder, CO: Lynne Rienner.

Yinger, John. 1995. *Closed Doors, Opportunities Lost: The Continuing Costs of Housing Discrimination*. New York: Russell Sage Foundation.

Yosso, Tara J. 2005. Whose Culture Has Capital? A Critical Race Theory Discussion of Community Cultural Wealth. *Race Ethnicity and Education* 8 (March): 69–91.

Young, Jeffrey R. 2003. Researchers Change Racial Bias on the SAT. *Chronicle of Higher Education* (October 10): A34–A35.

Zaidi, Arisha U. and Muhammad Shuraydi. 2002. Perceptions of arranged marriages by young Pakistani Muslim women living in a western society. *Journal of Comparative Family Studies* 33 (Autumn): 495–515.

Zambrana, Ruth Enid. 2011. *Latinos In American Society: Families and Communities in Transition*. Ithaca: Cornell University Press.

Zarembro, Alan. 2004. Physician, Remake Thyself: Lured by Higher Pay and Heavy Recruiting, Philippine Doctors Are Getting Additional Degrees and Starting Over in the U.S. as Nurses. *Los Angeles Times* (January 10): A1, A10.

Zeng, Zhen and Yu Xie. 2004. Asian-Americans' Earnings Disadvantage Reexamined: The Role of Place of Education. *American Journal of Sociology* (March), 109: 1075–1108.

Zhao, Yilu. 2002. Chinatown Gentrifies, and Evicts. *New York Times* (August 23): A13.

Zhou, Min. 2009. *Contemporary Chinese America*. Philadelphia: Temple University Press.

_____ and Carl L. Bankston, III. 1998. *Growing Up American: How Vietnamese Children Adapt to Life in the United States*. New York: Russell Sage Foundation.

Zittrain, Jonathan. 2008. *The Future of the Internet and How to Stop It. With a New Forward by Lawrence Lessig and New Preface by the Author*. New Haven: Yale University Press.

Zogby, John 2001a. *National Survey: American Teen-Agers and Stereotyping*. Submitted to the National Italian American Foundation by Zogby International. Accessed June 3, 2008, at www.niaf.org/research/report_zogby.asp?print=1&.

_____. 2010. *51% Expect Major Terror Attack This Year and 25% Plan to Fly Less* (February 4). Accessed March 2, 2011, at http://www.zogby.com.

_____. 2012. "The Partisan, Racial, and Generational Divide: How We View Arabs and Muslims." August 27. Accessed November 5, at http://www.aaiuse.org/dr-zogby/entry/the-partisan-racial-andgenerational-divide-how-we-view-arabs-and-muslims/.

Photo Credits

Chapter 1: p. 1, Monkey Business/Fotolia; **p. 2**, Robert F. Bukaty/ Associated Press; **p. 8**, Library of Congress, Prints & Photographs Division, [LC-USZ62-16767]; **p. 9**, Jeff Parker/www.politicalcartoons .com; **p. 10**, uwimages/Fotolia; **p. 22**, Marc Greiner/Newscom; **p. 25**, bikeriderlondon/Shutterstock; **p. 28**, Alex Brandon/Associated Press.

Chapter 2: p. 33, Russell Gordon/DanitaDelimont.com "Danita Delimont Photography"/Newscom; **p. 39**, Marcio Jose Sanchez/ Associated Press; **p. 43**, FILE PHOTO/Newscom; **p. 48**; KHALED DESOUKI/Getty Images; **p. 52**, Norman Jung/CartoonStock; **p. 53**, Bill Reitzel/Corbis; **p. 57**, Loren Fishman/CartoonStock.

Chapter 3: p. 62, Jim West/Alamy; **p. 63**, zwola fasola/Shutterstock; **p. 73**, JACK HOHMAN/UPI /Landov; **p. 76**, Stacy Walsh Rosenstock/Alamy; **p. 79**, CJ GUNTHER/Rapport Press/Newscom; **p. 81**, ROGERS Â© Pittsburgh Post-Gazette. Reprinted by permission of Universal Uclick for UFS. All rights reserved.

Chapter 4: p. 87, NICHOLAS KAMM/AFP/Getty Images/ Newscom; **p. 88**, Lloyd Fox/MCT/Newscom; **p. 92**, Bettmann/ CORBIS; **p. 94**, Jay Mallin/ZUMA Press, Inc/Alamy; **p. 95**, Kevin Fleming/Corbis; **p. 100**, John Darkow/www.politicalcartoons.com; **p. 101**, Steve Greenberg/CartoonStock; **p. 104**, David R. Frazier Photolibrary, Inc./Alamy; **p. 112**, Copyright Â© Mark Richards/ PhotoEdit.

Chapter 5: p. 123, Harley Schwadron/CartoonStock; **p. 129**, Matt York/Associated Press; **p. 130**, Copyright Â© Robert Brenner/ PhotoEdit; **p. 133**, Allstar Picture Library/Alamy; **p. 135**, SUMMIT

ENTERTAINMENT/Album/Newscom, **p. 141**, Jack Kurtz/ZUMA Press/Newscom.

Chapter 6: p. 145, janine wiedel/Janine Wiedel Photolibrary/Alamy; **p. 148**, Larry Lilac/Alamy; **p. 150**, David L. Moore - OR10/Alamy; **p. 154**, Mike Keefe/www.politicalcartoons.com; **p. 157**, Library of Congress Prints and Photographs Division Washington, D.C. 20540 USA; **p. 159**, Dawn Villella/Associated Press; **p. 170**, Image Source/ SuperStock; **p. 171**, Beowulf Sheehan/ZUMAPRESS/Newscom; **p. 172**, Jeff Parker/www.politicalcartoons.com; **p. 173**, KEVIN DIETSCH/UPI/Newscom; **p. 174**, Kerstin Joensson/AP Images.

Chapter 7: p. 178, Jeff Greenberg/Alamy; **p. 185**, Wild Geese/ Fotolia; **p. 189**, Exactostock/SuperStock; **p. 190**, William Randall/ E+/Getty Images; **p. 193**, J. Scott Applewhite/Associated Press; **p. 197**, David R. Frazier Photolibrary, Inc./Alamy; **p. 198**, Christian Kober/Robert Harding World Imagery/Alamy.

Chapter 8: p. 203, Fuse/Thinkstock; **p. 208**, Bettmann/CORBIS; **p. 212**, William Sutton/DanitaDelimont.com "Danita Delimont Photography"/Newscom; **p. 216**, Brian K. Diggs/Associated Press; **p. 217**, Preston Stroup/Associated Press; **p. 218**, TAKAAKI IWABU KRT/Newscom; **p. 224**, Joe Cavaretta/Associated Press; **p. 226**, ROGERS © Pittsburgh Post-Gazette. Reprinted by permission of Universal Uclick for UFS. All rights reserved.; **p. 229**, Warner Bros./Courtesy Everett Collection; **p. 232**, ZUMA Press, Inc./Alamy.

Chapter 9: p. 237, Abel Mitja Varela/E+/Getty Images ; **p. 240**, Katy Winn/Getty Images; **p. 243**, sippakorn/Shutterstock; **p. 246**, Blend Images/Alamy; **p. 248**, Glasbergen Cartoons; **p. 249**, Digital Vision./ Thinkstock.

Index